...ic Geography

Economic Geography

The Integration of Regions and Nations

Pierre-Philippe Combes

Thierry Mayer

Jacques-François Thisse

Princeton University Press
Princeton and Oxford

Copyright © 2008 by Princeton University Press

Published by Princeton University Press,
41 William Street, Princeton, New Jersey 08540

In the United Kingdom: Princeton University Press,
6 Oxford Street, Woodstock, Oxfordshire OX20 1TW

All Rights Reserved

ISBN: 978-0-691-12459-9 (alk. paper)

Library of Congress Control Number: 2008930613

British Library Cataloging-in-Publication Data is available

This book has been composed in LucidaBright

Typeset by T&T Productions Ltd, London

Printed on acid-free paper ∞

press.princeton.edu

Printed in the United States of America

10 9 8 7 6 5 4 3 2 1

To Emile, Anatole, Théo, Gaspar, Valérie, and Caroline

The economy, all-invading, mingling together currencies and commodities, tended to promote unity of a kind in a world where everything else seemed to be conspiring to create clearly distinguished blocs.

Fernand Braudel, *The Perspective of the World*

Contents

Foreword

Economic Geography as a Field

Economic geography seeks to explain the riddle of unequal spatial development. Ever since the emergence of civilization, human activities and standards of living have been unevenly distributed among both the continents and their territories. Diamond (1997) links spatial inequalities with differences in fauna and flora. Regions' differential endowments in terms of edible plants, with abundant nutrients, and wild animals, capable of being domesticated to help man in his agricultural and transport activities, largely explain why only a few regions in the world have become independent centers of food production. By producing a food surplus, these societies have succeeded in maintaining artisans devoted to elaborating new techniques and furthering knowledge. Writing came to play an important role among these artisans; it has reappeared several times over the course of history and has blossomed in areas that seem to have been the first sites in which agriculture flourished. We can safely conclude, therefore, that the spatial diffusion of economic and social development has been, and still is, very uneven. This book aims to familiarize the reader with economic theories and their empirical validations, which seek to explain why, even in societies where the circulation of people, goods, and ideas is becoming increasingly easy, economic activities are concentrated in a relatively limited number of areas. Although, as always in economics, everything depends on everything else, the results presented in this book will add a new element specific to economic geography: the fact that, in all places, *what is near has more influence than what is far.*

What Are the Main Concepts?

The fact that the spatial diffusion of progress has been so uneven leads one naturally to think of human history as a struggle undertaken by people and societies against the "tyranny of distance." Because the mobility of goods and people revolves around their movement across space, our first task is to specify the spatial unit of reference. This problem is often poorly understood by economists, as the forces that need to be mobilized on one spatial scale are not necessarily the same ones prevailing on another. One explanation can, for example, be relevant on one scale (e.g., a city) but irrelevant on another (e.g., a country). While it is true that a certain number of principles governing the spatial organization of economic activities are valid on every level, this does not mean that they are universally valid. Economic spaces do not fit into each other like little Russian dolls, identical apart from their size; they all have their own specific features.

The spatial unit of reference. Industrialization being more often a regional phenomenon than a national one, the internal economic development of a nation is unequal. Although globalization is often presented as a process affecting nations, it also has a major impact on a subnational level. In addition, armchair evidence shows that, within countries, the economic activity is concentrated in a few large metropolitan areas experiencing urban sprawl. Furthermore, the role of regional governments has been expanding and a growing number of countries are embarking on decentralization. These various considerations have led us to retain the *region* as our basic spatial unit. It is defined as a space open to trade, but in which internal exchanges are predominant. This definition is intentionally vague for, in contrast to an administrative region that has arbitrary but fixed borders, an economic region is both relative and changing (Isard 1956).

It is *relative* because the regions belonging to the same economic space result from a partition of this space. More precisely, this requires a relationship that considers some places to be identical and groups them together within a spatial entity, called a region. Consequently, the places that make up a region are entirely dependent on the relationship that has been selected to compare them. As various relationships can be chosen a priori, regions change as the relationship changes. An economic region is also a changing object because its borders vary over time along with the level of costs of moving goods and people. Regional contours, therefore, become blurred and unstable. Nevertheless, despite its imprecise nature, the choice of the region as our basic spatial unit has a clear implication: our spatial scale is *macroscopic* and our economic analysis must account for the presence of several regions.

Mobility of production factors. Having made this choice, the main objective of this book is to understand how, in a world characterized by an increasing opening-up of economies, *regions and their inhabitants are affected by the mobility of goods as well as by that of economic agents* (firms and consumers/workers). In other words, whereas international trade theory places the emphasis on the exchange of goods, while assuming that production factors are immobile, economic geography explicitly integrates the mobility of factors (capital and/or labor). To put it another way, *the locations of economic agents become endogenous*, whereas traditional economic theory considers them to be exogenous. We will see throughout this book that this modification, far from being a minor generalization of existing theories, often ends up overturning many standard results. Furthermore, instead of assuming that the comparative advantage preexists, we will see how it emerges from the location decisions made by firms and consumers. These two features are what really distinguishes economic geography from other fields.

First- and second-nature inequalities. Another assumption made in this book is that we put aside natural differences among regions, such as raw materials, climate features, geographical asperities, and natural means of transportation. These are what Cronon (1991) calls *first nature*, as opposed to *second nature*, which are the result of human actions to improve upon first nature. Without subscribing to any physical determinism, we do however agree with Landes (1998, pp. 4–5) when he writes that "geography ... tells an unpleasant truth, namely, that nature like life is unfair, unequal in its favors; further, that nature's unfairness is not easily remedied." Our vantage point is, therefore, the expression of a methodological choice, i.e., that of identifying *the microeconomic mechanisms that explain regional disparities in developed countries*, which form Cronon's second nature. In a world characterized by falling transport costs, we believe that the reasons for unequal spatial development, at least in relatively homogeneous areas like the European Union (EU), are to be found in the various relationships connecting the exchange of commodities, the mobility of production factors, and the working of markets.[1] By contrast, physical geography—Cronon's first nature—is much more critical if we want to explain why humanity has not progressed at the same rate on all the continents (Diamond 1997).

Interactions between agglomeration and dispersion forces. It should be stressed from the outset that both economists and geographers consider *economic space as the outcome of a system of countervailing forces*, some pushing toward the agglomeration of human activities (centripetal forces), others toward their dispersion (centrifugal forces). Depending on the respective intensity of the forces put into play, the economic landscape will be characterized by disparities of varying degrees. What economic geography intends to do is to determine the nature of these forces and the way in which they interact. One essential characteristic of

---

[1] It is worth bearing in mind here that spatial inequalities could be the result of a random process. This is because a uniform distribution has a zero probability of being the outcome of such a process.

the formation of economic spaces is that the cause often becomes the effect, and vice versa, thereby making the relationship of causality *circular* and the process of development *cumulative*, as noted by Allyn Young and Gunnar Myrdal several decades ago. For example, a greater number of activities in a region attracts more people, and this, in turn, fosters the creation of new jobs, and so on. As an added bonus, this observation allows us to understand the failure of many regional and local development projects: how can public, or private, intervention be efficient when causes and effects are so intimately related?

Increasing returns and imperfect competition. While the forces behind agglomeration and regional disparities are inherently numerous and diverse, our choice of retaining the region as the basic spatial unit leads us to zero in on two main forces. On the supply side, social sciences share the idea that human concentrations have permitted increased efficiency in trade, industry, and administration by bringing them to a level impossible to reach with a dispersed population. More precisely, an increase in population allows for more than proportional growth in the level of activity. In other words, *production involves increasing returns to scale*, at least at the aggregate level.

On the demand side, economic geography views firms' and households' access to a large variety of goods and jobs as one of the main reasons for the existence of large economic agglomerations. This leads us to think of an agglomeration as a portfolio of differentiated goods, services, and jobs.[2,3] Because product differentiation grants producers market power, we will assume throughout this book that *markets are imperfectly competitive.*

The Mechanisms of Agglomeration

This book will show that the interplay of trade costs, increasing returns, and preference for variety may lead to the emergence of a core–periphery structure. The *core* is formed by regions that supply a large array of differentiated and diversified products, whereas the regions belonging to the *periphery* specialize in the production of fairly standardized goods. It is, therefore, fair to say that the toolbox of economic geography is

---

[2] This idea is far from new. While Montaigne was praising Paris for the variety of things it had on offer, Descartes was writing about Amsterdam: "What place in the world could be chosen … in which all the commodities and all the curiosities one could desire are all as easy as here" (quoted on p. 20 of the English translation of Braudel (1979)).

[3] The recent growth in the number of varieties is truly amazing. For example, while the number of products imported to the United States increased from 7,731 in 1972 to 16,390 in 2001, the number of product variations for these goods increased from 74,667 to 259,215 (Broda and Weinstein 2006).

able to explain the *polarization* of economic spaces. Furthermore, the core–periphery structure emerges when trade costs are relatively low, that is, when distance seems to have less weight in the calculations of economic agents.

However, technological progress in transport and communication is such that distance-related costs can reach incredibly low levels, thus triggering the possible redispersion of activities, mainly because of the rise of congestion in the densest areas. This is suggested by the economic space of the United States, where regional discrepancies are much lower than in the European Union (Puga 2002). Without necessarily taking on board the arguments of Karl Marx, for whom "[t]he country that is more developed industrially only shows, to the less developed, the image of its own future" (preface to the first German edition of *Das Kapital*), we think that this opinion contains a sufficient amount of truth to make the economic and social reality of the United States worth considering. Let us recall that, for a region to benefit from the European Commission's "structural funds" it must have a gross domestic product (GDP) per capita of less than 75% of the EU average. After the addition of ten more countries in 2002, one quarter of the citizens of the European Union live in regions lying below this threshold, as against 18% before the enlargement—while only 2% of the American population lies below this threshold. As the American economic space was conceived as an integrated space from the outset, the circulation of goods, production factors, and ideas has always been high. It is therefore not unreasonable to venture that the gradual deepening of European integration will, ultimately, result in a more balanced organization of the continent.

In fact, as we will see, the most recent studies do suggest the existence of a *bell-shaped relationship*: as the costs of moving goods and people go down, thereby making markets spatially more integrated, economic activities may start to be concentrated in a fairly small number of large urban regions; in a second stage, activities may be redispersed toward a larger number of regions made up of small or medium-sized cities. Nevertheless, this evolution remains uncertain because of the very low spatial mobility of European workers, especially in comparison with that of American workers. Besides, not all territories will be affected in the same way by this possible redeployment—even today, the United States still has areas that can be considered as poor. Furthermore, only a limited number of very large cities are involved in the "game without frontiers"— a game in which they aim to attract high-tech activities. Finally, central core regions will probably retain significant pockets of poverty, just as rich cities have poor neighborhoods. Once again, there is nothing new under the Sun. As observed by Fernand Braudel in his study of the role of socioeconomic factors in the making of history, "the backward zones are not to be found exclusively in the really peripheral areas. They punctuate central regions too, with local pockets of backwardness" (Braudel 1979, p. 42 of the English translation).

Let us conclude by stressing that our choice of a macroscopic scale allows us to avoid looking closely at the goings-on inside agglomerations. Indeed, the very nature of local interactions implies that they can be overlooked on the interregional scale. Yet it is now widely accepted that a territory's success depends on micro-factors not captured by the market (Scott and Storper 2003). These are not examined in this book. More precisely, despite their indisputable interest, we do not analyze nonmarket exchanges within growth poles or industrial clusters, as they require a different set of tools from the ones used here. An integration of these different lines of research seems to be out of reach for the moment.[4] Similarly, we do not explore the spatial distribution of households in agglomerations, even though this is an important subject in which spatial externalities of another kind—often taking the form of neighborhood effects—play a determining role. Although the models studied in this book do throw new light on numerous aspects of the urbanization process, we do not examine the formation and structure of cities as such, because we do not focus on land markets and commuting costs. This choice does not reflect any prejudice on our part—quite the opposite. If we neglect the microcosm in favor of the macrocosm, it is because our aim is to highlight the basic principles that explain *macrospatial economic disparities*.

By contrast, this methodological approach allows us to extend our field of research to the international level and thereby tackle the question of globalization, described as the gradual integration of national and regional economies, as well as the relocation of activities that this integration might induce. This will lead us to propose analyses that diverge from both the knee-jerk reactions of some international organizations and the very different viewpoints of many anti-globalization groups. Having said this, it is perhaps worth recalling here that *the mobility of goods, ideas, and people is often experienced by sedentary societies as an invasion, and rarely as a positive contribution.*

Finally, this book also seeks to confront, as systematically as possible, the main theoretical contributions with their empirical counterparts. Unfortunately, although the numerous theoretical advances of recent years enable us to present the state of the art in a relatively integrated

---

[4] On an interregional level, it is reasonable to assume that most interactions across agents are mediated by the market.

way, the measurement of spatial inequalities remains considerably more heterogeneous, with respect to both the methods and data used. Empirical applications are still confined to a few areas or countries in which data are abundant and of high quality. Nevertheless, a wide range of empirical methods are available to illustrate the models developed in economic geography. These methods will be applied to a large spectrum of issues, ranging from descriptive approaches, which aim at evaluating the level of regional disparities and the overall effect of agglomeration on productivity, to structural approaches, which directly confront specific models with data.

Plan of the Book

This book is divided into three parts. The first comprises two chapters with a strong historical emphasis. Chapter 1 presents an overview of the evolution of the European economic space since the beginning of the Industrial Revolution, while chapter 2 is devoted to the place occupied by space in economic thought. The second part is theory oriented and focuses on the relationships between trade, integration, and the structure of the space-economy. To a large extent, it covers what is known as the "new economic geography"—rather cheekily, as the ideas that define it are sometimes fairly old (see, for example, Ottaviano and Thisse 2005). Finally, the third part is devoted to the empirical research that has run in parallel with the revival of economic geography.

Facts and Theories

Preindustrial economies are characterized by a low and roughly equal level of activity everywhere, with high transport costs and little trade. The first chapter offers some stylized facts regarding the formation of economic spaces since the start of the Industrial Revolution. It stresses, on the one hand, the phenomenal reduction in transport costs and, on the other, the massive urbanization and strong polarization of economic spaces. With this in mind, we provide a brief overview of the economic geography of the European Union and the United States, as well as a long-term perspective of the regional question in France.

The second chapter deals with the place occupied by space in economic thought. Its relative absence from mainstream economics probably stems from the inadequacy of the paradigm that has dominated economic theory for a very long time: perfect competition and constant returns. If production factors react to spatial inequalities by leaving regions where returns are low for others where returns are high, and if, as assumed by the neoclassical model, technology exhibits constant returns and markets are perfectly competitive, standards of living are equalized in equilibrium. In a context characterized by the progressive disappearance of distance—the traditional obstacle to the mobility of goods—it is therefore tempting to wait for the fulfillment of this prediction. The above setting implies, however, a second conclusion that is rarely spelled out: in equilibrium, every region is an autarky as it only needs to produce for its own domestic market. In other words, *if the assumptions of the standard neoclassical model are satisfied, the mobility of production factors between regions suppresses the need for trade.* We find it hard to accept such a conclusion. In chapter 2 we show in a precise way why the standard neoclassical model is not appropriate to study the simultaneous mobility of goods and economic agents.

Space, Trade, and Agglomeration

Because they occupy center stage in economic geography, we provide a survey of the main models of monopolistic competition in chapter 3. The following chapters are devoted to the most recent theoretical developments in economic geography, following a sequence that owes much to the chronology of research in this field. In chapter 4 we explore a spatial version of Dixit and Stiglitz's model of monopolistic competition. This version, attributed to Paul Krugman, can be seen as emblematic of the "new theories" of international trade, which do not encompass the mobility of production factors as economic geography does. In this context, international trade does not necessarily lead to the evening-out of levels of well-being, even when it seems to be in the interests of all the agents involved. We also discuss the idea that firms producing under increasing returns would be more than proportionally represented in large markets (the so-called home-market effect). The purpose of this chapter is to highlight two important results. On the one hand, the consequences of increasing integration of regional or national economies are not identical—far from it—when firms' locations are *exogenous* or *endogenous.* On the other hand, minor differences between regions are susceptible to *amplification* when the mobility of production factors is permitted.

Chapter 5 studies the microeconomic foundations of the *gravity model* widely used in the empirical literature. We should remember that this model is based on a formal analogy with Newtonian physics: two regions—or two countries—exchange goods at a rate proportional to their economic weight and at a rate inverse to the square of the distance separating them. This relationship has remained mysterious for a long time, even though it has a great capacity to describe and predict commodity flows between countries. The spatial model of monopolistic competition offers a plausible explanation of this relationship, while also enriching it.

Seeing the emergence of agglomerations as a symmetry-breaking process is a common feature of most economic geography models. In other words, the aim is to find the various channels through which the spatially uniform distribution of economic activity is either stable or unstable (Papageorgiou and Smith 1983). Unlike earlier contributions in the field, the acting centripetal and centrifugal forces are market based and are all endogenous. In this perspective, chapter 6 deals with the core–periphery model developed by Krugman, which lies at the root of economists' renewed interest in economic geography, while chapter 8 proposes an alternative version based on the linear model of monopolistic competition presented in chapter 3.

The conclusions of the core–periphery model are well-known and have raised controversy. Unlike new trade theories that do not consider factor mobility, allowing for the migration of workers may lead to the endogenous emergence of economic agglomerations. Specifically, the core–periphery model suggests that economic integration triggers a reinforcement of regional disparities. In view of the political and social implications of this conclusion, it is important to assess its robustness. In particular, the core–periphery model puts aside several major factors, such as the use of intermediate goods in production or the low spatial mobility of labor in Europe, which both lead to less pessimistic conclusions, as shown in chapter 7 within the Dixit–Stiglitz–Krugman framework and in chapter 8 by using the linear model. If economic integration is indeed capable of initially fostering a more intensive agglomeration of economic activities, its continuation is liable to generate a redeployment of activities that could lead to a kind of geographical evening-out. In short, one may expect the process of spatial development to unfold according to a bell-shaped curve.

The models of economic geography considered in chapters 4–8 all have their origin in the need felt by international trade theory to integrate the mobility of production factors with that of commodities. They focus on the entire economy. Chapter 9 turns its attention to location theory, where the focus is on specific markets, very much as in industrial organization. Instead of studying a small number of regions and a large number of firms, we turn this approach on its head and consider a small number of firms and a large number of regions. In this case, monopolistic competition must be abandoned because firms act strategically. On the other hand, the models lose their general-equilibrium character to become models of partial equilibrium, as a general-equilibrium model with oligopolistic competition is not yet available. In other words, what we gain on the one hand, we lose on the other. This exercise is worth the effort, however. As the two approaches are very different, if the conclusions are qualitatively the same, we can reasonably conjecture that they remain valid in more general contexts that are still out of reach.

Breadth and Determinants of Spatial Concentration

It should be stated from the outset that the confrontation between facts and theory in economic geography is still in its infancy. On the one hand, almost all the theoretical models suppose the existence of two regions and two sectors. Now, we know that a result valid in this context may not hold when more regions and sectors come into play, so a need for theoretical complements arises. On the other hand, regional data are often lacking, in which case we often have to work with national data, even though the nation is not our spatial unit of reference. We can nevertheless infer some important conclusions from this research, as well as acquiring a better understanding of the ins and outs of the methods used to reach these conclusions, as they are also applicable in other contexts (when data are available).

One initial question springs immediately to mind: how can we measure the spatial concentration of activities? This problem is considered in chapter 10, where a number of approaches are proposed. Although several of these are marred by serious deficiencies, some recent contributions have come up with more satisfactory solutions. Chapter 11 presents the determinants of spatial concentration by using measurements from the previous chapter, as well as econometric estimations of agglomeration economies that are much more convincing. As the second part will already have revealed, the main problem that economic geography attempts to tackle is that of the differential attractiveness of sites for businesses. In chapters 12 and 13, we will therefore study the determinants of firms' mobility. The first lesson of these investigations is of a methodological nature: in many cases the estimation of *reduced forms* oversimplifies matters, while the use of *structural* approaches allows one to interpret the facts more precisely. Furthermore, empirical validation varies greatly according to the type of prediction under consideration, somewhat mitigating the overall assessment. Nevertheless, further advances in a field in which research is booming are likely to solve many of the unsatisfying elements of the empirical strategy.

A final comment is in order. In a long list of publications, economic journalists have celebrated the "death of distance," the "weightless economy," or the "flattened world." We will see in this book that empirical studies do not confirm such predictions. Quite the opposite: *proximity still matters, but the form of proximity has vastly changed.* In particular, the new information and communication technologies do not seem to be a substitute but a complement to transport. Accordingly, we may safely conclude that questions raised in economic geography keep their theoretical and policy relevance.

Reader's Guide

This book is primarily aimed at students and researchers interested in economic geography. Chapters 1, 3, 4, 5-7, and 11-13 form what could be considered the core of the teaching material, while the remaining chapters dig deeper. However, we have organized the book so that it can be profitably used in other courses by grouping the chapters into large blocks. Chapters 3-7 and chapters 12 and 13 can be incorporated into a course on international trade, while chapters 3, 6, 8, and 9 can serve as illustrations for a course on industrial organization. Chapters 1, 6, 7, 10, and 11 could have a place in a course on development economics, while chapters 11-13 would be useful in a course on applied econometrics. Finally, chapter 2 could be used in a course devoted to the history of economic thought.

Acknowledgments

Any book is the outcome of a collective process in that it involves more people than just its author(s). This is especially true for this one since we have benefited from a large number of comments and suggestions made by friends, colleagues, and students.

Gilles Duranton made many insightful comments that led to substantial improvements throughout the book. For part I, our discussions with Bernard Walliser about the various relationships between facts and theories have been very useful to us. We have also greatly benefited from the comments made by Paul Hohenberg, Luc-Normand Tellier, and Jean-Claude Toutain when working on the economic history sections. Finally, Michel De Vroey has read chapter 2 carefully. His knowledge of the history of economic thought has allowed us to improve the final product, while Allen Scott has generously provided us with the opinion of a geographer about the history of spatial economic theory.

Parts II and III had more readers, some of whom read chapters in draft form. We would like to mention especially Kristian Behrens, Luisito Bertinelli, Jean Cavailhès, Sylvie Charlot, Francesco Di Comite, Jim Friedman, Jean Gabszewicz, Carl Gaigné, Pamina Koenig, Miren Lafourcade, Giordano Mion, Dominique Peeters, Susana Peralta, Sandra Poncet, Frédéric Robert-Nicoud, and Takatoshi Tabuchi. Jean-François Maystadt read the whole manuscript and pointed out several obscure explanations and typos, whereas Vianney Brandicourt was tremendously helpful when writing the English version of our initial manuscript.

Finally, we should thank CEPREMAP, CERAS (École nationale des ponts et chaussées), CIREM (International Trade in Cultural Goods, convention no. 2005/34-17/60), CORE (Université catholique de Louvain), GREQAM (Université d'Aix–Marseille), PSE, the University of Paris I, and the CEPR for providing friendly environments in which to work as well as for financial support. We also want to thank the *Review of Economic Studies*, the *Journal of International Economics, Regional Science and Urban Economics*, and North-Holland, the publisher of the *Handbook of Regional and Urban Economics*, for having granted us the permission to reproduce some diagrams and tables.

Last, but not least, we are very grateful to Sam Clark of T&T Productions Ltd and his colleague Emma Dain for their wonderful work in editing and typesetting this book.

Part I

Facts and Theories

1

Spatial Inequalities:
A Brief Historical Overview

During the second millennium, the world's population increased by a factor of twenty-two, while world income increased by a factor of three hundred. This development, however, was not uniform and did not affect all countries in the same way. Between 1000 and 1820, the annual growth rate of income per capita in the countries of Western Europe was estimated at around 0.15%, which is extremely low. That rate then rose to 1.5%, thus reaching a level ten times higher than it had been for the previous eight centuries. This change of pace was to have considerable consequences for economic disparities between nations. Indeed, income increases by less than 4% in a twenty-five year period (roughly one generation) when the annual growth rate is 0.15%, while it grows by 45% when the growth rate reaches 1.5%. To put it another way, income per capita doubles after 46 years in the second case, while the same doubling takes 463 years in the first. Thus, while the income per capita of Europeans hardly differed from that of other inhabitants of the planet at the beginning of the second millennium, it is currently seven times higher (Maddison 2001, chapter 1). The reason for this dramatic change is well-known: the Industrial Revolution.

In this chapter, we briefly discuss two major features of the Industrial Revolution that have been instrumental in reshaping the European economic space: (i) the existence of gigantic productivity gains and the tremendous lowering of transport costs; and (ii) the profound transformation of agricultural and rural societies into industrial and urbanized ones. Subsequently, we will see how, because of the Industrial Revolution, spatial inequalities became increasingly marked, not only between countries but also within them.

Our historical survey should ideally cover Europe, the United States, and Japan. However, in order to allow for meaningful long-run comparisons, we must consider economic spaces that have (more or less) the same borders. Furthermore, our aim is not to provide a detailed discussion of all the spatial implications of the Industrial Revolution. Instead, we are interested in a few facts that are directly relevant for economic geography. All of this has led us to focus mainly, but not solely, on Europe.

1.1   The Space-Economy and the Industrial Revolution

The Industrial Revolution began in Great Britain during the second half of the eighteenth century and then diffused to Continental Europe and North America. Since then, productivity gains have been steady and their accumulation has generated considerable multiplier effects.[1] This economic development was accompanied by spectacular decreases in transport costs and massive rural–urban migration. The old agricultural economy became industrial and then, in the twentieth century, services became the primary economic sector.

1.1.1   Productivity Gains and Falling Transport Costs

The most distinctive feature of the Industrial Revolution was the considerable increase in productivity. According to Bairoch:

> [I]t can be considered that, for the whole of the economy, the total factor productivity was multiplied on average in Western developed countries by 40 to 45 between 1700 and 1990. Even limiting ourselves to the years 1000 to 1700, which, in Europe, were on the whole a period of progress, it can be very roughly estimated that the productivity of the whole economy was, at best, multiplied by 2.
>
> Bairoch (1997, volume 1, pp. 97–98) [our translation]

Such productivity gains allowed an appreciable increase in individual incomes.[2] The question of whether European countries were richer than others before the Industrial Revolution is still discussed by historians— but this debate changes the global picture very little. For example, while Bairoch (1993) believes that China and other Asian civilizations were

---

[1] This does not mean that technological progress was absent before the Industrial Revolution, but it seems to have led to increased population and not higher living standards (Kremer 1993).

[2] Although some historians still debate the accuracy and relevance of the term "Industrial Revolution," we find it hard to deny the emergence of a completely new economic trend. This can be illustrated by means of the following counterfactual argument due to Joel Mokyr. In 1890, income per capita in the United Kingdom was about $4,100 in 1990 dollars. Had the United Kingdom been growing at a rate of 1.5% in the previous three hundred years, income per capita in 1590 would have been $63, which is far below the subsistence level. Indeed, the average income of the five poorest countries in the world was about $500 in 1990.

more advanced than Western Europe in the sixteenth century, he is "still inclined to think that there was no sizable difference in the levels of income of the different civilizations when they reached their preindustrial peak" (p. 106). Whatever the value of these differences, there is no longer any question that the Industrial Revolution generated income disparities between countries and regions of a completely different nature and on an unprecedented scale.

The transportation sector underwent the most stunning changes during the Industrial Revolution. In particular, the *great divergence* between nations appeared when all distance-related costs underwent a drastic and historically unprecedented fall. The scope of this decline led Cipolla to contend that:

> Fast and cheap transportation has been one of the main products of the Industrial Revolution. Distances have been shortened at an astonishing pace. Day by day the world seems smaller and smaller and societies that for millennia practically ignored each other are suddenly put in contact—or in conflict.
>
> Cipolla (1962, p. 13)

This was later confirmed by Bairoch in an evaluation of that spectacular transformation in the means of transportation:

> On the whole, between 1800 and 1910, it can be estimated that the lowering of the real (weighted) average prices of transportation was on the order of 10 to 1.
>
> Bairoch (1997, volume 2, p. 26) [our translation]

The cost of transporting maritime cargo dropped dramatically during the nineteenth century, leading to the convergence of prices of several goods and to the gradual integration of international markets. One example is the case of wheat, whose price in Liverpool exceeded that of wheat in Chicago by 57.6% in 1870 but by only 15.6% in 1913; the price of steel in London was 75% higher than it was in Philadelphia in 1870, but only 20.6% higher in 1913; the price differential of cotton between Liverpool and Bombay fell from 57% in 1873 to 20% in 1913, while the price difference of jute between London and Calcutta dropped from 35% to 4% (Findlay and O'Rourke 2003).

In the first half of the nineteenth century the costs of ground transportation were still very high and weighed heavily on the prices of commodities. France provides a good illustration of this. For example, the transport of coal from Saint-Etienne to the ironworks of Champagnes—a distance of 545 km—multiplied the sale price by five. The coal of Sarrebrück was sold for F 9.50 a ton locally, but the price in Saint-Dizier, located 220 km away, was F 51.50, with transport costs representing 82% of the total price (Léon 1976).

After the emergence of railroads, things changed dramatically. For example, prior to the Industrial Revolution the average cost of ground transportation of grains per ton–kilometer was equal to the average cost of buying 4 or 5 kg of grain, but this cost fell to 0.1 kg per ton–kilometer in 1910 thanks to long-distance transportation by rail. Once we account for the decrease in the price of grain generated by technological innovations in agriculture, the decrease in transport costs is even larger: they are divided by a factor close to 50 (Bairoch 1997, chapter 4). In the United States, the average cost of moving a ton a mile in 1890 was 18.5 cents, as opposed to 2.3 cents today (in 2001 dollars), while trucking costs have fallen 2% per year since 1980 (Glaeser and Kohlhase 2004).

Moreover, the actual cost of shipping commodities also involves time costs, along with the cost of inventory holdings and depreciation costs. We deal here with another dimension of falling transport costs, i.e., a big reduction in the time of transport. By 1910, steamships were crossing the Atlantic at five times the speed of seventeenth-century boats, and with twenty times more tonnage. Currently, the value of an additional day of transportation is worth an average of 0.5% of the value of manufactured goods. Because of decreases in transport times, the real drop in transport costs is thus even more marked than that revealed solely by the level of freight. The gains are even more considerable for ground transport. For example, it took 358 hours in 1650 to go from Paris to Marseille but only 38 hours in 1854 and just 3 hours in 2002.

The progressive integration of markets produced by this unprecedented decline in transport costs must have had a considerable impact on the international division of labor, distinguishing between industrialized countries and countries specializing in the supply of primary goods. Yet unlike transport costs, tariff barriers did not experience the same evolution. As shown in table 1.1, a slow advance of free trade is observed at the end of the Napoleonic Wars (up until 1875), and that is followed by a real revival in protectionism, which culminated in the 1930s. On the other hand, customs barriers have been lowered uniformly and constantly since 1950, driving customs duties to their lowest level in history.

Although a large range of factors affect the degree of openness of national economies, a rough estimate of the total impact of the decline in transport costs and tariff barriers may be obtained by looking at the variations of the share of exports in gross domestic product (GDP). Maddison (2001) shows that between 1820 and 1998 the share of world exports in

Table 1.1. Customs duties applied to manufactured goods in developed countries. (Sources: World Bank (1991) and World Trade Organization (2001).)

Year	1820	1875	1913	1925	1930	1950	1987	1998
Average tariff (%)	22	11–14	17	19	32	16	7	4.6

Table 1.2. Export/GDP ratio in the major developed countries. (Source: O'Rourke and Williamson (1999).)

Countries	1870	1913	1950	1973	1987	2000
Belgium	7.0	17.5	13.4	40.3	52.5	86.3
Brazil						10.8
China						25.9
France	3.4	6.0	5.6	11.2	14.3	28.5
Germany	7.4	12.2	4.4	17.2	23.7	33.7
Italy	3.3	3.6	2.6	9.0	11.5	28.4
Japan	0.2	2.1	2.0	6.8	10.6	10.8
Mexico						31.1
Netherlands	14.6	14.5	10.2	34.1	40.9	67.2
Poland						29.3
Russia						44.5
United Kingdom	10.3	14.7	9.5	11.5	15.3	28.1
United States	2.8	4.1	3.3	5.8	6.3	11.2

the world GDP has increased by a factor of 17. At a more disaggregated level, the pattern is similar.

Table 1.2 reveals another interesting, yet less widely known, fact: international trade had a more important role in the economy of industrialized countries in 1913 than it did in 1950. Even more surprisingly, on the eve of World War II, the share of production that was traded in the international marketplace fell back to the level observed in 1840, a century earlier. Protectionist policies, restrictive cartel and labor practices in transport, and the collapse of the gold standard were the main trade-reducing forces (Estevadeordal et al. 2003). The huge development in trade that preceded World War I suggests that the decline in transport costs had overcome fairly high tariffs between 1875 and 1913. This has allowed many economic historians to underline *the emergence during the second half of the nineteenth century of a first phase of globalization ending in 1914*, the main explanation of which lies in the dramatic drop in transport costs (O'Rourke and Williamson 1999).

By contrast, since 1950 the increase in trade seems to be due more to the progressive removal of trade barriers than to the decline in transport costs.[3] Between 1950 and 2000, the global production of commodities—which differs from the world GDP since it includes neither services nor construction—was multiplied by 6, while the volume of goods exported increased 17-fold (World Trade Organization 2000).

As for communication, the invention of the telegraph and then the telephone brought about big falls in the time taken to transmit information. For comparison, let us recall that it took an average of 15–16 days for a letter to travel between Avignon and Paris during the Renaissance, between 25 and 30 days to travel between Florence and London, and 20–22 days between Florence and Paris (Verdon 2003, p. 245). Things were pretty much the same for the next three centuries. For example, Bairoch (1997, chapter 18) notes that it took practically two years for an exchange of correspondence between England and India at the beginning of the nineteenth century. Even after the opening of the Suez Canal it still required several months. So, it is easy to guess that *long before the Internet, thanks to the invention of the telegraph and the telephone, information began to circulate at a speed previously unimaginable,* deeply affecting both the ways in which societies worked and the lives of individuals.

The following quotation from Stefan Zweig's autobiography, *The World of Yesterday,* illustrates probably better than many academic works the impact of the first revolution in the means of communication on lifestyle and on people's mentalities:

> There was no escape for our generation, no standing aside as in times past. Thanks to our new organization of simultaneity we were constantly drawn into our time. When bombs laid waste the houses of Shanghai, we knew of it in our rooms in Europe before the wounded were carried out of their homes. What occurred thousands of miles over the sea leaped bodily before our eyes in pictures. There was no protection, no security against being constantly made aware of things and being drawn into them. There was no country to which one could flee, no quiet which one could purchase; always and everywhere the hand of fate seized us and dragged us back into its insatiable play.
>
> Zweig (1944, p. 8 of the English translation)

---

[3] Baier and Bergstrand (2001) estimate that the decrease in customs duties explains 22% of the increase in trade between the countries of the Organisation for Economic Co-operation and Development (OECD) from 1960 to 1990, whereas the fall in transport costs explains only 8%. According to these authors, income growth is the major explanatory variable for the increase in commercial flows, accounting for 67% of it. Conversely, Hummels (2007) argues that technological change in air shipping and the declining cost of rapid transit have been critical in the growth of trade during the second half of the twentieth century.

Table 1.3. Indices of transportation and communication costs.
(Source: World Bank (1995).)

	1920	1930	1940	1950	1960	1970	1980	1990
Maritime transport	100	65	67	48	28	29	25	30
Air transport	—	100	70	45	38	25	18	15
Transatlantic telephone	—	—	100	30	28	18	3	1
Communication by satellites	—	—	—	—	—	100	15	8

This phenomenon underwent a drastic acceleration during the second half of the twentieth century. Table 1.3 compares the relative development of transportation and communication costs, with indices standardized at 100 at the first observation. If transport costs have continued to decrease, just not as fast as in the nineteenth century, then communication costs have fallen at an absolutely dizzying speed during the last few decades. For example, the costs of communication have fallen by more than 90% in the last twenty years.

In short, the questions raised by the current globalization of economies are far less new than is asserted in the general press. Keynes (1919) described marvelously the changes in the lifestyle and consumption habits of his contemporaries brought about by the globalization preceding World War I. The extract is a little long, but it is so relevant to this discussion that it is worth including:

> What an extraordinary episode in the economic progress of man that age was which came to an end in August 1914! ... [L]ife offered, at a low cost and with the least trouble, conveniences, comforts, and amenities beyond the compass of the richest and most powerful monarchs of other ages. The inhabitant of London could order by telephone, sipping his morning tea in bed, the various products of the whole earth, in such quantity as he might see fit, and reasonably expect their early delivery upon his doorstep; he could at the same moment and by the same means adventure his wealth in the natural resources and new enterprises of any quarter of the world, and share, without exertion or even trouble, in their prospective fruits and advantages; or he could decide to couple the security of his fortunes with the good faith of the townspeople of any substantial municipality in any continent that fancy or information might recommend. He could secure forthwith, if he wished it, cheap and comfortable means of transit to any country or climate without passport or other formality ... and would consider himself greatly aggrieved and much surprised at the least interference. But, most important of all, he regarded this state of affairs as normal, certain, and permanent, except in the direction of further improvement, and any deviation from it as aberrant, scandalous, and avoidable.
>
> Keynes (1919, p. 4)

1.1.2   Motorization of Transport and Urbanization

The second feature marking the economic development of Europe is the
almost perfect synchronization of the Industrial Revolution and urbanization due mainly to the advent of motorized transportation (steam-
boats, railroads, and finally automobiles). Steam navigation began in the
United States in 1807 and the first railroad line was built in England in
1825. Although the urban population in Europe (outside Russia) in 1800
corresponded to only 12% of the total population, it reached 41% in 1910
and it is now 75%; a similar evolution arose in the United States, where
the urban population share was 5% in 1800, 42% in 1910, and was close
to 75% by 2005 (Bairoch 1988, chapter 13). On a historical scale, such
figures are an indisputable sign of *an explosive growth in urbanization.*[4]

The beginning of the Industrial Revolution meant that agricultural
employment had to undergo an equally spectacular development in the
opposite direction, reaching its lowest historical level in the whole EU-
15 with 6.3 million farmers, while the United States had only 2.3 million by 2003. Although France has long preserved a considerably more
important agricultural sector than other industrial countries, its farm-
ing population represents only 2.5% of its current labor force. Note too
that without the steep drop in transport costs mentioned above such
human concentrations would have been impossible, as they had been
for centuries—except in a handful of big cities like London and Paris,
which were endowed by nature and royal power with dense networks of
navigable routes. Indeed, strong declines in freight costs were necessary
to allow for a rapid increase in urban population because larger volumes
of foodstuffs had to come from increasingly distant places.

The link between the structure of employment and the structure of
economic space was the same almost everywhere. Initially, the creation
of and boom in big industrial cities (e.g., Manchester, Saint-Etienne,
Charleroi) can be seen. As Bairoch noted:

> of the 228 cities of more than 100,000 inhabitants in the developed
> world (except Japan) in 1910, about 98 ... did not exist at all or were sim-
> ple villages at the beginning of the nineteenth century (or, for England,
> in the middle of the eighteenth century).
>
> Bairoch (1997, volume 2, p. 196) [our translation]

---

[4] Forcing the point a bit, Cipolla (1962) argued that, from a strictly economic standpoint, the city as we know it is a product of the Industrial Revolution. The economic
activity of traditional societies was so dominated by agriculture that cities were "often
nothing more than collecting centers of agricultural rents." Such an opinion, however, is
probably too extreme, for some cities played a crucial role in the development of banking
and financial institutions. They even welcomed the first industries of the Middle Ages,
which then left for the rural world (Hohenberg 2004).

Indeed, at the start of the Industrial Revolution the transportation of primary materials was still costly and hence the proximity of natural resources remained an essential location factor. This justified the establishment of new urban entities in the places where those resources were found. Moreover, industry used an unskilled labor force that it could borrow from the agricultural sector at a time when important productivity gains allowed the release of a large number of people (Bairoch 1997, chapter 4). Agricultural jobs were thus gradually replaced by industrial jobs, explaining the strength of rural–urban migration in all countries affected by the Industrial Revolution. The most representative case is probably England, for which historians have provided a complete reconstruction of population shifts between 1776 and 1871, a period covering the two phases of the Industrial Revolution in that country (Williamson 1990, chapter 1). The rate of urbanization in England was 25.9% in 1776 and 65.2% in 1871, making it the most urbanized country at the time. Yet for more than a century the annual growth rate of the urban population remained astonishingly stable, barely more than 2%.[5]

Because of the decline in transport costs, firms were progressively freed from natural factors of location—sources of primary material or energy—giving rise to what was to become known as "footloose industry." New location factors governing firms' spatial strategies then appeared. The new activities often needed workers who were more skilled than before, and they also needed a growing number of specialized services. These production factors were available mainly in an urban environment—especially in the big, old cities, because many cities created by the Industrial Revolution did not have a sufficiently diversified set of activities. Thus, a reverse causality emerges: it is the city that now favors the rise of industry. The intense urbanization that began in the preceding period enhanced the attraction of the cities insofar as they offered growing markets for new industrial products.

During the second half of the twentieth century, the preponderance of industrial jobs in modern economies decreased because of the productivity gains associated with advanced technologies. At the same time, industrial plants moved out of cities, where land and labor were too expensive. This departure was also facilitated by falling communication costs, which accelerated the vertical disintegration of firms into

---

[5] Contrary to general belief, such migratory movements were not limited solely to national economies. On the contrary, they had an increasingly international dimension. Before the formation of the welfare states that separate local people from foreigners, a sort of unregulated European labor market developed from the end of the nineteenth century, to such a degree that workers crossed borders more easily than commodities did (Bade 2002).

increasingly specialized and spatially separate units. In big cities, industrial jobs gave way to jobs in the various service sectors, which showed a common taste for urbanity. In addition, because of the variety of goods and services that they offer, contemporary cities are akin to gigantic public goods, which may be viewed as *consumer cities*: one lives in them to benefit from their commercial and cultural amenities, but one works in them less (Glaeser et al. 2001). On the other hand, in the older industrial regions, where cities are synonymous with concentrations of unskilled labor, redevelopment is still on the agenda. The economic fabric there is often too tenuous to allow their transformation into consumer cities.

Nevertheless, if the fall in transportation and communication costs generally favors the economic and social development of populations by permitting a greater spatial distribution of goods and ideas, this distribution is still quite unequal. Specifically, the economic development of Europe during the nineteenth century displays a major feature that seems paradoxical: *the various costs linked with the circulation of goods and ideas have dramatically decreased, but this has not contributed to a more equal distribution of prosperity among regions.* On the contrary, this reduction in distance-related costs instead seems to accompany a growing polarization of economic spaces. In other words, even when the costs of communication and transportation decline, growth processes are localized, are experienced only in certain regions, and are transmitted only very imperfectly to others, thus making regional development more uneven. This idea is confirmed by the English historian Sidney Pollard, who considers it misleading to speak of England and the continent as a whole when discussing the spread of the Industrial Revolution; it would be more appropriate to mention Lancashire and the valley of the Sambre and the Meuse (Pollard 1981, chapter 1).

It is precisely these complex bonds between economic development, transport costs, sectoral mutations, and spatial inequalities that the models of economic geography presented in the second part of this book intend to describe and understand. Beforehand, we want to complete the stylized facts presented in this chapter with some data highlighting the relationships between spatial inequalities and obstacles to trade.

1.2 Regional Disparities: When an Ancient Phenomenon Becomes Measurable

The existence of strong regional disparities is not new. During every great historical period, prosperous cities and small regions that were much richer than the average coexisted with poor zones within the major traditional societies of Europe and Asia. For Fernand Braudel, a "world-economy" is formed by at least three types of space:

> The centre or core contains everything that is most advanced and diversified. The next zone possesses only some of these benefits, although it has some share in them: it is the "runner-up" zone. The huge periphery, with its scattered population, represents on the contrary backwardness, archaism, and exploitation by others. This discriminatory geography is even today both an explanation and a pitfall in the writing of world history—although the latter often creates the pitfalls by its connivance.
>
> Braudel (1979, p. 39 of the English translation)

As a result, even if the differences in development between big preindustrial economies were small, regional inequalities were probably very important within those societies.

While the lack of reliable data does not allow evaluations comparable with those of today, there is broad agreement among social scientists in considering the "tyranny of location" to be one of the major causes of spatial inequalities. This includes the presence of navigable ways, the fertility of the soil, and the climatic characteristics of a zone, that is, factors that are almost all natural. These natural factors dominated choices about location for several centuries, but things changed a great deal with the revolution in transportation.

1.2.1 Spatial Inequalities in Nineteenth-Century Europe

GDP per capita is a standard indicator of the economic performance of a region or a nation. Paul Bairoch has estimated the GDP per capita from 1800 to 1913, a period of intense technological progress that preceded a long period of political turmoil; his results are presented in table 1.4.

These figures must be used with care, but even allowing for that they reveal clear tendencies. First, it is readily verified that, during the nineteenth century, all European countries experienced important development. Yet, while the initial levels of development were roughly the same, varying by about 10% around the European average (except perhaps in the Netherlands and, to a lesser extent, the United Kingdom), *countries were affected quite differently by the Industrial Revolution,* the income gains generated by it varying greatly. Indeed, international differences grow progressively and reach a ratio of 1 to 4 between the richest and poorest nations in 1913. While the average European GDP per capita increased gradually from $199 to $550—that is, by a factor slightly greater than 2.5—the standard deviation increased even faster, going from 24 in 1800 to 229 in 1913, which means a progression by a factor close to 10.

Table 1.4. GDP per capita in U.S. dollars and 1960 prices.
(Source: Bairoch (1997, volume 2, pp. 252–53).)

Countries	1800	1830	1850	1870	1890	1900	1913
Austria–Hungary	200	240	275	310	370	425	510
Belgium	200	240	335	450	555	650	815
Bulgaria	175	185	205	225	260	275	285
Denmark	205	225	280	365	525	655	885
Finland	180	190	230	300	370	430	525
France	205	275	345	450	525	610	670
Germany	200	240	305	425	540	645	790
Greece	190	195	220	255	300	310	335
Italy	220	240	260	300	315	345	455
Netherlands	270	320	385	470	570	610	740
Norway	185	225	285	340	430	475	615
Portugal	230	250	275	290	295	320	335
Romania	190	195	205	225	265	300	370
Russia	170	180	190	220	210	260	340
Serbia	185	200	215	235	260	270	300
Spain	210	250	295	315	325	365	400
Sweden	195	235	270	315	405	495	705
Switzerland	190	240	340	485	645	730	895
United Kingdom	240	355	470	650	815	915	1035
Mean	199	240	285	350	400	465	550
Standard deviation	24	43	68	110	155	182	229
United States	240	325	465	580	875	1070	1350

In other words, the Industrial Revolution produced a rise in the average level of well-being in all European countries. However, they were affected quite unequally by this process of development. Indeed, the disparities between nations grow more than proportionally, the coefficient of variation increasing from 0.12 in 1800 to 0.42 in 1913. As usual, such aggregate measures hide even stronger contrasts between countries: while the GDP per capita of the United Kingdom increased by a factor exceeding 4, that of the Balkans (Bulgaria, Greece, and Serbia) barely rose 50%. Observe also that *the United States was the leading industrial power from the end of the nineteenth century onward*, and also does better than Europe over the whole period.

Another aspect of this development process is worth stressing. Indeed, the countries that experienced the strongest growth (Belgium, France, Germany, the Netherlands, Sweden, and Switzerland) are almost all close to the new European center, the United Kingdom, despite the fact that

Table 1.5. Elasticity of GDP per capita with respect to the distance from the United Kingdom (European countries).

	1800	1830	1850	1870	1890	1900	1913
Elasticity	−0.090	−0.195	−0.283	−0.371	−0.426	−0.437	−0.436
Standard deviation	0.028	0.029	0.028	0.032	0.052	0.058	0.078
R^2		0.376	0.717	0.857	0.883	0.796	0.764	0.647

Note: all elasticities are significantly different from 0 at the 1% level.

their economic takeoff arose at different times. Thus, more generally, distance to the United Kingdom strongly influenced national rates of growth: *the further away from the United Kingdom a country was, the lower its level of growth.*

To show this more precisely, for each of the years and countries listed in table 1.4, we estimate the impact of the distance between a country and the United Kingdom on this country's GDP per capita by using the ordinary least squares method (OLS).[6] Table 1.5, which sums up the results of these regressions, confirms the initial intuition: the effect of distance to the United Kingdom on development is significantly negative. That is, the farther one is from the United Kingdom, the lower the GDP per capita, no matter what date is considered. Moreover, this effect regularly increases in absolute value, starting from a value of 0.090 in 1800, increasing to 0.426 in 1890, and then stabilizing. In other words, before the Industrial Revolution spread on the continent, a reduction of 10% in distance to the United Kingdom was associated with an increase of 0.9% in the GDP per capita. On the eve of World War I, the absolute value of that elasticity was multiplied by almost 5. In other words, a decrease in the distance of a given country from the United Kingdom from 1000 km to 900 km is associated with an increase of 4.4% in the per capita GDP of that country in 1913, as opposed to a 0.9% increase in 1800. We may thus safely conclude that *inequalities across European countries strongly increased over the nineteenth century, while the distance to the new center became increasingly important for the economic development of a country.* The data in table 1.5 provide a clear illustration of the process of divergence, which triggered here the emergence of a center and a periphery.

Will current economic integration accentuate this tendency toward a more unbalanced economic space in Europe? This is what Sicco Mansholt

---

[6] In the regression, we use the logarithm of both variables so that the coefficients can be interpreted directly in terms of elasticity.

thought as early as 1964. Mansholt, who was one of the major architects of the Common Market Agricultural Policy, worried that

> [i]f we do not conduct an active policy within some countries, we will see that, by the unification of Europe, the great stimulus and strong expansion it can and will give, the most advanced regions will develop fastest and will profit most from it. Marginal regions will then become submarginal.
>
> Quoted in Husson (2002, p. 28) [our translation]

However, even if the regional question retains its relevance within the European Union, it will subsequently be seen that the response to it needs qualification.

1.2.2   The Regional Question

The current standard of living is comparable across developed countries. These countries have reached similar stages of technological development and are governed by social rules and codes of behavior that are quite similar to those of other countries and to their own in the past. Yet there is another fact that cannot be denied: within each country or each block, striking contrasts between regions can be observed.

Figure 1.1 provides a map showing GDP per capita for the 269 NUTS2 regions of the EU-27, plus Norway and Switzerland, for the year 2004.[7] It reveals the existence of a bicentric structure: (i) the "Blue Banana" (an area that stretches from London to Northern Italy and goes through part of Western Germany and the Benelux countries) and (ii) the Nordic countries. It is also worth noting that several countries seem to belong entirely to what may be called the European economic periphery: Greece, Portugal, and the new Eastern European member states. However, regional disparities within some countries are also very striking. For example, Northern Italy contrasts strongly with Southern Italy, a textbook case frequently mentioned under the banner of the *Mezzogiorno*. While the Milan region groups with Switzerland in terms of wealth category, the southern part of Italy lies in the same income per capita category as Greece. To a lesser extent, the same holds in the United Kingdom, Spain, Belgium, and Germany, where the divide between western and eastern "Landers" remains strong. Note, however, that regions belonging to the new member states form most of the new periphery of Europe, whereas the old periphery, mainly made up of regions of Greece,

---

[7] NUTS ("nomenclature des unités territoriales statistiques") is the regional classification used by Eurostat, usually building on existing regional borders inside each country. It is organized by level of geographical detail: ranging from NUTS0 (countries) to NUTS5, which lists more than 100,000 areas in the EU-15.

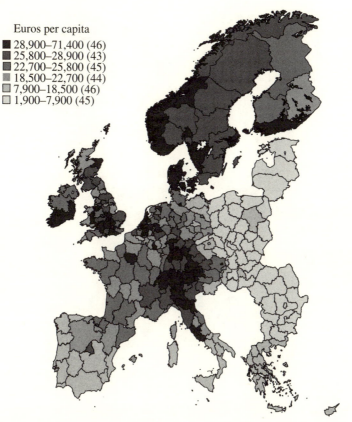

Euros per capita
- 28,900–71,400 (46)
- 25,800–28,900 (43)
- 22,700–25,800 (45)
- 18,500–22,700 (44)
- 7,900–18,500 (46)
- 1,900–7,900 (45)

Figure 1.1. GDP per capita of the NUT2 regions of the European Union in 2004 (number of regions in parentheses).

Ireland, Portugal, Spain, and Italy, has, at least partly, caught up with the core regions.

Finally, what is perhaps the most striking feature of the GDP per capita map is that the level of regional wealth seems to exhibit "spatial contagion": being close to rich regions makes it very unlikely that your region will be very poor. This is true inside countries and across national borders. This suggests some form of spatial diffusion of development. We will see in this book that economic geography theory has a lot to say about the source of such development, in particular through the concept of *market potential* proposed by the geographer Harris (1954).

GDP level provides a crude, but simple, measure of the economic size of a region. It thus gives us some insight into the potential of this region to attract new activities. Besides its size, one expects the accessibility of a region from others to be another critical determinant of firms' and workers' locational decisions. In order to account for this, we use Harris's

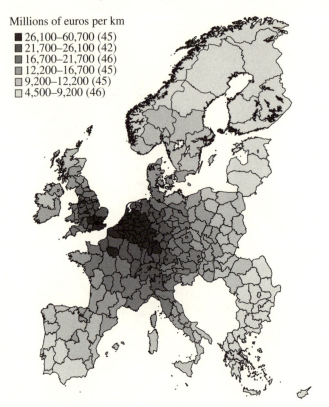

Figure 1.2. Market potential of the NUT2 regions of the European
Union in 2004 (number of regions in parentheses).

market potential of region r, as defined by Harris (1954), which is given
by the sum of regional GDPs, where the GDP of region s is weighted
by the inverse of its distance to region r.[8] By using these weights, the
market potential aims to capture the idea that being close to prosperous
regions makes a region more attractive because it offers good access to
several large markets.

Figure 1.2 depicts the market potential for all the regions considered
in figure 1.1. Much more than the latter, the former map reveals a very
strong core–periphery structure for the European Union in 2004: as the
distance to the old core regions increases, the market potential steadily
decreases. This is supportive of the idea that market potential is important for economic development. There are exceptions, however, the main
one being the group of Nordic countries. One possible explanation is

---

[8] This sum includes region r itself. Its GDP is divided by the intraregional distance,
which is equal to two thirds of the radius of a circle whose area represents that of region
r. We will return to the measurement of intraregional distance in chapters 5 and 12.

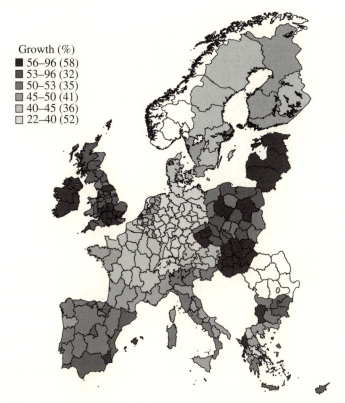

Growth (%)
■ 56–96 (58)
■ 53–96 (32)
■ 50–53 (35)
□ 45–50 (41)
□ 40–45 (36)
□ 22–40 (52)

Figure 1.3. The evolution of market potentials in the European Union from 1995 to 2004 (number of regions in parentheses).

that, although they suffer from poor accessibility to the rest of the European Union, the Nordic regions have been quite successful in overcoming their locational disadvantage. This is confirmed by figure 1.3, which shows the evolution of market potential from 1995 to 2004 (data for Norway and Romania are missing). More precisely, we see that *almost all regions located on the outskirts of the European Union have been more successful than the central regions in improving their market potential.* This in turn implies the existence of a catching-up process within the European Union. One of the objectives of economic geography is then to uncover (i) why being spatially central provides such a strong advantage in terms of GDP and (ii) how this advantage evolves over time when transport costs change? In particular, what are the main forces explaining why some initially disfavored and peripheral regions have caught up with the old European core.

Let us now turn to the United States. A glance at figure 1.4, which maps the GDP per capita for the forty-eight states of the continental

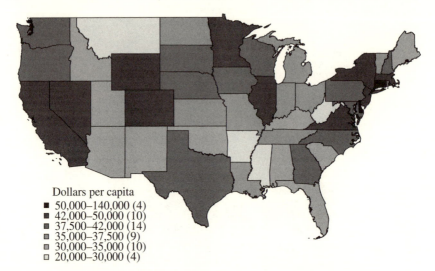

Dollars per capita
■ 50,000–140,000 (4)
■ 42,000–50,000 (10)
■ 37,500–42,000 (14)
□ 35,000–37,500 (9)
▫ 30,000–35,000 (10)
□ 20,000–30,000 (4)

Figure 1.4. GDP per capita of the states of the continental
United States in 2004 (number of states in parentheses).

United States, shows that there is more dispersion there than in the European Union, with prosperous states being scattered all over the country. Another major difference is worth noting. Looking at the extreme values taken by regional incomes, it appears that *regional disparities are much wider within the European Union than in the United States.*

As we did for the European Union, we map the market potential of each of the forty-eight U.S. states in figure 1.5. Even though there seems to be a core–periphery structure in the United States, it is not as strong as it is in the European Union. In particular, the gradient of the market potential becomes positive in the southwest (Arizona and California).

Repeating what we have done for the European Union, figure 1.6 shows that, from 1995 to 2004, the market potential has increased significantly in *all* the states of the U.S.'s western half as well as in the southeast, thus showing that a catch-up process is also at work in the United States. All in all, this confirms that *spatial development is more even within the United States than within the European Union.* This could be because the space-economy has been integrated for much longer in the former than in the latter. We will return to this important issue in subsequent chapters, especially chapters 7, 8, and 12.

1.2.3 Spatial Inequalities in France: A Long-Run Perspective

To the best of our knowledge, there exists no historical data available about GDP at the regional level that would allow one to estimate the evolution of spatial disparities within countries over a long time period.

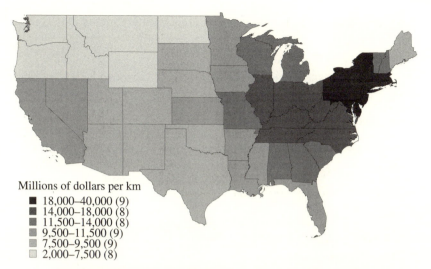

Figure 1.5. Market potential of the states of the continental
United States in 2004 (number of states in parentheses).

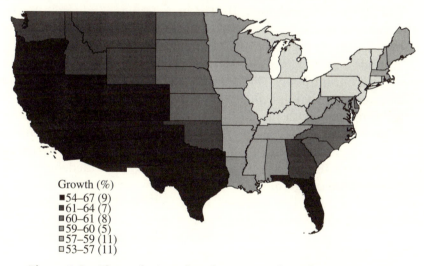

Figure 1.6. The evolution of market potentials in the United States
from 1995 to 2004 (number of states in parentheses).

However, thanks to the work of the economic historian Jean-Claude
Toutain, the case of France can be studied at a very fine geographical level
(eighty-eight continental "départements"), and the existence of strong
spatial disparities over a very long period is revealed. These data relate
to employment, population, and value-added (VA) for the years 1860
and 1930, distinguishing three large sectors: agriculture, industry, and

Table 1.6. Theil indices for French départements.

Variable	1860	1930	2000	Percentage change 1860–1930	Percentage change 1930–2000	Percentage change 1860–2000
Population	0.12	0.34	0.39	175.9	16.1	220.4
Employment	0.13	0.37	0.50	177.0	34.2	271.6
VA	0.30	0.68	0.71	124.9	5.0	136.1
VA/employee	0.05	0.03	0.01	−47.5	−76.7	−87.8
VA agriculture	0.10	0.10	0.22	−4.4	119.5	109.7
VA industrial	0.69	0.93	0.50	33.9	−45.8	−27.4
VA services	0.61	1.00	0.84	62.9	−15.7	37.4

services. We have gathered similar data for the year 2000 (Combes et al. 2008a).

In table 1.6 we give the value taken by an index measuring the spatial concentration of population, employment, and GDP across French départements. More precisely, we use the Theil index, whose properties will be studied in chapter 10. For now, let us simply note that a zero value means that the activity is uniformly distributed across space, while it reaches its highest value when all the activity is concentrated into a single region. More generally, the higher the index, the greater the spatial concentration. The first line of this table shows *the strong increase in spatial concentration of the French population* over nearly a century and a half, with the Theil index increasing by a factor of more than three. Thus, the French population gradually regrouped within a small number of départements. In terms of employment, the variation is even stronger. It is slightly weaker in terms of value-added, but this is more concentrated regardless of which period we are looking at.

A second striking fact emerges from this table. The value-added per employee, which can be interpreted roughly as the productivity or income per employee, became very homogeneous across regions. Even though inequalities in productivity were initially much lower than those observed in terms of production, they fell by two thirds between 1860 and 2000. Thus, the stronger concentration of the population and of economic activities that has been observed over the last 140 years has been accompanied by *a stronger decrease in regional inequalities in terms of labor income and productivity per worker.*

Looking at the maps of the total (figure 1.7) or per-employee (figure 1.8) value-added for the French départements confirms some of the facts observed today at the European level. There is a core region, the metropolitan area of Paris, and a periphery—a contrast that has

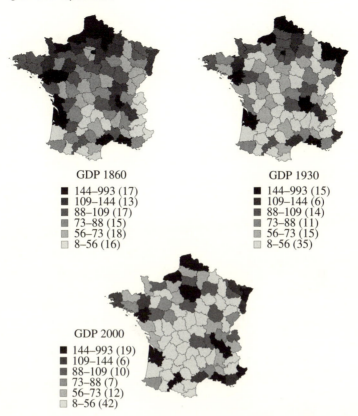

Figure 1.7. GDP of the French départements in 1860, 1930, and 2000 (annual average = 100; number of départements in parentheses).

been reinforced over time as the Parisian economic region gradually expanded. Nevertheless, apart for this well-known phenomenon, no strong tendency seems to appear among the other départements, apart from a rather strong mobility in the French hierarchy, since the three maps corresponding to the years 1860, 1930, and 2000 are ultimately quite different. Some industrial (and hence rich) areas at the end of the nineteenth century, like the north and the northeast, have seen their incomes collapse, while the takeoff of others, like the Rhône-Alpes region, is spectacular.

A breakdown of the data by sector is also worth considering. Table 1.6 shows that while the spatial distribution of agriculture, which is clearly less concentrated than industry and services, did not evolve strongly between 1860 and 1930, there has been a rather marked phenomenon of concentration since 1930. In addition, services are always more concentrated than industry. We also observe an important result that seems

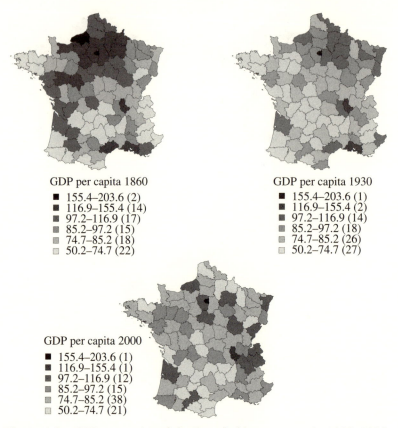

GDP per capita 1860
- ■ 155.4–203.6 (2)
- ■ 116.9–155.4 (14)
- ■ 97.2–116.9 (17)
- ■ 85.2–97.2 (15)
- ▨ 74.7–85.2 (18)
- ▢ 50.2–74.7 (22)

GDP per capita 1930
- ■ 155.4–203.6 (1)
- ■ 116.9–155.4 (2)
- ■ 97.2–116.9 (14)
- ■ 85.2–97.2 (18)
- ▨ 74.7–85.2 (26)
- ▢ 50.2–74.7 (27)

GDP per capita 2000
- ■ 155.4–203.6 (1)
- ■ 116.9–155.4 (1)
- ■ 97.2–116.9 (12)
- ■ 85.2–97.2 (15)
- ▨ 74.7–85.2 (38)
- ▢ 50.2–74.7 (21)

Figure 1.8. GDP per capita of the French départements in 1860, 1930, and 2000 (annual average = 100; number of départements in parentheses).

Table 1.7. Correlations between population density and value-added among French départements.

	1860	1930	2000
VA agriculture	−0.12	−0.16	−0.12
VA industry	0.94	0.95	0.84
VA services	0.96	0.98	0.96
VA agriculture/employee	0.37	0.11	−0.22
VA industrial/employee	0.31	0.45	0.44
VA services/employee	0.22	0.28	0.64

to validate the bell-shaped curve of spatial development mentioned in the foreword: *while the spatial concentration of industry and services increases over the period 1860–1930, it drops during the next seventy years.*

Table 1.7 provides correlations between the density of population and the levels of value-added and of labor productivity. The first three rows show that, in 1860, unlike agriculture both industry and services were located in densely populated regions, a tendency which is slightly reinforced in 1930. In 2000, such regions are slightly less attractive to industrial firms, while services remain in populated regions. The last three rows reveal that, in 1860, the correlation between labor productivity and population density was highest in agriculture and lowest in services. Since then, the ranking of sectors has undergone a complete reversal. Even though correlations increased for both manufacturing and services between 1860 and 2000, industrial productivity benefits most from population density in 1930; in 2000, the correlation is highest in services. As for agriculture, the correlation between productivity and density decreases and becomes negative in 2000, meaning that rural regions are now the most productive ones in this sector. Thus, as the economy gets more and more developed, agriculture, which has been the dominant sector for a long time, loses its comparative advantage in densely populated regions; industry then takes the lead but it is subsequently replaced by services. At first sight, these correlations might suggest that the spatial concentration of population is one of the main factors explaining the increase in labor productivity, and hence in growth. In fact, such a conclusion, at first sight correct, lacks solid foundations and we will see in chapter 11 that a finer analysis is needed to uncover the reasons for such correlations.

1.3 Concluding Remarks

Ever since the nineteenth century the downward trend in the costs of transporting goods, persons, and information has vastly relaxed the constraints imposed by natural factors over human activity. A rough economic analysis suggests that such a dramatic drop in transport costs allows economic agents to benefit from more freedom in their location choice, thus fostering a greater homogeneity across regions. Yet in most developed countries, wide spatial variations are still observed in the size and composition of populations, in average incomes, in regional structures of production, in the cost of living and the price of housing, and in the distribution of occupations. All these magnitudes are endogenous and the values they take are not imposed by nature. On the contrary, they are determined by the interaction between markets, public policies, and the mobility of production factors. It is the spatial facet of these numerous interactions that forms the realm of economic geography.

2
Space in Economic Thought

This chapter deals with the following two questions:

(i) Why is space peripheral to economic theory?

(ii) What issues and modeling constraints characterize the field of economic geography?

Economics textbooks give the impression that production and consumption take place on the head of a pin, as if space had no dimension. Neither land nor distance is mentioned. To a large extent, space and its major constituents are bracketed or ignored. Hence, it is no great surprise that Samuelson could write:

> Spatial problems have been so neglected in economic theory that the field is of interest for its own sake.
>
> Samuelson (1952, p. 284)

How, then, can such neglect be explained when, although it is the focal point of everyday economic life, *exchange almost always involves the movement of persons or commodities.* Moreover, in the widespread form of trade across regions or nations, exchange is spatial by its very nature.

Before proceeding, we want to stress the fact that the optimal location of an agent depends on the locations chosen by the agents with which it interacts. Thus, locational decisions are essentially interdependent and, consequently, must be studied within a general-equilibrium model encompassing the whole range of choices made by firms and households. A brief overview of the literature will show that the main reason for the (relative) absence of space in economic theory lies in the attempt made by economists to develop a rigorous theory of prices. This attempt has led them, through a series of simplifications and shortcuts taken long ago, to zero in on the combination "constant returns and perfect competition" with consequences for economic geography that are comparable to those for growth theory (Romer 1992). Subsequently, we will see that it is possible to *prove* how such a research strategy was bound to thwart the development of a relevant theory of the space-economy. Having done this, we will discuss alternative modeling strategies that enable us to cope with the mobility of goods and agents across space. Finally, we will show by means of two simple examples why increasing returns to scale are central to the formation of economic spaces.

2.1   Economics and Geography: A Puzzling History of Reciprocal Ignorance

The *costs of trade* are the costs of coordinating and connecting transactions between supplier and customer locations. This definition is extensive and includes all costs generated by distance and borders: transport costs of goods and services, of course, but also tariff and nontariff barriers, production standards, communication impediments, and cultural differences. Intuitively, these costs are expected to play an important role in economic theory since they are the inherent attributes of exchanges across space—yet they are usually absent.

The most common explanation for this negligence is that the value of transport costs has declined considerably since the middle of the nineteenth century (see chapter 1). Yet this does not make firms indifferent to their location. Indeed, tougher competition makes firms more sensitive to small differences in costs, thus implying that places where transport costs are low remain very attractive to firms. Moreover, if transport costs and trade costs are linked, they are not identical and we will see in chapter 5 that the latter remain high. Thus, the absence of space in economic theory cannot be justified solely by the fall in transport costs.

A second, fairly original, explanation is proposed by Jacobs:

> Nations are political and military entities, and so are blocs of nations. But it doesn't necessarily follow from this that they are also the basic, salient entities of economic life or that they are particularly useful for probing the mysteries of economic structure, the reasons for rise and decline of wealth. Indeed, the failure of national governments and blocs of nations to force economic life to do their bidding suggests some sort of essential irrelevance.
>
> Jacobs (1984, pp. 31–32)

Thus, the gradual emergence of the concept of *nation* in Europe has led the fathers of political economy to think of countries as the only entities of reference and, by definition, to consider them as homogeneous. Indeed, since the beginning of the nineteenth century, the concept of "nation-state" has gradually become the main referent in several social sciences. While economists have not played a major role in this development, they have not escaped it. Indeed, the only spatial dimension that has caught the attention of economists is the *national border*. As an example, think of David Ricardo, whose theory of international trade is based on the double postulate of the perfect immobility of factors between nations and their perfect mobility within them.[1] Recently, with the predominance of the nation-state having been challenged by the rise of both economic integration and political decentralization, it is reasonable to assume that the resurgence of economic geography is not alien to such economic and political changes.

Jane Jacobs's explanation can be augmented by the following remarks. First, because of the almost complete abolition of local tolls from the fifteenth century onward and important improvements in the transportation system during the last decades of the eighteenth century, the United Kingdom had the largest and most integrated internal market in Europe (Landes 1998, chapter 14). While in 1760 only large waterways could be used for navigation, thirty years later every urban center was connected to a national network of navigable rivers and 2600 km of newly dug canals (Bairoch 1997, chapter 3). This state of affairs quite naturally led observers of the Industrial Revolution to underestimate the role of transportation. Second, since sea trade—fundamental for the British economy, incorporated as it was into a colonial empire covering several continents—was already inexpensive, British economists were encouraged to build a theory of international trade without transport costs in which countries are reduced to dimensionless points.[2]

The same point of view is apparently still shared by several of the most prominent contributors to economic theory. Thus, in his *Theory of Value*, Debreu insists that

> a good at a certain location and the same good at another location are different economic objects, and the specification of the location at which it will be available is essential.
>
> Debreu (1959, p. 30)

---

[1] Otherwise, how can we interpret the following statement: "The labour of 100 Englishmen cannot be given for that of 80 Englishmen, but the produce of the labour of 100 Englishmen may be given for the produce of the labour of 80 Portuguese, 60 Russians, or 120 East Indians" (Ricardo 1817, section 7.17), except to admit that Ricardo considers the nation as a homogeneous entity within which production factors are identical and are rewarded equally.

[2] On the other hand, the unification of the national market was much slower and later in Germany, where ground transport, much more costly than maritime transport, played a larger role. This might explain why space has, conversely, caught the attention of several German economists (von Thünen, Landhardt, Weber, and Lösch, to mention just a few of them).

Indeed, the same good available in different locations can satisfy different needs depending on the specific characteristics of the places in question. This then leads Debreu to admit that the single-price law is meaningless whenever space is taken into account: *the same good available in different places is supplied at different prices.* However, in his discussion of the possible applications of his theory, Debreu deals only with rates of exchange between nations when he comes to spatial applications. Location choices do not catch his attention, the reason being that they are implicitly contained in the specification of the production or consumption plans selected by the agents.

To summarize, modern economic theory, when it does mention space, seems to do so only within the context of international trade and it focuses only on the differences in terms of technologies or factor endowments between countries. As observed recently by Leamer (2007), this implies a fairly strange geography in which countries are close enough for the cost of shipping goods internationally to be zero, but far enough apart that no workers or owners of capital can find their way from one country to another. This research strategy is especially surprising since, as stressed by Ohlin himself, theories of international trade and location are not independent of one another:

> international trade theory cannot be understood except in relation to and as part of the general location theory, to which the lack of mobility of goods and factors has equal relevance.
>
> Ohlin (1968, p. 97)

A last comment is in order. In his detailed study of economic thought in the eighteenth and nineteenth centuries, Lepetit (1988, chapter 10) sees the abandonment of space as a dividing line between preclassical and classical authors. Classical political economy focuses on general factors that are assumed to be the same in all places. Location-specific factors are confined to descriptive studies of particular regions and cities. When classical economists deal with the spatial organization of the economy, they do so quite crudely, thus leading Lepetit to summarize their approach as follows:

> from the countryside to the city, the nature of productions differs, but there is homology among the different levels of spatial organization (the country, the region, the city, the village) and an identity of their principles of functioning.... [Thus,] space appears like Russian dolls: unpacking the levels does not reveal any originality, but proves, on the contrary, the identical reproduction of similar principles of functioning.
>
> Lepetit (1988, pp. 370–71) [our translation]

Though fairly convincing, the foregoing arguments fail to provide a definite answer to the predominance of the dimensionless competitive model in economic theory. We will try to remedy this in section 2.4.

2.2   Integrating Space in Economics: The Main Attempts

It would be unfair, however, to claim that space was totally absent from economic theory before the upsurge of economic geography. Indeed, two bodies of research in spatial economic theory have attracted a lot of attention in the economics profession.

2.2.1   Urban Economics

The canonical model of urban economics originates in the pioneering work of von Thünen (1826), whose objective was to explain the location of crops around cities in preindustrial economies. Alonso (1964) took up this subject again later, but interpreted von Thünen's city as the "central business district" around which workers are distributed. Insofar as land is a perfectly divisible good and transactions take place in a center whose location is given exogenously, this model still belongs to the realm of constant returns and perfect competition. It is not surprising, therefore, that urban economics became a fashionable subject in academic circles in the late 1960s and early 1970s.

In the monocentric model, because consumers work in the central business district where firms are assumed to be located, the scarcity of land implies that they cannot all settle close to the center. They must, on the contrary, go farther away from it as their numbers increase. In other words, there is a trade-off between commuting and housing costs: the former increasing with distance while the latter decrease. Thus, urban economics uncovers an important force of dispersion, that is, *land consumption.*

The initial interest in this model gave way to a new economic field called urban economics. Remarkable progress has been made since the work of Alonso (see Fujita 1989). However, the area covered by urban economics was too narrow for the problems it posed to continue to occupy the center of the scientific stage. Yet it did get a second wind in the contemporary analyses of urban systems developed in relation to economic geography.

2.2.2   Spatial Competition

Hotelling (1929) is generally considered to be the father of the model of spatial competition. His contemporaries interpreted it as a model of duopoly illustrating market failures—but without really understanding all the ins and outs of it. It was only with the emergence of the new industrial economics almost fifty years later that it has become fully understood. Today, it is often presented as an illustration of a more general principle stating that economic agents strive to differentiate themselves from each other.

The model of spatial competition can be summarized as follows (see chapter 9 for more details). The market for a good, which is homogeneous in every respect except its place of sale, is formed of consumers whose individual demand is equal to a single unit. These consumers are assumed to be distributed uniformly along a straight line—let us call it Main Street. Two firms, aiming to maximize their respective profits, try to establish a foothold on this street. They correctly anticipate that each consumer will get his supplies from the seller who proposes the lowest full price, that is, including transport costs.[3] Hence, once located, firms have some market power over the consumers located in their vicinity because patronizing the firm's competitors is more expensive to those consumers in terms of transport costs. Firms are thus "price-makers." Their price choice is nevertheless limited by the possibility that consumers can get their supplies from the competing firm, even if the costs of getting there are higher. Thus, each firm having only a few neighboring competitors, *spatial competition is inherently strategic.* Hence, firms' choices of location and price must be modeled as a noncooperative game. We will return to this in chapter 9.[4]

The model of spatial competition encompasses a wide array of interpretations because it captures in a simple and intuitive way the fundamental idea of heterogeneity across agents (Rosen 2002). However, the fact that this model quickly becomes hard to handle once we deviate from simple assumptions probably explains why it has been neglected in recent developments in economic geography.

2.3 The Burden of Modeling Constraints

In this section, we are going to see that increasing returns and imperfect competition must be combined for a relevant integration of space into

---

[3] In this chapter, we talk only about transport costs, but everything also holds true for trade costs.

[4] Note also that the spatial competition model has been revisited and extended by Eaton and Lipsey in a series of papers published in the 1970s (see Eaton and Lipsey 1997). Their purpose was to build a spatial theory of value that would integrate the work of Lösch (1940). Very much as Krugman did almost twenty years later, Lipsey undertook this research program while he was already a well-established scholar in international economics.

economic theory. Combining these two elements within a fully fledged general-equilibrium model has so far been out of reach and this probably explains why space has been put aside for so long. This state of affairs has led some authors to use the concept of increasing returns external to firms (Henderson 1974). This research strategy allows them to work with the neoclassical model and explains why external economies first took center stage in economic geography. Consequently, it is useful to summarize how this work has been carried out.

Ever since the work of Marshall (1890, chapter X), it has been impossible to ignore externalities when space is mentioned. More precisely, we are thinking of the so-called *Marshallian economies*, which describe the advantages generated by the clustering of economic activities in space. Marshall distinguishes three types of external economies:

(i) the distribution of specialized inputs whose unit cost is low when demand for that input is sufficiently high;

(ii) the emergence of a local labor market large enough to permit good matching between jobs and workers, thus making firms and workers better-off; and

(iii) the most intense circulation of ideas and the existence of spillover effects raising productivity and fostering growth.

Yet Marshallian economies are often black boxes hiding richer microeconomic mechanisms that lead to increasing returns at the aggregate level. As a result, they cannot be considered as an economic concept *stricto sensu*, even if they retain their relevance in empirical works.

Things become more complex when we consider increasing returns *internal* to firms. As observed by Eaton and Lipsey,

> [o]nce the firm acts as if it faces a perfectly elastic demand curve, there is nothing to restrict size from the demand side. Size must be restricted from the cost side. Hence, the extreme importance of eventually diminishing returns to scale in any competitive model that seeks to limit the size of plants and firms.
>
> Eaton and Lipsey (1977, p. 63)

However, the level of demand and the fact that consumers are scattered across locations could be sufficient to explain why firms operating under increasing returns choose a finite size. Unfortunately, this is not enough to preserve the competitive model. Indeed, as seen above, a specific good in one location and the same good in another location must be considered as two different economic objects, thus implying that a good is defined by its characteristics as well as by the place where it is available.

Typically, the markets for such commodities involve a small number of firms. In such a context, how do we justify the assumption of price-taking firms since firms understand that they are large enough to manipulate market prices to their advantage? Even though it is not necessary to postulate the existence of a large number of agents to establish the existence of a competitive equilibrium, it is hard to escape this assumption if we want to justify the fact that agents are price-takers. Of course, it could be assumed, as in the work of von Thünen, that goods are made available in marketplaces (city centers, for example) in which a large number of agents must trade them. But that is simply to put off the evil day: why must transactions be made in such given places and how are their number and location determined?

Hence, in order to understand the nature of competition among a small number of firms in a spatial economy, we must account for the fact that firms operate under increasing returns (and imperfect competition). Otherwise, in a world where the geographical distribution of natural resources and technologies is uniform, each individual would be transformed into a Robinson Crusoe who would not even need the help of a Friday. When there are no scale economies, production activities may be divided up to the point where transport costs are zero without any loss of efficiency, thus turning each place into an autarky. This is what Eaton and Lipsey (1977) nicely called *backyard capitalism*. Mills very suggestively described the strange world without cities that would result from an economy with constant returns and perfect competition, allowing the perfect divisibility of activities without cost:

> each acre of land would contain the same number of people and the same mix of productive activities. The crucial point in establishing this result is that constant returns permit each productive activity to be carried on at an arbitrary level without loss of efficiency. Furthermore, all land is equally productive and equilibrium requires that the value of the marginal product, and hence its rent, be the same everywhere. Therefore, in equilibrium, all the inputs and outputs necessary directly and indirectly to meet the demands of consumers can be located in a small area near where consumers live. In that way, each small area can be autarkic and transportation of people and goods can be avoided.
>
> Mills (1972, p. 4)

Such a space is the quintessence of autarky. Thus, the paradigm combining constant returns and perfect competition seems unable to account for the emergence and growth of big economic agglomerations and the existence of trade flows generating large shipments of goods. In order to say something relevant about a spatial economy, it is necessary to assume that increasing returns are at work, which is tantamount to the existence of indivisibilities of some activities. This idea has been present in works devoted to economic geography for a long time, although it is unclear who it should be attributed to. It is now widely acknowledged, and Krugman summarizes it well in the following passage:

> in order to talk even halfway sensibly about economic geography it is necessary to invoke the role of increasing returns in some form.
>
> Krugman (1995, p. 36)

Interestingly, Koopmans seemed to say the same thing in 1957:

> without recognizing indivisibilities—in human person, in residences, plants, equipment, and in transportation—urban location problems, down to those of the smallest village, cannot be understood.
>
> Koopmans (1957, p. 154)

The question of increasing returns has retained the attention of economists for quite some time, since it is hard to reconcile them with the competitive assumption. Since the first efforts to model the working of competitive markets rigorously within a general-equilibrium model, it has seemed that the fixed-point theorems used to demonstrate the existence of a competitive equilibrium require several convexity assumptions. While it has been well-known since the work of Aumann (1966) that the convexity of preferences can be relaxed when the number of consumers is large enough, the same is not true for the convexity of technologies, which forbids the presence of increasing returns to scale.

At the same time, some theorists highlighted the fact that space generates imperfections in competition because the latter is the source of differentiation between agents. This idea, as we have just seen, was already discussed in the work of Hotelling (1929), who modeled competition between two producers separated spatially as a noncooperative game. Yet it is Kaldor (1935) who deserves credit for clearly demonstrating the specificity of the process of competition in space. Since consumers buy at the firm offering the lowest full price, competition occurs directly between a limited number of firms located in the same neighborhood, regardless of the total number of firms present in the industry (Eaton and Lipsey 1977; Gabszewicz and Thisse 1986; Scotchmer and Thisse 1992).

Thus, competition in space is inherently oligopolistic and its analysis must take place in a framework that allows for strategic decision making. This was one of the main messages of Hotelling (1929) and Kaldor (1935), but it was misunderstood by most economists until they became aware of the power of noncooperative game theory for the study of competition in market economies. New tools and concepts are now available to formalize questions raised by the first location theorists.

Increasing returns and strategic competition are, therefore, the basic ingredients of a relevant theory of spatial equilibrium. The magnitude and difficulty of the task have put off more than one scholar. To a large extent, the modeling constraints have quite spontaneously led economists to concentrate—probably for too long—on the combination involving constant returns and perfect competition, which is easier to handle. Exaggerating a little, it can be concluded that the elegance of the neoclassical model and, especially, the absence of alternative models have generated a lock-in effect that economists had a lot of trouble escaping.[5]

The elements necessary to understand fully the economists' neglect of the spatial dimension are now clear. Once more, Krugman summarizes the situation very well:

> So why did spatial issues remain a blind spot for the economic profession? It was not a historical accident: there was something about spatial economics that made it inherently unfriendly terrain for the kind of modeling mainstream economists know how to do. ... That something was ... the problem of market structure in the face of increasing returns.
>
> Krugman (1995, chapter 2, p. 35)

In the next section, we will show how these various observations may be given a formal and precise meaning.

2.4 The Breakdown of the Competitive Paradigm in a Spatial Economy

Because the competitive model is the starting point of any study in which the market plays an important role, it is natural to strive for a better understanding of the reasons why the competitive paradigm is unable to account for the main features of the space-economy. Note that the essence of the competitive model lies in the impersonal nature of exchanges: when agents make decisions regarding production or consumption, the only information useful to them is the price system given by the market, over which they have no influence.

The most elegant and general model of a competitive economy is indisputably the one proposed by Arrow and Debreu (1954). It can be described briefly as follows. The economy is made up of a finite number of agents (firms and households) and commodities (goods and services). A firm is characterized by a combination of production plans,

---

[5] The vocabulary itself confirms this impression as economists talk about "imperfect competition" and "impure public goods" once they move away from the standard paradigm, as if everything would be better in what Walter Isard has called "a wonderland of no spatial dimensions."

each production plan describing a possible technological combination between inputs and outputs. A household is identified by a preference relation, an initial endowment, and a portfolio of shares in the profits of firms. A competitive equilibrium is then described by a system of prices (one price per commodity), one production plan per firm, and one consumption plan per household satisfying the following conditions: at the equilibrium prices (i) the supply and demand of each commodity are balanced, (ii) each firm maximizes its profit subject to its technological constraints, and (iii) each household maximizes its utility under the budget constraint defined by the value of its initial endowment and its shares in firms' profits. In other words, all markets clear and each agent chooses the action it prefers at the equilibrium price.

As seen above, a good is defined by the place where it is available. Consequently, the choice of a good also entails the choice of a specific location. For example, when an individual chooses a consumption good or a type of work, he also chooses his place of consumption or work. Within the Arrow–Debreu model, spatial interdependencies are integrated in the same way as other market interactions. In other words, this model seems to be able to cope with the formation of a space-economy. Unfortunately, the spatial impossibility theorem, which we will discuss below, shows that things are not so simple.

To make our argument more transparent, we abandon the convention proposed by Arrow and Debreu and assume that *agents are not ubiquitous* and, therefore, have an "address." In such a context, instead of describing quantities of goods at different locations, a consumption (respectively, production) plan describes the quantities of goods consumed (respectively, produced) in a specific location. Space then is said to be *homogeneous* if (i) the utility function of each consumer is identical no matter what his location and (ii) the production set of each firm is independent of its location. In other words, location choice does not affect the characteristics of agents because they have a priori no preferences over the set of locations.[6]

To understand the nature of the difficulties posed by several agents simultaneously choosing their locations, we borrow the following example from Starrett (1978). Consider two agents, a firm and a consumer, involved in an exchange relationship, each consuming land. The consumer supplies one unit of labor to the firm, which then uses it as well as one unit of land to produce a quantity y of a good sold to the consumer. The latter also consumes one unit of land. Land is available in

---

[6] Of course, the consumption or production choices made by agents vary with their location, as relative prices change with the supply and demand of each good in each location.

two possible locations, A and B, and belongs to the consumer. Finally, resources are necessary to allow the movement of the worker and of the good between the two locations; in other words, transport costs are positive.

If the amount of land available in A is equal to or greater than 2 units, then the firm and the consumer can reside in the same place. In this case, the land rent in A is not negative ($R_A \geqslant 0$), while the land rent in B is zero ($R_B = 0$). If the rent R_A is not too high with respect to the level of transport costs, this configuration is an equilibrium, as no agent would be better off in B because the amount saved on the land rent would not compensate the agent for the transport costs. On the other hand, if the amount of land available in A is less than 2 units, either the firm or the consumer must reside in B so that the land rent in B also becomes nonnegative ($R_B \geqslant 0$). We will see that this configuration, which involves positive transport costs since the two agents are spatially separate, is *never* an equilibrium. More precisely, we are going to show that the firm can increase its profit or that the consumer can increase his income by changing location. The proof is done by contradiction.

Without loss of generality, it is assumed that the firm is located in A and that the consumer resides in B. If this configuration is an equilibrium, there are two prices for the good, p_A and p_B, two wage rates, w_A and w_B, and two land rents, R_A and R_B, such that the firm maximizes its profit by being established in A and the consumer his utility by being in B. The profit of this firm is equal to

$$\Pi_A = p_A y - w_A - R_A.$$

What would the profit of the firm be if it were established in B? To answer this question, it must be kept in mind that, in the competitive model, prices are not affected by agents' individual decisions. Moreover, since space is homogeneous, the firm is able to maintain the same input–output combination in B, and, thus, to produce the quantity y by using the same bundle of inputs. Consequently, its profit in B would be at least equal to

$$\Pi_B = p_B y - w_B - R_B.$$

Its incentive to change location (which can be positive, negative, or zero) is then given by

$$I_f = \Pi_B - \Pi_A = (p_B - p_A)y - (w_B - w_A) - (R_B - R_A). \qquad (2.1)$$

As for the consumer, his net income is equal to the sum of his wage and the income from his land minus his consumption expenses. Since he is located in B, this income is equal to

$$Y_B = w_B + (R_A + R_B) - R_B - p_B y = w_B + R_A - p_B y.$$

If, on the other hand, the consumer were located in A, his net income would be at least equal to

$$Y_A = w_A + R_B - p_A y,$$

his consumption being the same. In this case, his incentive to move is equal to

$$I_c = Y_A - Y_B = (p_B - p_A)y - (w_B - w_A) + (R_B - R_A). \qquad (2.2)$$

If the configuration considered is an equilibrium, no agent is induced to change location, which means that both (2.1) and (2.2) must be nonpositive. Now, by adding (2.1) and (2.2), we get

$$I = I_f + I_c = 2(p_B - p_A)y + 2(w_A - w_B). \qquad (2.3)$$

Because the market prices must reflect the relative scarcity of the good in each location, the difference between p_A and p_B is exactly equal to the unit cost of shipping the good between those two places (Samuelson 1952). As for the difference in salaries between w_A and w_B, this corresponds to the increase in the worker's salary that is needed for him to agree to work in A if he is located in B under the prevailing price system. Hence, I is equal to exactly twice the total transport cost of the good (given by $(p_B - p_A)y$) plus twice the cost to be paid for the worker to move (given by $w_A - w_B$). Consequently, when the two agents are separate, the total incentives to change location are positive and are of the same order of magnitude as aggregate transport costs.

In this example, the two agents must be located in the same place for a competitive equilibrium to exist. Using a general model in which each agent's consumption of land is endogenous, the number of agents is arbitrary, and where the sector of transportation is explicitly modeled, Starrett (1978) proves the following result.[7]

The spatial impossibility theorem. *Consider an economy with a finite number of locations. If space is homogeneous, transport is costly, and preferences are locally nonsatiated, then there exists no competitive equilibrium involving the transport of goods between locations.*

What is the meaning of this a priori unexpected result? Whenever economic activities are perfectly divisible, the spatial impossibility theorem implies that *the mobility of production factors is a perfect substitute for trade*. Such a result, proved by Mundell (1957) fifty years ago, is hardly surprising because every activity can be carried out on an arbitrarily

---

[7] It is worth stressing that no assumptions are made about the nonconvexity of preferences or technologies. The only nonconvexity is that agents are not ubiquitous.

small scale in every possible place, without any loss of efficiency. Firms and households are then induced to suppress all distance-related costs by producing exactly what they need where they are. By contrast, as pointed out by Starrett,

> so long as there are some indivisibilities in the system (so that individual operations must take up space) then a sufficiently complicated set of interrelated activities will generate transport costs.[8]
>
> Starrett (1978, p. 27)

In this case, the spatial impossibility theorem tells us something really new and important: whenever agents are mobile, there is no competitive equilibrium (hence the term "impossibility" in the name of the theorem) such that regions trade goods. In other words, *factor mobility and interregional trade are incompatible in a neoclassical world*. This result is especially meaningful insofar as it is internal to the theory itself.

Intuitively, the reason for this is that the only location factor that matters to an agent is its position with respect to the others. In this case, the price system must play two different roles: (i) it must allow trade between locations while guaranteeing that all local markets clear, and (ii) it must give firms and households the incentives not to change location. Once the economy is competitive and the space homogeneous, the spatial impossibility theorem tells us that it is impossible to kill two birds with one stone: *prices that sustain commodity flows between places send incorrect signals from the point of view of the stability of locations, and vice versa.*

The nature of this difficulty can be illustrated by means of a simple figure. Assume that one unit of good i is produced by a firm located in one of two places, A and B, using a fixed and given combination of inputs. To simplify, the cost of these inputs is assumed to be the same in each place. The product is transported by means of an *iceberg*-type technology: that is, if one unit of the good is moved between A and B, only a fraction $\theta < 1$ reaches the destination, the missing share $(1 - \theta)$ having "melted" on the way.[9] In figure 2.1, the horizontal axis represents the quantity of the output available in A and the vertical axis the quantity available in B. If the firm is located in A, the quantity of output available there is represented by point E on the horizontal axis. On the other hand, if all the output is shipped to B, only the quantity θ is available in B,

---

[8] Note again that the assumption of nonubuquitous agents is a special type of indivisibility.

[9] A more detailed discussion of this modeling of transport costs is presented in chapter 4.

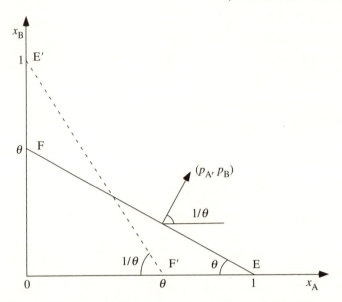

Figure 2.1. The production set when space is homogeneous.

which is represented by point F on the vertical axis. As a result, if the
firm is established in A, its production set is given by the triangle OEF.
Symmetrically, if the firm is set up in B, this set is given by the triangle
OE′F′. Hence, when the firm is not yet located, its production set is given
by the union of those two triangles.

Assume that the firm is located in A and that some fraction of the good
is shipped to B. In this case, every feasible allocation is represented by
one of the points of the segment EF, so that the equilibrium prices p_A and
p_B that prevail at A and B must satisfy the equality $p_B/p_A = 1/\theta > 1$, as
indicated in figure 2.1. Yet, at these prices, the firm can obtain a strictly
larger profit by choosing the production plan E′ since $p_B > p_A$, which
amounts to being established in B. The same holds, mutatis mutandis, if
the firm is located in B. Accordingly, there is no price system that allows
market clearing and profit maximization simultaneously.

This is because *activities are not ubiquitous* and *transport costs are positive*. Put together, these facts imply that every firm's production set—
and, consequently, the production set of the whole economy—is non-
convex. If shipping the output were free, the production set would be
given by the triangle OEE′ in figure 2.1, which is convex. In this case,
the firm would have no incentive to relocate. Similarly, if the production activity were perfectly divisible, the production set would again be
given by the triangle OEE′. Thus, we may safely conclude that the spatial

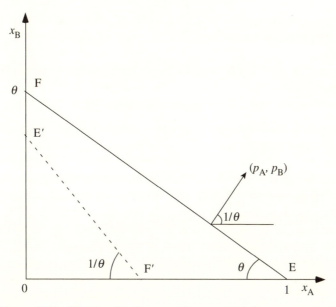

Figure 2.2. The production set when space is heterogeneous.

impossibility theorem stems from a combination of positive transport costs and of agents having an address in space.[10]

Finally, note that the spatial impossibility theorem no longer necessarily holds when available technologies vary with firms' locations. The role played by the assumption of a homogeneous space can be illustrated by reexamining the preceding example when the production set is now given by the triangle OE'F' (with OE' < 1) in figure 2.2 when the firm is established in B. When the firm is not yet located, its total production is then given by the triangle OEF, which is convex. In that case, the firm has no incentives to leave A.

2.5 What Are the Alternative Modeling Strategies?

Thus, if our objective is to explain the geographical distribution of economic activities, especially the making of agglomerations and the process of regional specialization, the spatial impossibility theorem tells us that we must start from at least one of the three following assumptions (Fujita and Thisse 2003a): (i) space is heterogeneous, as in the neoclassical theory of international trade; (ii) there are externalities in

---

[10] For more discussion regarding the spatial impossibility theorem and its consequences, see Fujita and Thisse (2002, chapter 2).

production and/or in consumption, as in urban economics; or (iii) markets are imperfectly competitive, as in spatial competition and economic geography.

While, in the real world, economic spaces are likely to be the result of various combinations of these three elements, it is convenient to separate them so that we can grasp the effects of each of them better.

(A) Comparative advantage. The heterogeneity of space presupposes an uneven distribution of "givens" (technologies, natural resources, amenities) and the existence of transport nodes (ports, points of transfer) and/or marketplaces (stock exchanges, city-markets).

In the Ricardian model, a given country is assumed to have a more efficient technology than the others. Each country then specializes in the production of the good for which its relative opportunity cost is lower. In the neoclassical model developed by Heckscher and Ohlin, countries have access to the same technologies but have different endowments in production factors. The international immobility of production factors implies that the relative prices of goods are different under autarchy, thus making trade desirable. Once trade is liberalized, each country specializes in the production of goods that use the production factor in which its relative endowment is higher. In both cases, what remains to be explained is why a specific country (or region) is more efficient than others, or why production factors are immobile while goods are not. Is building economic geography on such assumptions not like playing *Hamlet* without the prince?

(B) Externalities. Agglomeration forces are generated endogenously through *nonmarket interactions* among firms and/or households (knowledge spillovers, business communications, and social interactions).

According to Marshall, external effects are essential to understand the making of agglomerations. Marshallian economies aim to capture a fundamental idea: an agglomeration is the outcome of a snowball effect in which the concentration of a growing number of agents, who benefit from the advantages generated by a greater diversity and/or a greater specialization in activities, reinforces these advantages, thus attracting new agents, and so on. However, as seen above, working with such tools often amounts to using black boxes.[11] Although informational spillovers and learning processes are likely to be one of the engines of development at a microspatial level, it is hard to see how they could operate in

---

[11] Ever since Scitovsky (1954), two categories of external effects have been distinguished: *technological externalities* and *pecuniary externalities*. The former are restricted only to nonmarket interactions directly affecting individual utility or firms' production functions. The latter result from market interactions and affect firms or consumers/workers by means of exchanges involving prices.

the making of spatial inequalities at the interregional level because their scope is spatially bounded.

(C) Imperfect competition. When maximizing their profits, *firms no longer treat prices as given* but are price-makers. Because the level of prices typically depends on the spatial distribution of firms and consumers, the resulting interdependence between firms and households may yield agglomerations. Two approaches must be distinguished.

(i) Monopolistic competition. This type of competition involves a modest departure from the competitive model while allowing firms to be price-makers because they produce differentiated goods under increasing returns. However, strategic interactions are either absent or weak because the number of firms is large.

(ii) Oligopolistic competition. We now have a small number of big agents (firms, local governments, land developers) that interact strategically.

The consequences of choosing a modeling strategy are important. Models (A), (B), and (C i) are concerned with the economy as a whole and involve negligible agents. On the other hand, in models of (C ii) type, we want to know who is where, or with whom does each agent interact. Moreover, by emphasizing the heterogeneity of space (case (A)), the first theorem of welfare applies so that the market equilibrium is socially optimal. In the other two approaches (cases (B) and (C)), the presence of market failures implies that the market outcome is inefficient.

Comparative-advantage models have been used extensively in trade theory, as well as in standard urban economics. We do not wish to pursue this line of research. Quite the opposite, we will control for the impact of spatial heterogeneities by assuming that space is homogeneous. Furthermore, as models with externalities are relevant mainly at the urban level, they are not considered here either. In the rest of this book we are interested solely in models with imperfect competition, with or without strategic interactions. We will see that such models allow for the endogenous formation of specific comparative advantage or external effects.

2.6 Increasing Returns and Transport Costs: The Basic Trade-Off of Economic Geography

The point we want to make here is that *the trade-off between increasing returns and transport costs is fundamental to the understanding of the geography of economic activities.* Although it has been studied and understood for a long time, this trade-off has been rediscovered several times, including recently. By modifying both transport costs and firms' technologies, the Industrial Revolution profoundly changed the terms of that trade-off. Yet it is not only the level of transport costs that matters: it is also the way in which they vary with the distance covered. Less well-known is the impact of this variability on firms' locations.

2.6.1   The Optimal Number and Size of Firms

Archeologists have noted that the distances separating the regional capitals of ancient Egypt were very similar. The reason for this seems to be the capacity to store grain, one of the main justifications for the existence of those cities. Beyond a certain distance, shipping grain became so costly that it was preferable to build a new center.

The Industrial Revolution, as we have seen, brought lower transport costs, but also an increase in the size of production plants. The very first industrial plants had a very small optimal size. Indeed, as observed by Bairoch:

> In most manufacturing sectors, it was possible for a firm to have a competitive position with a very small size. The narrowness of the market, due to high transport costs, made it even easier to operate at a very low scale.
>
>   Bairoch (1997, volume 1, p. 347) [our translation]

Things changed after the second half of the nineteenth century. The minimal size of a firm grew because of the use of increasingly diversified equipment, which then required more workers. This growth in the size of firms was sustained by the expansion of markets areas, which in turn was possible because of the strong decline in transport costs. In brief, these simultaneous changes led to a gradual reduction in the number of firms, whose size increased. Take, for example, the case of Belgian steel enterprises: while their average workforce in 1845 was 26 people, it reached 446 people in 1930 (Bairoch 1997, volume I, p. 345).

Hence, it is no surprise that the trade-off between increasing returns and transport costs is at the heart of the work of the first contributors to location theory. Thus, for example, Lösch wrote:

> We shall consider market areas that are not the result of any kind of natural or political inequalities but arise through the interplay of purely economic forces, some working toward concentration, and others toward dispersion. In the first group are the advantages of specialization and of large-scale production; in the second, those of shipping costs and of diversified production.
>
>   Lösch (1940, p. 105 of the English translation)

The forces mentioned by Lösch refer to the fixed costs of production and the costs of transporting goods. The trade-off between these two forces is easy to understand. First, in the absence of fixed production costs, one plant could be built in each consumption place so that there would be nothing to ship (as in the case of backyard capitalism). Moreover, in the absence of transport costs, a single plant would be enough to satisfy the entire demand (except for the case where its marginal cost of production would increase). When transport costs increase with distance, this is formally equivalent to the case in which a fixed cost coexists with a growing marginal cost: each plant supplies consumers located within a certain radius, the length of which depends on the relative level of the transport costs and the intensity of increasing returns, but those located beyond this radius are supplied by another unit.

The nature of this trade-off can be illustrated by considering the simple case of two locations where the need for a given good is identical (δ). Two options are then available: either build a plant in each location at a cost of F per location, in which case the total cost is $2F$; or build one plant in a single location and ship the good to the other location at a cost proportional to the quantity transported $t\delta$, which gives a total cost of $F + t\delta$. The optimal solution, then, is to have a single unit if and only if

$$F + t\delta < 2F \iff t < F/\delta,$$

which is likely to hold when F is high and t is low. In the opposite case, it is optimal to have two plants. This example is enough to understand that *high fixed costs favor the concentration of production in a small number of units*, as in modern developed economies; on the other hand, the situation in which *high transport costs encourage the proliferation of establishments across space* characterizes preindustrial economies fairly well.

More generally, the trade-off between increasing returns and transport costs can be described as follows: given a spatial distribution of needs to be satisfied, what are the *number* and *location* of plants that minimize the sum of production and transport costs? On the demand side, the following simplifying assumption is made: consumers are distributed uniformly along a linear segment of unit length, while their individual needs are fixed and are equal to $\delta > 0$. In addition, the transport cost of a unit of a good is a linear function of the distance covered.

Let us first assume that locations need to be chosen for n plants. When the marginal cost of production c is constant and the same across plants, the uniformity of the density of needs implies that these plants must be set up equidistantly on the linear segment, two adjacent plants then being separated by a distance of $1/n$. To see this, consider the case of a plant to be set up between two existing plants installed at $x = 0$ and $x = 1$. Each consumer buys the good from the closest plant otherwise he would not minimize his transport costs. If the new plant is located at $x \in (0, 1)$, consumers located to the left of x are distributed equally between the new plant and the one at $x = 0$; similarly, consumers located to the right of x are also equally distributed between that plant and the one at $x = 1$. Therefore, the total transport cost is given by the sum of the costs borne by the consumers patronizing each of the three plants:

$$T(x) = \int_0^{x/2} \delta t\, y\, dy + \int_{x/2}^{(1+x)/2} \delta t\, |y - x|\, dy + \int_{(1+x)/2}^1 \delta t(1 - y)\, dy$$
$$= \delta t[\tfrac{1}{4}x^2 + \tfrac{1}{4}(1 + x)^2 - x],$$

which is a strictly convex function of x. It is readily verified that the first-order condition implies that $x^* = \tfrac{1}{2}$. In other words, to minimize total transport costs, the new plant must be set up in the middle of the two others. For each plant to be in the middle of the segment linking the two adjacent plants, the configuration must be symmetric.

Let us now determine the total costs of production and transport in the case of n equidistant plants. We have

$$C(n) = nF + c\delta + n \int_{-1/2n}^{1/2n} \delta t\, y\, dy$$
$$= nF + c\delta + \delta t\frac{1}{4n}.$$

This function is strictly convex, so the optimal number of plants is given by

$$n^* = \frac{1}{2}\sqrt{\frac{\delta t}{F}}.$$

This number, and hence the degree of spatial dispersion of production, then increases with the size of the market (measured here by the parameter δ) and with the unit transport cost t, but decreases with the level of fixed costs F. In the absence of fixed costs ($F = 0$), the number of plants tends to infinity: we fall back on backyard capitalism. On the other hand, in the case of zero transport costs, a single plant suffices to satisfy the total demand. There is, therefore, a trade-off between increasing returns and transport costs.

As will be seen in the subsequent chapters, the same trade-off is found, in different forms, in models of economic geography. What makes these models very appealing is the fact that we are not limited to a simple minimization of costs as we are here. On the contrary, each agent will choose his location in terms of his own interest only. One major consequence of this is that the cost parameters (*F* and *c*) and the demand level (δ) become endogenous and different across locations because they depend on the locational decisions made by all agents. This is what distinguishes them from models of international trade with imperfect competition in which the location of production factors is given and fixed.

2.6.2 The Optimal Location of a Firm

The simplest firm-location problem is the one in which the firm buys one input in one market and sells its output in another, with the two markets being connected by some transport link (which can be represented by a straight line). Assuming for simplicity that input and output can be shipped at the same unit cost, the value of the elasticity of this cost function with respect to distance allows measurement of the impact of a marginal increase in the length of a movement on the unit transport cost. It is, therefore, an indicator of the degree of increasing returns in transportation.

More precisely, a high value of this elasticity means that making the movement slightly longer increases its cost greatly. In this case, the value of transport costs is determined solely by the distance covered when shipping goods. Such a situation describes quite well periods in which moving commodities was both dangerous and difficult, thus necessitating coaching inns for ground transport and coastal navigation for maritime transport. On the other hand, a low elasticity implies that the share of transport costs due to investments in infrastructure and equipment grows, so that distance matters less. Clearly, such a situation is characteristic of modern economies.

In both of the cases discussed in the preceding paragraph, the optimal location of the firm can be viewed as the equilibrium point of a system governed by two forces generated by the need for proximity to the product market and the factor market. The intensity of these two forces depends, on the one hand, on the weight of each of these markets and, on the other, on the marginal cost of transport with respect to distance.

To start with, assume that the elasticity is much larger than 1. In that case, the intensity of each force increases rapidly with distance. By going away from the middle of the segment toward one of the two markets, the force exercised by the other market grows rapidly, thus coming to counterbalance the first. Consequently, the system of forces is in equilibrium when the firm chooses a location close to the middle of the segment connecting the two markets: increasing the length of a trip is so costly that it is desirable for the firm to reduce the distance to the farthest market. This is why a relay located somewhere in between is needed.

Once the elasticity starts to decrease, while remaining higher than 1, the optimal location gets closer to the market that has the largest weight. In other words, the firm chooses to set up nearer to its main market because the impact of an increase in distance to the other market has decreased as a result of the drop in elasticity. If the elasticity further decreases to reach a value equal to 1, the firm chooses to establish itself in the place with the highest weight. Because the intensity of the forces is now independent of the distances to the markets, every intermediary location becomes suboptimal. This remains true when elasticity takes on values less than 1, as the marginal cost of transport now decreases with distance.

The way in which distance has affected transport costs over time may then be described succinctly as follows. The long period during which all movement was very costly and risky was followed by another during which, thanks to technological and organizational advances, ships could cross longer distances in one go, thus reducing their number of stops. On land, it was necessary to wait for the advent of the railroad for appreciable progress to occur, but the results were the same. In both cases, long-distance journeys became less expensive and no longer demanded the presence of relays or rest areas. Such an evolution in technologies has favored places of origin and destination at the expense of intermediate places. Hence, we may safely conclude that *increasing returns in transport explain why places situated between large markets and transport nodes have lost many of their activities.*

2.7   Concluding Remarks

In this chapter, we have tried to explain the (relative) absence of space in economic theory. Differences in factor endowments and technologies are the major spatial variables considered in standard trade models because both are consistent with the paradigm involving constant returns and perfect competition. Two distinct examples have allowed us to understand why increasing returns are an essential ingredient of the space-economy. This explains to a large extent why space was so often ignored, as taking account of increasing returns demands either externalities or imperfectly competitive markets. Externalities are often black boxes that hide nonmarket mechanisms that deserve to be described and studied in and of themselves. They are outside the scope of this book, which zeroes in on the market-based micro-foundations of agglomerations. Therefore, we will consider general-equilibrium models with monopolistic competition (chapters 3–8) and partial-equilibrium models with oligopolistic competition (chapter 9). What is common to all these different models is the trade-off between increasing returns and transport/trade costs, which was briefly described in the preceding section.

Part II

Space, Trade, and Agglomeration

3
Monopolistic Competition

The standard model of economic geography relies on the Dixit–Stiglitz model of monopolistic competition, which makes it possible to integrate both *increasing returns* and *imperfect competition* in a very simple and elegant way. This combination is crucial for economic geography. Indeed, as seen in chapter 2, the presence of increasing returns is necessary to explain the agglomeration of activities in a homogeneous space. Under increasing returns at the firm level, the assumption of perfect competition becomes untenable, as marginal cost pricing results in negative profits. We therefore need a setting that integrates both increasing returns and imperfect competition to analyze the formation of economic agglomeration. Moreover, this setting must be of the general-equilibrium type as it has to include the interactions between product and labor markets. Finally, trade must arise in equilibrium if we want to avoid regions or countries ending up in autarky (see chapter 2). Of all the market structures studied in industrial organization, economic geography has focused on *monopolistic competition*, even though alternative approaches have been followed (see chapter 9). The aim of this chapter is to explain the reasons for this choice and to survey this family of models. We focus here on a closed economy; the case of an open economy will be dealt with in chapter 4.

The concept of monopolistic competition goes back to Chamberlin (1933).[1] It can be described by means of the following four assumptions:

  (i) Firms sell products of the same nature but they are not perfect substitutes—we refer to them as the *varieties* of a differentiated good.

  (ii) Every firm produces a single variety under increasing returns and chooses its price.

---

[1] The interested reader will find a more concise and, above all, clearer presentation of his ideas in Chamberlin (1951) than in the various editions of his earlier work. In this chapter, we shall focus solely on the formulations used in international economics and economic geography.

(iii) The number of firms belonging to the industry is sufficiently large for each of them to be negligible with respect to the whole group of firms.

(iv) Finally, there is free entry and exit, so profits are zero.

These assumptions bear a strong resemblance with those of perfect competition, the main difference being the fact that here each firm sells a specific product and chooses its own price. This endows each firm with a specific market, in which the firm has some monopoly power. However, the existence of other varieties implies that the size of this market depends on the behavior of the other firms, thus constraining each producer in their price choice. In other words, although the firm is not in a situation of perfect competition, neither is it in a situation of monopoly. Finally, since firms operate under increasing returns, the resources available in the economy impose a limit on the number of varieties capable of being produced. In general, this number depends on the entry barriers that firms face. In the case of monopolistic competition, it is assumed that the fixed cost associated with the launching of a new variety is the only effective barrier. Such an entry barrier is nonstrategic because it cannot be manipulated by the firms.

After having attracted a great deal of attention in the 1930s, Chamberlin's ideas lost most of their appeal until Spence (1976) and, above all, Dixit and Stiglitz (1977) brought them back onto the scientific stage by proposing a model capable of being used in various economic fields. Spence has developed a partial-equilibrium setting, whereas the Dixit–Stiglitz model places itself in a general-equilibrium context. We will therefore focus on the Dixit and Stiglitz model here. The main purpose of this chapter is to present an up-to-date discussion of this model and to study its principal properties. We will place special emphasis on the role played by the assumption of a continuum of firms. Hotelling (1929) and Aumann (1964) have shown that the idea than an agent (whether a consumer or a firm) has no influence on a market can only be captured by means of a continuum of agents, which are all negligible in the sense of measure theory.[2] Despite its appropriateness to describe Chamberlin's intuition, it took a long time for this idea to be integrated into the framework of monopolistic competition. In the second section of this chapter we will present a linear model of monopolistic competition recently put forward in economic geography to remedy certain weaknesses of the Dixit–Stiglitz model.

---

[2] Since then, the same assumption has been made in several economic fields.

3.1 The Dixit–Stiglitz Approach

The economy is made up of two sectors called *agriculture* (or the traditional sector) and *industry* (or the modern sector). The denomination of these two sectors is conventional and can vary according to the historical period under consideration. For example, for a long time the textile industry was the industry of reference, while this role was later taken by steel and, after that, by the automobile sector. What really matters for our purposes are the market and technological properties of these two sectors: in agriculture, a homogeneous good is produced under constant returns and is sold in a perfectly competitive market; in the manufacturing sector, firms produce a differentiated good under increasing returns and compete in a monopolistic competition setting.

3.1.1 Consumption and Production

3.1.1.1 Preferences and Demand Functions

The economy involves L consumers whose preferences are identical and are given by a Cobb–Douglas utility function:

$$U = CM^{\mu}A^{1-\mu}, \quad 0 < \mu < 1, \tag{3.1}$$

where C is a positive constant chosen so that the coefficient of indirect utility is normalized to 1.[3] In this expression, A denotes the quantity of the agricultural good and M denotes the quantity of a *composite* differentiated good defined by a CES-type index:

$$M \equiv \left(\sum_{i=1}^{n} q_i^{\rho} \right)^{1/\rho}, \quad 0 < \rho < 1,$$

where q_i is the quantity of variety i consumed, n is the total number of varieties available, and ρ is a parameter that, as we will see later, is an inverse measure of the degree of differentiation across varieties. We therefore assume that the varieties are differentiated and that they affect the value of M in a symmetric way.[4] Instead of using ρ, it will often prove convenient to use the parameter σ, the elasticity of substitution between any two varieties. These two parameters are related through the following expressions:

$$\sigma = \frac{1}{1-\rho} \quad \text{or} \quad \rho = \frac{\sigma-1}{\sigma}.$$

---

[3] It is readily verified that C is such that $C^{-1} \equiv \mu^{\mu}(1-\mu)^{1-\mu}$.

[4] The assumption that firms sell differentiated goods is in itself justified by the "principle of differentiation," which says that firms soften competition by selling differentiated goods (Tirole 1988).

The elasticity of substitution therefore ranges from 1 to ∞. The index M may then be rewritten as follows:

$$M = \left(\sum_{i=1}^{n} q_i^{(\sigma-1)/\sigma} \right)^{\sigma/(\sigma-1)}. \tag{3.2}$$

When σ tends to ∞ ($\rho = 1$), varieties are perfect substitutes as

$$M = \sum_{i=1}^{n} q_i.$$

By contrast, they are totally independent when $\sigma = 1$ ($\rho = 0$), as the index M boils down to a Cobb–Douglas subutility function with $M = \prod_{i=1}^{n} q_i$. For all intermediate values of σ, varieties are imperfect substitutes, ρ and σ being inverse measures of the degree of product differentiation across varieties.

Assume that a consumer has a quantity $\bar{M}$ of the composite good that is uniformly distributed among a limited number $k < n$ of varieties. Her well-being is therefore given by (up to the constant C)

$$\left[\sum_{i=1}^{k} \left(\frac{\bar{M}}{k} \right)^{(\sigma-1)/\sigma} \right]^{\mu(\sigma/(\sigma-1))} A^{1-\mu} = k^{\mu/(\sigma-1)} A^{1-\mu} \bar{M}^{\mu},$$

which is an increasing function of k since $\sigma > 1$. Consequently, rather than concentrating her consumption over a small number of varieties, every consumer prefers to spread it over a larger number of varieties until k is equal to the total n of varieties available. This property means that the CES index M incorporates what is called a *preference for diversity*—a preference that pushes consumers to purchase all the available varieties at an intensity that varies with the parameter σ (Bénassy 1996). This is because individuals want to avoid the boredom generated by the repeated consumption of the same variety: they prefer consuming different varieties, either one by one or simultaneously. Such an assumption also captures the basic idea, mentioned in the foreword, that a greater range of choices makes large urban regions more attractive to consumers.[5] As will be seen below, such preferences imply that the introduction of a new variety does not lead to the disappearance of existing varieties but rather to a reduction in their consumption.

If p_a denotes the price of the agricultural good and P the price index of the manufactured good (which will be defined in section 3.1.1.3), the budget constraint of a consumer, whose revenue is y, is

$$PM + p_a A \leqslant y.$$

---

[5] Remember that the preference for diversity is formally identical to the convexity of indifference curves and that this, in turn, is equivalent to the assumption of a quasi-concave utility function.

In this case, it is well-known that the aggregate demand functions take the form

$$M = \frac{E}{P} \quad \text{and} \quad A = \frac{E_a}{p_a},$$
(3.3)

where $E \equiv \mu L y$ and $E_a \equiv (1-\mu)L y$ are the expenditures of all consumers on the manufactured good and the agricultural good, respectively.

Expenditure E being given, the consumption of each variety is then obtained by maximizing (3.2) under the constraint $\sum_{j=1}^{n} p_j q_j \leqslant E$. The Lagrangian of this problem is

$$\mathcal{L} = M + \lambda\left(E - \sum_{j=1}^{n} p_j q_j\right),$$

and the first-order conditions are

$$\frac{\partial \mathcal{L}}{\partial q_i} = \frac{\partial M}{\partial q_i} - \lambda p_i = 0, \quad i = 1, \dots, n,$$
(3.4)

$$\frac{\partial \mathcal{L}}{\partial \lambda} = E - \sum_{j=1}^{n} p_j q_j = 0.$$
(3.5)

Conditions (3.4) are equivalent to

$$M^{1/\sigma} q_i^{-1/\sigma} = \lambda p_i, \quad i = 1, \dots, n,$$

which can be rewritten as follows:

$$q_i = M \lambda^{-\sigma} p_i^{-\sigma}.$$
(3.6)

If we multiply (3.6) by p_i, add the so-obtained terms over i, and substitute this sum in (3.5), we get

$$M \lambda^{-\sigma} = \frac{E}{\sum_j p_j^{-(\sigma-1)}},$$

which gives us, after substitution into (3.6), the aggregate demand function for variety i:

$$q_i = \frac{p_i^{-\sigma}}{\sum_j p_j^{-(\sigma-1)}} E, \quad i = 1, \dots, n.$$
(3.7)

The demand for a variety is, therefore, a function of the prices of *all* varieties, which is in contrast to what we will see later with models of spatial competition, in which each firm is in direct competition only with its immediate neighbors in space (see chapter 9 for further details). If one firm sets a higher price than its competitors, then consumers reduce their consumption of the corresponding variety, but their preference for variety has the effect of keeping the demand for this firm positive.

Expression (3.7) implies, moreover, that the introduction of a new variety increases the denominator and, consequently, leads to a reduction in the demand for the existing varieties $i = 1, \ldots, n$ so long as their prices remain unchanged. In other words, the entry of new varieties triggers the fragmentation of demand over more varieties. This is known as the "market-crowding" (or fragmentation) effect.

Finally, the relative demand of two varieties is given by

$$\frac{q_i}{q_j} = \left(\frac{p_i}{p_j}\right)^{-\sigma},$$

which is independent of the price of other varieties. This property, although restrictive, will prove very useful in various empirical applications in which the denominator of the CES demand function (3.7) is difficult to estimate. Furthermore, because the elasticity of substitution, which is given by

$$\frac{\partial \ln(q_i/q_j)}{\partial \ln(p_i/p_j)} = -\sigma,$$

is constant, it becomes clear why the term CES stands for "constant elasticity of substitution."

3.1.1.2 *Preference for Diversity and Heterogeneous Consumers*

The assumption of identical consumers is similar to that of the representative consumer used by Dixit and Stiglitz, which has long been known to have severe weaknesses (Kirman 1992). Furthermore, the fact that consumers have a taste for diversity implies that all individuals consume the whole array of varieties. Such behavior may seem unrealistic, but it is in fact less restrictive than it seems at first glance. Anderson et al. (1992, chapter 3) have demonstrated that the same demand functions can be obtained from a *population of heterogeneous consumers who buy a single variety*, while it was assumed above that consumers are identical and consume all varieties.

To show this, consider a situation in which each individual chooses a single variety i, which she consumes in quantity q_i; in this case, we have in mind mutually exclusive or discrete choices. In addition, each individual spends an amount E/L on the manufactured good, where L has been defined as the number of consumers. The utility function associated with the consumption of variety i, ignoring the agricultural good, is assumed to be given by

$$\tilde{U}_i = \ln q_i + \varepsilon_i, \quad i = 1, \ldots, n,$$

where ε_i is a random variable whose *realization measures the quality of the match between this consumer and variety i*. At identical prices, a specific consumer's ideal variety is the one for which the realization of the random variable is highest. Because they face different realizations of ε_i, different consumers have different matches with variety i. Given her own set of matches, each consumer chooses the variety i that provides her with the highest utility. The corresponding indirect utility is thus given by

$$\tilde{V}_i = \ln(E/L) - \ln p_i + \varepsilon_i,$$

since her consumption of variety i is equal to $q_i = E/Lp_i$, where p_i is the price of variety i. In this context, the distribution function of ε_i $(i = 1, \ldots, n)$, assumed to be the same for each variety, reflects the *heterogeneity* of consumers' tastes with respect to the varieties offered because the realizations of ε_i vary across consumers.

Our objective is to determine the aggregate demand for each variety. To do this, it is necessary to make certain assumptions about the heterogeneity of consumers, i.e., about the distribution of ε_i. Ever since the work of McFadden (1974), it has been known that the probability of a consumer choosing variety i is given by the *multinomial logit* (MNL),

$$P_i = \frac{\exp(-(1/v)\ln p_i)}{\sum_{j=1}^{n} \exp(-(1/v)\ln p_j)} = \frac{p_i^{-1/v}}{\sum_{j=1}^{n} p_j^{-1/v}},$$

if and only if the ε_i are independent and distributed according to the Gumbel distribution (the parameter v represents the degree of dispersion of consumers' preferences).[6] Moreover, if consumers' individual choices are independent, the expected aggregate demand is equal to L times the individual probability of choosing i, multiplied by the individual consumption of this variety:

$$D_i = LP_i q_i = \frac{p_i^{-1/v}}{\sum_{j=1}^{n} p_j^{-1/v}} \frac{E}{p_i}.$$

If $v = 1/(\sigma - 1) > 0$, we fall back on the CES-type demand (3.7). In other words, the assumption that consumers have a preference for diversity is equivalent to assuming the existence of a heterogeneous population in which each individual consumes a single variety chosen from the array of available varieties. Consequently, we can focus on the CES formulation

---

[6] The cumulative function of a random variable ε_i distributed according to the *Gumbel law* is given by $F(\varepsilon_i) = \exp[-\exp(-(\varepsilon_i/v + y))]$, where $y \approx 0.577$ is Euler's constant. Its mean is yv and its variance $v^2\pi^2/6$. The Gumbel law provides a fairly good approximation of the normal law and has the further advantage of having an explicit form for its cumulative function. It also has several appealing properties in discrete choice theory. The reader is referred to Anderson et al. (1992, chapter 2) for a detailed discussion of this distribution.

presented above without worrying too much about the assumption that all individuals consume all varieties.

Clearly, the expression

$$s_i \equiv \frac{p_i q_i}{E} = \frac{p_i^{-(\sigma-1)}}{\sum_{j=1}^n p_j^{-(\sigma-1)}}$$

denotes the market share of variety i. It is therefore equal to a logit-type probability, the interpretation of which is fairly straightforward: the probability that a variety is chosen depends negatively on its price and positively on the price of the competing varieties. This property has two interesting implications. First, it highlights some of the links between CES and MNL. In both cases, the probability of choosing a variety is the same. It is the quantity of the chosen variety that is consumed which distinguishes these two models. In the CES case, this quantity is equal to the income spent on the manufactured good divided by the price of the variety, while in the MNL the demand is totally inelastic and is equal to 1. Furthermore, as we have seen, the ratio of the CES demands for two varieties is independent of the price of the other varieties—a property also shared by the MNL case.

3.1.1.3 Price Index

We first show that the denominator of the demand function (3.7) is directly related to the price index of the manufactured good. Introducing the equilibrium consumption of each variety into the definition of the composite good (3.2) yields

$$M = \left[\sum_{i=1}^n \left(\frac{p_i^{-\sigma}}{\sum_j p_j^{-(\sigma-1)}} E \right)^{(\sigma-1)/\sigma} \right]^{\sigma/(\sigma-1)}$$

$$= E \left[\frac{\sum_i p_i^{-(\sigma-1)}}{(\sum_j p_j^{-(\sigma-1)})^{(\sigma-1)/\sigma}} \right]^{\sigma/(\sigma-1)}$$

$$= E \left[\left(\sum_{i=1}^n p_i^{-(\sigma-1)} \right)^{1-((\sigma-1)/\sigma)} \right]^{\sigma/(\sigma-1)}$$

$$= E \left(\sum_{i-1}^n p_i^{-(\sigma-1)} \right)^{1/(\sigma-1)},$$

so the total expenditure E on the manufactured good, which is a fraction of the total income, is given by

$$E = M \left(\sum_{i=1}^n p_i^{-(\sigma-1)} \right)^{-1/(\sigma-1)}.$$

This expression says that the level of expenditure on the manufactured good is equal to the CES aggregate of the quantities consumed, M, times a term that may be interpreted as the *price index* of the manufactured good:

$$P \equiv \left(\sum_{i=1}^{n} p_i^{-(\sigma-1)} \right)^{-1/(\sigma-1)}.$$

One important property of this index is that *it decreases with the number of varieties available*. Indeed, if all the prices are identical and equal to p, we come up with

$$P = \left(\sum_{i=1}^{n} p_i^{-(\sigma-1)} \right)^{-1/(\sigma-1)} = pn^{-1/(\sigma-1)}, \tag{3.8}$$

which is a decreasing function of the number n of varieties because $\sigma > 1$. This property is nothing but the counterpart in the price space of the preference for diversity in the variety space. Furthermore, the less differentiated the varieties, the lower the price index. This accounts for the fact that a larger elasticity of substitution makes the differentiated product less attractive to consumers. A lower price index may then be viewed as a compensation.

The demand functions (3.7) may then be rewritten as follows:

$$q_i = p_i^{-\sigma} P^{\sigma-1} E = \left(\frac{p_i}{P} \right)^{-\sigma} \frac{E}{P} \quad \text{and} \quad A = \frac{E_a}{p_a}. \tag{3.9}$$

Hence, the demand for a variety increases with the price index so that a low (respectively, high) price index means that the product market is more (respectively, less) competitive. In other words, *a firm's demand accounts for the aggregate behavior of its competitors via the price index*. This demand may thus be interpreted as the result of a two-stage process: consumers first choose the amount to spend on the manufactured good according to the index P, before sharing it among the varieties available according to their specific price. In other words, the term p_i/P encapsulates the competition effect between variety i and the other varieties, while the second term E/P denotes the aggregate demand for the manufactured good.

Introducing the demands (3.9) into the utility function (3.1) yields a consumer's indirect utility, which evaluates her well-being in terms of her income y and prices,

$$V = \frac{y}{P^\mu p_a^{1-\mu}} \equiv \omega, \tag{3.10}$$

which is here equal to her *real income*, the nominal income being divided by the price $P^\mu p_a^{1-\mu}$ of the batch consumed. As will be shown later on, in the standard model of economic geography with labor mobility, the consumer chooses her residence and her workplace by comparing the real incomes she can earn in the various regions.

3.1.1.4 Technologies

Agriculture uses only unskilled labor. We assume that there is perfect competition and constant returns in this sector, so that the price of the agricultural good (p_a) is equal to its marginal cost, which is equal to the marginal labor requirement (m_a) times the agricultural wage (w_a): $p_a = m_a w_a$. Without any loss of generality, we assume that one worker produces one unit of agricultural good, which means that $m_a = 1$. Consequently, the price of this good is equal to the wage of unskilled workers ($p_a = w_a$). The agricultural good being the numéraire ($p_a = 1$), we have

$$p_a = w_a = 1.$$

In the manufacturing sector, there are increasing returns at the firm level, but no scope economies that would induce a firm to produce several varieties. Each firm therefore produces a single variety. Furthermore, no two firms sell the same variety because this would allow them to relax price competition (see also chapter 9). Consequently, the n varieties of the manufactured good are produced by n different firms. We can therefore identify the set of varieties with the set of firms. The technology is identical in all locations—there are no comparative advantages—and for all the varieties—there are no specific advantages—so that space is homogeneous in the sense of chapter 2.

Three strategies for the modeling of technologies are found in the literature. They make use of various assumptions regarding production factors. In particular, labor is either homogeneous or heterogeneous, in which case we distinguish between skilled and unskilled workers. Each worker supplies one unit of her type of labor.

In the first modeling strategy, labor is homogeneous, and therefore perfectly mobile between sectors, which implies that the wage prevailing in the manufacturing sector is equal to w_a. The amount f denotes the fixed requirement and m denotes the marginal requirement of labor in each firm. The production of q_i units of variety i thus requires a total quantity of labor equal to $l = f + mq_i$. In this case, the production cost is given by

$$C(q_i) = f w_a + m w_a q_i = f + m q_i. \tag{3.11}$$

This cost function is therefore of the unique-factor type.

In the second strategy, labor is heterogeneous and specific to each sector. There are L_a unskilled workers employed in agriculture and L

skilled workers in the manufacturing sector. The cost of producing q_i units of variety i is now given by

$$C(q_i) = fw + mwq_i, \tag{3.12}$$

where w is the wage of skilled workers, which typically differs from w_a. This cost function is of the specific-factor type.

Finally, in the third strategy, labor and capital are the production factors. Labor is homogeneous and a worker's wage is equal to w_a, regardless of the sector. Each firm uses a fixed requirement f of capital and a variable quantity of labor mq_i. The production cost is therefore given by

$$C(q_i) = fr + mw_a q_i = fr + mq_i, \tag{3.13}$$

where r is the return on capital. In this case, the cost function is of the crossed-factor type.

We will use (3.12) later on in this chapter, while the other two specifications will be considered elsewhere in the book.

3.1.2 Market Equilibrium

3.1.2.1 Price

Let w be the wage of skilled workers. Firm i's profit is then

$$\pi_i = p_i q_i - C(q_i) = (p_i - mw)q_i - fw,$$

where the demand q_i is given by (3.9). Firm i's equilibrium price is determined by maximizing the profit π_i with respect to p_i. Letting the price elasticity of the demand (3.9) for variety i, denoted by ϵ_i, be given by

$$\epsilon_i = -\frac{\partial q_i}{\partial p_i}\frac{p_i}{q_i},$$

the first-order condition gives the following classical result:

$$p_i\left(1 - \frac{1}{\epsilon_i}\right) = mw,$$

provided $\epsilon_i > 1$, otherwise the left-hand side of this expression would be negative. Here lies one of the key assumptions of the Dixit–Stiglitz model: *the absence of strategic interactions between firms*—an assumption that explains both its simplicity and its success in various applications. This point deserves further elaboration.

First, if we assume that the firm takes expenditure E as constant, we have

$$\frac{\partial q_i}{\partial p_i} = \frac{-\sigma p_i^{-\sigma-1} \sum_j p_j^{-(\sigma-1)} + p_i^{-\sigma}(\sigma-1)p_i^{-\sigma}}{(\sum_j p_j^{-(\sigma-1)})^2} E$$

$$= -\sigma \frac{p_i^{-\sigma-1}}{\sum_j p_j^{-(\sigma-1)}} E + \left(\frac{p_i^{-\sigma}}{\sum_j p_j^{-(\sigma-1)}}\right)^2 (\sigma-1)E$$

$$= -\sigma \frac{q_i}{p_i} + q_i^2 \frac{\sigma-1}{E},$$

so

$$\epsilon_i = \sigma - \frac{(\sigma-1)q_i p_i}{E} = \sigma - (\sigma-1)s_i. \tag{3.14}$$

In a symmetric market, when the number of firms increases, each of them experiences a drop in its market share, s_i. Ultimately, when n tends to ∞, s_i tends to 0, so that the price elasticity is such that

$$\epsilon_i = \sigma.$$

Therefore, if we assume that the number of firms is large, the first-order condition determining the equilibrium price boils down to a very simple expression:

$$p^* = \frac{\sigma}{\sigma-1} mw, \tag{3.15}$$

so *the relative markup is constant* and equal to $\sigma/(\sigma-1)$, with $\sigma > 1$. The second-order condition is also satisfied. For a given wage, the Lerner index is independent of the number of firms and is equal to

$$\frac{p^* - mw}{p^*} = \frac{1}{\sigma},$$

which increases with the degree of differentiation across varieties. The expression (3.15) agrees with what we know from industrial economics: the equilibrium price exceeds the marginal cost (mw) as soon as varieties are differentiated, i.e., as soon as σ takes on a finite value greater than one, and the profit margin increases with the degree of differentiation, i.e., as soon as σ decreases. Consumers being less sensitive to price considerations, firms are then able to charge higher prices. Conversely, in the special case of homogeneous varieties (σ tends to ∞), we fall back on Bertrand's solution: the equilibrium price is equal to the marginal cost.[7]

---

[7] Even though the number of firms is arbitrarily large, a finite value for σ implies that the equilibrium price remains greater than the marginal production cost. This result runs against the conventional wisdom that a very large number of producers is equivalent to perfect competition.

The above expressions have been obtained under price competition (Bertrand). Let us now assume that there is quantity competition (Cournot). Applying the first-order condition yields

$$p_i\left(1 - \frac{1}{\epsilon_i^C}\right) = mw,$$

where

$$\frac{1}{\epsilon_i^C} \equiv -\frac{\partial p_i}{\partial q_i}\frac{q_i}{p_i}.$$

Using the inverse demand function

$$p_i = \frac{q_i^{-1/\sigma}}{\sum_j q_j^{1-1/\sigma}} E,$$

we can determine ϵ_i^C as follows:

$$\frac{1}{\epsilon_i^C} = \frac{1}{\sigma} + \left(1 - \frac{1}{\sigma}\right)s_i. \tag{3.16}$$

When the number of firms tends to infinity, we again find that $\epsilon_i^C = \sigma$.

To sum up, when there are many firms, everything works as if each firm had a zero market share. Consequently, when it chooses its strategy, a firm anticipates that its decision has no significant impact on the market, so that it does not affect its competitors' own choices of strategies. In other words, *everything works as if the best-reply functions were horizontal*. Unlike in the case of oligopolistic competition, therefore, there are no strategic interactions because a firm's profit-maximizing strategy does not depend on the strategies of the other firms.

From a more formal point of view, this amounts to saying that, when it maximizes its profit, a firm assumes that its price choice has no impact on the price index P or on consumers' expenditure E, which both appear in the demand (3.9). We thus obtain $\epsilon_i = \epsilon_i^C = \sigma$. We will see in section 3.1.2.2 how an alternative model makes it possible to justify such a behavioral assumption. Furthermore, competition on price or on quantity leads to the same equilibrium in monopolistic competition, while these two forms of competition give different results in oligopolistic competition. Finally, the assumption of symmetry between varieties, with respect to both consumer preferences and firms' technologies, is reflected in the same equilibrium price for all varieties.

3.1.2.2 Quantity

We can substitute the equilibrium price (3.15) into the demand function (3.9) to determine the quantity produced by each firm as a function of the number of varieties (and wages). Then, by reintroducing prices and quantities into the free-entry condition, $\pi_i = 0$, we can obtain the number of firms, and therefore the number of varieties, existing in equilibrium.

It is in fact simpler, but strictly equivalent, to proceed in the reverse order by first determining the volume of production thanks to the free-entry condition given by

$$\pi_i = (p - mw)q - fw$$
$$= \frac{mw}{\sigma - 1}q - fw = 0,$$

which makes it possible to obtain the equilibrium production of each firm:

$$q^* = \frac{(\sigma - 1)f}{m}. \tag{3.17}$$

Regardless of the total number of firms, they all have the same size. This result is a direct consequence of the fact that the markup is constant, and it is one of the major weaknesses of the Dixit–Stiglitz model. More generally, in this model, the entry of new firms does not generate any procompetitive effect: the markup is independent of the number of firms n, while industrial economics suggests that it decreases with n.[8] Second, there is no scale effect, as q^* is independent of both the share of the manufactured good μ in consumption and the number of consumers L. It is important to keep these two limitations in mind. Although the Dixit–Stiglitz model is very useful for its great simplicity, it fails to capture some important effects.

3.1.2.3 The Number of Firms

As the quantity of skilled labor used by a firm is equal to $l^* = f + mq^* = f\sigma$, the number of firms is thus determined by the full-employment condition:

$$L = nl^* = n(f + mq^*),$$

from which it immediately follows that

$$n^* = \frac{L}{\sigma f}. \tag{3.18}$$

One difficulty should be pointed out right away: n^* is not necessarily an integer, so the number of firms in equilibrium is given by the largest

---

[8] This observation needs qualification, however. Indeed, even if the equilibrium price remains unchanged when the number of firms increases, the consumption of the manufactured good is fragmented over a greater number of varieties. This in turn implies that each firm's profits go down. In other words, we come back, albeit very indirectly, to a kind of competitive effect (which has been called the market-crowding effect), as the entry of new firms has a negative effect on the profitability of the incumbents.

of the integers lower than or equal to n^*. Such an approximation only makes sense when n^* is large. Having said that, the zero-profit condition is equivalent to the famous Chamberlinian condition of tangency between the firm's demand and its average cost at the free-entry equilibrium. This implies that increasing returns are not totally exploited in equilibrium, as the average cost is not minimized, which is explained by the fact that consumers value diversity in their consumption of the manufactured good.

Although firms' sizes are unaffected when the economy gets larger, there is a scale effect at the market level. It takes the specific form of a growth in the number of varieties. The greater the increase in the number of workers/consumers L, the greater the increase in the number of firms—and consequently in the number of varieties. The price index then decreases, as seen above, thus contributing to making all consumers better-off. Likewise, the greater a drop in fixed costs f is, the smaller the firms and the higher their number in equilibrium, with the same consequences on the price index and on individual welfare. We should note, however, that, *so long as the fixed costs are positive, the number of firms and varieties is finite.* Indeed, if the demand for a new variety proves to always be positive, consumers are not numerous enough for the profits that they create to cover the fixed cost associated with the launching of an additional variety. The entry process must therefore come to a halt.

The number of varieties obtained in this way has little chance of being the socially desirable number. Indeed, when a new firm enters the market, it ignores the fact that its entry triggers a loss in earnings for its competitors. This force favors an excessive number of varieties. On the other hand, due to the absence of price discrimination, no single firm can capture the whole social surplus created by the introduction of its variety. This force, in contrast, favors an insufficient number of varieties. Consequently, the equilibrium and optimal outcomes are generally different. In addition, there is a priori no reason to expect the market to supply too many or too few varieties.

3.1.2.4 Wages

It remains for us to determine the wage, w, of the skilled workers in the manufacturing sector. We do this by using the equilibrium conditions of the product market. Indeed, the equilibrium output q^* depends only on the exogenous parameters of the model, while the demand (3.7) varies with the price set by firm i and the number of varieties n^*. As this number depends only on the exogenous parameters, and since the markup is constant, the equilibrium price varies only with w. Wages are indeed the only parameter of adjustment left. More precisely, we have

$$q^* = \left(\frac{p^*}{P}\right)^{-\sigma} \frac{\mu(L_a + wL)}{P},$$

where $yL = L_a + wL$ is the total income in the economy. Combining (3.8), (3.15), (3.17), and (3.18), it is readily verified that the equilibrium wage is given by

$$w^* = \frac{\mu}{1 - \mu} \frac{L_a}{L}. \tag{3.19}$$

Because each firm takes the wage level as given, this wage is similar to the equilibrium wage of a competitive labor market. This also implies that all the operating profits are redistributed to the skilled workers. The equilibrium wage increases with the consumption share of the manufactured good because the demand for this good increases. It decreases with the number of skilled workers because there is more competition on the skilled labor market. Furthermore, the zero-profit condition has another important implication: a consumer's income is equal to her wage ($y = w_a$ for agricultural workers and $y = w^*$ for industrial workers) and the overall income is given by the total wage bill. The free-entry assumption thus enables us to avoid having to tackle the question of how profits are distributed.

To sum up, *the monopolistic competition equilibrium is unique and is described by the expressions* (3.15), (3.17), (3.18), *and* (3.19). The welfare of an industrial or agricultural worker is given by her indirect utility (3.10) evaluated at equilibrium prices and wages (recall that $p_a = 1$):

$$V = w^*[(n^*)^{-1/(\sigma-1)}p^*]^{-\mu} = \left(\frac{\sigma m}{\sigma - 1}\right)^{-\mu}\left[\frac{\mu L_a}{(1-\mu)L}\right]^{1-\mu}\left(\frac{L}{\sigma f}\right)^{\mu/(\sigma-1)}$$

$$V_a = [(n^*)^{-1/(\sigma-1)}p^*]^{-\mu} = \left[\frac{(\sigma-1)(1-\mu)L}{\sigma\mu m L_a}\right]^{\mu}\left(\frac{L}{\sigma f}\right)^{\mu/(\sigma-1)}.$$

All else being equal, a large labor force ($L_a + L$) favors both industrial and agricultural workers provided that the relative sizes of the two groups remain the same. On the other hand, an increase in the size of one of the two groups has contrasting effects on their welfare. A larger number of agricultural workers proves favorable to the industrial workers, by increasing their relative wage, but it is obviously unfavorable to the agricultural workers. A larger number of industrial workers enhances the welfare of agricultural workers, who have access to a greater number of varieties sold at lower prices. Likewise, more industrial workers leads to a higher number of varieties; however, this also makes competition in the skilled-labor market more fierce. Inspecting V tells us that the net impact is positive if and only if $1 > \sigma(1 - \mu)$, i.e., when the size of the manufacturing sector is large and the manufactured good is very differentiated.

3.1.2.5 The Continuum of Firms

The assumption of nonstrategic behavior has generated considerable controversy. So long as the number n of firms is described by an integer, the elasticity (3.14) varies with s_i and, therefore, with the prices chosen by the other firms. As a result, a firm's equilibrium price is never equal to $mw\sigma/(\sigma - 1)$. More precisely, when n is an integer and a finite number, it must be that $\partial P/\partial p_j > 0$ for every $j \neq i$, as the demand for i depends on the price set by each of the other producers. In such a context, the price game among firms has a unique symmetric Nash equilibrium given by (see Anderson et al. 1992, chapter 7):

$$p^* = mw\left(1 + \frac{n}{n-1}\frac{1}{\sigma-1}\right) > \frac{\sigma}{\sigma-1}mw.$$

To obtain the results derived above, we must therefore assume that the number of firms is infinitely large, in which case we come up with $p^* = mw\sigma/(\sigma - 1) > mw$. Nevertheless, this assumption contradicts the endogenous determination of the number of firms. Moreover, the number n^* is small when f or σ is large, which automatically rules out the absence of nonstrategic behavior. Finally, in a general-equilibrium context, a firm's pricing strategy also influences, albeit only slightly, consumers' income and therefore their demand for the variety produced by this firm. The same is true of the wage rate, which depends, if only to a minor degree, on every firm's hiring policy.

It is possible, however, to resolve these contradictions in a rigorous and elegant manner by assuming the existence of a *continuum* of firms whose total mass is N. This leads us to assume that the composite good entering the utility function takes the form

$$M = \left[\int_0^N q(i)^{(\sigma-1)/\sigma}\, di\right]^{\sigma/(\sigma-1)}, \tag{3.20}$$

where $q(i)$ is the quantity of variety i consumed. Intuitively, as each variety is assumed to be infinitely close to its neighboring varieties in $[0, N]$, we may treat $q(\cdot)$ as a continuous density function.[9]

This assumption implies that *each firm is negligible*. Indeed, it is easy to show that the price index, in the demand function (3.9), may be

---

[9] Note that in the first version of their working paper, which has been republished in Brakman and Heijdra (2004), Dixit and Stiglitz describe the manufacturing sector by means of a continuum of firms. Such a formulation does not appear in the subsequent versions of their paper, where they assume a finite number of firms.

rewritten as follows:

$$P \equiv \left[\int_0^N p(i)^{-(\sigma-1)} \, di \right]^{-1/(\sigma-1)}.$$

Consequently, a firm's price choice has no impact on either the value of P (i.e., $\partial P / \partial p(i) = 0$) or on the level of income y (i.e., $\partial y / \partial p(i) = 0$), as each firm is equally negligible in both the product and labor markets. Such a modeling strategy captures in a very neat way the essence of the Chamberlinian idea of monopolistic competition as summarized in the following quote:

> A price cut, for instance, which increases the sales of him who made it, draws inappreciable amounts from the markets of each of his many competitors, achieving a considerable result for the one who cut, but without making incursions upon the market of any single competitor sufficient to cause him to do anything he would not have done anyway.
>
> Chamberlin (1933, p. 83)

The demand elasticity that any firm faces is therefore constant and equal to σ. In this case, the equilibrium price is given exactly by (3.15), the other equilibrium magnitudes being unchanged. Furthermore, the assumption of the existence of a continuum of firms does not contradict what we have seen regarding the equilibrium values of the other variables. The only difference is that *all magnitudes related to firms and varieties are now described by continuous densities over the interval of varieties* $[0, N]$. Once we have derived firms' equilibrium prices, the free-entry condition and the full-employment constraint allow us to determine the output of each firm and the mass N^* of varieties/firms.

The assumption of a continuum enables us to grasp the simple, but fundamental, idea that *a firm can be negligible with respect to the economy as a whole while having some monopoly power on its market.* And indeed, each firm faces a downward-sloping demand for its product. Furthermore, with a continuum of firms, the difference between price competition (Bertrand) and quantity competition (Cournot) disappears—a distinction that plagues oligopoly theory.

The assumption of a continuum presents another advantage that is little known but nevertheless fundamental. In a general-equilibrium model with imperfect competition, the choice of the numéraire matters for the equilibrium.[10] If oligopolistic competition prevails in the product market, taking variety i as a numéraire changes the behavior of its producer,

---

[10] See Bonanno (1990) for a detailed discussion of this problem. Dierker et al. (2003) have recently shed light on the difficulties associated with the choice of numéraire in some models of international trade with imperfect competition.

as its profit function is no longer the same, thus also changing the behavior of the other producers. This results in the emergence of a new market equilibrium. To put it another way, the market solution changes with the choice of numéraire. By contrast, in a situation of monopolistic competition with a continuum of firms, the behavior of producer i has no impact on the other agents because it is negligible. In consequence, the equilibrium remains the same, regardless of the choice of numéraire (Neary 2003).

Finally, this assumption greatly simplifies the analysis of the distribution of firms between regions that will occupy us later, as all the variables are continuous. With a discrete number of firms, a firm's relocation from one region to another always has a nonnegligible impact on the regions of origin and destination, which in turn implies discrete jumps in the variables. The conditions of spatial equilibrium must therefore be described by inequalities. With a continuum, the move of a single firm is negligible and we can work with equalities. Furthermore, the question of whether or not n^* is an integer no longer needs to be asked.

It is important to understand the precise meaning of the continuum assumption. If we want to work with a model in which agents are negligible, this approach is formally the right one, even though it does not seem realistic. In addition, it allow us to avoid the formidable difficulties posed by the existence of a market equilibrium, once we account for strategic behavior in a general-equilibrium setting. Finally, the monopolistic competition model with a continuum of firms allows for a combination of increasing returns and imperfect competition, something that has not been achieved in other contexts. Wether or not using such a setting is reasonable must, therefore, be evaluated on the basis of its overall implications, and not just its realism. In this respect, it can hardly be denied that monopolistic competition presents real advantages over oligopolistic competition, even though, as we will see in chapter 9, the latter brings new effects to light.

3.2   Monopolistic Competition: A Linear Setting

We have just seen that the Dixit–Stiglitz model takes away all forms of strategic interaction among firms. It is therefore legitimate to wonder whether we can keep the flexibility inherent to a model of monopolistic competition while introducing certain forms of interaction that agree with what we know from industrial economics. This is precisely the objective of the *linear model*, introduced into economic geography by Ottaviano et al. (2002), which we examine in this section. In addition, this setting, unlike the Dixit–Stiglitz model, allows us to account for a particularly robust empirical fact: namely, that larger markets have lower markups but larger output (see, for example, Campbell and Hopenhayn 2005).[11]

3.2.1   Quadratic Utility with a Continuum of Varieties

In the case of two varieties, the utility function generating a system of linear demands is given by the quasi-linear utility encapsulating a *quadratic subutility*:

$$U = \alpha(q_1 + q_2) - \tfrac{1}{2}\beta(q_1^2 + q_2^2) - \gamma q_1 q_2 + A, \tag{3.21}$$

where α, β, and γ are three positive parameters. For the utility function U to be quasi-concave, it must be that $\beta > \gamma$. As the function U is linear in the numéraire A, income effects are absent from individual consumption: a variation in income only affects the demand for the numéraire, not the demand for varieties.

The demand function for variety i, obtained by maximizing (3.21) under the budget constraint, takes the following form:

$$D_i(p_1, p_2) = a - bp_i + c(p_j - p_i), \quad i, j = 1, 2, \ i \neq j. \tag{3.22}$$

The parameter $a \equiv \alpha/(\beta + \gamma)$ expresses the desirability of the differentiated product with respect to the numéraire and may, therefore, be viewed as a measure of the size of this market; $b \equiv 1/(\beta + \gamma)$ gives the link between individual and industry demands: when b rises, consumers become more sensitive to price differences. Finally, $c \equiv \gamma/[(\beta-\gamma)(\beta+\gamma)]$ is an inverse measure of the degree of product differentiation between varieties: when $c \to \infty$, varieties are perfect substitutes, whereas they are independent for $c = 0$.

In the case of $n > 2$ varieties, the utility function (3.21) can be generalized as follows:

$$U = \alpha \sum_{i=1}^{n} q_i - \tfrac{1}{2}\beta \sum_{i=1}^{n} q_i^2 - \tfrac{1}{2}\gamma \sum_{i=1}^{n}\sum_{j \neq i} q_i q_j + A$$

$$= \alpha \sum_{i=1}^{n} q_i - \tfrac{1}{2}(\beta - \gamma) \sum_{i=1}^{n} q_i^2 - \tfrac{1}{2}\gamma \sum_{i=1}^{n}\sum_{j=1}^{n} q_i q_j + A$$

$$= \alpha \sum_{i=1}^{n} q_i - \tfrac{1}{2}(\beta - \gamma) \sum_{i=1}^{n} q_i^2 - \tfrac{1}{2}\gamma \left(\sum_{i=1}^{n} q_i \right)^2 + A.$$

---

[11] Also note that the Dixit–Stiglitz model presupposes homothetic preferences—an assumption that is rarely validated by empirical consumption studies. We assume here quasi-linear preferences. Although they rank far behind homothetic preferences in general-equilibrium models of trade and geography, Dinopoulos et al. (2007) show that "quasi-linear preferences behave reasonably well in general-equilibrium settings."

When n tends to ∞ and q_i to 0, we obtain the following expression in the case of a continuum of varieties:

$$U = \alpha \int_0^N q(i)\, di - \tfrac{1}{2}(\beta - \gamma) \int_0^N [q(i)]^2\, di - \tfrac{1}{2}\gamma \left[\int_0^N q(i)\, di \right]^2 + A. \quad (3.23)$$

The condition $\beta > \gamma$ means that a consumer is endowed with a preference for diversity. To see this, let us assume that she consumes a quantity $\bar{M}$ of the manufactured good such that her consumption is uniform over $[0, x]$ and zero over $]x, N]$. The density over $[0, x]$ is thus $\bar{M}/x$. The utility (3.23) evaluated at this consumption structure is given by

$$U = \alpha \int_0^x \frac{\bar{M}}{x}\, di - \tfrac{1}{2}(\beta - \gamma) \int_0^x \left(\frac{\bar{M}}{x} \right)^2 di - \tfrac{1}{2}\gamma \left[\int_0^x \frac{\bar{M}}{x}\, di \right]^2 + A$$

$$= \alpha \bar{M} - \frac{\beta - \gamma}{2x} \bar{M}^2 - \tfrac{1}{2}\gamma \bar{M}^2 + A,$$

which is an increasing function of x, the maximum of which is achieved for $x = N$, i.e., when all varieties are consumed. In other words, as soon as $\beta > \gamma$, the quadratic utility exhibits a preference for diversity, this preference being stronger when β is larger.[12] Even though consumers do value variety, they do so at a decreasing rate, as $d^2 U / dx^2 < 0$.

Besides her labor, every consumer is endowed with $\bar{A} > 0$ units of the numéraire. Her budget constraint is then written as

$$\int_0^N p(i)q(i)\, di + A = \bar{A} + y.$$

We assume that the initial endowment $\bar{A}$ is sufficiently high for the equilibrium consumption of the numéraire to always be positive. This assumption aims to capture the idea that consumers like to consume both agricultural and manufactured goods.

Solving the budget constraint with respect to the numéraire, substituting the corresponding expression into (3.23), and computing the first-order condition with respect to $q(i)$, we obtain[13]

$$p(i) = \alpha - (\beta - \gamma)q(i) - \gamma \int_0^N q(j)\, dj, \quad i \in [0, N]. \quad (3.24)$$

We obtain the demand function for variety $i \in [0, N]$ as follows.

---

[12] This interpretation is very close to the one underpinning Herfindahl's index, used to measure industrial concentration, which will be discussed in chapter 10. By fixing the total quantity of the differentiated good, the absolute value of the quadratic term of (3.23) decreases as soon as the consumption is dispersed over a greater number of varieties, thus leading to an increased level of utility.

[13] Differentiating a function on a zero measure set gives rise to technical problems that cannot be tackled here. The reader is referred to Pascoa (1993) for a detailed discussion of these problems.

Integrating (3.24) over i yields

$$\int_0^N p(i)\,di = \alpha N - (\beta - \gamma)\int_0^N q(i)\,di - \gamma N\int_0^N q(j)\,dj,$$

from which it follows that

$$\int_0^N q(i)\,di = \frac{\alpha N - \int_0^N p(i)\,di}{\beta + \gamma(N-1)}.$$

Substituting this expression into (3.24) gives

$$p(i) = \alpha - (\beta - \gamma)q(i) - \gamma\frac{\alpha N - \int_0^N p(i)\,di}{\beta + \gamma(N-1)},$$

which in turn implies

$$(\beta - \gamma)q(i) = \frac{\alpha(\beta - \gamma)}{\beta + \gamma(N-1)} - p(i) + \frac{\gamma}{\beta + \gamma(N-1)}\int_0^N p(i)\,di.$$

Adding and subtracting $N\gamma p(i)/(\beta + \gamma N)$, we obtain, after simplification,

$$q(i) = a - bp(i) + c\int_0^N [p(j) - p(i)]\,dj,$$
$$= a - (b + cN)p(i) + cP, \qquad\qquad (3.25)$$

where $a \equiv \alpha/[\beta + (N-1)\gamma]$, $b \equiv 1/[\beta + (N-1)\gamma]$, $c \equiv \gamma/(\beta - \gamma)[\beta + (N-1)\gamma]$, and where the price index

$$P = \int_0^N p(j)\,dj$$

expresses the aggregate pricing behavior of firms.[14]

This demand system has a very appealing property: *the consumption of variety i decreases when its price p(i) gets larger than the average price P/N prevailing on the market.* More precisely, when firm i sells its variety at a price higher than the average market price P/N, the term

$$c\int_0^N [p(j) - p(i)]\,dj = cN\left(\frac{P}{N} - p(i)\right)$$

is negative, thus implying that its demand is pushed downwards. In other words, when the average price takes on a low value, the elasticity of a firm's demand increases for any given value of its own price. This leads the firm to charge a lower price. Clearly, the opposite holds when firm i sells its variety at a price lower than the average market price. Moreover, provided that $N > 1$, the direct price effect on the demand for a variety,

---

[14]Note that (3.25) is meaningful so long as $q(i)$ is positive: that is, so long as $p(i)$ is not too large.

measured by $b + cN$, always exceeds the crossed price effect, measured by c.

At this stage, it is useful to compare the structure of preferences and demand in the Dixit–Stiglitz and linear models. In the Cobb–Douglas case, the income share spent on any type of good is constant, while in the case of a quasi-linear function these shares are variable (the two goods being perfect substitutes). Furthermore, firms' demands have a constant price elasticity in the Dixit–Stiglitz model, while here they are linear, and thus exhibit a decreasing price elasticity. In contrast, the absence of an income effect in the linear model is a strong simplification that eliminates certain effects that we would like to take into account in economic geography. We can therefore conclude that the two functional forms fit fairly different preference settings.

Remark. We have seen that CES preferences can represent a heterogeneous population in which each consumer buys a single variety. Similarly, quadratic preferences can be obtained from such a heterogeneous population. To illustrate this, assume that consumers are uniformly distributed along Main Street. Two stores, denoted 1 and 2, selling the same good are located at $x_1 = -k$ and $x_2 = k$. Each consumer wants to buy one unit of the good, provided that its price, augmented by the cost of reaching the selected store, does not exceed her willingness-to-pay $r > 0$. If the consumer located in x purchases from store i, the full price she pays is given by $p_i + t|x - x_i|$, where p_i denotes the price set by store i and $t > 0$ is the shopping cost per unit of distance. This price must be less than (or equal to) its competitor's full price, but it must also be less than (or equal to) the consumer's willingness-to-pay. Hence, the market is divided into three areas: (i) one inhabited by the consumers who shop in store 1; (ii) one by the consumers who shop in store 2; and (iii) one by the consumers who choose not to consume the good. If we assume that k is sufficiently small for areas 1 and 2 to be adjacent, the third area consists of consumers who are located outside these two areas, either to their left or to their right. The marginal consumer, who is indifferent between patronizing one or the other of the two stores, is located at $\bar{x}$, for which we have

$$p_1 + t(\bar{x} - x_1) = p_2 + t(x_2 - \bar{x}),$$

the solution of which is given by

$$\bar{x}(p_1, p_2) = \frac{p_2 - p_1}{2t}$$

since $x_1 + x_2 = 0$. Moreover, the consumer located to the right of store 1 who is indifferent between buying or not buying is located to the left of x_1; her location is obtained by finding the solution $\bar{x}_1$ to

$$p_1 + t(x_1 - \bar{x}_1) = r,$$

i.e.,

$$\bar{x}_1(p_1) = x_1 - \frac{r - p_1}{t} < x_1 < 0,$$

where $p_1 < r$, otherwise store 1 would not have any customers. The demand addressed to this store is therefore given by

$$D_1(p_1, p_2) = \bar{x}(p_1, p_2) - \bar{x}_1(p_1) = \frac{r}{t} + k - \frac{p_1}{t} + \frac{p_2 - p_1}{t}.$$

The demand addressed to store 2 is obtained in a similar manner. We thus again find a system of linear demands identical to (3.22) provided that $a = r/t + k$, $b = -1/t$, and $c = 1/t$. The last condition amounts to saying that the parameter t can be considered as a direct measure of the degree of differentiation of the two varieties. To put it another way, *higher transport costs are formally equivalent to more differentiated varieties.* Once again, we can go from an interpretation where identical consumers consume all the varieties to an interpretation where heterogeneous consumers consume only one variety. We will come back to this interpretation in chapter 9.

3.2.2 Market Equilibrium with Weak Interactions

Although the linear model shares several features with the Dixit-Stiglitz model, we are going to see that prices are determined through a very different mechanism. When a firm determines its equilibrium price, unlike what we saw in the Dixit-Stiglitz model, it must take into account the distribution of prices. This is achieved by means of an aggregate statistic given by the price index P. Hence, the market solution is given by the Nash equilibrium of a game with a continuum of players, where *each firm disregards its impact on the market but is aware that the market as a whole has a nonnegligible impact on its own choice.* There are interactions between firms, therefore, but these interactions are weaker than those encountered in standard models of oligopolistic competition.

In order to understand how this model works, we study in detail how the equilibrium prices are determined. Firm i maximizes its profits, which are defined by

$$\pi(i) = [p(i) - mw]q(i) - fw,$$

where $q(i)$ is given by (3.25). By applying the first-order condition with respect to p_i, i.e., $a + cP - [2p(i) - mw](b + cN) = 0$, we obtain p_i^* as a function of P. Varieties being symmetric, this expression is independent of i and is given by

$$p^*(P) = \frac{a + mw(b + cN)}{2(b + cN)} + \frac{cN}{2(b + cN)} \frac{P}{N}. \tag{3.26}$$

The natural interpretation of this expression is that it represents a firm's *best-reply function* to the market conditions. These conditions are defined by the *aggregate behavior* of all producers, which is summarized here by the average price P/N. The best-reply function is upward sloping because varieties are substitutable: a general price rise in the market for the manufactured good enables each firm to sell its variety at a higher price.[15] In addition, the more differentiated the varieties, i.e., the lower the parameter c, the weaker a firm's reaction to a variation in the average price.

For an equilibrium to arise, each firm's expectation with respect to the average price must be accurate, which amounts to imposing the following fixed-point condition:

$$p^*(P) = \frac{P}{N}.$$

Substitution into (3.26) thus allows us to determine the equilibrium value of P, and hence the common equilibrium price of varieties:

$$p^* = mw + \frac{a - bmw}{2b + cN} = mw + \frac{(\alpha - mw)(\beta - \gamma)}{2(\beta - \gamma) + \gamma N}.$$

As the equilibrium value of the index P is unique and given by $P^* = p^*N$, the Nash equilibrium is also unique. The equilibrium quantity sold by each firm is given by

$$q^* = a - bp^* = \frac{\alpha - mw}{2(\beta - \gamma) + \gamma N}.$$

Note that the condition $a > bmw$ must hold for the equilibrium price to exceed the marginal cost. In particular, as in the Dixit–Stiglitz model, the equilibrium price is equal to the marginal production cost as soon as varieties are homogeneous ($\beta = \gamma$). This shows, once again, the importance of product differentiation for monopolistic competition. In contrast to what we have seen in the Dixit–Stiglitz model, it is readily verified that both the equilibrium price and the markup decrease as the mass N of firms increases. In other words, the linear model accounts for the pro-competitive effect stressed above. This property is particularly important in economic geography, as the mobility of firms affects the intensity of competition in each local market. Another effect of the varieties

---

[15] Recall that the best-reply function is flat in the Dixit–Stiglitz model.

being differentiated is that the equilibrium quantity also decreases with the mass of firms, which means that the market-crowding effect among varieties dominates the price effect that increases the total demand for the manufactured product. Also, it is easy to check that $\partial(q^*N)/\partial N > 0$, which amounts to saying that consumers' total demand for the manufactured product increases with the number of varieties available. This is because a higher number of varieties makes this good more attractive relative to the agricultural good.

Furthermore, the linear model displays a scale effect to the extent that the quantity q^* increases with the parameter α that expresses the desirability of the manufactured good. Finally, instead of applying a proportional and constant markup, firms apply an additive markup that varies with the structural parameters of the economy. As will be seen later on in the book, although the linear model is also able to deal with *mill pricing*, it allows for the study of segmented markets in which firms choose a specific *delivered price* for each spatially separate market.[16]

In summary, unlike the Dixit–Stiglitz model, in which all forms of interaction are taken away, the linear model integrates what we may call "weak interactions" between firms, which in turn give rise to effects similar to those observed in differentiated oligopoly models (Anderson et al. 1992; Tirole 1988). Plugging the equilibrium quantities and prices into the zero-profit condition allows us to determine the equilibrium mass of firms:

$$N^* = \frac{(\alpha - mw)\sqrt{(\beta - \gamma)/fw} - 2(\beta - \gamma)}{\gamma}.$$

Finally, the wage of skilled workers can be obtained implicitly from the nonlinear equilibrium condition in the labor market with N^* firms, each one demanding a quantity $f + mq^*$ of skilled labor.

In the linear model, the equilibrium variables are therefore determined by a more intuitive chain of relationships than the very indirect one used in the Dixit–Stiglitz model. However, in the latter model, equilibrium is described by simpler expressions. The main limitations of the linear model are very different from those of the Dixit–Stiglitz model: first,

---

[16] Mill pricing is equivalent to "free on board" (FOB) pricing. This terminology has been borrowed from the vocabulary of maritime transport to designate the value of a cargo before the payment of transport and insurance charges. It is used to designate the price upon departure from the factory. By contrast, delivered or CIF (cost, insurance, and freight) pricing includes all the charges associated with shipping a good between two places.

there is no income effect; second, we must assume that consumers have an initial endowment of the numéraire.[17]

Depending on whether one's primary interest is in price or income effects, one should work with the Dixit–Stiglitz or the linear model, respectively. Clearly, the objective is to have a model incorporating both these effects. A first step in this direction has been taken recently by Behrens and Murata (2007). Ideally, such a model should remain simple enough to serve as a building block that could be used in more general frameworks.

3.3 Concluding Remarks

In the present state of the art, it is fair to say that models of monopolistic competition fall short of achieving the degree of generality found in general-equilibrium theory. They should be considered as, at best, a collection of examples that form a satisfactory compromise between the two approaches, as general-equilibrium theories with imperfect competition are almost nonexistent.

Unlike the Dixit–Stiglitz model, the linear model makes it possible to integrate weak interaction between firms. It is therefore incorrect to claim that monopolistic competition necessarily rules out all forms of interaction, even though it does exclude strategic interactions proper. This limitation is less restrictive than it appears at first sight, as most of the effects present in models of oligopolistic competition are also present in the linear model and, to a large extent, in the Dixit–Stiglitz model. Yet there are some fundamental differences between oligopolistic and monopolistic competition. For example, in the two models presented above, the market outcome is the same with price-setting and quantity-setting firms. While the choice of quantity or price as a strategy is a crucial one in oligopolistic competition, it is immaterial for monopolistic competition.

Despite their numerous limitations, models of monopolistic competition allow us to tackle issues that cannot be handled in the Arrow–Debreu model of a perfectly competitive economy (Matsuyama 1995). This is because they allow us to combine market power and scale economies. The trade-off thus seems simple: either some economic problems, fundamental in several respects, are ignored, or attempts are made to derive results by means of specific models, while taking all precautions required by such an approach.

---

[17] The income effect can be reintroduced by assuming that the consumption of the homogeneous good is zero. Conversely, we could eliminate the income effect in the Dixit–Stiglitz model by introducing a CES in a quasi-linear utility.

In this book, we choose the second option. To start with, we will compare the results obtained by using the two models discussed in this chapter, with special emphasis being placed on the properties that hold in both settings (chapters 6—8). We will then test the degree of robustness of the results thus obtained by studying models of partial equilibrium in which firms operate in a strategic setting in the sense of game theory (chapter 9).

3.4 Related Literature

Unfortunately, there is no complete and integrated survey of monopolistic competition. Matsuyama (1995) remains the best synthesis of the main contributions based on the Dixit–Stiglitz model. A recent discussion of the contributions of this model to modern economic theory is proposed in the book edited by Brakman and Heijdra (2004). The microeconomic foundations of the CES model have been studied by Anderson et al. (1992, chapters 3 and 4). In the case of a finite number of firms, the market solution integrating all the effects generated by a price change can be found in d'Aspremont et al. (1996). Melitz (2003) has proposed an extension of the Dixit–Stiglitz model that makes it possible to work with heterogeneous firms in terms of their marginal input requirement. Finally, Bénassy (1991) offers an (incomplete) list of the attempts made to model Chamberlin's ideas.

Finally, it is worth noting that Kaldor (1935) criticized Chamberlin (1933) for providing an inadequate description of competition in the space-economy (which we will examine in chapter 9). By founding economic geography on Chamberlinian models of monopolistic competition, modern scientists have thumbed their noses at the pioneers of location theory.

4

Interregional Trade and Market Size

In the previous chapter, we undertook a detailed study of the two models of monopolistic competition that will be used later on in this book. They can be interpreted as models that describe closed economies. In order to familiarize the reader with the use of these models in economic geography, which requires working with open economies, we present a *spatial* version of the Dixit-Stiglitz model in the next section. It is by marrying this model with trade costs that we can shed light on the role played by these costs in economic life. This extension can be considered as a model of trade, as the goods are shipped from one region to the other, while production factors are immobile. It is largely inspired by Krugman (1980) and will be designated hereafter as the DSK model. In this setting, although regions are not specialized, there is trade. One of the main conclusions that will be derived is that falling trade costs are favorable to the consumers of both regions and enhance the convergence of welfare levels. This is because lower trade costs allow better access to the goods produced in the other region. It is worth noting, however, that regional disparities persist so long as trade costs remain positive.

In the next section, we study an extension of the DSK model in which capital is mobile, just as goods are, thus allowing us to highlight the impact that the size of each region may have on the spatial distribution of firms. Indeed it is to be expected that market size is one of the basic determinants of firms' choices of location. Likewise, accessibility to markets is a crucial element in determining the attractiveness of a location. Weber (1909), one of the pioneers of location theory, developed this idea by assuming that a firm chooses its location to minimize the sum of trade costs—which amounts to admitting that it seeks the best possible access to markets. Formally, this can be expressed as the minimization of the weighted sum of distances to a given number of points representing the factor or product markets, the weights being defined by the quantities bought or sold, multiplied by the freight rate of the corresponding good. A firm's location can therefore be seen as the resultant of a system of forces, each market attracting the firm with an intensity that depends on the weight associated with it. A market is said to be *dominant* when its weight exceeds the sum of the others. In this case, the dominant market is always the optimal location (Witzgall 1964). Despite its simplicity, such a result allows us to understand, at least partially, location decisions that are apparently very different: for example, a firm choosing to set itself up in a large metropolis that offers it a wide variety of services; or a steel firm in the nineteenth century deciding to situate itself in a location close to sources of coal or iron ore.

Weber's model, however, does not take into account competition, or, more generally, market forces: the prices of goods bought or sold are assumed to be fixed and potential competitors are ignored. If, at least at first sight, these assumptions seem reasonable in the case of a single firm, they are considerably less so as soon as we focus on the location of several firms belonging to the same sector. And indeed, we will see that firms have an incentive to relax competition by separating themselves geographically from each other. By selling differentiated products, firms relax, but do not eliminate, competition, which is a dispersion force. We will see that it is essential to integrate competition within location models to make predictions that rest on solid foundations. This subject has been studied by Helpman and Krugman (1985), and their approach has given rise to a new family of models that intend to study the resultant of a system of centripetal forces (the proximity of markets) and centrifugal forces (competition between firms). This setting will be studied in greater detail in section 4.2, which explores the impact of market size on the location of firms. We will see that, in contrast to the case of immobile capital, *falling trade costs—though still favorable to consumers as a whole—may be at the root of a growing divergence between regions.*

4.1   The Dixit–Stiglitz–Krugman Model of Trade

Let us consider an economy in which farmers and manufacturing firms are located in two regions A and B. The agricultural sector is identical in every respect to the one described in section 3.1. Furthermore, we assume that the trade costs of this good are zero.[1] Thus, its price is the same in each region, so the agricultural good can still be the numéraire. The wages in the agricultural sector are, therefore, identical in both regions and equal 1. Hereafter, the expressions will be given only for

---

[1] This assumption is relaxed in chapter 8.

region A (unless explicitly stated), while those corresponding to region B can be obtained by symmetry.

Let us now turn to the manufacturing sector. The varieties produced in each region enter into the definition of the composite good in a *symmetric* way:

$$
M_A = \left\{ \int_{i \in \mathcal{N}_A} [q_{AA}(i)]^{(\sigma-1)/\sigma} \, di + \int_{i \in \mathcal{N}_B} [q_{BA}(i)]^{(\sigma-1)/\sigma} \, di \right\}^{\sigma/(\sigma-1)},
$$

where $\mathcal{N}_r$ is the set of varieties produced in region $r = A, B$. The definition of M_A implies that the varieties produced by the domestic and foreign firms are different; however, they obey the same elasticity of substitution. Moreover, consumers' welfare depends on the quantity of each variety consumed, but not its place of production. These two assumptions are undoubtedly fairly strong. Since the varieties exchanged between the two regions belong to the same sector, there is *intraindustry trade.*[2]

Although foreign varieties are not distinguished by their place of origin in individual preferences, their consumption imposes a trade cost when the consumption does not occur in the region of production.[3] In the DSK model, we assume that this cost is an *iceberg-type cost.* This means that if a good is exported from region A to region B, and if q units of this good must arrive at the destination, τq units must be sent from A, where $\tau \geqslant 1$ (the case in which $\tau = 1$ amounts to admitting that transport costs are zero). The fraction of the good lost during transport, $(\tau - 1)q$, represents the amount of resources required to transport one unit of the good. The level of trade cost is thus defined by this value multiplied by the price of the variety prevailing in the region where it is produced.

This modeling strategy, proposed by Samuelson (1954), enables us to consider positive trade costs without having to deal explicitly with a transport sector.[4] One illustration of this type of transport cost—which

---

[2] One of the main goals of new trade theories was to incorporate the growing importance of intraindustry trade, which cannot occur according to the traditional theories of international trade.

[3] This asymmetry in the treatment of the transport of agricultural and manufactured goods can be explained, at least partially, by the fact that in 2003 the latter accounted for 74% of world trade, while the former comprised only 10% (World Trade Organization 2005).

[4] It should be noted, in passing, that von Thünen (1826) proposed a similar specification of the transport cost, consisting of a fraction of the initial cargo that "disappeared" during transportation because it was eaten by horses hitched up to the cargo (Samuelson 1983).

allows us to evaluate the value of τ in societies in which goods are transported on a man's back—is proposed by Bairoch:[5]

> it can be estimated that a man can transport 35–40 kilograms of freight over a distance of 30–35 km per day (or 1.1–1.3 ton-kilometers per day.) Now in order to sustain himself, a man must eat each day 1 kilogram of food, so when the return is taken into account, a man needs 1 kilogram for every 17 km of ground he covers in transporting agricultural goods. Taking the simplest possible case, this implies that if food is transported over a distance of 300 km, half of the cargo will be absorbed in the cost of transportation alone, and if the distance reaches 600 km, the cargo will be consumed.
>
> Bairoch (1988, p. 11)

For the rest of this book—except for the chapters devoted to the linear model (chapter 8) and to spatial competition (chapter 9)—we assume that trade costs are borne by consumers.[6] Firms therefore follow a *mill pricing policy*. In other words, if $p_A(i)$ denotes the mill price of variety i produced in region A, its delivered price in B, including trade costs, is given by the following expression:[7]

$$p_{AB}(i) = \tau p_A(i) \geqslant p_A(i). \tag{4.1}$$

Indeed, to consume one unit of the good, the consumer is required to make a payment of $\tau \geqslant 1$ units. An iceberg-type trade cost is proportional to the price of the variety, and thus has the nature of an ad valorem tax. Such a formulation is reasonable when modeling a customs tariff, but it is probably less so when dealing with a transport cost.

The behavior of a region A consumer with a disposable income y takes on the same form as in section 3.1.1, once we have accounted for the fact that prices are region specific. As a result, his demand for variety i is given by

$$q_{AA}(i) = \left[\frac{p_A(i)}{P_A}\right]^{-\sigma} \frac{E}{P_A},$$

if variety i is produced in region A, and by

$$q_{BA}(i) = \left[\frac{\tau p_B(i)}{P_A}\right]^{-\sigma} \frac{E}{P_A},$$

---

[5] Another striking example of an iceberg-type transport cost is provided by the cargo of a ship partly made up of food and drink required by the crew: "[The] *Anthoine*, which made the Hull–Bordeaux journey in 1459, loaded up with six months worth of provisions, namely five barrels of flour and biscuits, ten barrels of salted meat, thirteen barrels of salted fish." It also took on board twenty barrels of fresh water, "while the other beverages, particularly wine, amounted to thirty barrels" (Verdon 2003, p. 109).

[6] See, however, the remark at the end of the section.

[7] Remember that the terms mill (or FOB) price and delivered (or CIF) price are defined in chapter 3.

if it is imported from region B. In each of these two expressions, the price index in region A is given by

$$P_A = \left\{ \int_{i \in \mathcal{N}_A} [p_A(i)]^{-(\sigma-1)} \, di + \int_{i \in \mathcal{N}_B} [\tau p_B(i)]^{-(\sigma-1)} \, di \right\}^{-1/(\sigma-1)}.$$

At the same mill price, the consumption of an imported variety is lower by a factor of $\tau^{-\sigma}$ than the consumption of a domestic variety because its delivered price is higher. The resulting difference in purchasing power explains why firms seek to set up close to their customers, all other things being equal.

Let the total mass of unskilled workers be L_a and let the share of them residing in region A be θ_a (with $1 - \theta_a$ in region B). Additionally, let the total mass of skilled workers be L and let the share of them residing in region A be θ (with $1 - \theta$ in region B). The income of region A is then given by

$$Y_A = \theta_a L_a + w_A \theta L$$

and that of region B is given by

$$Y_B = (1 - \theta_a) L_a + w_B (1 - \theta) L,$$

where w_A and w_B denote the wage of skilled workers in regions A and B, respectively (these wages need not be equal because the prices of varieties are different between regions). Consequently, the *total demand* for variety i produced in region A is given by

$$q_A(i) = \frac{p_A(i)^{-\sigma}}{P_A^{-(\sigma-1)}} \mu(\theta_a L_a + w_A \theta L)$$

$$+ \tau \frac{[\tau p_A(i)]^{-\sigma}}{P_B^{-(\sigma-1)}} \mu[(1 - \theta_a) L_a + w_B (1 - \theta) L].$$

The first term on the right-hand side of this expression represents the *domestic demand* for variety i, and the second one represents the *external demand*, which in turn is multiplied by τ because every unit consumed in the other region requires shipping $\tau > 1$ units. The external demand is lower than the domestic demand due to the higher price paid by consumers, as expressed by the term $\tau^{-\sigma} < 1$. We have just seen, however, that the firm must produce $\tau > 1$ times this demand. This second effect does not, though, dominate the first, as the total effect is given by $\tau^{-(\sigma-1)} < 1$. Consequently, with identical regional incomes and price indices, a firm produces more for the local market than for the external market. A firm located in the larger region also produces more than if it were established in the smaller one. All of this shows how trade costs affect the extent of the market.

Note that $q_A(i)$ can be rewritten in a more suggestive way:

$$q_A(i) = \mu p_A(i)^{-\sigma} \{ P_A^{\sigma-1} (\theta_a L_a + w_A \theta L) + \phi P_B^{\sigma-1} [(1-\theta_a) L_a + w_B (1-\theta) L] \},$$

where

$$\phi \equiv \tau^{-(\sigma-1)} \in [0,1]$$

can be interpreted as a "spatial discount" factor, which varies inversely with the level of trade costs and the elasticity of substitution across varieties.[8] Hence, a firm's market is not the sum of the local markets, but their spatially discounted sum.

Because the firm takes as given the price indices and the regional incomes, the only term affected by its strategy is $p_A(i)^{-\sigma}$, which implies that *the elasticity of its aggregated demand is constant and equal to the elasticity of substitution σ*. The former is, therefore, independent of the spatial distribution of the demand, i.e., the share of agricultural and industrial workers located in each of the two regions. Although convenient, this is a fairly restrictive property since, all other things being equal, the demand price elasticity typically increases with the distance from the market. The idea is simple: at a given delivered price, the demand for a product decreases as the distance from the firm increases, on account, for example, of more competition with local producers or different consumption habits. The regional price indices, however, influence a firm's profits because the aggregated behavior of the competing firms affects its market share. Indeed, a high price index makes its variety more competitive on the market by pushing its demand curve upward. Finally, note that an increase in trade costs leads to a drop in the total demand by triggering a reduction in exports.

For centuries people have sought out other areas and cultures for their specific products. In the first century C.E., Pliny the Elder observed that, since the constitution of the Roman Empire and the development of its transport systems, "all products, even those that were previously unknown, have become common usage" (quoted by Ferri 2005, p. 24). Much more recently, Hicks claimed something similarly:

> The extension of trade does not primarily imply more goods.... [T]he variety of goods is increased, with all the widening of life that entails. There can be little doubt that the main advantage that will accrue to those with whom our merchants are trading is a gain of precisely this kind.
>
> Hicks (1969, p. 56)

---

[8] Richard Baldwin coined the expression "ϕ-ness of trade" for this measure of the freeness of trade.

Nowadays, both economists and business analysts agree to consider product variety as one of the main benefits of globalization (Broda and Weinstein 2006; Spulber 2007). The DSK model captures this important idea through changes in the intensity of trade flows. High trade costs—due, for example, to high customs duties—reduce the penetration of foreign varieties, thus making competition predominantly *local*. By contrast, lowering trade costs enhances the supply of varieties in all regions and makes competition more *global*.

If production involves specific factors and the cost of producing $q(i)$ units is given by

$$C[q(i)] = fw + mwq(i),$$

we can follow the same approach as in the previous chapter to show that the equilibrium price of variety i produced in region A is equal to

$$p_A^* \equiv p_A^*(i) = \frac{\sigma}{\sigma - 1} m w_A,$$

and the quantity that is produced is equal to

$$q^* \equiv q^*(i) = \frac{(\sigma - 1)f}{m}.$$

A firm's price and production strategies are, therefore, independent of both trade costs and the spatial distribution of consumers and firms. Moreover, each firm hires $(1 + m(\sigma - 1))f$ skilled workers, so that the mass n_r of firms located in region r is proportional to the mass of skilled workers living therein. Hence, in the DSK setting, even though the number of varieties produced in each region remains the same, trade gives consumers access to a much larger mass of varieties.

Observe that when firms operate under constant returns ($f = 0$), all varieties are produced in each region, the number of which is infinite. Hence, there would be no gains to trade and regions would not be involved in trade. This result once again shows the importance of having either different factor endowments or increasing returns to scale for trade to occur between regions or countries. It is, therefore, hardly surprising that these two notions crop up as the basic ingredients of standard and new theories of international trade.

As the varieties produced in the same region are sold at the same mill price, the regional price index takes the following form:

$$P_A = \frac{\sigma m}{\sigma - 1} [n_A w_A^{-(\sigma-1)} + n_B (\tau w_B)^{-(\sigma-1)}]^{-1/(\sigma-1)}. \tag{4.2}$$

At identical wages ($w_A = w_B$), it is readily verified that P_A is lower than P_B if and only if the number of firms in region A exceeds the number in region B.

When wages are higher in region A than in region B, the varieties produced in A prove more expensive than those produced in B. In this case, the demand stemming from the inhabitants of A for the varieties of B is strong, except when trade costs are themselves sufficiently high to protect the producers of A. In such a context, an abrupt drop in these costs facilitates the penetration of manufactured products from B into A. The present trade relations between the West (A) and China (B) will come to the reader's mind as a perfect illustration of this situation. We must not forget that it is not new, however. Great Britain was flooded with German products at the end of the nineteenth century, leading one contemporary journalist, Ernest Williams, to describe it in terms that seem astonishingly modern in tone:

> A gigantic commercial State is arising to menace our prosperity, and contend with us for the trade of the world. Take observations, Gentle Reader, in your own surroundings. You will find that the material of some of your own clothes was probably woven in Germany. Still more probable is it that some of your wife's garments are German importations. The toys, and the dolls, and the fairy books which your children maltreat in the nursery are made in Germany. Roam the house over, and the fateful mark will greet you at every turn, blazoned though it be with the legend, "Made in Germany."
>
> Williams (1896, pp. 10–11 of the third edition)

All else being equal, and taking into account the fact that the indirect utility is given by $V = yP^{-\mu}$ (chapter 3), a consumer's welfare is higher in the region offering the highest nominal wages and/or the lowest price index. These two effects lie at the root of the trade-off driving the mobility of workers. Furthermore, we should point out that *deeper economic integration* (meaning lower trade costs) *increases workers' welfare in both regions* because it allows them better access to the entire range of varieties, which sparks a drop in both price indices. Although the benefits of trade between trade partners are unequally distributed, as the region producing less varieties benefits most from deeper integration, the discrepancy nevertheless dwindles as trade costs diminish.

Note, finally, that *the intensity of trade increases with lower trade costs* so long as firms' locations remain unchanged. The trade deficit of the manufactured good is compensated for by exchanges, in the opposite direction, of the agricultural good, so that the balance of trade is in equilibrium. In other words, intraindustry flows are accompanied by interindustry flows, with one region exporting more of the industrial good and the other region exporting more of the agricultural good. The assumption of zero trade costs for the latter good means that it is sold at the same price in both regions; hence this price is independent of the volume of trade because the agricultural good is produced under constant returns. It should, therefore, be clear how these two assumptions allows for a fairly simple resolution of the model. Either of these two assumptions can be relaxed by determining the price of the agricultural good—either by using the corresponding market-clearing condition or by using the equilibrium condition of the trade balance.

A comparable spatialization of the linear model, which we introduced in chapter 3, does not give rise to any special difficulties; it leads to the same types of conclusions as the DSK model. We will use it in chapter 8 together with additive trade costs, which match the linear model better than iceberg-type trade costs.

Remark. The results above, along with those presented in the following chapters, do not depend on the assumption of a mill pricing policy. Indeed, if each firm is free to select a specific delivered price in each of the two regions, as the demand elasticity is the same in both regions, each firm does choose a mill pricing policy. In other words, every firm chooses not to discriminate, as the two prices maximizing its profits are such that $p_B^* = \tau p_A^*$ if the variety is produced in region A or $p_A^* = \tau p_B^*$ if it is produced in region B. To show this, it is sufficient to repeat the preceding argument by replacing $\tau p_A(i)$ with $p_B(i)$ in the demand and the price indices before computing the first-order conditions.

4.2 The Home-Market Effect

Both economists and geographers agree that a large market tends to increase the profitability of the firms established in it.[9] More generally, the idea is that locations that have good access to several markets offer firms a greater profit. Indeed, we have just seen that a region's demand increases with the accessibility and size of this region. The profitability of firms is further enhanced by increasing returns, since the growth in their volume of production also generates a drop in their average production costs. Hence, we expect that the firms that set up in the large region enjoy higher profits than the ones installed in the small one. In the long term, the core region should therefore attract new firms, thereby heightening the inequalities between the core and the periphery. Nevertheless, as firms set up in the core region, competition there is also heightened, thereby holding back the tendency to agglomeration. Studies that aim to

---

[9] There are several historical examples showing the importance to firms of belonging to a large market. It is less well-known that the entrance of Luxembourg into the Zollverein greatly enhanced the development of Luxembourg's steel industry between 1870 and 1900 by guaranteeing it privileged access to the German market.

determine the resultant of these two forces have led to what is known as the "home-market effect" (HME).

The economy is similar to the one described in the previous section. However, because we focus here on the interregional mobility of capital, the DSK model must be modified as follows: (i) the two production factors of the manufacturing sector are *labor* and *capital*; (ii) labor is homogeneous and each worker possesses one unit of it; (iii) workers are free to work across sectors and the regional supply of labor is large enough to support some production of the agricultural good for any interregional allocation of capital, which implies that the wage is the same in both sectors and is equal to 1; (iv) the capital belongs collectively to the workers, hence without any loss of generality we may assume that each worker owns one unit of capital; and finally (v) the production cost of the variety i is given by

$$C[q(i)] = fr + mq(i),$$

where f is the fixed requirement of capital, r is the rental rate of capital, and m is the marginal requirement in labor (remember that the wage rate is equal to 1).[10]

4.2.1 The Two-Region Case

The total mass of workers is L. The share of workers living in region A is $\theta \geqslant \frac{1}{2}$, while $1 - \theta$ is the share of those living in region B. Consequently, the capital incomes are distributed between the regions according to the same fractions. Although any Heckscher–Ohlin-type comparative advantage has been eliminated, since the relative factor endowment is the same in the two regions, region A has an advantage in terms of size.[11]

Capital searches for the higher rental rate in either A or B, but labor is spatially immobile, perhaps because there are more barriers to labor migration than there are to capital flows. The overall stock of capital is equal to the overall population L. Because each firm requires the use of $f > 0$ units of capital, market clearing leads to a total number of firms equal to

$$N^* = L/f.$$

Then

$$n_A = \frac{\lambda L}{f}, \qquad n_B = \frac{(1 - \lambda)L}{f}, \tag{4.3}$$

---

[10] The uniform distribution of capital ownership has no influence here, so long as the mass of capital belonging to the inhabitants of region A is equal to θ.

[11] To illustrate this point, think of the EU-15, where the relative endowments are very similar across member countries, while national market sizes vary considerably.

where λ denotes the share of capital invested in region A.[12] Moreover, $(\theta - \lambda)L < 0$ (respectively, $(\theta - \lambda)L > 0$) measures the amount of capital imported (respectively, exported) by the large region.

Although capital is mobile, capital-owners are immobile and spend the income earned from capital in the region where they live. Hence, regional incomes are given by

$$Y_A(\lambda) = [1 + r_A(\lambda)]\theta L, \qquad Y_B(\lambda) = [1 + r_B(\lambda)](1 - \theta)L. \qquad (4.4)$$

The quantities demanded by each consumer vary with their nominal income, which is endogenous, via the return from capital, which itself depends on the distribution of firms. Because capital-owners do not move, at the spatial equilibrium, the nominal rental rate of capital must be the same everywhere:[13]

$$r_A(\lambda) = r_B(\lambda) = r(\lambda). \qquad (4.5)$$

As above, and remembering that $w_A = w_B = 1$ here, the first-order conditions yield

$$p_A^* = \frac{m\sigma}{\sigma - 1}, \qquad p_{AB}^* = \frac{\tau m\sigma}{\sigma - 1}, \qquad (4.6)$$

which are identical for all region A firms. The price index thus becomes

$$P_A = \frac{m\sigma}{\sigma - 1}(n_A + \phi n_B)^{-1/(\sigma-1)}. \qquad (4.7)$$

Although firms' equilibrium prices are independent of their distribution, any change in the distribution of firms in favor of the large region has a downward effect on the price index of this region, thus pushing up the local demand. This effect is due to falling trade costs. On the other hand, this change also sparks a downward effect in the demand for each variety produced therein, because of the greater fragmentation of the market for the differentiated product, thus pushing profits downward. This is the market-crowding effect, which impedes the agglomeration of firms.

Furthermore, we assume that a sufficiently high number of potential entrepreneurs who seek to attract capital exist in each region. To achieve their goal, they offer the capital-owners higher and higher returns, and this goes on until the profits that they make are zero. In other words, although the total number of active firms N^* is fixed, everything works as if there were free entry. Consequently, operating profits must exactly cover the cost of the capital:

$$\pi_A \equiv p_A^* q_{AA} + p_{AB}^* q_{AB} - m(q_{AA} + \tau q_{AB}) - fr(\lambda) = 0. \qquad (4.8)$$

---

[12] Note here another advantage of the continuum assumption: it enables us to work with a continuous distribution of capital shares, while each firm has only one location.

[13] Thus, in equilibrium, there is factor price equalization.

If $q_A = q_{AA} + \tau q_{AB}$ denotes the production of a region A firm, the expressions (4.6) and (4.8) imply that

$$r_A(\lambda) = \frac{m q_A}{f(\sigma - 1)}. \tag{4.9}$$

Furthermore, we have seen in the preceding section that the demand for the variety i produced in region A is given by

$$q_A = \mu (P_A^{\sigma-1} Y_A + \phi P_B^{\sigma-1} Y_B) p_A^{-\sigma}. \tag{4.10}$$

Variety i's market-clearing condition allows us to determine the equilibrium output of a firm, which varies with the distribution of capital, unlike what we had in the DSK model. By substituting (4.6) and (4.7) into (4.10), we obtain

$$q_A^*(\lambda) = \frac{\mu(\sigma - 1)}{m\sigma} \left(\frac{Y_A}{n_A + \phi n_B} + \frac{\phi Y_B}{\phi n_A + n_B} \right). \tag{4.11}$$

Substituting (4.3) and (4.4) into (4.11) and inputting the resulting expression into (4.9), we obtain, after simplification,

$$r_A(\lambda) = \frac{\mu}{\sigma} \left[\frac{\theta(1 + r_A)}{\lambda + \phi(1 - \lambda)} + \frac{\phi(1 - \theta)(1 + r_B)}{\phi\lambda + (1 - \lambda)} \right]. \tag{4.12}$$

Using the corresponding expression for $r_B(\lambda)$, the equilibrium condition (4.5) then gives

$$\frac{\theta}{\lambda + \phi(1 - \lambda)} + \frac{\phi(1 - \theta)}{\phi\lambda + (1 - \lambda)} = \frac{1 - \theta}{\phi\lambda + (1 - \lambda)} + \frac{\phi\theta}{\lambda + \phi(1 - \lambda)},$$

the solution of which yields the equilibrium firm distribution:

$$\lambda^*(\theta) = \tfrac{1}{2} + \frac{1 + \phi}{1 - \phi} (\theta - \tfrac{1}{2}) \geqslant \theta \geqslant \tfrac{1}{2}. \tag{4.13}$$

So long as $\theta > \tfrac{1}{2}$, we have $\lambda^* > \theta$, since $\phi > 0$. Consequently, *the large region* (in terms of population and demand) *attracts a more than proportional share of firms* into the sector characterized by increasing returns. In other words, the small region exports capital to the large one: the home-market effect. Because of its comparative advantage in terms of size, it is of course natural that the large region attracts more firms. What is more unexpected is that the share of firms exceeds the relative size of this region, thus implying that the initial advantage is magnified. In addition, the relationship (4.13) linking λ^* and θ is linear. This property will vastly simplify the econometric estimation of the HME. We will return to this in chapter 12.

As the large region is also the one that offers the wider array of varieties, it is a net exporter of the manufactured good and a net importer of the agricultural good. The two regions are, therefore, partially specialized: the large one in the production of the manufactured good and the small one in that of the agricultural good. This type of specialization owes nothing to a Ricardian comparative advantage, the nature of the forces at work here being totally different. Indeed, they rest on the interplay between the market-access and the market-crowding effects.

In order to emphasize the trade-off between the agglomeration and dispersion forces, it is worth rewriting (4.13) as follows:

$$(1 + \phi)(\theta - \tfrac{1}{2}) = (1 - \phi)(\lambda^* - \tfrac{1}{2}). \tag{4.14}$$

The left-hand side of this equation denotes the agglomeration force and the right-hand side the dispersion force. If $(1 + \phi)(\theta - \tfrac{1}{2}) > (1 - \phi)(\lambda^* - \tfrac{1}{2})$, then $r_A(\lambda) > r_B(\lambda)$, thus inducing a higher fraction of capital to be invested in the large region. The intensity of the agglomeration force gets stronger as the size of the large market increases and the trade costs decrease. Conversely, if $(1 - \phi)(\lambda^* - \tfrac{1}{2}) > (1 + \phi)(\theta - \tfrac{1}{2})$, a higher fraction of capital is induced to establish itself in the small region. Hence, the dispersion force depends on the distribution of firms (λ) and gets stronger as trade costs increase. In equilibrium, these two forces are exactly balanced at λ^*.

The intensity of the HME varies with the level of trade costs: for a given value of θ, it is readily verified that $\lambda^*(\theta)$ increases with ϕ. Specifically, when economic integration gets deeper, (4.14) shows that the intensity of the agglomeration force increases whereas the intensity of the dispersion force decreases. This result can be understood as follows. On the one hand, a higher degree of integration makes exports to the small market easier, which allows firms to exploit their scale economies more intensively; on the other hand, the deepening of integration reduces the advantages associated with geographical isolation in the small market, where demand is less fragmented. These two effects push toward more agglomeration of the manufacturing sector, thus implying that, *as trade costs go down, the small region gets deindustrialized to the benefit of the large one.*

By replacing λ by its equilibrium value in (4.5), we obtain the equilibrium level of capital return:

$$r^* = \frac{\mu}{\sigma - \mu},$$

which is independent of the regions' sizes and of their degree of integration. This is because the capital market is totally integrated: that is, it can be invested in either of the two regions regardless of the location of the capital-owners. Moreover, this expression shows that more differentiated varieties and a larger manufacturing sector allow firms to make higher operating profits, thereby guaranteeing both regions a higher capital return.

Another important implication of the HME is the fact that deeper economic integration leads to growing regional disparities, so long as $\phi < 1$. Indeed, as the equilibrium capital return is independent of ϕ, so are the nominal regional incomes. Consequently, the welfare of individuals depends entirely on the differences in the regional price indices, which both decrease as trade costs go down. However, the drop in P_A is stronger than the drop in P_B. As a result, although all the consumers benefit from the pursuit of integration, deeper economic integration generates more regional disparities at the expense of the small region. Here, trade liberalization enhances the mobility of capital, rather than substitutes for it, and makes the two economies less similar.

The HME is also liable to have unexpected implications for transport policy, such as that implemented by the European Union in its cohesion program. By making the transport of goods cheaper in *both* directions, the construction of a new infrastructure permits an increase in both imports to and exports from the small region. We have just seen that lower transport costs may induce some firms to pull out of the small region, thus failing to reduce regional disparities. This result could explain the disillusion regarding the effectiveness of EU policies that aim for a more balanced distribution of activities across the European Union (Midelfart-Knarvik and Overman 2002; Vickerman et al. 1999).

At this point, some remarks are in order. First, it is readily verified that

$$\frac{d\lambda^*}{d\theta} = \frac{1 + \phi}{1 - \phi} > 1,$$

which means that the share of firms in the large region increases faster than the share of consumers located there. It is easily verified that this property is itself the equivalent of the HME described above. Second, having varieties that are more differentiated (a lower σ) leads to more regional disparities as $d^2\lambda^*/d\theta d\phi > 0$ and $d\phi/d\sigma < 0$, thus $d^2\lambda^*/d\theta d\sigma < 0$. The reason for this is to be found in the fact that a higher degree of differentiation allows firms to charge higher prices and, therefore, weakens the market-crowding effect. Third, firms, although a priori identical, do not make the same choice: some of them set up in the small region and the others set up in the large one.

Before investigating the case of three regions, we should also point out that $\lambda^* = 1$ as soon as θ exceeds the threshold value

$$\bar{\theta} \equiv \frac{1}{1 + \phi} \geq \frac{1}{2},$$

in which case all firms are agglomerated in the large region. In view of the definition of $\bar{\theta}$, full agglomeration is more likely to arise, the lower the trade costs. Moreover, as expected, the greater the asymmetry between regions in terms of size (that is, the greater θ is), the more the large region is liable to attract the entire manufacturing sector. In contrast, if the two regions are identical ($\theta = \frac{1}{2}$), the firms are always evenly distributed between the two regions ($\lambda^* = \frac{1}{2}$).

4.2.2   The Multi-Region Case

Although the results presented above tell us something important, they depend on the assumption of an economy made up of two regions. Dealing with more than two regions gives rise to at least two new questions that are not easy to answer. The first one concerns the fact that we would like to find, for any pair of regions, a definition of the HME similar to the one obtained in the two-region setting. Along these lines, if θ_r is the share of consumers located in region r and λ_r is the share of capital invested there, one possible definition of the HME would be to require that $\lambda_r/\theta_r > \lambda_s/\theta_s$ if and only if θ_r exceeds θ_s. In other words, for every pair of regions, the region with the higher share of expenditure would attract a more than proportional share of firms. Moreover, another fundamental facet of a multi-region setting is that *the accessibility to markets varies across regions.* More precisely, trade costs between two regions are likely to vary with the regions considered, which means that the relative positions of regions within the whole network of interactions matters.[14] Consequently, we can foresee that the locations and sizes of *all* regions have an impact on the locations of firms. In this context, what does the HME become? In this section, we aim to shed light on these issues by studying the case of three regions A, B, and C. We will use the indices r and s, with $r, s =$ A, B, or C.

Let us assume that A and C have the same size ($(1 - \theta)/2$), while B is larger ($\theta > \frac{1}{3}$). Furthermore, the geography of markets is described by an isosceles triangle in which regions A and C are equidistant from region B. In the two extreme cases, this region is situated in the middle of the segment joining A and C, or at an arbitrarily large distance along the perpendicular passing through the middle of this segment. The economy that we are considering is therefore described by the following

---

[14] This point has long been stressed in location theory: see, for example, Beckmann and Thisse (1986).

parameters:[15]

$$(\theta_A, \theta_B, \theta_C) = (\tfrac{1}{2}(1 - \theta), \theta, \tfrac{1}{2}(1 - \theta)), \quad \text{with } \tfrac{1}{3} < \theta < 1,$$

$$\phi_{AC} = \phi_{CA} = \phi, \quad \phi_{AB} = \phi_{BA} = \phi_{BC} = \phi_{CB} = \frac{\phi}{\delta}, \quad \text{with } \delta \in [\sqrt{\phi}, \infty).$$

While the value of ϕ expresses the overall evolution of trade costs, by varying δ between its two boundaries $\sqrt{\phi}$ and ∞, we can describe a wide range of market configurations. First, if $\delta = \sqrt{\phi}$, region B is located in the middle of the segment linking regions A and C; when $\phi < \sqrt{\phi} < \delta < 1$, the three regions form an obtuse triangle within which region B retains a relative advantage in terms of accessibility to the two others. In this case, region B can be interpreted as the "hub" of the global economy; when $\delta = 1$, the three regions are equidistant; and finally, if $\delta > 1$, the three regions form an acute triangle and region B occupies a "peripheral" position, this effect being exacerbated as δ increases. In the limit, region B approaches autarky as δ tends to ∞.

Because the variety market equilibrium conditions are linear in the mass of varieties produced in each region (see (4.11)), they have a unique solution. Furthermore, the symmetry of the market space suggests that regions A and C accommodate the same share of firms in equilibrium, which is equal to $(1 - \lambda_B^*)/2$. As a result, determining the spatial equilibrium is equivalent to finding the value λ_B^* that solves the equation $r_A(\lambda_B) = r_B(\lambda_B)$. By following the same approach as in the two-region case, it can be shown that the share of firms located in region B is given by the following expression:

$$\lambda_B^*(\delta) = \frac{\delta^2(1 + \phi)\theta - \delta\phi(1 + \phi) + 2\phi^2(1 - \theta)}{(\delta - \phi)(\delta + \delta\phi - 2\phi)}$$

$$= \frac{\delta(1 + \phi)}{\delta(1 + \phi) - 2\phi}\theta - \frac{\phi}{\delta - \phi}(1 - \theta), \tag{4.15}$$

where the second expression is obtained from the first one by multiplying $\delta\phi(1 + \phi)$ by $(\theta + 1 - \theta)$. Using $\theta_A + \theta_C = 1 - \theta$ and $\theta_B = \theta$ yields

$$\lambda_B^*(\delta) = -\frac{\phi}{\delta - \phi}\theta_A + \frac{\delta(1 + \phi)}{\delta(1 + \phi) - 2\phi}\theta_B - \frac{\phi}{\delta - \phi}\theta_C,$$

which means that $\lambda_B^*(\delta)$ is given by a linear combination of the market sizes, the coefficients of which depend upon only the accessibility between regions.

---

[15] We assume that δ is larger than or equal to $\sqrt{\phi}$ for the following reason. When A, B, and C are collinear, going from A to C through B implies a freeness of trade equal to $\phi_{AB}\phi_{BC} = \phi^2/\delta^2$, which is equal to the freeness of trade when going directly from A to C, i.e., ϕ, if and only if $\delta = \sqrt{\phi}$.

Using (4.15), it is readily verified that

$$\frac{\lambda_B^*(\delta)}{\theta} > 1 > \frac{\lambda_A^*(\delta)}{(1-\theta)/2} = \frac{\lambda_C^*(\delta)}{(1-\theta)/2}$$

because θ exceeds $\frac{1}{3}$ and $\delta \in [\sqrt{\phi}, 1)$. In other words, *when the large region has a locational advantage, the HME always holds.* For $\delta = 1$, we have

$$\lambda_B^* = \frac{1+2\phi}{1-\phi}\theta - \frac{\phi}{1-\phi},$$

which is greater than θ so long as $\theta > \frac{1}{3}$. Hence, the HME is also present when the market configuration is symmetric ($\delta = 1$), confirming what we have seen in the two-region case. What happens when δ exceeds 1?

It is readily verified that $\lambda_B^*(\delta)$ always decreases with δ when

$$\frac{1}{3} < \frac{1+\phi}{3+\phi} < \theta < 1. \tag{4.16}$$

On the other hand, if

$$\frac{1}{3} < \theta < \frac{1+\phi}{3+\phi}, \tag{4.17}$$

then $\lambda_B^*(\delta)$ decreases in the interval $[\sqrt{\phi}, \hat{\delta})$ but increases on $[\hat{\delta}, \infty)$, where

$$\hat{\delta} \equiv \frac{\phi[2 - 4\theta + 2\phi - 4\theta\phi + (1-\phi)\sqrt{2\theta(1-\theta)(1+\phi)}]}{(1+\phi)[1+\phi-\theta(3+\phi)]} > 1.$$

To sum up, $\lambda_B^*(\delta)$ always decreases with δ over the interval $\sqrt{\phi} \leqslant \delta \leqslant 1$, which implies that region B accommodates its highest share of the manufacturing sector when it is located in the middle of the segment linking regions A and C. Hence, *improving the accessibility of the central region makes it more attractive.*[16]

Things may change when $\delta > 1$. When (4.16) holds, region B always receives a share of firms that exceeds θ. In addition, for a given value of ϕ, the stronger the locational disadvantage of region B (i.e., as δ gets larger), the weaker the HME. Indeed, the minimum of $\lambda_B^*(\delta)$ is reached when δ tends to ∞, with $\lambda_B^*(\infty) = \theta$. Consequently, *so long as the size of region B is sufficiently large, the HME remains true regardless of the relative position of the region.* Despite its locational disadvantage ($\delta > 1$), the market of region B is big enough for it to attract a more than proportional share of firms.

---

[16] Note, however, that (4.15) also shows that region B no longer imports capital but exports it instead once its market size becomes small enough. In other words, improving the accessibility of a *small* region through building new transport infrastructure is likely to be ineffective if the purpose is to make this region more attractive.

On the other hand, if (4.17) holds, the relationship between $\lambda_B^*(\delta)$ and δ ceases to be monotone decreasing and becomes U-shaped. The minimal value of $\lambda_B^*(\delta)$, which is equal to

$$\max\left\{\frac{2\sqrt{2\theta(1-\theta)(1+\phi)}-1-\phi}{1-\phi},0\right\},$$

is now lower than θ. In this case, the large region loses a great deal of its attractiveness because it is too far from the other two regions, its size advantage being too weak to counterbalance its poor accessibility to the rest of the economy. Of course, in such a case, there is no HME anymore: the large region no longer keeps its role as a magnet to firms. Consequently, we may safely conclude that *the attractiveness of a large region crucially depends on its relative position in the market space*, confirming the conclusions of Gallup et al. (1999), who observed that physical geography affects the level of economic development.

Yet when the large region is barely accessible from the others (that is, when δ is very large), it attracts more capital than when the other two regions have better access to its market. This is so because the firms located in region B are better protected from foreign competition. As in the foregoing, but in a different setting, improving accessibility is not necessarily a good way of boosting the industrial development of a large and landlocked region.

4.3   Concluding Remarks

We saw, in section 4.1, how the DSK model allows us to determine trade flows (both intraindustry and interindustry) between two open economies when interregional exchanges imply trade costs. In the absence of mobile production factors, all the agents benefit from more economic integration. However, a difference in size does have an impact on the regions: the unequal distribution of the manufacturing sector in the two regions generates inequalities in the corresponding levels of welfare. However, this welfare gap tends to be whittled away as trade costs diminish.

In section 4.2, we looked into the idea that large markets are more profitable than small ones and are, in consequence, likely to attract more firms. The idea of the dominant market is an old one that belongs equally to economics and geography. In contrast, the force of dispersion—which here depends on the competition between firms—has been introduced only recently. It is the balance between these two forces that determines the degree of agglomeration of the manufacturing sector in the large market, which magnifies the initial size advantage. In other words, regional disparities triggered by size differences widen with market integration once it is recognized that the location of firms is endogenous. Having said that, trade liberalization is likely to produce contrasting results for the economies involved, depending on whether capital is mobile. The difference between international trade, where all the factors are immobile, and economic geography, where some factors are mobile, is therefore crucial. In addition to the market size effect, the analysis of the multi-region case has shown us that the relative position of markets is another critical factor in determining the spatial distribution of firms. In other words, *both market size and market access matter for the locational choice of firms.* We will see in the next chapter how this observation may be used to understand and predict the intensity of flows of goods and factors across space.

One critical feature of the HME model is the fact that firms' locations need not be the same as those of the capital-owners. Indeed, while the location of capital-owners is exogenous, capital itself is mobile and can be invested in any region. As capital-owners repatriate their income, they spend it in the region in which they live. The production and consumption capacities are therefore disassociated. In contrast, in chapter 6 we will assume that it is no longer physical capital but human capital, in the form of skilled workers, that is mobile. This implies that these workers spend in the region in which they produce. Such a reformulation has the effect of substantially enriching the model by bringing new agglomeration and dispersion forces.

In many scientific fields, the passage from one to two dimensions raises fundamental conceptual difficulties. In economic geography, the difficulty begins with the apparently innocuous passage from two to three regions. The reason for this is that when there are just two regions, there is only one way in which these regions can interact: directly. With three regions, however, there are two ways in which these regions can interact: directly and indirectly. In other words, in multi-region systems the so-called "three-ness" effect enters the picture and allows one to *combine first- and second-nature ingredients.* This introduces complex feedbacks into the models, and these significantly complicate the analysis. Dealing with this richer pattern of spatial interdependencies constitutes one of the main theoretical and empirical challenges that economic geography will have to face in the future.

Although the models presented in this chapter highlight the role of economic geography, they are still quite restrictive. For example, it is essential to assume from the outset a degree of *exogenous* asymmetry between regions ($\theta > \frac{1}{2}$ in the context of two regions, $\theta > \frac{1}{3}$ in the case of three regions) for the HME to appear.[17] Conversely, we will see in chapters 6 and 7 that new endogenous income effects make it possible for identical regions to diverge when integration gets sufficiently deep, thus generating spatial inequalities endogenously.

4.4   Related Literature

Iceberg-type costs were introduced to model different types of transaction costs, so the reader has plenty of opportunities to explore them in various economic fields. Helpman and Krugman (1985) remains the primary reference regarding new trade theories. Feenstra (2004) has recently presented a detailed synthesis of various new lines of research in trade theory. The HME was spotlighted by Krugman (1980), but the reader should consult Head et al. (2002) for a more detailed analysis. In this chapter we have followed the formulation of the HME proposed by Martin and Rogers (1995), called the footloose capital model. Behrens et al. (2005) have generalized the Helpman and Krugman model to an arbitrary number of regions and any matrix of trade costs. Ago et al. (2006) focus on the special case of three regions. The linear version of the HME can be found in Ottaviano and Thisse (2004). Yu (2005) shows that the HME can arise, disappear, or reverse in sign depending on the demand elasticity of substitution between the homogeneous and the differentiated goods. The assumption of perfect capital mobility made in HME models is not fully satisfying, as empirical evidence highlights the existence of a significant home bias in international equity holdings (Ahearne et al. 2004). To the best of our knowledge, there is to date no model of economic geography dealing with home bias in investment decisions. Finally, for detailed surveys of spatial price theory, the reader is referred to Beckmann and Thisse (1986) as well as to Greenhut et al. (1987).

---

[17] When regions are the same size, they remain so whatever the level of trade costs, thus showing that the standard assumption of identical regions or countries is very restrictive.

5
Gravity and Trade Costs

According to Newton's theory of gravitation, two bodies are attracted to each other in proportion to the product of their mass and in inverse proportion to the square of the distance separating them. In physics, a body is defined as a point mass with no spatial extension, which is reminiscent of standard theories of international trade in which countries are considered as dimensionless entities. When several bodies come into play, the law of gravitation generates a system of forces that organizes them in the solar system. Consequently, it does not seem unreasonable to think of economic entities, such as countries or regions, as bodies subject to push and pull forces, the intensity of which depends on their sizes and the distances between them. Pursuing the analogy further, just as gravitation aggregates matter in a small number of planets, economic activity aggregates firms and households in a fairly limited number of human settlements. Just as both large and small planets exist, there are also large and small settlements, involving different combinations of firms and households. However, these places exchange flows of people, goods, and information that are far more visible than gravitational forces.

It is therefore no surprise that the idea of "social physics" emerged in the nineteenth century, bringing to the fore the human propensity to interact with others, very much as bodies do in physics (Carey 1858). One of the first applications of social physics was the study of migration flows between countries, regions, or cities (Ravenstein 1885; Young 1924). The *gravity model*, as social scientists call the modified law of gravitation, takes into account the population size of two places and the distance between them. Because larger places attract people more than smaller places and closer places interact more, the gravity model incorporates these two features. The same idea was later readopted to describe consumers' shopping behavior when choosing between various urban areas (Reilly 1931). Finally, the same idea was again successfully explored by Tinbergen (1962) in the context of international trade; flows are now measured by the imports and exports of countries, with their sizes being given by their GDPs. Despite the absence of early microeconomic foundations, the gravity model thus displays an empirical relevance rarely found in social sciences (Leamer and Levinsohn 1994).[1]

The gravity model builds on some characteristics of the spatial entities under consideration, as well as on their relative positions in space. Consequently, it takes geographical proximity as a major cause of trade between countries. This might seem at odds with the common belief that one of the main engines of the trade growth in the years after World War II was the progressive disappearance of the tyranny of distance and, more generally, the weakening of the impact of proximity on international trade. Contrary to that belief, trade costs remain high, especially between nations. Anderson and van Wincoop (2004) estimate that, for developed countries, average trade costs represent 170% of the FOB price of manufactured goods. This is quite a high rate for a world in which distance and space are supposedly disappearing from economic life. In the same vein, Hummels (2007) shows that international shipping costs still increase sharply with distance and matter much more than tariffs.

This chapter aims to provide an assessment of the various links between the location of activities, the level of trade costs, and the intensity of trade flows. The gravity model is presented in the first section. One of the most important aspects of the gravity model is the quality of its empirical fit. The success of this model in predicting bilateral flows is pervasive, and this calls for a theoretical foundation: why does the gravity model provide such a good description of actual trade flows? We will show that this model can be linked to the DSK model presented in chapter 4, thus endowing the gravity model with sound microeconomic foundations.[2] At the same time, this relationship allows us to better understand the advantages and limitations of the gravity model. Finally, from an economic viewpoint, it seems natural to believe that the geodesic distance between countries is not a rich enough description of trade costs. The question of how to evaluate these costs is the subject of section 5.2.

---

[1] It should be emphasized that the gravity model lies at the heart of one of the most fertile branches of human geography, i.e., *spatial interaction theory*, which seeks to predict flows of various kinds between entities all located in geographical space (Anas 1987; Sen and Smith 1995; Wilson 1970).

[2] The existence of a close relationship between these two models is not surprising. Indeed, it has long been known that both are closely related to the logit model (Anas 1983; Anderson et al. 1992).

5.1 The Gravity Model

We start by giving details of estimates related to trade flows, and then proceed to other types of flows, such as capital and knowledge flows, that also seem to be ruled by gravity forces.

5.1.1 Gravity and Bilateral Trade

In the traditional version of the gravity model, bilateral trade flows are positively correlated with the size of each partner and negatively affected by the level of trade costs. Countries' sizes are often measured by their GDPs and trade costs by the distance separating them.[3] Denoting the GDP of country r by Y_r, exports from r to s by X_{rs}, and the distance separating them by d_{rs}, the basic version of the gravity model can be written as follows:

$$X_{rs} = G \frac{Y_r^\alpha Y_s^\beta}{d_{rs}^\delta}, \tag{5.1}$$

where G, α, β, and δ are parameters to be estimated. The parameter δ is an indicator of the sensitivity of trade to the distance between trading partners. A high value of δ means that proximity is a crucial element in determining bilateral trade between those two countries, while a low value indicates that trade is of a similar intensity between partners that are close to each other and those that are far apart.

The multiplicative structure of (5.1) implies that its parameters can be estimated by taking its logarithm, which gives us the following log-linear relationship:

$$\ln X_{rs} = \ln G + \alpha \ln Y_r + \beta \ln Y_s - \delta \ln d_{rs} + \varepsilon_{rs}, \tag{5.2}$$

where ε_{rs} denotes an error term that has no economic meaning but controls for measurement errors.

In (5.2), the parameter δ measures the elasticity of trade with respect to distance. In a world in which distance no longer had an impact on the intensity of trade, the parameter δ would be zero. Although the estimates of this elasticity tend to vary across studies, they are significantly positive in a very systematic way. We can therefore interpret (5.1) as the outcome of the interplay between economic forces. In this context, Y_r is the amount that country r is willing to sell and Y_s the amount that country s is willing to buy, while the distance would represent the price to be paid for the goods to be shipped between the two countries. Although it is not possible to provide details of all the results of such estimates,

---

[3] We refer to countries in this chapter because most analyses were initially performed on that basis, but the same logic can be applied to regions.

it is worth illustrating the strength of the gravity model by means of an example that does not come immediately to mind, namely trade between cities in Ancient Mesopotamia (Bossuyt et al. 2001).

The archeological excavations undertaken on several urban sites in this area have unearthed a significant number of clay tablets mentioning the names of cities involved in a trade system 5,000 years ago. Needless to say, no one has any idea about the intensity of the corresponding trade flows. However, it seems reasonable to assume that the number of times a city is mentioned in tablets discovered in another city can be viewed as a good proxy of the intensity of the bilateral trade between these two cities. This may thus be used to represent X_{rs} in an estimation of (5.2). On the basis of a sample of thirty cities that have a precise and known location, the value of Y_r is approximated by the number of times all the other cities in the sample are mentioned in the archives of city r.[4] Finally, the value of d_{rs} is obtained from the distance, calculated in kilometers, along routes that have been identified by archeologists; it depends on the means of transport used (mules or boats) and ranges from half a day to eighty days of transport.

The general fit of equation (5.2) proves to be excellent. The most surprising result is the estimation of the parameter δ, with a value of 0.21, which is markedly lower, as we will see, than values obtained for modern economies. Bossuyt et al. infer from this that *Ancient Mesopotamia must have been an extremely integrated trading block,* possibly because the lack of natural resources in the region made trade between cities essential to their survival.

On reflection, the fact that distance reduces trade flows is barely surprising, as it is hard to imagine cases where proximity would not enhance exchanges. More interesting is the evolution of this relationship over a long period. The variety observed in both the data and the methods of estimation makes it difficult to draw conclusions from a mere comparison of existing studies. However, Disdier and Head (2008) have done a meta-analysis of seventy-eight articles devoted to estimates of the gravity model from data on bilateral trade. This type of survey obviously runs the risk of comparing apples with pears. Nevertheless, by carefully choosing their sample, the authors demonstrated how to significantly reduce the impact of the methodological differences in the various

---

[4] It is worth bearing in mind the fact that many archives are missing, as a great number of tablets have disappeared, and the excavations were of varying intensity from one site to the next. Thus, only part of the available material has been brought to light. Bossuyt et al. (2001) therefore added several binary variables to the specification in order to take into account the intensity of the excavations, the access to the tablets, and the position of a city with respect to the river network delineated by the Euphrates and the Tigris.

studies. Their main conclusions are as follows. As expected, the impact of distance on bilateral trade flows tended to decrease slightly between 1870 and 1950 but, more surprisingly, it started to increase again after 1950. Disdier and Head also observed that the impact of distance is more pronounced in developing countries. This result is probably due to the inferior quality of their transportation infrastructures (a point we will return to in the final section of this chapter). Finally, they calculated the mean distance elasticity to be 0.89, attesting to the fact that *distance significantly influences the intensity of trade flows*. Hence, doubling distance typically divides trade flows by a factor close to two.

It is worth stressing that this average value is bound to hide significant heterogeneity across traded goods. For example, as expected, trade in construction materials is much more sensitive to distance than trade in many other goods. At the other extreme, one might think of services as being free of the tyranny of distance because of the development of modern communication devices. For overall services or, more specifically, commercial services, this intuition happens to be wrong. Distance elasticities for services are comparable with, if not larger than, those obtained for material goods (Ceglowski 2006; Head et al. 2007). This is likely to be due to the face-to-face contacts that are needed in this type of trade. Yet, in a recent study, Tharakan et al. (2005) go into even greater detail and find that distance has very little impact on exports of software by India. It could therefore be the case that distance loses its relevance in the case of nonmaterial goods.

5.1.2 Is Gravity Universal?

The gravity model has been applied to the study of the impact of distance on a very wide range of flows, such as portfolio investments, foreign direct investments, and the diffusion of technologies. In the first instance, Portes and Rey (2005) obtain a distance elasticity equal to 0.88, which is considerable in a world where finance is considered as being globalized. These authors show that this impact is partially derived from distance-related informational asymmetries between countries.

In the case of foreign direct investments (FDIs), which typically entail a long-run strategic commitment on the part of the investor, Di Mauro (2000) finds an elasticity of 0.42. Stein and Daude (2002), who use a larger sample, find a distance elasticity of 0.51. Here, distance undoubtedly represents a cost of a type unlike those involved in portfolio investments. Specifically, the coordination of activities by headquarters is crucial in the FDI decision. Distance makes the task of monitoring the operations of overseas subsidiaries harder, thus reducing the attractiveness of far-away destinations, all else being equal. Stein and Daude come up with another interesting finding: distance does not have the same impact on investment flows along a north–south axis as it does along an east–west axis. The costs of coordinating multinational activity are clearly higher when a subsidiary operates in a country belonging to a different time zone. If a problem is discovered at 11:00 A.M. in Los Angeles, it is already 8:00 P.M. in Paris, and those responsible for solving this problem will only discover it the following morning, by which time it will be midnight in Los Angeles. As a solution cannot be implemented until later in the day, this type of delay proves costly. When the time difference between countries is introduced into the regression, the result is spectacular: the impact of distance disappears completely, whereas a time difference of one hour reduces the bilateral stock of direct investments by almost 24%. In the same vein, one expects advances in transportation and communication technologies to cancel out the impact of distance. This need not be the case. If the drop in the impact of distance on investment flows is relatively high for investments in countries situated in nearby time zones, the impact of east–west distance grows with time, rather than decreasing.

Ever since the pioneering work of Ravenstein (1885), it has been known that distance has a significant impact on migration flows (Clark 1986). One may wonder to what extent ideas also diffuse over space and how such a spatial diffusion has evolved in societies in which the transfer of information across space is getting much cheaper and less dependent on distance, especially in an age in which new communication technologies make cheap and easy circulation of information possible. As this type of flow is difficult to assess, one line of research involves exploring the impact that a country's research and development (R&D) expenses can have on productivity in other countries through spillover effects. The studies carried out to date are unanimous in their conclusion: *the effects of technological spillovers are very localized*, which refutes the idea that knowledge is disseminated very quickly across space. For example, Keller (2002) observes that, while the R&D expenses of the five countries where such investments are highest (France, Germany, Japan, the United Kingdom, and the United States) have a positive impact on the total productivity of the firms located in other OECD countries, this impact decreases markedly with the distance between the country of origin and the country where the investment is made. Another line of research tries to measure the flow of ideas more directly, via the traces they leave in their wake. Jaffe et al. (1993) and, more recently, Peri (2005) observe that a firm that registers a patent must mention all patents used in the new process/product, which makes it possible to reconstruct the flow of knowledge. On the basis of a sample containing 147 regions in eighteen countries, Peri computes in each case the number of patent citations registered in another region. Somewhat surprisingly, the tyranny of distance is again at work. All else being equal, the crossing of the first regional border reduces the flow of knowledge by 80%, while the crossing of the national border has an impact identical to that of a linguistic frontier. This striking impact of spatial frictions on the flow of knowledge is, however, obviously less important than the impact on the flow of goods. In this respect, Peri (2005) compares the elasticities obtained with those affecting trade flows, using the same specification of the gravity model. The impact of distance and national borders on the flow of knowledge remains significant, but is six to seven times lower than the impact on trade flows.

These results, along with many others, challenge the idea of an economy free from geographical constraints.[5] We must be wary, however, of too readily inferring a relationship of causality. These studies only show the existence of *a negative correlation between trade and distance*. The analysis should be developed in order to determine how and why distance has such a negative impact at a time when, as seen in chapter 1, transport and communication costs are continuously falling, and have been doing so since the start of the Industrial Revolution. The answer is probably that *the significance of distance for economic activities has changed*. Indeed, it should be kept in mind that, in the gravity model, distance is nothing more than an *aggregate* of variables influencing trade between countries, which hides other far more complex phenomena.[6] Distance, therefore, has the status of a black box—one that we will open in section 5.2. Before we do, though, we must make sure that the estimated relationships do not suffer from any major bias of specification and estimation. This is what we will explore below, using the DSK model as our reference framework.

5.1.3 Gravity and Monopolistic Competition

Consider a DSK-like economy made up of R countries, denoted by $r = 1, \ldots, R$, keeping the notation of chapter 4.[7] The iceberg trade cost between countries r and s is now specific to these countries (the pair

---

[5] For example, borders and distance also matter for telephone calls, business traffic, and passenger transport.

[6] Note also that transport costs involves several important dimensions that are often overlooked in attempts made to measure trade costs (Rietveld and Vickerman 2004).

[7] In this chapter, we focus on countries instead of regions because the literature has mainly studied international flows.

of countries is also called a dyad) and is denoted by $\tau_{rs} \geqslant 1$; the internal trade cost τ_{rr} is also larger than 1. Moreover, we allow consumers to have a bias toward some countries in their preferences, so that the utility of a consumer residing in country s becomes

$$U_s = \left(\sum_{r=1}^{R} a_{rs}^{(\sigma-1)/\sigma} \int_{i \in \mathcal{N}_r} q_r(i)^{(\sigma-1)/\sigma} \, di \right)^{\sigma/(\sigma-1)},$$

where a_{rs} is the weight attributed by consumers in country s to varieties supplied by country r, $\mathcal{N}_r$ being the set of varieties produced in r. We will see that this formalization of preferences, due to Armington (1969), gives us a better understanding of empirical studies of trade flows. Such a specification of preferences does not, however, significantly affect the main conclusions derived in economic geography models. So, in the theoretical chapters of the book, we retain the symmetric framework in which $a_{rs} = 1$ for all possible r and s.

Denoting by μ_s a country's income share spent on manufactured goods, the demand functions are obtained as in chapters 3 and 4:

$$q_{rs} = a_{rs}^{\sigma-1} \left(\frac{\tau_{rs} p_r}{P_s} \right)^{-\sigma} \frac{\mu_s Y_s}{P_s}.$$

Hence, the biased preferences do not affect the elasticity of demand, which implies that all varieties produced in a country are sold at the same FOB price, as in chapter 4. In equilibrium, the price index of country s is thus expressed as follows:

$$P_s = \left[\sum_{r=1}^{R} n_r \left(\frac{p_r \tau_{rs}}{a_{rs}} \right)^{-(\sigma-1)} \right]^{-1/(\sigma-1)},$$

where n_r is the mass of varieties produced in country r. The bilateral flow in value from r to s is given by

$$X_{rs} \equiv n_r p_{rs} q_{rs} = n_r p_r (\tau_{rs}/a_{rs})^{-(\sigma-1)} \left(\frac{p_r}{P_s} \right)^{-\sigma} \frac{\mu_s Y_s}{P_s}. \qquad (5.3)$$

At first sight, this expression seems to correspond to a gravity-like prediction. On the right-hand side we find the GDP of the country of destination (Y_s) and the mass of varieties produced in the country of origin (n_r), which is proportional to the GDP of country r. Indeed the number of firms in a country is proportional to the value of its production, since, in equilibrium, all firms have the same volume of production. Hence, the DSK model predicts $\alpha = \beta = 1$, which agrees with many estimations. Equation (5.3) also incorporates parameters that depend on both the country of origin and that of destination, i.e., the trade cost (τ_{rs}) and the bias in preferences (a_{rs}). As a first approximation, we may assume that they both depend upon the distance between countries r and s. More precisely, τ_{rs} increases with distance, while a_{rs} decreases with distance because consumers are expected to prefer the goods they are accustomed to and know best. Consumers may even feel a pride in their domestic industry (the often-cited home bias in favor of domestic products). Note, however, that the perceived quality of some products is associated with their country of origin because of the reputation that some industries have acquired in specific countries (think of German cars and French cheese).[8] We will return to these issues in the next section.

However, a more careful inspection suggests that it is difficult to consider (5.1) as a good approximation of (5.3) since Y_s is the only term common to both expressions. Specifically, (5.3) is much more involved than (5.1). In particular, *the DSK model yields a gravity equation that involves price terms* (p_r and P_s), which are missing from (5.1). Nevertheless, we are going to see that it is possible to use the DSK model further to narrow the gap between the two expressions.

Letting v_r denote the total value of production in country r, q_r the amount produced by a firm located in r, and p_r the FOB price of its variety, the following relationship must hold:

$$v_r = n_r q_r p_r.$$

Furthermore, if preferences and technologies are the same across countries, a firm's equilibrium output is the same everywhere, $q_r = q$ (chapter 3). We can thus use the relationship $n_r p_r = v_r / q$ to eliminate the variable n_r in (5.3). Taking the logarithm of the resulting expression leads to

$$\ln X_{rs} = \ln \mu_s Y_s + \ln v_r - (\sigma - 1) \ln(\tau_{rs}/a_{rs}) - \sigma \ln p_r + I_s, \qquad (5.4)$$

where

$$I_s = \ln P_s^{\sigma-1} = (\sigma - 1) \ln \left\{ \sum_{k=1}^{R} \left[v_k + \left(\frac{\tau_{sk}}{a_{sk}} \right)^{-(\sigma-1)} + p_k^{-\sigma} \right] \right\}.$$

Expression (5.4) seems to have a partial-equilibrium flavor because bilateral flows are described by variables depending on r and s only. However, it should be kept in mind that I_s captures general-equilibrium effects associated with the rest of the world. Unfortunately, estimating this equation remains a hard task because I_s is highly nonlinear in the unknown parameters, especially σ, and contains some variables that are

---

[8] Neven et al. (1991) discuss the contributions of marketing studies that demonstrate the reality of these two phenomena.

difficult to measure accurately.[9] We now move on to discuss the various strategies used to tackle these difficulties.

5.1.4 Empirical Implementations

There are three types of implementations that have been followed.

(i) Equation (5.4) can be consistently estimated by a simple fixed effects regression, a path followed by Harrigan (1996), Hummels (1999), Eaton and Kortum (2002), and Redding and Venables (2004), among others. The method rewrites (5.4) as[10]

$$\ln X_{rs} = \text{FX}_r - (\sigma - 1)\ln(\tau_{rs}/a_{rs}) + \text{FM}_s + \varepsilon_{rs}, \tag{5.5}$$

where FX_r and FM_s are exporter and importer specific dummy variables, which take the value 1 for the country in question and 0 otherwise; these variables account for the terms $\ln v_r - \sigma \ln p_r$ and $\ln \mu Y_s + I_s$, respectively; and ε_{rs} is an error term. Because FX_r and FM_s are estimated without imposing any constraints on their values, the fixed-effect method is fairly general. Indeed, (5.5) is compatible with explanations of the gravity model other than the DSK model (Anderson and van Wincoop 2003). This method bypasses the need to gather the data required for the construction of $\ln v_r - \sigma \ln p_r$ and $\ln \mu_s Y_s + I_s$. It avoids the problems of nonlinearity in (5.4) and does not require sophisticated estimation methods. It also allows us to obtain estimates of two groups of variables that appear in (5.3), namely

$$\widehat{n_r p_r^{-(\sigma-1)}} = \exp(\text{FX}_r) \quad \text{and} \quad \widehat{\mu_s Y_s P_s^{\sigma-1}} = \exp(\text{FM}_s), \tag{5.6}$$

which can be used to study other questions (see chapter 12).[11]

Applying the fixed-effect method allows us to study the impact of distance on trade over a very long time period and for many countries. We

---

[9] The term I_s has the nature of a weighted distance index, in the sense used by Anderson and van Wincoop (2003): it incorporates not only the size of the potential suppliers, through v_k, and the distance separating them from region s, but the prices of their varieties as well.

Note also that I_s is supposed to account for *all* the regions producing the manufactured good, that is, the entire set of trading partners. Such information is generally not available in existing databases.

[10] This subsection and the next require some very basic knowledge of panel data econometrics and endogeneity issues. An introductory textbook such as Wooldridge (2006) might be useful for readers who are not familiar with such econometric techniques.

[11] The use of variables in an estimation resulting from another econometric estimation is plagued with a number of difficulties. In particular, the degree of uncertainty with which these variables are estimated must be taken into account in the second estimation. There are methods for correcting the standard deviations, but they are too complex to be discussed here. Redding and Venables (2004) present an application of such methods.

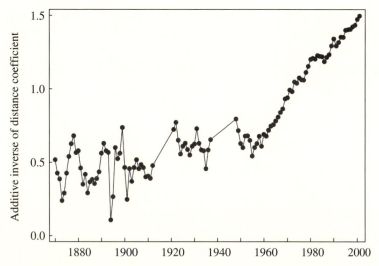

Figure 5.1. The impact of distance on trade, 1870–2001.

illustrate it for the period 1870–2001 by using IMF annual bilateral trade data as well as those collected by Barbieri (2003).[12] For this purpose, trade costs and preferences must be specified. We assume that

$$\ln(\tau_{rs}/a_{rs}) = \delta \ln d_{rs} - \beta \operatorname{cont}_{rs} - \lambda \operatorname{lang}_{rs}. \tag{5.7}$$

Following our discussion above, distance is the most obvious candidate to take into account. Two additional variables are introduced: cont_{rs} and lang_{rs}. These two dummy variables take a value of 1 when countries r and s have a common border and share a common language, respectively.

Figure 5.1 shows how the coefficient of distance varies over time. The main result comes as a surprise: since 1870, a marginal increase in distance has increasingly reduced the intensity of trade. In other words, the impact of distance has become stronger, especially since World War II. This does not mean that trade has decreased, nor that short-distance trade has grown while long-distance trade has shrunk. Instead, this suggests that the former has grown more rapidly than the latter. Although the reasons for this phenomenon are still unclear, we may safely conclude that, *far from diminishing, the importance of geography in the determination of international trade flows has increased.*[13]

---

[12] The appendix to this chapter gives more details about the main sources that can be used to carry out gravity estimations.

[13] The coefficient of distance is equal to $-(\sigma-1)\delta$ in the DSK interpretation. Therefore, an alternative interpretation is that products become less differentiated.

(ii) When internal flows, i.e., the quantities sold by firms within their host country (X_{ss}), are available,[14] a second method for estimating (5.4) involves using the fact that the term I_s depends on only the importer, and not on the exporter. We can rewrite (5.4) when $r = s$, which gives an expression for $\ln X_{ss}$. By subtracting this from (5.4), we obtain

$$\ln\left(\frac{X_{rs}}{X_{ss}}\right) = \ln\left(\frac{v_r}{v_s}\right) - (\sigma - 1)\ln\left(\frac{\tau_{rs}\,a_{ss}}{\tau_{ss}\,a_{rs}}\right) - \sigma \ln\left(\frac{p_r}{p_s}\right). \qquad (5.8)$$

When no data on prices are available, we can once again use the DSK model to replace the relative prices with relative wages, which are equal to each other because markups are the same:

$$\ln\left(\frac{X_{rs}}{X_{ss}}\right) = \ln\left(\frac{v_r}{v_s}\right) - (\sigma - 1)\ln\left(\frac{\tau_{rs}\,a_{ss}}{\tau_{ss}\,a_{rs}}\right) - \sigma \ln\left(\frac{w_r}{w_s}\right). \qquad (5.9)$$

In both cases, a slightly less constrained model may be estimated by allowing the coefficient on $\ln(v_r/v_s)$ to be different from 1 (its value in (5.9)).

These expressions make it possible to analyze the way in which the consumers of a given country s split their expenditure between domestic varieties (X_{ss}) and varieties produced in a foreign country r (X_{rs}). Moreover, this equation is linear in the unknown parameters, thereby permitting a simple estimation of (5.9). Another characteristic of this expression is the fact that it provides a direct estimate of the price elasticity σ, which is useful from the point of view of economic geography, where it plays a central role. This in turn allows us to check the model's internal coherence, since σ must be greater than 1. Once σ is determined, the parameters δ, β, and λ can be obtained by plugging (5.7) into (5.9). Then, using (5.7) again, we can compute τ_{rs}/a_{rs} for any r and s, i.e., the trade costs normalized by preferences. By contrast, the fixed-effect method only enables us to identify $(\sigma - 1)\delta$, $(\sigma - 1)\beta$, and $(\sigma - 1)\lambda$.[15]

(iii) Two alternative methods are also worth mentioning.

First, as we said above, one of the key problems in estimating (5.4) lies in the nonlinearity of the term I_s. Anderson and van Wincoop (2003) suggest the use of nonlinear estimation techniques. This approach is appropriate provided that the estimates are stable. Furthermore, convergence algorithms used in nonlinear econometrics may be sensitive to the chosen initial values for parameters.

---

[14] The simplest way of obtaining these data consists of subtracting total exports from the production value of manufactured goods. For this, the two data sets must be consistent, which is not often the case. In some countries, though, such as Canada, France, Spain, and the United States, reliable internal trade data are available.

[15] The interested reader will find various applications of this method to European and French data in Head and Mayer (2000) and Combes et al. (2005), respectively.

Second, if data for the variety price index in each country were available, one could replace the term I_s with its actual value. However, the most sophisticated existing price indices are often pretty bad approximations of those that appear in the DSK model, which would require a simultaneous estimation of the elasticities of substitution across varieties.

5.1.5 The Limits of the Gravity Model

Even though economic integration has been deepening for quite a while, the foregoing analysis suggests that distance still has a strong impact on trade flows. Two explanations can be put forward. First, as discussed above, trade costs include several elements, other than transport costs and tariff barriers, that may have increased over time. Second, this phenomenon could also be explained by the fact that some econometric problems have not been properly addressed.

Endogeneity is the main problem to address. Typically, an unobservable shock to a country's trade flows must have an impact on its income. As a consequence, the variables related to the (absolute or relative) sizes of the countries of origin and destination are likely to be correlated with the error term, thereby introducing a bias into the ordinary least square (OLS) estimates. Instrumenting these variables is rarely done, except when the GDPs are proxied by population sizes or factor endowments (which are less likely to be endogenous). Another solution is to use the theoretical prediction of a unit elasticity of trade flows with respect to country size in (5.4), (5.8), or (5.9). In this case, the corresponding term, i.e., $\ln(v_r/v_s)$, is moved to the left-hand side of (5.8), say, to obtain

$$\ln\left(\frac{X_{rs}}{v_r}\right) - \ln\left(\frac{X_{ss}}{v_s}\right) = -(\sigma - 1)\ln\left(\frac{\tau_{rs}\, a_{ss}}{\tau_{ss}\, a_{rs}}\right) - \sigma \ln\left(\frac{p_r}{p_s}\right). \quad (5.10)$$

Some authors view the problem of endogeneity of country size variables as a minor one because a specific trade flow accounts for a low share of total trade, and an even lower share of GDP. The reverse influence of this specific flow on GDP is, therefore, likely to be weak. This argument is not entirely convincing, however, since the endogeneity bias may also stem from the endogenous location choices made by firms. We will come back to this question in chapters 11 and 12.

Another endogeneity problem arises in the structural estimation of relative flows. Indeed, in (5.10), relative prices are determined simultaneously with relative flows, which creates a new source of bias in OLS estimates, even when using fixed effects. When the analysis is carried out at a sufficiently disaggregated level, this problem can be partially alleviated by introducing prices at a more aggregated level into the right-hand side of the equation. This is because the impact of a sector's trade on the overall price index and wage level is likely to be low when the sector is small and labor is sufficiently mobile between sectors. Yet when the appropriate tools are available, it remains preferable to instrument the price variables.

One of the most popular applications of the gravity model is for estimating the impact of regional trade agreements on the intensity of trade flows between member countries. For example, dummy variables, which identify countries involved in the same regional trade agreement (the European Union, NAFTA, MERCOSUR), can be added to the specification of trade costs (5.7). The coefficients thus obtained then reveal the excess or lack of trade (with respect to theoretical prediction) between the corresponding countries. For example, in a simple cross-sectional gravity regression for the year 2000, Baier and Bergstrand (2004) find a coefficient of 0.29, which means that, all else being equal, two countries involved in the same trade agreement trade $\exp(0.29) - 1 = 33.6\%$ more than two countries that are not involved in that agreement. However, countries choose to sign a trade agreement because they expect the corresponding benefits to be substantial. In this respect, geographical proximity and other factors facilitating trade make the prospects of such agreements more appealing, as they make actual trade flows fairly high. On the contrary, countries that are very unlikely to sign a trade agreement are often characterized by political and/or historical antagonisms, which in turn imply that the countries probably have low bilateral trade. Hence, *it is the strength of trading relationships that determines the level of trade costs through the creation of a regional trade agreement, not the other way round*. This is the source of another bias in OLS estimates.

This reverse causality also arises when a trade shock gives rise to internal tensions by kindling the demands of protectionism, thereby reducing the probability of signing a regional agreement. Once more, a possible solution is to use instruments that provide an independent explanation for the creation of preferential agreements, or to use the probability of signing agreements rather than the signature itself to explain trade flows. However, it often proves very difficult to proceed very far with this method, as the variables that are likely to foster the signature of a trade agreement—for example, geographical proximity or historical ties—are often correlated with the volume of trade. The results obtained from using such an instrumentation strategy are thus disappointing (Baier and Bergstrand 2004). When data for several years are available, another solution, adopted by Carrère (2006), is to integrate a fixed effect for each pair of countries. Unobservable characteristics that are specific to each dyad and are constant over time are then taken into account; the effect of preferential agreements is then identified purely through the time dimension: that is, through the impact of creations of agreements or entries into them or exits from them.[16]

Apart from endogeneity problems, it is also worth stressing that exports from a given country, region, or firm are often zero for many destinations. This fact is neither compatible with the underlying theoretical models, such as DSK, nor taken into account in most estimations. Recent contributions try to provide solutions by introducing heterogeneity in production costs (Melitz 2003). From an empirical viewpoint, the presence of a large number of zero values requires a specific treatment via Tobit or Poisson econometric models (Santos Silva and Tenreyro 2006).

There are further problems linked to the specification of trade costs. Above all, the assumption that they are *ad valorem* costs is neither neutral for estimates nor, in many cases, realistic. These costs could be additive, involving a fixed part as well as a variable one. One solution, used by Eaton and Kortum (2002), is to replace the distance variable with a group of dummies for a certain number of intervals of distance (0-100 km, 100-200 km, etc.); this discretization yields a more flexible specification for the impact of distance. Further progress still needs to be made in this direction, however. Moreover, as we are now going to see, choosing the variables that will enter the specification of trade costs remains a difficult task.

5.2 Trade Costs

Gravity models tackle trade costs in a very crude way as they often retain the physical distance as the sole barrier to trade. This approach has attracted many criticisms. There are, indeed, a large number of restrictions imposed on trade that are not directly linked to the distance between countries. One solution is to collect all the information available on transport costs, tariffs, nontariff barriers, and even more sophisticated factors, such as cultural differences or informational costs between origin and destination. They are then introduced into the specification of trade costs to be estimated. This estimation makes it possible to evaluate the overall magnitude of trade costs and to recalculate the weight of some of their components. We will then show how the DSK

---

[16] As a final remark on endogeneity, note that most of the variables used as proxies for trade costs can be subject to the same type of bias. For example, a country may decide to improve its transport infrastructure following a positive shock on trade flows, which also has the effect of making trade costs endogenous. This difficulty calls for the use of instruments or fixed effects.

model may be used to get an indirect measure of trade costs, which does not require data about the various trade barriers.

5.2.1 How to Measure Trade Costs

One major disadvantage of the specification approach lies in the fact that the various restrictions to trade must be chosen a priori. As there are many of them, there is a need to resort to several simplifications. Four types of trade barriers are generally considered. First, natural barriers that result from physical geography—distance, mountains, access to the sea—are grouped together in what we call transport costs, T_{rs}. Second come all types of trade policy measures, P_{rs}, or those with an environmental or phytosanitary focus, as well as exchange rate transaction costs for countries that do not share the same currency. The last two types of trade barriers deal with information costs, I_{rs}, and cultural differences, D_{rs}. All these elements influence the level of trade costs, τ_{rs}, and/or the intensity of preferences, a_{rs}. What they have in common is that they restrict trade, although it is often difficult to know the exact channel through which each of these barriers acts. In many applications, it is assumed that these effects are log-separable: that is,

$$\tau_{rs} = P_{rs}T_{rs}I_{rs} \quad \text{and} \quad a_{rs} = 1/(I_{rs}D_{rs}) \tag{5.11}$$

if only trade policies and transport costs affect trade costs, only cultural differences affect preferences, while information costs affect the magnitudes of both.

Despite their simplicity, such expressions shed light on the above-mentioned results. If we have very few variables that can be used as proxies for P, T, I, or D (e.g., distance), then the estimated effect of these proxies can just as easily apply to transport costs, preferences, policies, information costs, or cultural differences. The same holds true for the evolution of that effect. This could explain why, as seen above, the impact of distance seems to become stronger over time. While government trade restrictions and transport costs have decreased markedly, as we saw in chapter 1, home bias might have risen. It is even more likely that information costs could have risen as a result of the increasing complexity of products (Duranton and Storper 2008). Hence, other modeling strategies must be selected to make the interpretation of the trade cost effect more precise.

As well as distance, the gravity literature has added trade costs proxies like contiguity and common-language dummy variables. Added to geographic distance, contiguity introduces a nonlinear impact of proximity into trade costs and preferences. People speaking the same language often share other common characteristics, which can reduce trade costs. This is why both contiguity and common-language dummy variables are introduced into the regressions used to obtain figure 5.1. The effects of contiguity and common language are large, even today, as they are estimated to multiply trade by 2 and 2.6, respectively. Furthermore, as for distance, contiguity and common-language effects have risen over time, so that *sharing a common language or border has an impact on trade that is higher now than it was thirty, forty, or fifty years ago.*

A novel addition to the set of distance-related variables has been proposed by McCallum (1995), who focuses on trade flows between Canadian provinces and U.S. states in 1988. He introduces a dummy variable $bord_{rs}$ that is equal to 1 for trade flows that do not cross the border with the United States (trade between different Canadian provinces) and to 0 otherwise (trade between a Canadian province and a U.S. state). The econometric estimate of the impact of $bord_{rs}$ on trade flows provides a quantification of the famous *border effect.* McCallum obtains a value close to 20, which means that, for equal size and distance, two Canadian provinces trade twenty times more than a U.S. state would with a Canadian province. Even though more sophisticated estimation methods yield substantially reduced values, the border effect remains large. In the decomposition (5.11), the effect of national borders can enter into any of the components. It can come from trade policy restrictions (which are probably unimportant in North America but are not in other cases) or from transport costs (which increase with distance but possibly in a nonlinear manner, which leaves room for a border effect). Difficulties in acquiring the information required for trading goods can also be markedly affected by crossing borders, as can the home bias that naturally emerges from the existence of national borders.

Despite their empirical relevance, accounting for distance, contiguity, borders, and sharing a common language in the estimation provides an oversimplified description of trade barriers. For example, they fail to account for all the differences arising from protectionist policies or for the size and quality of transport infrastructures, to mention only two of the many determinants of trade costs. Moreover, the inability to explain the border effect through specific components of trade costs or preferences may generate serious difficulties in the interpretation of results.

Some of these drawbacks can be solved by focusing on the impact of specific trade barriers for which precise data are available. For example, Hummels (1999) seeks to isolate the roles played by transport costs and tariffs. To this end, he selects seven countries (the United States, New Zealand, and five Latin American countries) with detailed data on

transport costs, tariffs, and imports at a very high level of sectoral disaggregation (15,000 products for the United States and around 3,000 for
the others). He then estimates via a gravity specification the following
expression:

$$\ln(\tau_{rs}/a_{rs}) = \delta \ln d_{rs} - \beta \, \text{bord}_{rs} - \lambda \, \text{lang}_{rs} + \ln(P_{rs} T_{rs}).$$

The results obtained are very stimulating. First, since the two variables
P_{rs} and T_{rs} (available in Hummels's data) directly capture tariffs and
transport costs, the effects of distance, contiguity, and language are
purged from these two components and are, therefore, lower. Moreover,
once (5.11) is plugged into (5.5), the coefficient of $\ln(P_{rs} T_{rs})$ being equal
to $-(\sigma - 1)$, we obtain an estimate of the elasticity σ.[17] The parameter
σ is estimated to vary between 5 and 8 according to the level of disaggregation. The distance elasticity of trade flows, given by $-(\sigma - 1)\delta$,
ranges from -0.54 to -1.28 (Hummels 1999, table 6). We can therefore
conclude that *the influence of distance on trade considerably exceeds the
effects of transport costs and policy-related trade restrictions alone.*

This type of study illustrates the recent progress that has been made
in measuring tariffs and transport costs. Going well beyond proxies such
as geodesic distance, Hummels (1999) and Limão and Venables (2001)
use real freight costs as charged by carriers. This is a much richer measure of shipping costs because freight rates are both origin specific and
destination specific, and they can sometimes be broken down according to the transport mode and the type of shipped goods. Along these
same lines, Combes and Lafourcade (2005) have built what is as yet the
most detailed measure of transport costs by road for the ninety-five
départements (administrative divisions) of France. First, these costs take
into account the type of each road (toll freeways, no-toll freeways, four-
lane highways, national, regional, and urban roads). Second, the data
allow for a very accurate description of all costs associated with using a
truck: gas consumption for each type of road, the cost of replacing tires,
the maintenance costs of trucks, possible tolls, drivers' wages as well
as their accommodation and eating expenses, the cost of replacing the
truck, insurance policies, and general overheads. The results obtained
by Combes and Lafourcade confirm that, between 1978 and 1998, transport costs significantly decreased, by 38.3%. However, this decrease owed
very little to the improvements made to French transport infrastructure

---

[17] See Chaney (2007) for a recent criticism of the interpretation of these coefficients. His
argument (which goes beyond the scope of this chapter) rests on the fact that a reduction
in trade costs leads to the entry of new exporters. These newcomers capture a market
share that varies directly with the intensity of the competition, and therefore with the
value of σ.

(only 3.2%). Indeed, the deregulation of the transport sector—which has led to substantial reductions in drivers' wages and transport firms' overheads and maintenance costs (a drop of 21.8%)—and also the various technological improvements that have led to a substantial drop in gas consumption (accounting for 10.9% of the decrease) have had a much larger impact. Interestingly, for any given year, the correlation between transport costs and simpler measures, such as distance or travel time, is extremely high (0.99). By contrast, this correlation is much lower for intertemporal variations (between 0.4 and 0.8, depending on which measure is used). This suggests that, in cross-sectional estimates, distance provides an extremely good proxy of transport costs, whereas detailed data about transport costs are needed for time series analyses.

It is worth stressing that the almost perfect correlation between freight costs and geodesic distance might not hold in other countries. France is not crossed by major natural barriers and is almost entirely covered by a very efficient transport network. In the case of developing countries, some of which are landlocked, Limão and Venables (2001) find that the size and quality of the transport infrastructure still has a big impact on transport costs, thus making distance inadequate as a proxy.[18] Note, finally, that estimations of trade costs may be obtained by comparing FOB and CIF import prices, as registered by customs or the IMF. Hummels and Lugovskyy (2006) have shown, however, that such estimates are plagued by errors. In addition, such estimates do not contain enough useful information for us to compare freight rates across products or over time.

Recent studies have tried to include new variables that embrace other elements of trade costs. In particular, some empirical works have focused on the effects of social and business networks that affect information-related trade costs (I_{rs}). As an example, Combes et al. (2005) use French data on migrations and financial linkages between firms to capture these networks. They show that the existence of business and social networks has a strong trade-promoting effect. Networks of migrants almost double trade, while financial linkages between firms have a multiplicative effect estimated to lie between 4 and 5. Introducing network effects also significantly reduces the estimated impact

---

[18] A country with a median level of transport infrastructure trades around 28% more than an identical country with a quality of infrastructure in the lowest quartile. This difference is the equivalent of a difference in distance between trading partners of 1627 km. In a similar vein, Clark et al. (2004) demonstrate that if Peru or Turkey were to raise the quality of their port infrastructures to the level of Iceland's or Australia's, they could increase their volume of trade by about 25%.

of distance and contiguity.[19] Regarding portfolio investments, Portes and Rey (2005) integrate two variables measuring the quality of bilateral information for investors: telephone traffic between the two countries and the number of bank branches installed in the partner country. The estimated impact of distance on bilateral portfolio investment then drops from 0.88 to 0.67. In the same spirit, Guiso et al. (2004) show that the degree of bilateral trust between nations, measured by using Eurobarometer opinion polls, has a positive impact on trade. One may expect this type of research to contribute to a better understanding of the elements defining trade costs.

A major difficulty is worth mentioning here. As seen above, some methods require the evaluation of trade costs within a region or a country. Although trade policy and some other variables have no impact on internal trade costs, internal distance does. However, measuring the internal distance is not an easy task. A simple expression may be obtained by using the country's area, S_r, and by making some simplifying assumptions about the shape of the country and the internal distribution of supply and demand. Assume, for example, that the country is a disk of radius R_r. If consumers are uniformly distributed over this disk, with firms all located in its center, the average distance between a consumer and a producer is $d_{rr} = \frac{2}{3}R_r = \frac{2}{3}\sqrt{S_r/\pi} \approx 0.376\sqrt{S_r}$, which may be used as a measurement of internal distance. These are, of course, very ad hoc assumptions. We could instead assume that consumers or firms are distributed over a fraction of the disk, or that the shape of the country is depicted by a square. When data are available at an infranational level, one alternative consists of calculating an average distance between the subunits (regions or cities), weighted by their size. These various methods can yield significant differences in the estimates (Head and Mayer 2002).

Anderson and van Wincoop (2004) provide a very detailed overview of the different approaches used to evaluate trade costs. They conclude that trade costs incurred between countries reach a level approximately equal to 170% of the average FOB price of manufactured goods. Trade costs consist of 55% internal costs and 74% international costs (2.7 = 1.55 × 1.74). The international costs are in turn broken down into 21% transport costs and 44% costs connected with border effects (1.74 = 1.21 × 1.44). Tariff and nontariff barriers account for no more than 8% of the border effects (exceptionally 10 or 20% in the case of developing countries), language differences for 7%, currency differences for 14%, and

---

[19] See also Rauch and Trindade (2002) for the impact of Chinese migrants on international trade.

other costs, including information, for 9% ($1.44 = 1.08 \times 1.07 \times 1.14 \times 1.09$). It is worth noting, however, that the variance across goods is large.

5.2.2 Indirect Measures of Trade Costs

We have considered different approaches to the direct measurement of trade costs. This direct measurement offers the advantage of identifying, at least partially, the various elements that determine these costs. Its main disadvantage is that it amounts to an endless quest. An alternative method makes use of the tractability of the DSK model to *indirectly* identify the overall degree of market segmentation, without using gravity estimations. Two sources of data are used for this purpose: price differentials, which will not be discussed here (see Anderson and van Wincoop 2004), and the gap between actual trade flows and those that are predicted if integration were perfect. These methods therefore cover trade barriers as a whole, without being able to isolate their determinants separately.

Following this idea, Head and Ries (2001) propose an approach based on the comparison of interregional and intraregional trade flows. Using (5.8), they multiply X_{rs}/X_{ss} by the symmetric ratio and take the logarithm of the corresponding expression to obtain

$$\ln\left(\frac{X_{rs}X_{sr}}{X_{ss}X_{rr}}\right) = -(\sigma - 1)\ln\left(\frac{\tau_{rs}\tau_{sr}}{\tau_{ss}\tau_{rr}}\frac{a_{ss}a_{rr}}{a_{rs}a_{sr}}\right). \tag{5.12}$$

If trade is costless within countries ($\tau_{ss} = \tau_{rr} = 1$), trade costs between countries are symmetric ($\tau_{rs} = \tau_{sr}$), and consumer preferences are not biased ($a_{rs} = a_{sr} = a_{ss} = a_{rr} = 1$), then the parameter

$$\phi_{rs} \equiv \tau_{rs}^{-(\sigma-1)}$$

measures the freeness of trade between countries r and s (see chapter 4). It takes a value of 0 in the case of complete autarky and a value of 1 when trade is costless. Using (5.12), we obtain an estimator of ϕ_{rs},

$$\hat{\phi}_{rs} = \sqrt{\frac{X_{rs}X_{sr}}{X_{ss}X_{rr}}},$$

which is indeed an *indirect measure* of trade costs. One important advantage of this procedure is the low data requirement: bilateral trade and internal flows for the sector in question. Finally, it should be pointed out that $\hat{\phi}_{rs}$ is obtained by a simple calculation, rather than by an econometric estimation.

This approach has several disadvantages, however. First, it rests on the DSK model and is, as a result, subject to the simplifying assumptions made in this model. Even when the DSK model is accepted, it still presents some other shortcomings. To start with, the hypothesis $\tau_{rr} = \tau_{ss} = 1$ represents an approximation whose validity varies according to the characteristics of the countries involved. Although it may seem reasonable for two countries like Belgium and the Netherlands, it is far more questionable in the dyad of Germany and Slovenia, as here the internal trade costs are very different due to the countries' respective sizes. Actually, what $\hat{\phi}_{rs}$ really measures are the bilateral trade costs with respect to internal ones. Similarly, if the terms a_{rs} were not assumed to be equal to 1, we would be measuring not just trade costs but also the intensity of bilateral preferences. In other words, an increase in $\hat{\phi}_{rs}$ can reflect either a homogenization of preferences or an increase in internal trade costs. Furthermore, $\hat{\phi}_{rs}$ varies in inverse proportion to the elasticity of substitution σ. If, for whatever reason, varieties become more differentiated, σ and $\hat{\phi}_{rs}$ decrease together, but this should not be interpreted as signaling an increase in trade barriers. To sum up, caution is required and it is best not to make an overly strict interpretation of this indicator, particularly with respect to its absolute level. On the other hand, the drawbacks just pointed out should have a less systematic impact on the *differences* across sectors and, above all, on the *evolution* over time of this indicator. The index $\hat{\phi}_{rs}$ therefore seems to be better suited for this type of comparison.

We want to emphasize that the above index is, in itself and independently of any theoretical consideration, fairly intuitive. Indeed, it seems quite natural to assess the openness of country s to the goods produced in country r by comparing bilateral imports to internal consumption, i.e., the ratio X_{sr}/X_{rr}. In this ratio, the size of country r is irrelevant, as it presumably affects both the numerator and denominator. Hence, comparing the values of this index for countries of origin having different sizes is reasonable.

The same is true for the differing sizes of partner countries. Let us assume that s is France and its trading partners are the three members of NAFTA. These are situated at comparable distances from France but have very different GDPs: the United States accounts for almost a third of the world production, while the GDP of Canada is more than ten times lower, and that of Mexico more than twenty times so. If French imports from country r are high when r denotes the United States, it is reasonable to expect that the United States imports little from France. This brings us back to the proposition that the ratio X_{sr}/X_{rr} incorporates a size effect: all else being equal, a large country will tend to import less. Nevertheless, this effect is neutralized in $\hat{\phi}_{rs}$: if the United States (r) has a ratio X_{sr}/X_{rr} that is low for most of the exporting countries s, thereby reducing the value of $\hat{\phi}_{rs}$, each country s will have a high ratio X_{rs}/X_{ss},

Table 5.1. Median freeness of trade ($\hat{\phi}_{rs} \times 100$) between France, Germany, Italy, and the United Kingdom.

Sector	1980	1985	1990	1995	1998
Industrial chemistry	6.6	8.0	13.3	16.4	15.2
Transport	5.2	7.9	10.3	14.1	11.1
Instruments	11.9	14.0	39.7	13.3	11.4
Electrical machinery	3.0	3.9	5.4	9.3	11.6
Leather	4.6	5.6	7.7	9.1	28.6
Nonelectrical machinery	5.6	8.7	9.1	8.4	11.3
Textiles	4.0	4.1	6.3	7.4	6.9
Rubber	3.4	4.2	6.2	7.3	9.8
Glass	3.5	4.5	6.4	6.9	5.8
Nonferrous metal	5.8	4.2	5.9	6.8	7.8
Metal and iron	2.3	3.0	5.4	6.3	5.8
Shoes	2.5	3.4	5.0	5.3	7.2
Other chemical products	5.6	5.5	5.3	5.3	5.6
Pottery	2.8	3.0	3.9	4.4	4.9
Paper	1.8	2.5	2.9	4.4	4.8
Clothes	2.1	2.2	4.4	3.6	4.3
Drinks	1.8	2.4	2.8	3.0	3.0
Metal products	2.3	2.8	3.1	2.8	2.6
Plastics	2.0	2.0	2.4	2.3	2.3
Food	1.0	1.2	1.7	1.7	1.9
Nonmetal furniture	1.4	1.5	2.3	1.5	1.6
Other mineral products	1.3	1.4	1.8	1.3	1.6
Wood, except furniture	0.8	1.1	1.4	1.2	1.6
Publishing and printing	0.8	0.8	0.9	0.7	0.6
Petroleum products	1.4	1.5	1.0	0.6	0.6
Tobacco	0.4	0.6	0.7	0.6	0.6

thus compensating for this effect by increasing the value of $\hat{\phi}_{rs}$. Hence, we may conclude that the index $\hat{\phi}_{rs}$ is purged of size effects and captures most of the elements of trade costs mentioned above (P, T, I, or D), obviating the need for data on each of those elements.

Let us now see how this index has evolved over time and whether, for example, countries that are members of regional trade agreements have experienced specific trends. To this end, we first consider the case of European integration, using a database developed by CEPII. Table 5.1 shows the values of $\hat{\phi}_{rs}$ obtained by focusing on the median of the values calculated for six combinations of four large countries in the EU-15 (France, Germany, Italy, and the United Kingdom) for the years 1980, 1985, 1990, 1995, and 1998. The sectors are classified in decreasing order of their degree of integration in 1995. We should make it clear that all the values have been multiplied by 100 in order to make the results easier to read—something that suggests immediately their low level.

The highest values are around 15 (with the exception of instruments in 1990 and leather in 1998).[20] Such low values run against expectations regarding the level of integration of European markets. They are probably the counterpart of the border effects mentioned above. It is worth comparing these figures with those obtained in the literature. For example, McCallum's (1995) result about trade between the United States and Canada suggests a value of $\hat{\phi}_{rs} \times 100 = 5$, while the results obtained in more recent studies lie between 17 and 20. If we assume that product differentiation is similar in both continents, this suggests that, in the last two decades, *the European Union has not been more integrated than the North American market.*

The above index can also be used to compare the European market (supposedly integrated since at least 1993) and the American market, which has been integrated for more than 200 years (recall that the U.S. Constitution expressly forbids any impediment to trade between states). Wolf (2000) shows that the United States is far from being an entirely integrated market. Nevertheless, with an average index of $\hat{\phi}_{rs} \times 100 = 33$ for interstate and intrastate flow, *the freeness of trade seems to be two to three times higher within the United States than in Europe's most integrated markets.* It is not impossible that this low level of integration of European markets is partly due to firms' collusion, which the United States manages to protect against with more success owing to the greater severity of its antitrust policies. Unfortunately, the DSK model, which serves as a basis for the above indicator, is incompatible with any type of strategic behavior by firms, such as collusion. Furthermore, there are many other possible explanations, such as the greater impact of cultural differences in Europe (integration is much more marked in European countries sharing the same language) or the coexistence, until recently, of several currencies.

The other important message of this table lies in the hierarchy of sectors. The sectors characterized by a high degree of segmentation are petroleum industries, wood, publishing/printing, and nonmetallic mineral products (which incorporate construction materials). These sectors seem to be those in which transport matters most, which would explain why the internal trade of these goods dominates their international trade. Right after those sectors come the food and beverage industries, in which trade freeness is also relatively low, although it does increase

---

[20] The high value for instruments is the result of a very sharp drop in production and, therefore, in internal trade after the German reunification.

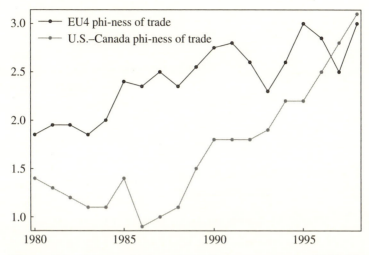

Figure 5.2. Degree of integration of beverages sector, 1980–98.

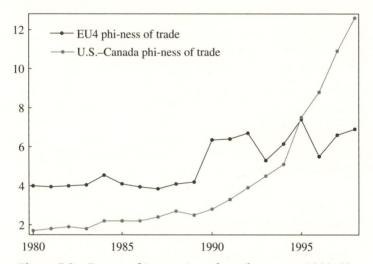

Figure 5.3. Degree of integration of textiles sector, 1980–98.

over time. The most integrated sectors in the European Union are those of industrial chemistry, machinery, instruments, and transport material. These are also the sectors in which integration has taken place most rapidly. It must be pointed out, however, that it is difficult to distinguish the respective roles of trade costs and degrees of product differentiation in such comparisons.

Finally, let us compare the level of integration among European countries to the level of integration found in the United States–Canada dyad. The results of our calculations for a few sectors are summarized in

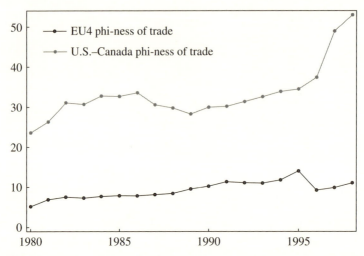

Figure 5.4.   Degree of integration of transport equipment sector, 1980–98.

figures 5.2–5.4. The most striking feature is *the growth of the freeness of trade in both cases.* Nevertheless, in most sectors, the level of integration rises at a higher rate between the United States and Canada than it does between the member countries of the European Union. There seems therefore to be a catching-up effect, if not an overtaking effect, in North America.

It should be kept in mind that the value of $\hat{\phi}_{rs}$ accounts for the impact of distance. As the United States and Canada are separated by an average distance of 2064 km, against 896 km in the case of the four largest countries in the European Union, the European coefficient should therefore be higher, while the United States and Canada appear to be notably more integrated in some sectors.[21] This is the case with the transport equipment market, which is likely to be related to the existence of the automobile production complex around the Great Lakes. In more traditional sectors, such as textiles and drinks, the European Union was more integrated at the beginning of the period, but progress has been so rapid in North America that the level of integration has proved higher there in recent years. In short, it seems that, in a large number of sectors, there was a fairly clean break in the evolution of exchanges after the Canada–United States free trade agreement was implemented in 1989—a break that does not manifest itself in Europe, neither in 1986 with the signing of the Single European Act nor in 1993 when the single market was achieved.

---

[21] These distances are calculated by using all of the regions in each country and weighting each of them by its share in the country's total population (see Head and Mayer (2002) for more details).

5.3   Concluding Remarks

This chapter is aimed at understanding the simple but far-reaching idea that market size is a critical factor in the determination of trade flows. More surprisingly, while we are constantly hearing about the "death of distance" in economies connected by new and efficient communication devices, we have seen that both distance and borders remain critical for the intensity of trade flows. We have discussed various strategies for estimating obstacles to trade, all of them going beyond mere physical distance. In all cases, we have found that *trade costs remain high*, especially at the international level. Even though transport costs have dropped steeply for almost two centuries (along with, more recently, trade policy barriers), other barriers, especially those linked to information costs, could have been reinforced by, for example, the increasing complexity of products. For example, there is still a strong home bias within the EU, since intranational trade is about twelve times as high as international trade with a comparable EU partner (Fontagné et al. 2005). According to business analysts (see, for example, Spulber 2007), trade costs remain an important driver of international business strategies. Recall that economists estimate that they reach a staggering level of 170% of the average FOB price of manufactured goods. In view of the large number of results presented in this chapter, we can therefore safely conclude that distance and borders still matter in developed economies, although their impact on agents' behavior is felt in different ways than it was in the past.

5.4   Related Literature

The first study of the theoretical foundations of the gravity equation can be attributed to Anderson (1979), who used an Armington-like product differentiation setting with perfect competition. It was not until Anderson and van Wincoop (2003) that the Armington model became more widely recognized as one of the possible foundations of the gravity model because of its application to the border effect between the United States and Canada. Regarding monopolistic competition as an alternative foundation, Bergstrand (1985) was undoubtedly the first to present a clear formulation of the gravity model derived from a DSK framework. Evenett and Keller (2002) offered an analysis of the general conditions for gravity prediction in models of international trade. As far as estimation methods are concerned, Harrigan (1996) seems to have been the first to have proposed estimating the DSK version of the gravity model with fixed effects. Feenstra (2004), as well as Anderson and van Wincoop (2004), put forward very complete syntheses of the theoretical foundations and empirical methods of the gravity model. The applications of both traditional and recent versions of this model are uncountable, but we want to single out two contributions that have aroused great interest. First, the impact of regional agreements is thoroughly explored by Frankel (1997), even though it is based on old formulations of the gravity model. Second, Baldwin (2006) studied the impact on trade of monetary unions, especially the eurozone. His review of the conceptual and methodological problems proves to be very useful. A fairly comprehensive overview of international *price differences* for five industrialized countries can be found in the Economist Intelligence Unit (2001) survey. Last, but not least, Leamer (2007) has recently provided a witty, and entertaining, appraisal of the (too) many claims made regarding the death of distance and the flattening of the globe.

Appendix. Data and Methods for Gravity Equations

Economic Data

1. Andrew Rose has put the main elements of the economic data used in his gravity estimates online (aggregated data on 1960–2000). The main underlying sources are, for trade, the IMF DOTS (a database going back to 1948) and, for GDP and populations, the *Penn World Tables* (from 1950) or the *World Development Indicators* of the World Bank (from 1960).

2. When the analysis focuses on a more refined disaggregation, the trade data are mainly drawn from the COMTRADE database of the United Nations (from 1962). They have been made easily usable by Robert Feenstra and Robert Lipsey via the NBER. Structural estimation requires the use of data on bilateral trade, production values, and prices (or wages) in the same statistical classification. This is not simple, as trade is classified by means of a logic based on products, while production and prices or wages are collected based on the type of activity. The main source in which trade and production data have been collected under a common classification on a large geographical scale is the *Trade and Production* database, developed by Olleaga and Nicita at the World Bank. It covers the years 1976 to 1999 and some thirty sectors for more than sixty countries. Its sources include the United Nations (COMTRADE for trade and UNIDO for the remaining variables). As data are very

scarce after 1993, CEPII has completed them on the basis of original data and the STAN database of the OECD. The resulting database is freely available on CEPII's website.

Geographical Data

1. Jon Haveman has collected data on distance, common language, and contiguity that cover a large number of countries. Andrew Rose's databases also include colonial ties. CEPII supplies the most complete database to date on bilateral distances, taking into account, for example, the internal geography of each country. Measures of internal distance for all countries can thus be obtained, which is useful not only for gravity estimates but also for computing the market potential, which we will discuss in chapter 12. This database includes several variables related to colonial links, as well as various measures of linguistic proximity. CEPII also provides a database that collects geographical data for each country, such as their main city and its coordinates, a dummy for whether or not a country is landlocked, the area of the country, etc.

2. World Gazetteer (http://gazetteer.de/) is a Web site with abundant data on cities and regions of the world, most notably a database covering nearly 55,000 cities with their latest available population sizes and their geographical coordinates. Vernon Henderson offers an extract from this database.

6

The Core–Periphery Structure

In chapter 1, we emphasized one of the most salient features of economic history, namely the existence of large disparities in the spatial distributions of wealth and population. In all cases, the facts are the same: in a particular historical period, economic activities are concentrated in a limited number of regions, which form the *core* of a civilization, while the other regions stagnate, or even regress, and these are known as the *periphery*. In other words, *economic development is unequal*, thereby giving rise to one (or several) pattern(s) having a core–periphery (CP) structure. It is therefore important to ponder the reasons underlying such a universal phenomenon.

In the 1950s, several theorists put forward a principle that allowed them to uncover the underpinnings of unequal development—a principle that has been ignored, however, for several decades—that of *circular* or *cumulative causation*.[1] Myrdal (1957, p. 13) sums up these ideas in the following paragraph:

> The idea I want to expound in this book is that … there is no such tendency towards automatic self-stabilisation in the social system. The system is by itself not moving towards any sort of balance between forces, but is constantly on the move away from such a situation. In the normal case a change does not call forth countervailing changes but, instead, supporting changes, which move the system in the same direction as the first change but much further. Because of such circular causation a social process tends to become cumulative and often to gather speed at an accelerating rate.

Applied to economic geography, this principle says that the phenomenon of agglomeration is driven by a "snowball" effect, which results in its continuous reinforcement once it is set in motion. Krugman (1991a, p. 486) states the same idea when he writes:

> manufactures production will tend to concentrate where there is a large market, but the market will be large where manufactures production is concentrated.

---

[1] This idea had already been put forward by Young (1928) as a possible explanation of economic growth and development. It is, then, no surprise that the same idea reappears in modern analyses of the industrial takeoff (Murphy et al. 1989; Matsuyama 1992).

To explain this phenomenon, Krugman then extends the DSK model to this new context.[2]

Krugman's point is that economic agglomeration is very much an economic phenomenon, and thus so are regional disparities. To show this, Krugman zeroes in on the mobility of labor rather than capital. We have seen in chapter 4 that, despite the fact that capital-owners spend their income in their region of residence, the large market attracts a more than proportionate share of firms. By contrast, when skilled workers move, they spend their income in their host region, where the demand thus increases, while it decreases in their region of origin. To put this another way, skilled workers produce in the region where they settle, just like capital, but they also spend their income there, which is not generally the case with capital-owners. We can thus maintain that *the migration of workers, because it sparks the combined move of production and consumption capacities, modifies the relative size of markets*, thus generating new agglomeration forces. It also triggers new dispersion forces, however. Moreover, workers' migration is governed by the difference between nominal wages as well as by the difference between costs of living, while capital mobility is driven by the difference in nominal rates of return.

We therefore have at our disposal (almost) all the elements needed to understand how the snowball forms and grows bigger. Two effects are intertwined; one involves the firms and the other the workers. First, the increase in the number of workers, and therefore of consumers, pushes up the local demand for the manufactured good, triggering the installation of more firms in this region ("backward linkages"). The HME implies that an increase in the size of the large market, at the expense of the small market, generates a more than proportional increase of the share of the manufacturing sector established there. This pushes nominal wages upward. Second, if the number of firms located in a region increases, the number of locally produced varieties also increases and, in consequence, the equilibrium price index of the manufactured goods decreases in this region. The two effects, in turn, spark an increase in real wages and thus a new flow of workers from the small region to the big one, where, all else being equal, they benefit from a higher standard

---

[2] Note that the American geographer Harris (1954, p. 315) seems to say the same thing when he writes: "[t]he interrelationship between this [manufacturing belt] and other manufacturing areas and location of markets has been reciprocal; manufacturing has developed partly in areas or regions of largest markets and in turn the size of these markets has been augmented and other favourable conditions have been developed by the very growth of this industry." However, Harris's analysis does not integrate any element accounting for competition on the product and labor markets, so that his analysis is necessarily incomplete.

of living ("forward linkages"). If these two effects are combined, migration toward the large market should continue, ending when the whole industry is concentrated there.

However, if this process seems to imply an ineluctable cumulative dynamics, it will not always unfold according to Myrdal's prediction. Indeed, the above argument ignores the various modifications affecting the labor market. In particular, it fails to take into account the fact that the arrival of new workers leads to an increase in the supply of skilled labor in the destination region, which pushes wages downward. On the other hand, this larger pool of workers leads to an increase in the demand for the manufactured good and, therefore, to an increase in the demand for labor from the firms producing this good. If we add the fact that the larger number of firms tends to push wages upward through an indirect crowding effect on the market for varieties, we can safely conclude that the overall impact on nominal wages is very hard to predict. Consequently, as we will see, the foregoing elements can also be combined to *melt* the snowball, thus leading to the geographical redistribution of the manufacturing sector.

Krugman (1991a) has been able to knit together the different effects generated by the mobility of firms and workers in a model where labor and product markets are interdependent, and to identify the conditions on the level of trade costs that lead to the possible formation of a Myrdal-like snowball. More precisely, Krugman has identified the cases in which the manufacturing sector becomes concentrated on the basis of a difference (perhaps a minimal one) between regions from the cases in which such a difference vanishes to yield a dispersed industrial pattern. An unsuspected implication of this analysis is that *migrants are substitutes when trade costs are high, but complements when they are low.* In the former case, the departure of a region A worker for region B triggers the departure of a region B worker for region A. In the latter, the departure of a worker from A induces another worker to follow suit.

The main difference between Krugman's approach and earlier studies is the emphasis he places on *pecuniary externalities*; his predecessors focused more on technological externalities, usually postulated a priori (Henderson 1988). Krugman's approach is particularly relevant on the interregional scale considered in this book, as it is to be expected that spillovers, whose role is stressed in local development, play a minor role on this spatial scale. As competition is imperfect, pecuniary externalities find their origin in the fact that prices do not reflect the social value of individual decisions. Consequently, *when firms and workers move, they do not account for all the effects caused by their decisions.* To put it another way, the move of workers and firms unintentionally affect the welfare of all agents through pecuniary externalities.

In short, the spatial equilibrium of Krugman's model can be seen as the resultant of a complex game involving several dispersion and agglomeration forces. The centrifugal forces have two origins: (i) the immobility of unskilled workers whose demand for the manufactured good needs to be satisfied; and (ii) the now-standard market-crowding effect that accompanies the agglomeration of a growing number of firms. The centripetal force is given by the HME, which is strengthened by the larger size of the local market triggered by the migration of skilled workers.

In section 6.1, we show by means of a diagrammatic argument proposed by Casetti (1980) how increasing returns can generate multiple equilibria and catastrophic transitions from a configuration without spatial inequality to a CP structure. Section 6.2 is devoted to the analysis of Krugman's model (1991a).[3] Although this is a model in which all functional forms are specified, it cannot be solved analytically. This difficulty leads us to consider in section 6.3 a simplified version, which has been put forward by Forslid and Ottaviano (2003).

6.1 Increasing Returns and Industrialization

In this section, we will show by means of simple diagrams how sudden changes in the spatial distribution of workers may arise when increasing returns to scale are at work. To do this, we consider an economy made up of two sectors and two regions; agricultural activities are confined to a single region, denoted as A, while industry is entirely concentrated in the other region, denoted as B. Whereas the agricultural sector is characterized by decreasing returns, the industrial sector can exhibit either decreasing or increasing returns. We will see that quite different patterns of activities emerge according to the technology prevailing in the industrial sector.

The total workforce is made up of L individuals. They are willing to work in either region or, equivalently, in either sector. Initially, the workforce in regions A and B is given by L_A and L_B, with $L_A + L_B = L$. The output levels in agriculture and industry depend on the number of workers in each sector:

$$Q_A = F_A(L_A), \qquad Q_B = \kappa F_B(L_B),$$

---

[3] Note that, in his conclusion, Krugman (1979) suggested the development of such a model. An analysis anticipating several elements of Krugman's model was proposed by Faini (1984). Using a different approach, Arthur (1994, chapter 4) has shown the importance of positive feedbacks and history in the formation of regional disparities.

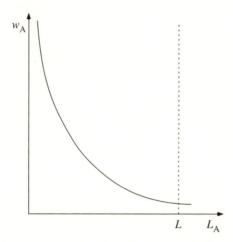

Figure 6.1.   Marginal productivity of labor in agriculture.

where κ is a positive constant scaling the productivity of labor in the industrial sector, and F_r $(r = A, B)$ is a production function that depends on the sector under consideration. The marginal labor productivity in each sector becomes arbitrarily large when the number of workers becomes arbitrarily small. Hence, the equilibrium will always be achieved at an interior point: $0 < L_A^* < L$ and $0 < L_B^* < L$.

The prices of the agricultural good and the industrial good are constant and the same in the two regions; they are denoted, respectively, by p_A and p_B. The two regional labor markets are perfectly competitive, so that workers are remunerated at their marginal productivity:

$$w_A = p_A \frac{dF_A}{dL_A}, \qquad w_B = \kappa p_B \frac{dF_B}{dL_B}.$$

Workers distribute themselves between the two regions according to the wage gap. A *spatial equilibrium*, i.e., a pattern in which no worker has an incentive to relocate, is given by a distribution of workers involving the same wage in both sectors. The stability of a spatial equilibrium is studied by means of the following equation of motion:

$$\frac{dL_B}{dt} = w_B - w_A = \kappa p_B \frac{dF_B}{dL_B} - p_A \frac{dF_A}{dL_A}.$$

To put it another way, the population of the industrial region B increases if and only if the industrial wage w_B exceeds the agricultural wage w_A. Because $L_A + L_B = L$, we only need to describe the evolution of one population to obtain, by inversion, that of the other.

Recall that agriculture exhibits decreasing returns, so that the marginal productivity of labor is decreasing, as depicted in figure 6.1. As

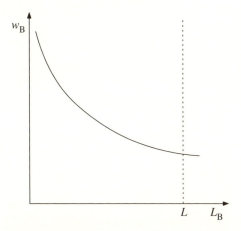

Figure 6.2. Marginal productivity of labor in industry under decreasing returns.

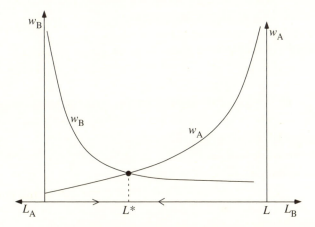

Figure 6.3. Spatial equilibrium under decreasing returns in both sectors.

a first step, we admit that the same holds in the industrial sector (see figure 6.2).

Figures 6.1 and 6.2 can thus be superimposed to produce figure 6.3, where the size of the industrial sector is measured positively along the horizontal axis from the point $L_B = 0$, while that of the agricultural sector is measured negatively from the point $L_B = L$. In this way, every point belonging to the segment $[0, L]$ corresponds to a single distribution of workers between the two sectors or regions. A spatial equilibrium arises at any point where the two curves w_A and w_B cross, thus equalizing the marginal productivity of labor in the two sectors. In the present case, there is a unique point of intersection given by $L_B^* = L^*$ and $L_A^* = 1 - L^*$.

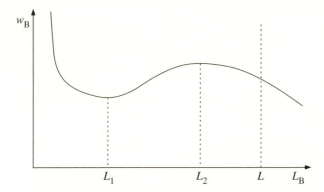

Figure 6.4. Marginal productivity of labor
in industry under nonmonotonous returns.

Furthermore, it is readily verified that migration plays here an equilibrat-
ing role, thus making this equilibrium stable (this is what the arrows in
figure 6.3 mean). For example, if L exceeds L^*, the wage prevailing in the
industrial region is lower than the wage in the agricultural region, which
induces some industrial workers to become farmers, and vice versa.

We now suppose that industry exhibits increasing returns, at least for a
range of intermediate output levels, represented by the segment $[L_1, L_2]$
in figure 6.4. The shape of this curve can be explained as follows. For low
levels of output, returns to scale are decreasing, because a traditional
technology is still used. When the output level crosses a certain threshold, it becomes profitable to use a mass-production technology, thus
giving rise to increasing returns. However, when the volume of production becomes very high, technology in the industrial sector again exhibits
decreasing returns because various constraints slow down the benefits
derived from having a larger size. By superimposing figures 6.1 and 6.4,
we obtain figure 6.5.

The determination of the spatial equilibrium yields results that differ
vastly from those obtained above. Let us assume for the moment that
the marginal productivity of labor in the industrial sector is given by the
curve w_1 in figure 6.5. In this case there is only one spatial equilibrium,
$L_B^* = L^*$, and this is stable. When the parameter κ increases, possibly
because of the accumulation of knowledge, the marginal productivity
curve in the industrial sector is shifted upward. When this curve occupies
the position w_2 in figure 6.5, there are three spatial equilibria, ($L_B^* = L_1^*$,
L_2^*, and L_3^*), instead of one equilibrium. The equilibria L_1^* and L_3^* are
(locally) stable, as shown above. In contrast, L_2^* is unstable, as any wage
gap in favor of one region sparks a new migration of workers toward
it. If the economy is initially in $L_B^* = L^* < L_1^*$, it is situated within the

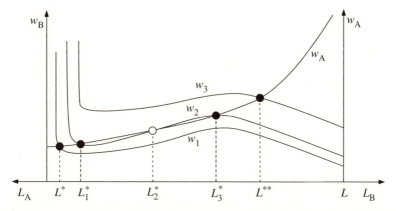

Figure 6.5. Spatial equilibrium under increasing returns in industry.

basin of attraction of the equilibrium L_1^*. In this case it is reasonable to believe that, after a technological shock that shifts the productivity curves from w_1 to w_2, the number of industrial workers increases by a quantity of $L_1^* - L^*$ units, thereby triggering a slight growth in the rate of industrialization. If knowledge keeps accumulating, the parameter κ continues to increase, and the new curve w_3 intercepts the curve w_A at a single point. The latter point is situated in L^{**}, far to the right of point L_1^*. Consequently, the economy now experiences a huge migration from region A to region B, bringing sudden industrialization and urbanization in its wake. It is worth pointing out that *such an abrupt industrialization and massive urbanization is due to increasing returns.*

The above argument brings to light two basic characteristics of economic geography: (i) increasing returns and the mobility of workers enhance the formation of regional disparities, and (ii) small variations in structural parameters can cause a sudden change in the spatial pattern of economic activity. By contrast, the economy never displays such behavior when returns to scale are decreasing. Once more we observe that increasing returns are critical to our understanding of the space-economy. Of course, Casetti's analysis suffers from several pitfalls, e.g., the prices of goods are exogenous, while the absence of transport costs implies that workers care only about nominal wages. Krugman's model, which is the subject of the following section, incorporates these variables as well as others.

6.2 Regional Disparities: The Krugman Model

Krugman (1991a) considers a two-region economy of the type described by the DSK model presented in chapter 4. There is one major difference, however. Distinguishing between unskilled workers operating in the agricultural sector and skilled workers operating in the manufacturing sector, Krugman assumes that the skilled are mobile between regions while the unskilled are not. To a large extent, this assumption fits modern migration patterns fairly well (Greenwood 1997), although the relationship between workers' mobility and skill was less clear-cut in the past (Bade 2002). It should be stressed, however, that the interpretation of the two production factors retained in this chapter is made only for expositional convenience. The critical point is that the mobile production factor is related to labor, while the other factor, such as unskilled labor but also land or nontradable goods, is immobile.

The difference in migration behavior has an important consequence in Krugman's model: places of residence (and therefore of consumption) and of work are now the same, whether or not the workers are skilled. To put this another way, *all workers earn and spend all their income in the region where they live.* This is a major difference with respect to the HME model developed in chapter 4, where we assumed that the incomes earned from investing abroad were repatriated in the region in which the capital-owners live. This also explains the reason for the presence of the agricultural sector in the model: as the unskilled workers are immobile, a certain proportion of them necessarily remains located in the periphery. Their demand for the manufactured good thus constitutes a dispersion force; this is a point which we will return to later. From now on, we assume that unskilled workers are equally distributed between the two regions ($\theta_a = \frac{1}{2}$), so that their total expense on the manufactured product is the same everywhere. We want to stress the fact that this assumption is intended to avoid favoring a priori one region at the expense of the other, thus making the symmetric pattern our benchmark case. As noted in the conclusion to chapter 4, one of the goals of the Krugman model is precisely to uncover the underpinnings of spatial inequalities on the basis of market mechanisms alone, that is, without presupposing any exogenous asymmetry between regions. The share of skilled workers living in region A is endogenous; it is denoted by $\lambda \in [0, 1]$. This implies that λ replaces θ in the DSK model. However, we will see that the interregional distribution of demand changes with the distribution of skilled workers. It is therefore endogenous, unlike in the HME model.

The production cost of variety i is of the specific-factor type:

$$C[q(i)] = fw + mwq(i),$$

where f is the fixed requirement and m the marginal requirement of skilled labor. The profit function of the firm producing variety i, installed in region A, and exporting toward region B at a trade cost τ is, therefore, given by

$$\pi_A(i) = p_{AA}(i)q_{AA}(i) + p_{AB}(i)q_{AB}(i) - mw_A[q_{AA}(i) + \tau q_{AB}(i)] - fw_A, \tag{6.1}$$

where $p_{AA}(i)$ and $p_{AB}(i)$ are the prices of variety i produced in region A paid by the consumers in region A and B, respectively, $q_{AA}(i)$ and $q_{AB}(i)$ are the quantities that they consume, and w_A is the wage prevailing in region A.

It is both convenient and relevant to think of the market equilibrium in which the locations of firms and workers are fixed as being a *short-run equilibrium*. The distinction between short-run and long-run is justified here by the fact that adjustments in the agents' locations are slower than adjustments in market prices. In other words, for a given distribution of population, we will determine the equilibrium prices and wages prevailing in the two regions. We will then study how firms and skilled workers are distributed between the regions. As the Krugman model involves a large number of parameters, we normalize some of them to ease the burden of notation. In particular, we choose the unit of skilled labor for the marginal requirement to be equal to one: $m = 1$.

6.2.1 Short-Run Equilibrium

We saw in chapter 4 that the equilibrium prices of the varieties produced in the same region are identical and independent of the distribution of the manufacturing sector, λ:

$$p_{AA}^* = \frac{\sigma}{\sigma - 1}w_A, \qquad p_{AB}^* = \frac{\sigma}{\sigma - 1}\tau w_A. \tag{6.2}$$

However, wages vary with λ, as will become apparent soon, so the equilibrium prices depend indirectly on the distribution of workers.

Plugging p_{AA}^* and p_{AB}^* into $\pi_A(i)$ yields

$$\pi_A = \frac{w_A}{\sigma - 1}q_A - w_A f = \frac{w_A}{\sigma - 1}[q_A - (\sigma - 1)f], \tag{6.3}$$

where $q_A = q_{AA} + \tau q_{AB}$. Under free entry, profits are zero, so the equilibrium output of a firm is given by the solution to (6.3):

$$q^* \equiv q_A^* = q_B^* = (\sigma - 1)f. \tag{6.4}$$

A firm's output is thus the same for all varieties and is independent of the distribution of firms. A firm's demand for labor, given by $l^* = f + q^*$, is therefore the same in each region and independent of the distribution:

$$l^* = \sigma f.$$

The share of the fixed requirement in firms' demand for labor f/l^* is an index of the intensity of scale economies, which is equal to $1/\sigma$. Hence, the parameter σ plays two different roles in Krugman's model: it is, by assumption, the degree of product substitutability, but it is also an index of the extent of increasing returns exploited at the market equilibrium. This greatly facilitates the estimation of this parameter, as discussed in chapter 12. However, this versatility of σ blurs the nature of some results because it does not permit us to separate scale and price effects.

Another consequence of the demand for labor is that the total number of firms operating in the manufacturing sector is constant and equal to $N = L/l^* = L/\sigma f$, where L denotes the total mass of skilled workers. The labor-market clearing conditions therefore imply that

$$n_A = \frac{\lambda L}{\sigma f}, \qquad n_B = \frac{(1-\lambda)L}{\sigma f}. \tag{6.5}$$

Hence, *the number of firms in a region is linked by a one-to-one relationship to the number of skilled workers living there*: firms and skilled workers move together. There is no need, therefore, to describe the evolution of the distribution of firms, as it automatically follows that of the skilled workers. This vastly simplifies the analysis. Everything unfurls as if the supply of potential entrepreneurs was sufficiently large in every region for all skilled workers to find a job at a wage that cancels out profits. Despite its restrictive nature, this approach captures in a very simple way the fact that what we face here is a chicken-and-egg problem, as already stressed by Muth (1971) in his famous quote: "Do people follow jobs or do jobs follow people?" Here, it does not matter whether we talk about the distribution of firms or that of (skilled) workers.

Furthermore, as the total number of firms is equal to $L/\sigma f$, the CP model does not allow us to deal with cases in which the total number of firms varies with their spatial distribution, as is the case in the next chapter. The model only permits the analysis of the interregional distribution of the manufacturing sector when its size is fixed.

Plugging the equilibrium prices (6.2) into the regional price indices defined in chapter 4 leads to the following two expressions:

$$P_A(\lambda) = \left[\frac{\lambda L}{\sigma f} \left(\frac{\sigma w_A}{\sigma - 1} \right)^{-(\sigma-1)} + \frac{(1-\lambda)L}{\sigma f} \left(\frac{\sigma w_B}{\sigma - 1} \tau \right)^{-(\sigma-1)} \right]^{-1/(\sigma-1)}$$

$$= \kappa_1 [\lambda w_A^{-(\sigma-1)} + (1-\lambda)(w_B \tau)^{-(\sigma-1)}]^{-1/(\sigma-1)} \tag{6.6}$$

and

$$P_B(\lambda) = \left[\frac{\lambda L}{\sigma f} \left(\frac{\sigma w_A}{\sigma - 1} \tau \right)^{-(\sigma-1)} + \frac{(1-\lambda)L}{\sigma f} \left(\frac{\sigma w_B}{\sigma - 1} \right)^{-(\sigma-1)} \right]^{-1/(\sigma-1)}$$

$$= \kappa_1 [\lambda(w_A \tau)^{-(\sigma-1)} + (1-\lambda)w_B^{-(\sigma-1)}]^{-1/(\sigma-1)}, \qquad (6.7)$$

where

$$\kappa_1 \equiv \frac{\sigma}{\sigma - 1} \left(\frac{L}{\sigma f} \right)^{-1/(\sigma-1)} = \frac{\sigma}{\sigma - 1} N^{-1/(\sigma-1)}.$$

All else being equal, this expression implies that the two regional price indices decrease when the total number of varieties rises, thus capturing the idea that a greater number of firms makes the crowding-out effect stronger in product markets. In addition, the indices P_A and P_B depend not only on regional wages and the spatial distribution of workers, which are endogenous, but also on the level of trade costs.

There are two additional constraints to be considered to close the model. First, we must determine the regional incomes. As profits are zero in equilibrium, incomes are defined by the sum of wages:

$$Y_A(\lambda) = \tfrac{1}{2}L_a + \lambda w_A(\lambda)L, \qquad Y_B(\lambda) = \tfrac{1}{2}L_a + (1-\lambda)w_B(\lambda)L, \qquad (6.8)$$

where L_a denotes the total mass of unskilled workers. In each of these expressions, the first term on the right-hand side corresponds to the incomes of the unskilled and the second term to those of the skilled. Second, the equilibrium conditions in the regional markets for varieties must be satisfied. The demand for a variety produced in A, evaluated at the equilibrium prices (6.2), is given by

$$q_A(w_A) = \mu \left(\frac{\sigma}{\sigma - 1} \right)^{-\sigma} w_A^{-\sigma} (Y_A P_A^{\sigma-1} + Y_B \tau^{-(\sigma-1)} P_B^{\sigma-1}).$$

As this expression must be equal to the equilibrium supply, $(\sigma - 1)f$, we thus obtain an implicit expression for the *equilibrium wage* in region A since both the incomes and price indices also depend on wages:

$$w_A^*(\lambda) = \kappa_2 [Y_A(\lambda)P_A^{\sigma-1}(\lambda) + Y_B(\lambda)\tau^{-(\sigma-1)}P_B^{\sigma-1}(\lambda)]^{1/\sigma}, \qquad (6.9)$$

where

$$\kappa_2 \equiv \frac{\sigma - 1}{\sigma} \left[\frac{\mu}{(\sigma - 1)f} \right]^{1/\sigma} = \frac{\sigma - 1}{\sigma} \left(\frac{\mu}{q^*} \right)^{1/\sigma}.$$

By proceeding in a similar manner, the equilibrium wage in region B is given by the following implicit expression:

$$w_B^*(\lambda) = \kappa_2 [Y_A(\lambda)\tau^{-(\sigma-1)}P_A^{\sigma-1}(\lambda) + Y_B(\lambda)P_B^{\sigma-1}(\lambda)]^{1/\sigma}. \qquad (6.10)$$

These two expressions are called *wage equations*. They give us the wage that prevails in a region as a function of regional incomes, price indices, and trade costs. Their simultaneous resolution give us the equilibrium wages in terms of λ.

Even though we now have all the equations characterizing the short-run equilibrium, it turns out to be impossible to determine the explicit form of the nominal wages, as the above system cannot be solved analytically. This obviously complicates the analysis but, as will be seen later, this will not prevent us from developing a detailed analysis of the long-run equilibrium. In addition, it is possible to solve the model numerically.

Finally, the Walras law implies that the agricultural sector is in equilibrium once the above equilibrium conditions are satisfied. To sum up, when the spatial distribution of firms λ is fixed, the short-run equilibrium is given by the solution of six expressions (6.6)–(6.10) (the expressions of the two regional incomes being contained in (6.8)), of which the six unknowns are Y_A, Y_B, w_A, w_B, P_A, and P_B.[4] It now remains to describe how the spatial equilibrium is determined by the mobility of skilled workers in the long run.

6.2.2 Long-Run Equilibrium

The equilibrium distribution of workers, i.e., the equilibrium value of λ, is obtained from the comparison of the welfare levels that workers can achieve in regions A and B. The well-being of a worker in a region depends on the wage that she can earn as well as the cost of living prevailing there. A low nominal wage in the core region can, indeed, be more than compensated for by low prices for the manufactured good, if this region accommodates a higher number of firms, and vice versa. The goal here is to determine whether we obtain a dispersed structure, with two regions of the same size, or a CP structure, with the core region receiving a large share of the manufacturing sector.

A worker's welfare is measured by the value of her indirect utility, which is equal here to her real wage. As $p_a = 1$, because of the choice of numéraire, the value of her indirect utility is given by the following expression (chapter 3):

$$V_A(\lambda) = w_A(\lambda)P_A^{-\mu}(\lambda). \tag{6.11}$$

A *spatial equilibrium* is obtained when no skilled worker can obtain a higher utility level in the other region. Such an equilibrium arises in $0 < \lambda < 1$ when

$$\Delta V(\lambda) \equiv V_A(\lambda) - V_B(\lambda) = 0 \tag{6.12}$$

---

[4] Mossay (2006) has shown that this system of equations has a unique solution.

or in $\lambda = 0$ when $\Delta V(0) \leqslant 0$, or in $\lambda = 1$ when $\Delta V(1) \geqslant 0$. As the functions $V_A(\lambda)$ and $V_B(\lambda)$ are continuous with respect to λ, proposition 1 from Ginsburgh et al. (1985) implies that such an equilibrium always exists. However, it is not necessarily unique. There is therefore a need to be able to discriminate between the different equilibria in order, if possible, to select one of them.

To this end, we use the concept of stability, which requires specifying a dynamic adjustment process. The mobility of skilled workers being governed by the real wage differential, we retain a myopic best response dynamics in which skilled workers gradually move at a speed $\varphi > 0$ to the region offering them a higher level of welfare:

$$\dot{\lambda} = \varphi \Delta V(\lambda), \tag{6.13}$$

where $\dot{\lambda}$ is the temporal derivative of λ. When $\Delta V(\lambda)$ is positive and $0 < \lambda < 1$, workers migrate from B to A because their welfare in region A exceeds that prevailing in region B; if it is negative, they move in the opposite direction. Such a process rests on the assumption that regional prices and wages instantaneously adjust in reaction to a move of skilled workers. In particular, nominal wages are adjusted for profits to be zero in each region where skilled workers reside. The migration process stops when $\Delta V(\lambda) = 0$, or the variable λ takes the value 0 (and $\Delta V \leqslant 0$) or 1 (and $\Delta V \geqslant 0$). Moreover, it is clear that any spatial equilibrium is a stationary state of (6.13); conversely, a stationary state of (6.13) is a spatial equilibrium. Although this adjustment dynamics is fairly intuitive, it lacks explicit microeconomic foundations. Indeed, workers being identical, they should all move together once some of them choose to move. One possible way of overcoming this is to assume that workers face different migration costs (see chapter 8).

A spatial equilibrium is said to be *stable* when, for every marginal modification of the equilibrium distribution $0 < \lambda^* < 1$, the adjustment process (6.13) leads the skilled workers back to their initial distribution. The existence of a corner equilibrium ($\lambda^* = 0$ or 1) also implies its stability. This is because the inequality defining such an equilibrium is not affected by a small perturbation in the distribution. In what follows, any unstable equilibrium is discarded.[5] Indeed, an unstable equilibrium has practically no chance of being observed, since even the slightest error made by some agents will be enough to dispel it. Regarding the role of time, note that it is merely conceptual here and does not refer to a specific evolutionary process.

The equation (6.12) defining a spatial equilibrium is both implicit and transcendental. It is implicit because we do not have the expression for

---

[5] This corresponds to the trembling-hand refinement in game theory.

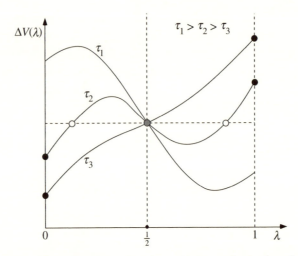

Figure 6.6. Migration dynamics for different values of trade costs.

the nominal wages $w_A^*(\lambda)$ and $w_B^*(\lambda)$. It is transcendental because it involves noninteger powers. It is, therefore, impossible to solve analytically. Krugman thus started by proceeding with numerical simulations; his results are presented in figure 6.6, where the interregional utility differential is plotted against the share of population located in A. They can be summed up as follows. When τ takes high values (for example, τ_1), there is a single stable equilibrium which corresponds to the full dispersion of the manufacturing sector ($\lambda^* = \frac{1}{2}$). Because the utility differential ΔV is decreasing in the neighborhood of $\lambda^* = \frac{1}{2}$, if region A were bigger, the indirect utility there would fall and workers would move to B. When τ takes on intermediate values (τ_2), four additional equilibria emerge; all are nonsymmetric in the sense that one region incorporates a larger share of the manufacturing sector than the other. As the two interior equilibria are unstable, we are left with three stable equilibria: the symmetric configuration ($\lambda^* = \frac{1}{2}$) and the CP structure with a complete concentration of the manufacturing sector in region A ($\lambda^* = 1$) or in region B ($\lambda^* = 0$). Finally, when τ takes a sufficiently low value (τ_3), the symmetric equilibrium becomes unstable and only the CP structure remains a stable equilibrium ($\lambda^* = 0, 1$). These results suggest that two specific stable equilibria need to be examined: the core-periphery pattern and the symmetric pattern.

6.2.2.1 The Core-Periphery Structure

Assume that the manufacturing sector is concentrated in one region, region A say, with $\lambda = 1$. For such a configuration to be a spatial equilibrium, the skilled workers must have a higher level of welfare there than they would have in B. By setting $\lambda = 1$ in the equations describing the short-run equilibrium, we obtain the following expressions:

$$Y_A = w_A^* L + \tfrac{1}{2} L_a, \qquad Y_B = \tfrac{1}{2} L_a \tag{6.14}$$

given (6.8),

$$P_A = \kappa_1 w_A^*, \qquad P_B = \kappa_1 \tau w_A^* \tag{6.15}$$

given (6.6) and (6.7), which, after substitution in (6.9) and (6.10), yields

$$w_A^* = \kappa_2 [Y_A (\kappa_1 w_A^*)^{\sigma-1} + Y_B \tau^{-(\sigma-1)} (\kappa_1 \tau w_A^*)^{\sigma-1}]^{1/\sigma} \tag{6.16}$$

and

$$w_B^* (w_A^*) = \kappa_2 [Y_A \tau^{-(\sigma-1)} (\kappa_1 w_A^*)^{\sigma-1} + Y_B (\kappa_1 \tau w_A^*)^{\sigma-1}]^{1/\sigma}. \tag{6.17}$$

It is now possible to determine the equilibrium nominal wages. As profits are zero, the total income of the skilled workers is equal to the sum of the expenditure on the manufactured good: $w_A^* L = \mu (Y_A + Y_B)$. Substituting $w_A^* L$ into (6.14) and solving with respect to Y_A and Y_B, we obtain the regional incomes

$$Y_A = \frac{1+\mu}{1-\mu} \frac{L_a}{2}, \qquad Y_B = \frac{L_a}{2},$$

so the economy's GDP is equal to $Y_A + Y_B = L_a/(1-\mu)$. From $w_A^* = \mu (Y_A + Y_B)/L$, we then obtain

$$w_A^* = \frac{\mu}{1-\mu} \frac{L_a}{L}. \tag{6.18}$$

This expression is independent of trade costs because all varieties are produced in A. By using (6.17), the wage w_B^* is given by

$$w_B^* = \kappa_3 \left[\frac{1}{2} \left(\frac{1+\mu}{1-\mu} \right) \tau^{-(\sigma-1)} + \frac{1}{2} \tau^{\sigma-1} \right]^{1/\sigma}, \tag{6.19}$$

where

$$\kappa_3 \equiv \kappa_2 \kappa_1^{(\sigma-1)/\sigma} L_a \left(\frac{\mu}{1-\mu} \frac{1}{L} \right)^{(\sigma-1)/\sigma} = \frac{\mu}{(1-\mu)^{(\sigma-1)/\sigma}} \frac{L_a}{L} > 0.$$

The equilibrium wage in region B does depend on τ because all varieties are imported.

The equilibrium wage w_A^* is higher, and w_B^* is lower, when the manufacturing sector's share μ in total consumption rises. The macroeconomic implications of this result are straightforward: if consumers demand more of the manufactured good, the nominal wage paid by firms located in the core goes up, while the wage they are able to pay in the periphery goes down, thus making the latter even less attractive.

Using (6.2), we can determine the varieties' common equilibrium price:

$$p_A^* = \frac{\sigma}{\sigma - 1} \frac{\mu}{1 - \mu} \frac{L_a}{L}.$$

This means that the prevailing price of the manufactured good in the agglomeration rises with the degree of differentiation of the varieties $(\sigma/(\sigma - 1))$, the ratio between unskilled and skilled workers (L_a/L), and the manufacturing sector's share in the economy (μ); remember that the variable labor requirement, m, has been normalized to 1.

Given (6.15), the welfare level in region A is given by

$$V_A \equiv w_A^* (P_A)^{-\mu} = \kappa_1^{-\mu} (w_A^*)^{1-\mu}.$$

This expression is also independent of τ as all varieties are produced in A. Similarly,

$$V_B \equiv w_B^* (P_B)^{-\mu} = w_B^* \kappa_1^{-\mu} \tau^{-\mu} (w_A^*)^{-\mu}.$$

Thus,

$$\frac{V_B}{V_A} = \frac{w_B^*}{w_A^*} \tau^{-\mu}$$

or, by using (6.18) and (6.19) as well as the definition of κ_3 and $\phi = \tau^{-(\sigma-1)}$,

$$\frac{V_B}{V_A} = \tau^{-\mu} \left[\frac{1-\mu}{2} \left(\frac{1+\mu}{1-\mu} \phi + \frac{1}{\phi} \right) \right]^{1/\sigma}.$$

This expression can be given a nice interpretation. The term $\tau^{-\mu}$ accounts for the fact that region B imports the total mass of varieties, thus making this region relatively unattractive to workers. The bracketed term contains two terms (up to a common factor). In the first one, the income in the core is multiplied by $\phi < 1$ because of the transport disadvantage that a region B firm has to bear when shipping its variety to region A. In the second, the income in periphery is weighted by $1/\phi > 1$ to reflect the fact that firms in the core have a cost disadvantage in supplying region B. Together, they mean that a firm in region B does pretty well in this region but rather poorly in the other. In the special case where shipping the manufactured good is costless ($\phi = 1$), we always have $V_B/V_A = 1$, because the location of activities no longer matters.

Since $\rho = \sigma/(\sigma - 1)$, the expression above may be rewritten as

$$\frac{V_B}{V_A} = \left[\frac{1+\mu}{2} \tau^{-\sigma(\mu+\rho)} + \frac{1-\mu}{2} \tau^{-\sigma(\mu-\rho)} \right]^{1/\sigma}. \tag{6.20}$$

Observe that the first term on the right-hand side of (6.20) is always decreasing with respect to τ. If $\mu \geqslant \rho$, the second term is also decreasing,

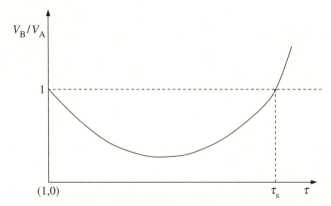

Figure 6.7. Determination of the sustain point.

so that V_B/V_A always decreases with τ. This implies that $V_B < V_A$ for every $\tau > 1$. In other words, the CP structure is a stable equilibrium for every value of $\tau > 1$. Therefore, when $\mu \geqslant \rho$ (known as the "black hole" condition) holds, the varieties are so differentiated that the demands to firms are relatively insensitive to the differences in trade costs, thus making the agglomeration very strong. In this case, *the core can be seen as a black hole attracting the entire manufacturing sector* whatever the level of trade costs.

More interesting is the case where $\mu < \rho$, as the second term of (6.20) ceases to be decreasing with respect to τ. As the varieties are less differentiated, the demand to firms becomes sufficiently elastic to weaken the agglomeration force. In this case, the second term of (6.20) tends to ∞ when τ tends to ∞. The slope of (6.20) being always negative in $\tau = 1$, it is readily verified that the curve V_B/V_A is as described in figure 6.7.

This figure allows us to identify the existence of a single value $\tau_s > 1$ such that $V_B/V_A = 1$. Consequently, the agglomeration is a stable equilibrium for every $\tau \leqslant \tau_s$. In other words, *when trade costs are sufficiently low, all firms locate in the same region.* For completeness, it should be pointed out there are two stable equilibria with agglomeration: one in which the agglomeration occurs in A and one in which it occurs in B. In what follows, we will retain only one of these equilibria, as the results also hold for the other.

Spatial concentration here stems from the fact that firms can enjoy all the benefits associated with agglomeration without bearing a strong drop in their exports. The threshold τ_s is called the *sustain point* because, once firms are agglomerated, they remain so for all the values of τ lower than this threshold value. The size of the local market becomes large enough to sustain the agglomeration of all firms. In contrast, when trade costs are sufficiently high ($\tau > \tau_s$), exports fall markedly, thus leading some firms to depart for the other region, so that the CP structure ceases to be an equilibrium.

6.2.2.2 The Symmetric Structure

We have just seen that the agglomeration is no longer an equilibrium when trade costs are sufficiently high. This leads us naturally to study the stability of the symmetric configuration, in which the manufacturing sector is equally spread across space ($\lambda = \frac{1}{2}$). In this case, the nominal wages and the price indices are the same in both regions, since the short-run equilibrium is unique. Consequently, we have $V_A = V_B$ when $\lambda = \frac{1}{2}$, which means that *the symmetric pattern is always a spatial equilibrium.* However, this equilibrium need not be stable, which we study now. The short-run equilibrium conditions become

$$Y_A = Y_B = Y = \tfrac{1}{2}Lw^* + \tfrac{1}{2}L_a,$$

where $w^* = w_A^* = w_B^*$ is the wage common to the two regions. Given (6.9) and noting that $P_A(\frac{1}{2}) = P_B(\frac{1}{2}) \equiv P$, the equilibrium wage is given by

$$w^* = \kappa_2 (YP^{\sigma-1} + Y\tau^{-(\sigma-1)}P^{\sigma-1})^{1/\sigma}$$
$$= \kappa_2 (YP^{\sigma-1})^{1/\sigma}(1 + \tau^{-(\sigma-1)})^{1/\sigma}.$$

By using (6.6), the price index common to the economy is equal to

$$P = \kappa_1[\tfrac{1}{2}(w^*)^{-(\sigma-1)} + \tfrac{1}{2}(w^*\tau)^{-(\sigma-1)}]^{-1/(\sigma-1)}$$
$$= \kappa_1 2^{1/(\sigma-1)}w^*(1 + \tau^{-(\sigma-1)})^{-1/(\sigma-1)}.$$

The common welfare level is therefore given by

$$V = w^*P^{-\mu}.$$

As mentioned above, for a given value of $\tau > 1$, the symmetric equilibrium is stable if the slope of $\Delta V(\lambda)$ evaluated in $\lambda = \frac{1}{2}$ is negative; conversely, this equilibrium is unstable when the slope of $\Delta V(\lambda)$ is positive. Checking when this condition holds is very tedious. We will confine ourselves here to a heuristic argument; the reader is referred to Fujita et al. (1999, chapter 5) for a detailed proof.

The idea behind this proof is standard. Consider a linear approximation of the conditions (6.6)–(6.10) in the neighborhood of the equilibrium by totally differentiating these conditions. This process is simplified hereby by the fact that the derivatives are evaluated in $\lambda = \frac{1}{2}$, so that the variation of a variable in region A corresponds to a variation with the opposite sign of the same variable in region B. For example, the total differential of (6.8) gives us the following two expressions:

$$\mathrm{d}Y_A = w_A L \, \mathrm{d}\lambda + \lambda L \, \mathrm{d}w_A, \qquad \mathrm{d}Y_B = -w_B L \, \mathrm{d}\lambda + (1 - \lambda) L \, \mathrm{d}w_B.$$

As symmetry implies that $\lambda = \frac{1}{2}$, $w_A = w_B = w$ and $Y_A = Y_B = Y$, as well as $\mathrm{d}Y_A = -\mathrm{d}Y_B$ and $\mathrm{d}w_A = -\mathrm{d}w_B$, these two equations can be reduced to the single equation

$$\mathrm{d}Y = wL \, \mathrm{d}\lambda + \lambda L \, \mathrm{d}w.$$

By proceeding in the same way for the price indices, the nominal wages, and real wages, we obtain four equations with four unknowns: $\mathrm{d}Y$, $\mathrm{d}P$, $\mathrm{d}w$, and $\mathrm{d}V$. By successively substituting the so-obtained expressions in $\mathrm{d}V$, we get an expression that depends only on τ. It then remains to determine the condition to be imposed on this parameter for the derivative $\mathrm{d}V/\mathrm{d}\lambda$ to be negative (the equilibrium is stable) or to be positive (the equilibrium is unstable).

The expression $\mathrm{d}V/\mathrm{d}\lambda$ is positive for all admissible values of τ, which means that the symmetric equilibrium is always unstable, when the black-hole condition is verified. This result confirms what we have seen above: if $\mu \geqslant \rho$, the agglomeration is the only stable spatial equilibrium. Let us now consider the case in which the black-hole condition is not satisfied ($\rho > \mu$). When trading goods is costless ($\tau = 1$), the spatial distribution of workers has no impact on workers' welfare, so $\mathrm{d}V/\mathrm{d}\lambda = 0$. Under autarky (i.e., $\tau \to \infty$), an increase in λ implies a larger labor supply, which pushes the wages downward. However, more workers implies more firms and, therefore, a larger labor demand. The former effect dominates the latter here. Yet the wage drop is not compensated for by an increase in the price index, so $\mathrm{d}V/\mathrm{d}\lambda < 0$. For the intermediary values of τ, it can be shown that $\mathrm{d}V/\mathrm{d}\lambda$ changes sign just once, which implies that $\mathrm{d}V/\mathrm{d}\lambda < 0$ provided that τ exceeds the solution to the equation $\mathrm{d}V/\mathrm{d}\lambda = 0$. Although we cannot obtain an analytical solution for the equilibrium wages, it is possible to determine the value of τ such that $\mathrm{d}V/\mathrm{d}\lambda = 0$:

$$\tau_b = \left[\frac{(\rho + \mu)(1 + \mu)}{(\rho - \mu)(1 - \mu)} \right]^{1/(\sigma - 1)}, \tag{6.21}$$

which is greater than 1 (remember that $\rho > \mu$). The symmetric equilibrium is therefore stable (respectively, unstable) if and only if τ is higher (respectively, lower) than τ_b, a threshold known as the *break point* because the symmetric pattern ceases to be stable for values of τ lower than τ_b. It follows from this result that when trade costs are high firms do not congregate, as the access to what would become the periphery is very poor, thus making it profitable for firms to focus on

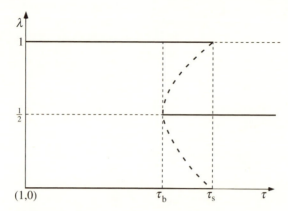

Figure 6.8.   Set of equilibria in the CP model.

their local market; in contrast, when these costs are low, firms benefit from an "endogenous" HME triggered by the relocation of skilled workers, without experiencing a large drop in their exports to the periphery. Note, in passing, that the break point depends on the same parameters as the sustain point, i.e., σ and μ.

We have now established the characteristics of the symmetric and CP equilibria. What about the existence of other equilibria and, more generally, the evolution of all these equilibria when trade costs go down? The answers to these questions are too complex to be analyzed in the context of this book. We will therefore confine ourselves to summarizing the main results obtained by Robert-Nicoud (2005) when the black-hole condition does not hold. When τ exceeds τ_s, the symmetric configuration is the only spatial equilibrium and it is stable. Since $\tau_b < \tau_s$, several stable equilibria may coexist with unstable equilibria in this range. More precisely, when $\tau_b \leqslant \tau \leqslant \tau_s$, both agglomeration and dispersion are stable equilibria, which implies that both the intervals $(0, \frac{1}{2})$ and $(\frac{1}{2}, 1)$ contain an unstable equilibrium (see the case for τ_2 in figure 6.6). In other words, there are five equilibria (two equilibria with partial agglomeration, two with agglomeration, and the symmetric configuration), represented in figure 6.8 by solid lines for the stable equilibria and broken lines for the unstable ones. Finally, when trade costs decrease sufficiently ($\tau < \tau_b$), the agglomeration of the manufacturing sector occurs discontinuously, with the economy jumping from dispersion to agglomeration in one of the two regions. This result is reminiscent of the sudden growth of the industrial region highlighted in the first section. The mobility of human capital thus leads to a dramatic amplification of the HME in which only physical capital is mobile.

The main results may be summarized as follows.

Proposition 6.1. *Consider an economy made up of two regions.*

(i) *If $\mu \geqslant \rho$, then the core-periphery structure is the only stable spatial equilibrium.*

(ii) *If $\mu < \rho$, then there is a unique solution, $\tau_s > 1$, to the equation*

$$\frac{1 + \mu}{2}\tau^{-\sigma(\mu+\rho)} + \frac{1 - \mu}{2}\tau^{-\sigma(\mu-\rho)} = 1,$$

such that the core-periphery structure is a stable equilibrium for every value $\tau \leqslant \tau_s$. Moreover, when $\tau \geqslant \tau_b$, with

$$\tau_b = \left[\frac{(\rho + \mu)(1 + \mu)}{(\rho - \mu)(1 - \mu)}\right]^{1/(\sigma-1)} < \tau_s,$$

the symmetric configuration is a stable equilibrium.

In which of the two regions will firms be concentrated in the case of an agglomerated equilibrium? Krugman's model has nothing to tell us on this matter. Many scientists seem to be happy with the idea that history, or path dependency, is all that matters in the selection of a spatial equilibrium. By this we mean that agglomeration will occur in the region favored by history, because it has better endowments or slightly better technologies than the other. This result is valid if the agents do not commit any error of prediction. On the other hand, if a large number of errors blurred the foresight of the agents (they compare regional utilities up to a random term that has a high variance), then it might be that, despite one region holding an initial advantage, the other will predominate in the long run. Furthermore, if a group of individuals anticipates that one initially smaller region will develop, this expectation may become self-fulfilling.[6] Conversely, expensive urban infrastructure implies that we rarely see such historical turnarounds (chapter 12). This is illustrated by Zipf's law, which shows the extremely strong stability of the urban hierarchy based on city size.[7]

Product differentiation plays a key role in the model. To see this, consider the case of homogeneous varieties. So long as the black hole condition does not hold, it is easily verified that $\tau_b = \tau_s = 1$ when σ tends to infinity. In other words, *when varieties are homogeneous, dispersion is the only stable equilibrium.* Conversely, when varieties are more differentiated, the likelihood of agglomeration is higher because the competition effect is weakened. Likewise, as σ is also a measure of the competitiveness of the manufacturing sector, we may expect a more competitive

---

[6] Krugman (1991b) develops this idea within the context of the model presented in the first section of this chapter.

[7] See Nitsch (2005) for a synthetic analysis of empirical studies devoted to the distribution of city size within various countries.

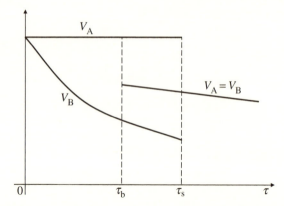

Figure 6.9. Unskilled workers' welfare and trade costs.

economy to be less concentrated than a less competitive one. Along
the same lines, we have seen that a low σ implies strong economies
of scale. Hence, we may say that a high degree of increasing returns fosters agglomeration. Regarding the share of the manufactured good, it is
readily verified that the values of τ_s and τ_b increase with μ, and so does
the probability that agglomeration occurs. This is because a larger share
of the manufacturing sector, on which the snowball effect is built, makes
the agglomeration force stronger.

6.2.3   Some Key Implications of the Krugman Model

Let us now examine the main strengths and weaknesses of Krugman's
model. We will proceed in stages, starting with its main implications for
economic theory.

6.2.3.1   Spatial Economic Theory

1. Despite its simplicity, Krugman's model incorporates a large number of effects, which allows it to come up with new and unexpected
results. The progressive integration of economies first leaves the spatial
structure of production unchanged, merely yielding an intensification
of trade. So long as dispersion prevails, a deeper integration increases
the level of welfare in the two regions, as the real wage goes up everywhere. As in new trade theories, there is intraindustry trade; integration
has only positive effects because the spatial pattern remains the same
(see the locus where $V_A = V_B$ in figure 6.9, which plots the indirect utility
achieved in the two regions as a function of trade costs).

It would be naive, however, to think that things will stay that way. If
economic integration is pursued, some firms relocate and the economy

is shifted to a state characterized by stronger spatial inequalities, i.e., a new effect not captured by the new trade theories. Indeed, a shift toward the CP structure, even if it benefits all the core's workers by increasing their real wages, has a negative effect on those remaining in what has become the periphery (see figure 6.9, where $V_A > V_B$ once the CP structure prevails). This is because the relocation of firms leads to a higher price index in region B, thus reducing the purchasing power of its inhabitants. In this case, regional disparities arise, and their intensity depends on this price effect. The differences in the welfare levels of unskilled workers depend on the manufacturing sector's share in consumption and degree of product differentiation. When these two rise, the gap in welfare grows, thus fostering more spatial inequality. The resulting pattern of trade now involves intersectoral trade because one region has a Ricardian comparative advantage in producing the industrial good. Note, however, that this advantage is endogenous here, not exogenous.

In this new configuration, however, the pursuit of integration does make possible a progressive catching-up in the welfare level of the unskilled living in the periphery. As illustrated in figure 6.9, where V_B keeps rising up to V_A, their access to the manufactured good improves and the gap is completely reabsorbed when trade costs are canceled out. In contrast, workers in the core no longer gain any benefit from further integration since all varieties are produced there, implying that the integration process loses one of its main engines.

2. The idea that interregional economic integration enhances the geographical concentration of activities may at first sight seem counterintuitive as agents are less sensitive to the costs of distance. One could thus think that the economic activity can locate anywhere and, therefore, specifically on the periphery. Proposition 6.1 does not say anything new, however. It has been anticipated (but not proven) by various authors, such as Kaldor (1970, p. 241), that

> When trade is opened up between them, the region with the more developed industry will be able to supply the need of the agricultural area of the other region on more favourable terms: with the result that the industrial centre of the second region will lose its market and will tend to be eliminated.

Likewise, Giersch (1949, p. 94) observed over half a century ago, in the context of the first debates about European unification, that

> production would tend to be centered in those industrial countries which already provide large domestic markets before the formation of the federal state.

The reason for this unexpected result, as seen above, is that *the migration of skilled workers widens the initial gap* (even if very small) once trade costs are sufficiently low. When trade costs are high, the conclusion is just the opposite: the initial size advantage shrinks and, eventually, disappears. The mobility of skilled workers' purchasing power thus markedly changes the conclusions derived from the HME model discussed in chapter 4.

The equilibria obtained by Krugman should not be interpreted literally. Dispersion means that industry is spread over a large number of regions, with small or medium-sized cities. At the other extreme, agglomeration is to be seen as a situation in which industry is concentrated in a small number of very urbanized regions. The coexistence of agglomeration and dispersion as simultaneous stable equilibria is a by-product of the two effects discussed in section 6.1, while the catastrophic nature of the transition between these two situations, which agrees with the sudden industrialization uncovered in section 6.1, finds its origin in the assumption that workers are identical. This assumption will be relaxed in chapter 8.

3. If the space-economy shifts from dispersion to agglomeration, this is not the result of a collective decision. Agglomeration, which is a macroscopic phenomenon, is caused here by a host of microeconomic decisions. It is not pursued for its own sake, to the extent that firms and workers do not choose to be concentrated or dispersed. Each chooses its location without making a binding agreement with the others. The gathering of skilled workers has nothing to do with the "peer" effect either. In other words, here *agglomeration is the unintended consequence of the aggregation of a wide range of individual choices.*[8] In such a context, regional policy makers have no impact on the structure of the space-economy if the initial advantage required for a region to become the core is not the result of any action on their part.

If the initial gaps are not too big, however, agents' expectations are liable to play a significant role in enabling them to choose one region over another. Some players (e.g., local governments or land developers) can thus help coordinate these expectations in favor of a particular region, at a cost that is both low and temporary. The winning region can thus rightfully claim that its expansion only required a small push in the right direction at the right time. The fact remains that its contribution to the agglomeration process is also very limited.

---

[8] In an urban setting, Bénabou (1994) obtains a similar result: social mixing is unstable, while a pattern formed by homogeneous socioeconomic categories is stable, but for reasons other than the ones discussed here.

4. The cumulative nature of an agglomeration makes it particularly robust to external shocks. Indeed, the gathering of skilled workers (and firms) within a region allows it to benefit from an *agglomeration rent*, which can be measured by the gap between the real wage in the agglomeration and the wage that a skilled worker would receive if she came to live on the periphery. This rent being positive, it follows that the agglomeration can be affected only by external shocks that are sufficiently strong. As a result, subsidizing skilled labor on the periphery will not involve (at least up to a certain threshold) changes in the residential choices made by the targeted workers, and will leave the agglomeration as it is. Building on the same effect, Baldwin and Krugman (2004) stress the fact that fiscal harmonization can, by definitively perpetuating the core's advantage, stifle any opportunity for the periphery to attract firms.

Those effects are absent in the case of mobile capital. Compared with the HME model studied in chapter 4, the CP model illustrates the difference between the mobility of capital and the mobility of labor, the two models being otherwise identical. In the former, if the two regions have the same size, capital is always divided equally between them. Any perturbation gives rise to mechanisms that lead the economy back to the symmetric pattern, whatever the level of trade costs. In the latter, as soon as trade costs are sufficiently low, any perturbation, however small, suffices to unleash a cumulative mechanism that comes to a halt when all skilled workers are concentrated in a single region. Conversely, if the two regions initially have different sizes, this gap is widened in the case of mobile capital, regardless of the level of trade costs. On the other hand, it shrinks when labor is the mobile factor and trade costs are sufficiently high.

5. One important implication of the cumulative nature of the agglomeration process, which can be viewed as its spatial counterpart, is what we may call a *putty-clay geography*. If there is a great deal of flexibility in locational choices, i.e., firms can settle in region B just as well as in region A, then once the agglomeration process is set into motion it keeps developing in the same region. Individual choices become more rigid because of the self-reinforcing nature of the agglomeration mechanism (the snowball effect mentioned in the introduction). In other words, the process of agglomeration sparks a "lock-in" effect. If, for whatever reason, the population of skilled workers was to increase once agglomeration had been developed, these new workers would come to settle in that particular region and make it grow, as the value of the sustain point is independent of L. On the other hand, the winning region is by definition indeterminate, to the extent that its selection may depend on

small events. The contrast with the tyranny of distance mentioned in the foreword is striking, though often misunderstood.

To sum up: both firms and workers are (almost) freed from natural constraints in their locational choices; this does not mean, however, that they do not pay attention to their respective location choices.

6. Whether there is too much or too little agglomeration is an issue that has triggered endless debate. Quite the opposite: it is fair to say that this is one of the primary questions that policy makers wish to address. Besides the standard inefficiencies generated by firms pricing above marginal costs, the CP model contains new sources of inefficiency whose origin lays in the mobility of agents. Firms and workers move without taking into account the benefits and losses they bring about to the agents residing in their new region, nor the benefits or losses they impose on those left behind. Accordingly, *there is a priori no general indication as to the social desirability of agglomeration or dispersion.*

Even though the setting provided by Krugman involves no technological externalities, its welfare analysis does not deliver a simple and unambiguous message. Neither of the two configurations (agglomeration or dispersion) Pareto dominates the other: workers living in the periphery always prefer dispersion, whereas all those living in the core always prefer agglomeration. In order to compare these two market outcomes, Charlot et al. (2006) use compensation mechanisms put forward in public economics to evaluate the social desirability of a move, using market prices and equilibrium wages to compute the compensations to be paid either by those who gain from the move (Kaldor), or by those who are hurt by the move (Hicks). They show that, *provided that trade costs are sufficiently low, agglomeration is preferred to dispersion* in that all workers in the core can compensate those staying in the periphery. However, those staying in the periphery are unable to compensate the workers who choose to move into what becomes the core. This implies that neither of the two configurations is preferred to the other with respect to the Kaldor and Hicks criteria. Such an indetermination may be viewed as the "synthesis" of the many contrasting views that prevail in a domain in which the two tenets have many good reasons to be right.

This partial indetermination may be resolved by resorting to specific social welfare functions. Charlot et al. consider the CES family that encapsulates different attitudes toward inequality and includes the utilitarian and Rawlsian criteria as polar cases. As expected, the relative merits of agglomeration then critically depend on societal values. If society does not care much about inequality across individuals, then agglomeration is socially desirable once trade costs are below some threshold, the value of which depends on the fundamental parameters of the economy; conversely, when trade costs are above such thresholds, dispersion is the socially optimal outcome. Even though these results are derived from social preferences defined on individualistic utilities, it is worth noting that they lead to policy recommendations that may be regarded as being *region based.* This is because the market yields highly contrasting distributions of workers and income in the CP model. We will return to this problem in chapter 8.

6.2.3.2 *Deindustrialization of the Peripheral Regions*

Krugman's model can be used to shed light on the geographical aspects of the transition between the two phases preceding and following the Industrial Revolution (chapter 1). When dispersion prevails, markets are fragmented and consumers primarily have access to local varieties. Firms, for their part, have limited outlets and operate on a reduced scale. In contrast, in the case of agglomeration, the whole market is more or less unified, as even consumers living on the periphery have a good access to the varieties produced in the core region. Moreover, the production of firms increases as the demand in the core grows, without any major decrease in the demand from the periphery. Although the present setting does not allow one to deal with mass production, agglomeration makes possible a change in scale. In particular, despite the fact that Krugman's model does not account for the rise in the number of firms observed during the historical transition, or for their output, we have seen how decreases in trade costs have positively affected the consumption of households.

In order to assess the relevance of the above argument, we can turn to Pollard (1981), who paid special attention to the geographical characteristics of the Industrial Revolution. His main conclusions can be summarized as follows. First, before the Industrial Revolution,

> the gaps between different parts of Europe were much smaller than they were to become later and some industrial activity not unlike that in Inner Europe was to be found almost everywhere.
>
> Pollard (1981, p. 201)

This allows us to say that the symmetric configuration provides a fairly good approximation of the space-economy in preindustrial societies.[9]

---

[9] One statistic is particularly striking in this context: Bairoch (1997, chapter 13) calculates the share of exports in the GDP in European countries around 1830 as being a mere 2%. This suffices to show that, in traditional economies, activities were essentially devoted to the satisfaction of local needs. We can therefore conclude that the spatial distribution of production largely corresponded to that of the population.

After the Industrial Revolution,

> the industrial regions colonize their agricultural neighbours [and take]
> from them some of their most active and adaptable labour, and they
> encourage them to specialize in the supply of agricultural produces,
> sometimes at the expense of some preexisting industry, running the
> risk thereby that this specialization would permanently divert the
> colonized areas from becoming industrial themselves.
>
>   Pollard (1981, p. 11)

Therefore, there was a simultaneous move of workers and firms toward
the new industrial regions. As in Krugman, a CP structure thus emerged
in Europe in the aftermath of the Industrial Revolution.

Bairoch (1997) reflected Pollard's ideas by arguing that the polarization of the European space that accompanied the Industrial Revolution
owes a great deal to the profound transformations observed in transport costs. In the first phase of the Industrial Revolution, high transport
costs protected the scattering of emerging small businesses, at a time
when technological and financial means were still unfavorable to larger
firms. Falling transport costs in the second half of the nineteenth century allowed firms to take full advantage of scale economies linked with
new energy sources, by enabling their market area to expand on a regular
basis (see also Wrigley 1988). In addition, the fact that transport costs
were still high at the beginning of the Industrial Revolution encouraged
the development of regions close to England, while the subsequent drop
probably put a stop to the growth of regions further away, as imports
became a great deal less expensive. Finally, rich regions that took on a
large share of the industrial production began to emerge, with the (relative) standard of living going down as the distance from these regions
increased.[10]

When he comes to the world consequences of the Industrial Revolution, Bairoch (1997, volume II, pp. 116–17) asserts:

> There began a massive sales flow of manufactured articles toward what
> was gradually becoming the Third World, with the notable appearance
> of one of its characteristics: the more or less complete and rapid dis-
> appearance of all its industries. As a counterpart to these sales of

---

[10] Other approaches, on a different spatial scale, are also possible. For example, Tirado
et al. (2002) use an econometric model to show that the progressive integration of the
Spanish economy in the second half of the nineteenth century has enhanced the concentration of industry in a few regions, particularly Catalonia. In contrast, Crafts and
Mulatu (2005) found that the location of English industries, which took shape in a period
when transport costs were markedly higher, is more readily explained by the natural
distribution of resources.

manufactured articles, a massive flow of untreated products (tropical goods and raw materials) went to the West, which had more and more means to absorb them.

Again, once trade costs were sufficiently low, deindustrialization occurs in some regions to the benefit of others. The same idea, i.e., that high transport costs can constitute a trade barrier that protects the formation of a national industry, was anticipated by Adam Smith himself and is strongly reaffirmed by Bairoch:

> if the transport costs had not proved a burden on the price of importing machines, the development of countries other than England would have been greatly prejudiced.
>
> Bairoch (1997, volume II, p. 360) [our translation]

6.2.3.3 Limits and Shortcomings of the Krugman Model

By now, the implications of Krugman's model for economic policy should be clear. If this model correctly describes the prevailing trends in modern economies, this means that the growing integration of markets should lead to stronger regional disparities. In the CP model, industrial agglomeration does not rely on any exogenous comparative advantage. On the contrary, it is induced by the interaction between the market and the process of economic integration. In the case of the European Union, the resulting interregional gaps would thereby threaten the process of European unification, as this process would be responsible for the desertification of various regions. As a result, it is fundamental, on the one hand, to ascertain whether the somewhat alarming conclusions of Krugman's model remain true when reasonable changes in the model are made and, on the other hand, to confront these conclusions with data.

From the theoretical viewpoint, Krugman's model is unsatisfying in many respects. (i) It only accounts for two sectors and two regions. (ii) It ignores strategic interactions between firms. (iii) It is fairly cumbersome to handle and does not lead to an analytical solution: something frustrating for a specific model. (iv) Some parameters, such as σ, are given different interpretations, thereby hindering a precise analysis of some results. (v) It overlooks other costs whose origin lies in the space-economy (for example, the congestion costs generated by the emergence of an agglomeration) and, conversely, overlooks other agglomeration benefits, such as a better matching on labor markets, the proximity of intermediate inputs and knowledge spillovers. (vi) The agricultural sector is given a very restricted role, its main role being to guarantee the equilibrium of the trade balance. Along the same line, it is hard to see why trading the agricultural good is costless in a model seeking to ascertain the overall impact of trade costs.

Although this rather long list is not exhaustive (Scott 2004), it nevertheless seems to us that Krugman has identified a major channel yielding regional disparities. In this book, we will attempt to answer some of the above criticisms and to evaluate their impact on Krugman's main results, as summarized in proposition 6.1. However, the reader must be aware that, in the present state of knowledge, it is impossible to work with a model that could answer all the criticisms mentioned above.

6.3   The Krugman Model Revisited

One possible attempt to make Krugman's model amenable to an analytical treatment is to relax the assumption of marginal requirement in skilled labor. Although this assumption turns out to be reasonable in some sectors (think of restaurants, where production requires skilled labor), it is true that only the fixed requirement calls for skilled labor in many other sectors, the production itself being undertaken by unskilled workers. In fact, in a growing number of industries, production is divided into several activities, starting with the product design and ending with its marketing and distribution, which all require skilled workers, while the actual production can often be performed by unskilled workers. Consider, for example, the case of Nike. The production of sporting footwear is characterized by high fixed costs, which depend on the wages of the designers and engineers that conceive the shoes. This activity is largely carried out in the United States. In contrast, production itself is outsourced toward countries with very low wages, such as Indonesia, China, Thailand, or Vietnam, as it almost exclusively involves workers with a very low level of skill. All of this is confirmed by the fact that, in 1990, while the sale price of a pair of basketball shoes was $70, its marginal production cost was $2.75 (Cohen 2007).

This has led Forslid and Ottaviano (2003) to propose a simplified version of the CP model, where firms use unskilled labor to produce the manufactured good. More precisely, the production of a variety requires a fixed requirement f of skilled labor and a marginal requirement $m = 1$ of unskilled labor. This amounts to assuming that mobility differs according to the type of labor: unskilled workers are mobile between sectors but not between regions, while skilled workers are mobile across space. In this context, skilled workers can also be considered as entrepreneurs, whose action is needed to launch a new variety in the manufacturing sector. Such a modeling strategy allows us to provide a complete analytical solution for the short-run equilibrium, because the marginal costs, and hence the equilibrium prices, no longer depend on the wages of the skilled and, therefore, on their location. This cancels out some interesting effects but vastly simplifies the analysis.

Equation (6.1) becomes

$$\pi_A(i) = p_{AA}(i)q_A(i) - w_A f - q_A(i) = [p_{AA}(i) - 1]q_A(i) - w_A f.$$

As the marginal cost is now equal to 1 instead of w_A, the mill price of a variety is the same for all the firms, regardless of the region in which the variety is produced:

$$p_{AA}^*(i) = p_{BB}^*(i) = \frac{\sigma}{\sigma - 1}, \qquad p_{AB}^*(i) = p_{BA}^*(i) = \frac{\tau \sigma}{\sigma - 1}.$$

The equilibrium conditions in the regional labor markets now become

$$n_A = \frac{\lambda L}{f}, \qquad n_B = \frac{(1 - \lambda)L}{f},$$

so that the regional price indices take the form

$$P_A(\lambda) = \frac{\sigma}{\sigma - 1} \left(\frac{L}{f}\right)^{-1/(\sigma-1)} [\lambda + \tau^{-(\sigma-1)}(1 - \lambda)]^{-1/(\sigma-1)}$$

and

$$P_B(\lambda) = \frac{\sigma}{\sigma - 1} \left(\frac{L}{f}\right)^{-1/(\sigma-1)} [\tau^{-(\sigma-1)}\lambda + (1 - \lambda)]^{-1/(\sigma-1)}.$$

As in Krugman, the region receiving the larger number of skilled workers is the one in which consumers' purchasing power is higher. This is due to the fact that the price index there is lower, as the number of imported varieties is smaller there than in the other region.

The production volume that cancels out the profits of a region A firm is now equal to

$$q_A^* = (\sigma - 1)f w_A. \tag{6.22}$$

In Krugman's model, the fixed and marginal costs, the income, and the price index of a region all depend on this region's nominal wage, whereas only the fixed cost and the income vary with this wage in the model by Forslid and Ottaviano (2003). This vastly simplifies the analysis. Equalizing expression (6.22) in region A to the demand for any variety ($q_A + \tau q_B$) evaluated at the equilibrium prices, we obtain

$$w_A = \frac{\mu}{\sigma} \left\{ \frac{1}{\lambda L + (1 - \lambda)L\tau^{-(\sigma-1)}} [\tfrac{1}{2}L_a + \lambda L w_A] \right.$$

$$\left. + \frac{\tau^{-(\sigma-1)}}{\lambda L\tau^{-(\sigma-1)} + (1 - \lambda)L} [\tfrac{1}{2}L_a + (1 - \lambda)L w_B] \right\}$$

and

$$w_{\mathrm{B}} = \frac{\mu}{\sigma}\left\{\frac{\tau^{-(\sigma-1)}}{\lambda L + (1-\lambda)L\tau^{-(\sigma-1)}}[\tfrac{1}{2}L_{\mathrm{a}} + \lambda L w_A]\right.$$

$$\left. + \frac{1}{\lambda L\tau^{-(\sigma-1)} + (1-\lambda)L}[\tfrac{1}{2}L_{\mathrm{a}} + (1-\lambda)L w_{\mathrm{B}}]\right\},$$

which form a system of two linear equations, the solution of which is given by the equilibrium wages:

$$w_A^*(\lambda) = \frac{\mu/\sigma}{1-\mu/\sigma}\frac{L_{\mathrm{a}}}{2}$$

$$\times \frac{2\phi\lambda + [1-\mu/\sigma + (1+\mu/\sigma)\phi^2](1-\lambda)}{\phi[\lambda^2 + (1-\lambda)^2]L + [1-\mu/\sigma + (1+\mu/\sigma)\phi^2]\lambda(1-\lambda)L},$$

$$w_B^*(\lambda) = \frac{\mu/\sigma}{1-\mu/\sigma}\frac{L_{\mathrm{a}}}{2}$$

$$\times \frac{2\phi(1-\lambda) + [1-\mu/\sigma + (1+\mu/\sigma)\phi^2]\lambda}{\phi[\lambda^2 + (1-\lambda)^2]L + [1-\mu/\sigma + (1+\mu/\sigma)\phi^2]\lambda(1-\lambda)L}.$$

By deriving the ratio $w_A^*(\lambda)/w_B^*(\lambda)$ with respect to λ, we find that the region with the larger number of skilled workers offers a higher wage than the other region if and only if

$$\phi > \frac{1-\mu\sigma}{1+\mu\sigma}$$

which amounts to saying that *the large region offers higher nominal wages so long as the share of the manufacturing sector is sufficiently high.*

We are now able to determine all the short-run equilibrium variables and to write the migration equation (6.12) explicitly. This equation remains transcendental, however, and cannot be solved analytically. Nevertheless, Robert-Nicoud (2005) has been able to show that the revisited model has the same equilibria as the original model. The simplification proposed by Forslid and Ottaviano therefore does not affect the main properties of the CP model. It is retained in several applications and extensions of Krugman's model.

6.4 Concluding Remarks

Spatial inequality is the involuntary consequence of a myriad of individual decisions made by firms and workers. Somewhat unexpectedly, we have seen that the manufacturing sector is spatially concentrated when trade costs are sufficiently low. Such a result contradicts the general belief that falling trade costs would lead to more flexibility in the choice of locations, thereby permitting the development of the periphery. In fact, we may also observe the opposite: the progressive disappearance of the traditional location factors allows for newer determinants to become predominant, thus leading firms to congregate in regions that do not offer natural comparative advantage. In other words, *although firms are footloose, they gradually lose their malleability once the effects of the new agglomeration forces associated with increasing returns come into play.* This is mapped into a putty–clay geography: the regions may be similar at the outset, but they can diverge considerably later on.

While the neoclassical theory of international trade assumes that labor is homogeneous and mobile between sectors but not between countries, Krugman's model of economic geography assumes that labor is divided between two watertight categories, one spatially immobile and the other mobile. Instead of confirming the convergence of factor prices predicted by standard trade theory, Krugman provides a support to substantial and persistent regional disparities. Under increasing returns, imperfect competition, and trade costs, it would therefore appear that the alarmist forecasts of Sicco Mansholt, mentioned in chapter 1, may become concrete within the European Union. As we will see, however, things are not quite that simple.

Spatial inequalities generated here by the agglomeration of activities take on the form of a concentration of skills in a limited number of regions. This process is indeed unfurling in some regions. For example, in 2000 the fraction of college graduates went from about 10% in the least-educated American cities to above 40% in the highest-educated cities, thus suggesting a very uneven spatial distribution of skills (Moretti 2004).[11] However, the assumption of spatially mobile labor, even skilled labor, describes more accurately the United States than the European Union (see, for example, Braunerhjelm et al. 2000). The relative immobility of European workers therefore makes it unlikely for the European Union to be structured around a single core and a large periphery. It is reasonable, on the other hand, to think that *skilled labor is becoming increasingly mobile within some areas of the European Union.* For example, in the United Kingdom, regional disparities are widening because of the progressive concentration of human capital in Greater London and southeast England (Duranton and Monastiriotis 2002). If this scenario had indeed to be replicated elsewhere, one could expect the emergence of several CP structures on the subcommunity level. In other words, it

---

[11] Note that the absence of strong regional disparities in the United States is likely to be due to the fact that the American economy has been integrated from the very beginning (see chapters 8 and 12).

seems more likely that the European space will be formed by a collection of prosperous and stagnating regions (chapter 12).

Furthermore, e-work, by allowing the separation of the location of production and consumption capacities, could prevent, or at least hinder, the emergence of strong agglomerations. Indeed, as seen in chapter 4, in this case lower trade costs lead to a market outcome in which the manufacturing sector is shared, although unequally, across regions. By allowing skilled workers to keep their residence in the smaller region while supplying their work in the large region, *new communication technologies could foster a greater dispersion of activities*. Of course, more research is called for here.

Finally, although the CP model leads to clear-cut conclusions and testable predictions, it must be recognized that these have been achieved under some fairly strong assumptions. In particular, as the agglomeration of activities is also found in countries characterized by a low spatial mobility of labor, it must be that forces other than those identified in this chapter drive toward agglomeration. In the following chapters, we will turn our attention to alternative explanations, as well as extensions, before going on to an empirical evaluation of the main results of economic geography.

6.5 Related Literature

Fujita et al. (1999) provided the first synthesis of the economic geography literature based on the DSK approach. It remains a key reference, while Neary (2001) provides an indispensable complement to it. Another valuable reference is Baldwin et al. (2003), which contains a wide range of applications. Finally, Fujita and Thisse (2002) integrated the CP model into a broader perspective, which aims to understand the formation of economic agglomerations on different spatial scales. Note, in passing, that Casetti's article took ten years to be published.

There are countless extensions of the Krugman model. The most general framework that admits Krugman's model as a special case is the work of Puga (1999). It was not until Robert-Nicoud (2005) that a detailed study of the correspondence of equilibria was provided. Baldwin (1999) developed a model in which agglomeration is the outcome of the demand effects generated by the accumulation of physical capital. Pflüger (2004) revisited the CP model in the case where preferences are quasi-linear, $U = \alpha \log M + A$, and showed that the transition from dispersion to agglomeration is gradual.

Amiti and Pissarides (2005) consider a horizontally heterogeneous workforce, which allows firms to have market power in regional labor markets. Mori and Turrini (2005) assume, on the contrary, that skilled workers are vertically heterogeneous. They show that a new type of equilibrium may emerge: the population of skilled workers is spatially segmented, the most skilled being in one region and the least skilled in the other.

Finally, by combining the CP model and a Grossman–Helpman–Romer-type model of endogenous growth, Fujita and Thisse (2003b) show that growth and agglomeration go hand in hand. Their welfare analysis supports the idea that the additional growth spurred by agglomeration of the R&D sector may lead to an outcome in which workers in the periphery are better-off than under dispersion.

Intermediate Goods and the
Evolution of Regional Disparities

The CP model underscores one specific mechanism of agglomeration: consumers' demand is greater in core regions; this attracts firms and leads to a wider array of local varieties, which, in turn, attracts more workers, thus generating a snowball effect. As it turns out, soon after the publication of Krugman's work, the CP model was subject to several criticisms. The agglomeration force discussed in this chapter will serve as a response to two of these shortcomings. As a first glimpse, recall from chapter 6 that a key point in the Krugman model is that skilled workers' spatial mobility is much greater than that of unskilled workers. From the empirical point of view, however, this fact dwindles in importance. For example, even though labor mobility in the United States is twice as high as in the European Union, the share of American workers moving for job-related reasons is only 4% of the U.S. labor force (U.S. Department of Labor 2002).[1] Moving beyond the Krugman model in search of alternative explanations appears to be warranted in order to understand *the emergence of large industrial regions in economies characterized by a low spatial mobility of labor.* A second shortcoming of the CP model is that it overlooks the importance of intermediate goods. Yet the demand for consumer goods does not account for a very large fraction of firms' sales, being often overshadowed by the demand for intermediate goods.[2] Therefore, in making their location choices, it makes sense for intermediate-goods producers to care about the places where final goods are produced; similarly, final-goods producers are likely to pay close attention to where intermediate-goods suppliers are located. This

---

[1] Evidence regarding the low mobility of labor in the European Union may be found in Braunerhjelm et al. (2000). See also Eichengreen (1993), who shows that worker elasticity with respect to wage differentials is twenty-five times greater in the United States than in the United Kingdom.

[2] For example, in the United States, intermediate goods account for 59% of the total amount of manufactured goods produced in 1997 (computed on the basis of the input–output tables of the *Bureau of Economic Analysis*).

reciprocal influence of location decisions is overlooked by the CP model. Yet this idea is nothing new, and can be traced back to Marshall (1890, chapter X), who suggested that the availability of specialized inputs is a key variable in accounting for the existence of industrial clusters:

> subsidiary trades grow up in the neighbourhood, supplying it with implements and materials, organizing its traffic, and in many ways conducing to the economy of its material.... [T]he economic use of expensive machinery can sometimes be attained in a very high degree in a district in which there is a large aggregate production of the same kind, even though no individual capital employed in the trade be very large. For subsidiary industries devoting themselves each to one small branch of the process of production, and working it for a great many of their neighbours, are able to keep in constant use machinery of the most highly specialized character, and to make it pay its expenses, though its original cost may have been high.
>
> Marshall (1890, p. 225)

In a different but related context, Lampard (1955, p. 341) makes a similar point by suggesting that "the city is the only feasible locus for the mass of specialized servicing."[3]

In this chapter, our objective is to determine whether core–periphery structures may emerge in economies characterized by a low spatial mobility of labor. In the original CP model no such mobility constraints are imposed, meaning that in this new context one could expect the degree of spatial inequality across regions to be low. Yet even a quick glance around the globe is sufficient to undermine this hasty conclusion. For example, the European Union is characterized by a low mobility of labor and strong regional disparities in employment and/or income. Then what other factors might account for the existence of a core–periphery structure? As suggested above, a good candidate might be the demand for intermediate goods. And indeed, Venables (1996) has shown that a core–periphery structure can emerge even in the absence of labor mobility. To see this, assume that many firms belonging to the final sector are concentrated in one region. Quite naturally, the high demand for intermediate goods within this region attracts producers of intermediate goods. In turn, these intermediate goods are supplied at a lower cost in the core region, which induces even more final sector firms to move to the core. Such a cumulative causation process feeds on itself, so that the resulting agglomeration can be explained solely by the demand for intermediate goods, without having recourse to labor mobility as in Krugman's setting.

---

[3] Note also that a number of empirical studies confirm the importance that firm-specific services have in fostering regional development (see Hansen (1990) for one of the first contributions).

Giving intermediate goods a prominent role is a clear departure from the CP model, which allows one to focus on other forces that are at work in modern economies. To this end, note that, once workers are immobile, a higher concentration of firms within a region translates to an increase in wages for this region. This gives rise to two opposite forces. On the one hand, final demand in the core region increases because consumers enjoy higher incomes. As in Krugman, final demand is an agglomeration force; however, it is no longer sparked by an increase in population size, but by an increase in income. On the other hand, an increase in the wage level generates a new dispersion force, which lies at the heart of many debates regarding the deindustrialization of developed countries, i.e., their *high labor costs*. In such a context, firms are induced to relocate their activities to the periphery when lower wages there more than offset lower demand.

This chapter will study these new forces, which are both related to the role of intermediate inputs and the working of local labor markets. It should be clear that introducing these forces into the picture will considerably modify the mechanisms that shape the spatial distribution of economic activity. Furthermore, this will bring to light an important threshold effect, whereby spatial inequality obeys a *bell-shaped relationship*. Specifically, while the first stage of economic integration still exacerbates regional disparities, once a certain threshold is reached, additional integration starts undoing them. This amounts to the *reindustrialization* of the periphery, and possibly a simultaneous *deindustrialization* of the core. The existence of such regional convergence at very high levels of economic integration has major implications for the space-economy, which will be discussed later in this chapter. This also agrees with our intuition, as it seems natural for a very large drop in trade costs to correct for spatial inequalities. As suggested in previous chapters, it turns out that this conventional wisdom, shared by many European policy makers, is both unfounded and incomplete. The framework discussed in this chapter will allow us to reconcile conventional wisdom with theoretically founded models.

Finally, a few policy implications can be teased from the bell-shaped relationship. In the early stages of economic integration, there is a trade-off between economic efficiency and spatial equity. Improving the former is achieved at the expense of the latter. However, once some critical level of integration has been reached, this trade-off gives way to a win–win scenario: more integration implies both an increase in efficiency and a decrease in spatial inequality. Thus, partial integration is to be avoided, as it entails the "worst of both worlds." An economy characterized by partial integration is uncomfortably perched at the top of the inequality hill, and only benefits from relatively modest efficiency gains. We will see, however, that even when efficiency and equality go hand in hand, some redistribution of income from the core to the periphery must occur.

7.1 The Role of Intermediate Goods

Krugman and Venables (1995) provide a model that encapsulates the effects mentioned above, while Venables (1996) goes on to offer a more detailed version. These models introduce two important changes due to Krugman (1991a): (i) workers are bound to their native region (i.e., they are spatially immobile), and (ii) firms use intermediate goods produced by other firms.

7.1.1 Population, Labor Market, and Final Demand

Consider again an economy made up of two regions, A and B. The population size in each region is constant and identical, a simplifying assumption that removes any exogenous source of asymmetry. Without loss of generality, the unit of labor is chosen for the population in each region to be equal to 1. Workers are employed in one of two sectors: agricultural or manufacturing. In contrast to the CP model, labor is taken to be homogeneous, meaning that workers can be hired in either of these two sectors. We also assume that *sectoral mobility is costless, while spatial mobility is prohibitively costly*, two assumptions that are at odds with those made in the CP model. This new framework is helpful in discriminating between the roles played by different types of labor mobility.

Because workers are free to choose between the agricultural and manufacturing sectors, the wage rate must be the same in the two sectors within each region, provided the two of them exist in the region under consideration. As in the CP model, the agricultural sector is perfectly competitive and exhibits constant returns to scale; the cost of shipping the agricultural good is zero. This allows us to choose the agricultural good as the numéraire and to set the agricultural wage to 1. Then, let w_A be the manufacturing wage in region A, and let λ_A be the number (and share) of industrial workers in this region. Region A's labor market can be characterized by one of the following three scenarios. If both sectors are active, wages are as follows:

$$w_A = 1 \quad \text{and} \quad 0 \leqslant \lambda_A \leqslant 1. \tag{7.1}$$

If one of the two sectors disappears from region A, then either

$$w_A > 1 \quad \text{and} \quad \lambda_A = 1 \tag{7.2}$$

or manufacturing firms would be willing to pay a wage smaller than 1, thus implying that $\lambda_A = 0$.

As before, the good produced by the manufacturing sector is horizontally differentiated, and n_A is the number of varieties/firms in region A. These varieties are exported to region B; trade costs are the same across varieties, and of the iceberg type with $\tau > 1$. Region A consumers' preferences are given by

$$U_A = C_y M_A^y A_A^{1-y},$$

where $C_y \equiv y^{-y}(1-y)^{y-1}$ is a constant with $0 < y < 1$, A_A is the quantity of the agricultural good, and M_A is a CES-composite of varieties defined by

$$M_A = \left[\sum_{r=A,B} \int_{i \in \mathcal{N}_r} q_{rA}^{\text{fin}}(i)^{(\sigma-1)/\sigma} \, di \right]^{\sigma/(\sigma-1)},$$

where $q_{rA}^{\text{fin}}(i)$ is the quantity of variety i produced in region $r = A, B$ and consumed by an individual residing in region A, and $\mathcal{N}_r$ is the set of varieties produced in region r. Note that the share y of the manufactured good in consumption is identical to the parameter μ used in the CP model. This change in notation will be justified later on.

Hence, a region A consumer's *final demand* for variety i is given by

$$q_{rA}^{\text{fin}}(i) = \left[\frac{p_{rA}(i)}{P_A} \right]^{-\sigma} \frac{E_A}{P_A}, \tag{7.3}$$

where $p_{rA}(i)$ is the (delivered) price in region A of variety i produced in region r. Let $E_A \equiv y(w_A \lambda_A + 1 - \lambda_A)$ be the region A workers' total expenditure on the manufactured good, while the price index for varieties in region A is still denoted as P_A and defined by

$$P_A = \left[\sum_{r=A,B} \int_{i \in \mathcal{N}_r} p_{rA}(i)^{-(\sigma-1)} \, di \right]^{-1/(\sigma-1)}. \tag{7.4}$$

7.1.2 Technology, Cost, and Intermediate Demand

Another key departure from the CP model has to do with technology: varieties are now produced using both labor and intermediate goods. Following Ethier (1982), *intermediate goods in the firm's production function mirror final goods in the consumer's utility function*. Specifically, it is assumed that the *same* aggregate of varieties enters both the production and utility functions. In particular, this means that (i) the elasticity of substitution is identical for both final and intermediate consumption and (ii) each variety enters its own production.[4] Moreover, technology is once more characterized by the simplest form of scale economies in that both fixed and marginal requirements are constant, the latter being normalized at 1 as in chapter 6. In the DSK model, the amount of labor required to produce q_A units of a variety was given by $l_A = f + q_A$. Here it becomes

$$f + q_A = C_\mu l_A^{1-\mu} K_A^\mu, \tag{7.5}$$

where $C_\mu \equiv \mu^{-\mu}(1-\mu)^{\mu-1}$ and where K_A is the CES aggregate of input varieties:

$$K_A = \left[\sum_{r=A,B} \int_{i \in \mathcal{N}_r} q_{rA}^{int}(i)^{(\sigma-1)/\sigma} \, di \right]^{\sigma/(\sigma-1)},$$

$q_{rA}^{int}(i)$ being the quantity of variety i produced in region $r = A, B$ and used as an input by a firm set up in region A. In other words, to produce a variety, a firm needs a fixed amount f and a unit marginal amount of a composite good, which is defined by a Cobb–Douglas function of two inputs. The former input is labor and the latter is given by a CES function of all varieties. We will see in section 7.3.2 that the Cobb–Douglas parameter μ plays the same role here as in the CP model's utility function, thus explaining why we use the same notation.

To determine firms' prices, we need first the cost function of firms located in each region. For a production volume equal to $\bar{q}_A$, this function is obtained in region A by solving the following minimization problem:

$$\min_{l_A,(q_{rA}^{int}(i))} \left(w_A l_A + \sum_{r=A,B} \int_{i \in \mathcal{N}_r} p_{rA}(i) q_{rA}^{int}(i) \, di \right)$$

$$\text{subject to } \bar{q}_A = C_\mu l_A^{1-\mu} K_A^\mu - f. \tag{7.6}$$

We could solve this optimization problem by writing out its Lagrangian, but it is more straightforward to appeal to a standard duality result. Indeed, minimizing

$$w_A l_A + \sum_{r=A,B} \int_{i \in \mathcal{N}_r} p_{rA}(i) q_{rA}^{int}(i) \, di$$

subject to producing $\bar{q}_A$ is equivalent to maximizing production

$$q_A = C_\mu l_A^{1-\mu} K_A^\mu - f$$

---

[4] The latter hypothesis is more realistic than it may seem at first glance. It is a well-established fact that input–output matrices have "thick" diagonals, meaning that a significant fraction of intermediate goods are used to produce final goods from the same sector. This is particularly true of industrial sectors, especially when working on a highly aggregated level as is the case here.

subject to the cost constraint

$$\overline{C}_A = w_A l_A + \sum_{r=A,B} \int_{i \in \mathcal{N}_r} p_{rA}(i) q_{rA}^{int}(i) \, di,$$

that is

$$\max_{l_A,(q_{rA}^{int}(i))} (C_\mu l_A^{1-\mu} K_A^\mu - f)$$

$$\text{subject to } \overline{C}_A = w_A l_A + \sum_{r=A,B} \int_{i \in \mathcal{N}_r} p_{rA}(i) q_{rA}^{int}(i) \, di. \qquad (7.7)$$

Because C_μ and f are constants, *a firm's optimization problem is thus formally equivalent to that of the consumers' in the Dixit-Stiglitz model.* The analogy becomes clear when observing that, in the present context,

(i) the amount of labor is the counterpart of the consumption of the agricultural good,

(ii) the wage rate corresponds to the price of the agricultural good,

(iii) production costs $\overline{C}_A$ take on the role of income, and

(iv) intermediate varieties replace final varieties.

Aside from a few minor details, it follows that the value function of program (7.7) is identical to the indirect utility obtained by consumers in the Dixit-Stiglitz model (see chapter 3):

$$l_A^{1-\mu} K_A^\mu = \frac{\overline{C}_A}{C_\mu w_A^{1-\mu} P_A^\mu}.$$

Using (7.5), we obtain a firm's cost function for producing a given variety in region A:

$$\overline{C}_A(q_A) = w_A^{1-\mu} P_A^\mu (f + q_A).$$

This firm has, therefore, a marginal production cost given by

$$c_A \equiv w_A^{1-\mu} P_A^\mu \qquad (7.8)$$

and a fixed cost equal to

$$f_A \equiv f w_A^{1-\mu} P_A^\mu, \qquad (7.9)$$

which both depend not only on the nominal wage w_A, as in the CP model, but also on the price index P_A.

At this point, note the emergence of the new force of agglomeration mentioned in the introduction. Regions in which the number of local varieties is large benefit from a low price index, just as in the CP model. The novelty of the present context is that the decrease in prices leads to a drop in *both fixed and marginal production costs in the manufacturing sector*, which is nothing short of introducing a Marshallian externality through intermediate inputs. All else being equal, it follows that *producers have an incentive to locate in the region hosting the largest number of varieties, as they will benefit from lower production costs.*

Applying to (7.7) the techniques used in the Dixit–Stiglitz model, we get the *intermediate demand* of a region A firm for a variety i produced in region r:

$$q_{rA}^{\text{int}}(i) = \left[\frac{p_{rA}(i)}{P_A}\right]^{-\sigma} \frac{\mu \overline{C}_A}{P_A}, \tag{7.10}$$

where the firm spends $\mu \overline{C}_A$ on each of the varieties produced in region r.

Finally, the demand for labor from a firm in region A is given by

$$l_A = \frac{(1 - \mu)\overline{C}_A}{w_A}. \tag{7.11}$$

7.1.3 Short-Run Equilibrium

In the analysis of the CP model, we have defined the short run as any market situation in which the overall population is fixed and (arbitrarily) split between the two regions. Thus, in the short run, for both regions, prices and wages as well as the corresponding indirect utilities, which all depend on regional population size, can be determined. Then, allowing for spatial migration yields the long-run (or spatial) equilibrium. By adopting a similar approach in which the intersectoral distribution of labor is now given within each region, we can determine the number of varieties, prices, and wages in each region, which characterizes a short-run equilibrium. We will then go on to examine the long-run mobility of labor between sectors.

Firms' profit-maximizing prices are obtained by noting that, regardless of the origin or nature of demand (be it domestic or foreign, final or intermediate), its elasticity is constant and equal to σ. This major simplification arises because the CES functions' parameters are assumed to be identical for final and intermediate consumption. Furthermore, the number of varieties being large, each firm may accurately disregard their own impact on price indices and wages. In other words, the population in each region being 1, (7.3) and (7.10) lead to a total demand for the variety produced by any region A firm that is given by

$$q_A = q_{AA}^{\text{fin}} + \tau q_{AB}^{\text{fin}} + n_A q_{AA}^{\text{int}} + \tau n_B q_{AB}^{\text{int}}$$
$$= p_A^{-\sigma} \times \{[y(w_A \lambda_A + 1 - \lambda_A) + \mu n_A \overline{C}_A]P_A^{\sigma-1}$$
$$+ \tau^{1-\sigma}[y(w_B \lambda_B + 1 - \lambda_B) + \mu n_B \overline{C}_B]P_B^{\sigma-1}\}, \tag{7.12}$$

where the bracketed term is treated as a constant by each firm. This has a major implication: the equilibrium mill price p_A^* chosen by a region A firm is the same regardless of the demand and region of destination. This price is the markup $\sigma/(\sigma-1)$ discussed in chapter 3, multiplied by the marginal production cost (7.8):

$$p_A^* = \frac{\sigma}{\sigma-1} w_A^{1-\mu} P_A^{\mu}. \tag{7.13}$$

Applying the free-entry condition to regional product markets implies that firms' profits are zero:

$$\pi_A = (p_A^* - c_A) q_A - f_A = 0,$$

where c_A, f_A, and p_A^* are given by (7.8), (7.9), and (7.13), respectively. The equilibrium production of a firm in region A is thus given by

$$q_A^* = q^* = (\sigma-1)f. \tag{7.14}$$

We are now equipped to rewrite the three equations defining the short-run equilibrium in a much simpler way. First, by using the price index (7.4), a firm's profit-maximizing price (7.13) becomes

$$p_A^* = \frac{\sigma}{\sigma-1} w_A^{1-\mu} [n_A (p_A^*)^{-(\sigma-1)} + n_B (\tau p_B^*)^{-(\sigma-1)}]^{-\mu/(\sigma-1)}. \tag{7.15}$$

This is another important departure from the CP model; p_A^* is now proportional to $w_A^{1-\mu} P_A^{\mu}$, which depends implicitly on both wages and the number of varieties.

Note also that the number of employees per firm is not constant, which implies that *the size of the manufacturing sector is no longer proportional to the number of varieties.* Since this number is given by the ratio of the industry and firm sizes, it becomes an independent variable in its own right. Noting that the zero-profit condition implies $\overline{C}_A = p_A^* q^*$ and using (7.11) and (7.14), we find that the total demand for labor in region A, $\lambda_A = n_A l_A$, is given by

$$\lambda_A = (1-\mu)(\sigma-1)f \frac{n_A p_A^*}{w_A}. \tag{7.16}$$

Finally, market clearing for a given variety (7.12) reads as follows:

$$(\sigma-1)f = (p_A^*)^{-(\sigma-1)}$$
$$\times \left\{ \left[y + \frac{\mu w_A + y(1-\mu)(w_A - 1)}{1-\mu} \lambda_A \right] \right.$$
$$\times \left[n_A (p_A^*)^{-(\sigma-1)} + n_B (\tau p_B^*)^{-(\sigma-1)} \right]^{-1}$$
$$+ \tau^{1-\sigma} \left[y + \frac{\mu w_B + y(1-\mu)(w_B - 1)}{1-\mu} \lambda_B \right]$$
$$\left. \times \left[n_A (\tau p_A^*)^{-(\sigma-1)} + n_B (p_B^*)^{-(\sigma-1)} \right]^{-1} \right\}. \tag{7.17}$$

In short, given the regional shares of labor used in the manufacturing sector (λ_A and λ_B), the short-run equilibrium is defined by the following six unknowns: the number of varieties produced in each region (n_A^* and n_B^*), the mill prices (p_A^* and p_B^*), and the wage rates in the manufacturing sector (w_A^* and w_B^*). To solve for these unknowns, the three equations (7.15)–(7.17) are available for both regions, summing up to six equations.

7.1.4 Long-Run Equilibrium

The long-run equilibrium is obtained by allowing workers to move costlessly between sectors (but not between regions). This necessarily implies one of the following two outcomes: (i) *the equalization of nominal wages across sectors in each region* or (ii) *the disappearance of one sector in one or both of the two regions.* As usual, stability can ascertain whether one spatial equilibrium is likely to emerge (chapter 6). Studying analytically the stability of long-run equilibria is prohibitively difficult here, thus making numerical and graphical analysis a convenient choice.[5]

Defining the long-run equilibrium requires determining the size of the manufacturing sector in each region (λ_A^* and λ_B^*) under the assumption of intersectoral mobility of workers. This is achieved by means of one of the conditions (7.1) or (7.2). Only four scenarios are possible (up to a permutation between regions).

(1) *Both the agricultural and manufacturing sectors exist in each region.* In this case, wages in the manufacturing sector are equal to 1 in both regions ($w_A^* = w_B^* = 1$). Rewriting (7.15)–(7.17) for each region leads to a system of six implicit nonlinear equations. The six unknowns are the number of varieties, n_A^* and n_B^*, the profit-maximizing prices, p_A^* and p_B^*, and the shares of manufacturing employment, $\lambda_A^* < 1$ and $\lambda_B^* < 1$.

(2) *One region completely specializes in manufacturing, while both sectors are present in the other region.* Assuming region A undergoes complete specialization, we have $\lambda_A^* = 1$ and $w_B^* = 1$. In (7.15)–(7.17), the variable $w_A^* > 1$ replaces the unknown λ_A^*, which is equal to 1.

(3) *One region completely specializes in agriculture, while both sectors are present in the other region.* Assuming this time that region B undergoes complete specialization, we have $\lambda_B^* = 0$, $n_B^* = 0$, and $w_A^* = w_B^* = 1$. In region A, the share of manufacturing employment, the number of varieties, and price of these varieties ($\lambda_A^* < 1$, n_A^*, and p_A^*) are simultaneously determined by solving (7.15)–(7.17) written for region A only.

---

[5] We refer the reader to Puga (1999) for the only (albeit incomplete) analytical treatment of this model.

(4) *One region completely specializes in manufacturing, while the other completely specializes in agriculture.* Again, $\lambda_B^* = 0$, $n_B^* = 0$, and $w_B^* = 1$ in the agricultural region, while $\lambda_A^* = 1$ in the industrial one. Compared with the previous scenario, $w_A^* > 1$ replaces λ_A^* in region A's system of equations (7.15)–(7.17).

This would leave us with one final possible case, in which *both regions completely specialize in the same sector, i.e., manufacturing or agriculture.* In fact, this situation cannot be an equilibrium. To see this, note that if the supply for a good were to approach zero in both regions, its price would approach infinity because its marginal utility would tend toward infinity (recall that individual utilities are of the Cobb–Douglas type). Under such circumstances, there is necessarily a point at which it would become profitable to produce in the missing sector. To sum up, only the four previous scenarios are possible.

At this stage, it is important to grasp the economic contexts corresponding to the different values each of the parameters can take, and how different parameter values influence the spatial distribution of economic activity as well as the degree of spatial inequality. This requires a deeper understanding of the properties of equilibria, which we leave to the next section. There are five main parameters of interest: the trade cost, τ, the share of the manufactured good in final consumption, y, the share of the manufactured good in intermediate consumption, μ, the elasticity of substitution, σ, and the fixed requirement, f. In the rest of this chapter, we mainly focus on the impact of the first three parameters.

7.2   The Spatial Distribution of the Manufacturing Sector

Finding an analytical solution for the CP model is difficult, not to say impossible. The present framework bears the added challenge of dealing with the existence of four different scenarios, instead of two. This involved task is likely to have discouraged Krugman and Venables from pursuing the formal analysis of their model further. In what follows, at the risk of trading in rigor for pragmatism, we use simulations drawn from Fujita et al. (1999, chapter 14) to present the main results. The manufactured good's share in household consumption plays a key role in determining the spatial equilibrium. More precisely, it is important to discriminate between the following two cases: $y < \frac{1}{2}$ and $y > \frac{1}{2}$.

7.2.1   Incomplete Specialization of the Core ($y < \frac{1}{2}$)

Figures 7.1–7.5 are helpful in understanding which of the various possible equilibria are more likely to emerge in the long run. The x-axis (respectively, y-axis) represents the fraction of labor used in region A's (respectively, B's) manufacturing sector, meaning that each point in the positive quadrant corresponds to a short-run equilibrium that satisfies equations (7.15)–(7.17). The curve labeled $w_A = 1$ (respectively, $w_B = 1$) traces out all possible combinations (λ_A, λ_B) for which the wage in region A (respectively, B) is equal to 1 in the short run. Note that curves $w_A = 1$ and $w_B = 1$ are both decreasing. To the left of curve $w_A = 1$, the wage is such that $w_A > 1$, which implies that the number of manufacturing employees is too low to satisfy labor demand. In turn, this causes an upward pressure on their wage, which becomes higher than the wage in agriculture. This leads to higher prices in the manufacturing sector, hence a drop in the demand for this good as well as in firms' labor demand. The reverse holds true to the right of $w_A = 1$, where $w_A < 1$. In the long run, since workers are sectorally mobile, they choose the sector with the higher wage. In the first case (to the left of $w_A = 1$), wages are higher in the manufacturing sector, which leads to an inflow of workers; in the second case, we would expect an outflow. The same reasoning holds for region B. These dynamic labor flows are illustrated by a horizontal (respectively, vertical) arrow for region A (respectively, B), pointing either right or left (respectively, up or down).

7.2.1.1 High Trade Costs and Symmetric Equilibrium

Figure 7.1 illustrates the two iso-wage curves when trade costs are high. Note that they intersect at point S, which lies on the bisector. At this point, both the wages and shares of labor are identical across regions ($w_A^* = w_B^* = 1$ and $\lambda_A^* = \lambda_B^*$), which means that the equilibrium is symmetric: the number of varieties and the price indexes are identical. As in the CP model, we are faced with the following two questions:

(i) Is this equilibrium stable?

(ii) Are there other equilibria?

Before tackling these questions, it should be noted that in a symmetric pattern, the share of manufacturing employment in each region is equal to y. This result can be obtained analytically by solving the equations (7.15)–(7.17) in which we set $w_A^* = w_B^* = 1$, $p_A^* = p_B^*$, and $n_A^* = n_B^*$.

The symmetric equilibrium appears to be stable when trade costs are sufficiently high. In particular, in the neighborhood of this equilibrium, curve $w_A = 1$ has a greater slope than curve $w_B = 1$.[6] When the economy moves away from the symmetric equilibrium, an intersectoral labor flow

---

[6] Under autarky, $w_A = 1$ is given by a vertical line at y, and $w_B = 1$ is given by a horizontal line at y.

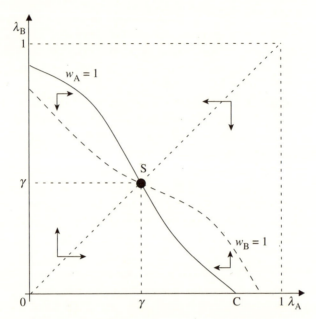

Figure 7.1. Employment distribution when trade costs are high and final demand is low.

brings the economy back to the initial point. To see this, imagine decreasing the number of industrial workers in both regions (we move slightly southwest from point S), thus implying that the wage in the manufacturing sector becomes greater than 1 in both regions. This wage differential induces some agricultural workers to move back into the manufacturing sector, thereby lowering the number of agricultural workers until the economy is back to the symmetric equilibrium. Alternatively, imagine increasing the number of industrial workers in region A while decreasing their number in region B (we move slightly southeast from point S), such that the economy now finds itself poised between the two curves: in region A workers are encouraged to turn to the better-paid agricultural sector, while the inverse holds in region B, since the wage in the manufacturing sector is greater than 1. Once again, market forces bring the economy back to symmetric equilibrium. To sum up, when trade costs are high, the pattern in which both regions host the same share of the manufacturing sector is a stable equilibrium.

Are there other equilibria? When moving to the right or to the left of the symmetric equilibrium S, the two iso-wage curves fail to intersect again, meaning that no other interior equilibria exist. However, this does not preclude the existence of corner equilibria, in which complete specialization occurs in at least one of the two regions. Imagine an economy

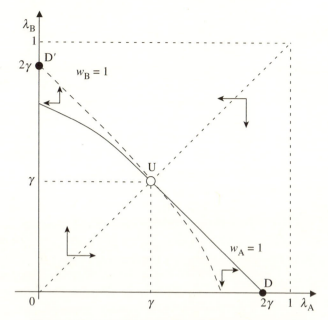

Figure 7.2. Employment distribution when trade
costs are low and final demand is low.

situated to the left of the point C where curve $w_B = 1$ intersects the
x-axis. In this case, region B would only have agricultural workers. However, these workers want to switch to the manufacturing sector because
the corresponding wage is greater than 1. Thus, such a configuration
cannot be an equilibrium. To the right of point C, the absence of the
manufacturing sector in region B is in itself stable, but workers from
region A's manufacturing sector wish to move into agriculture. This net
outflow of agricultural workers pushes the economy back to point C.
Once again, this scenario is not an equilibrium. We can apply the same
logic to all other potential corner equilibria, meaning that *when trade
costs are high and the share of manufacturing in final consumption lower
than* $\frac{1}{2}$*, the symmetric equilibrium is the only stable equilibrium.*

7.2.1.2 Low Trade Costs and Asymmetric Equilibria

Figure 7.2 traces out the same curves, but under low trade costs. As for
the situation when trade costs are high, these curves intersect only once,
at point U (that is, on the bisector), but curve $w_B = 1$ now has a steeper
slope than curve $w_A = 1$ at this point. In this case, the symmetric equilibrium is no longer stable. To see this, imagine increasing the size of the
manufacturing sector in region A while reducing it in region B, so that the
economy lies between the two curves. The manufacturing wage is thus

higher than 1 in region A. This gives rise to a further inflow of workers into the manufacturing sector and moves the economy away from the symmetric equilibrium. Similarly, a wage differential in favor of agriculture arises in region B, thus inducing this region's workers to work in agriculture. Again, the economy strays from the symmetric equilibrium.[7]

On the other hand, an equilibrium does emerge when the whole manufacturing sector is agglomerated in region A. Geometrically, this corresponds to the intersection of curve $w_A = 1$ and the x-axis at point D. Furthermore, this equilibrium turns out to be stable. Recall that in figure 7.1, all points located to the right of point C were stable for region B's labor market. In this case, when moving away from D toward the right, we increase the size of the manufacturing sector in region A, making for a relatively lower wage and triggering the now familiar move that brings the economy back to D. The same proves to be true when moving leftward from D. In the same manner, it can be shown that the intersection point D′ of curve $w_B = 1$ and the y-axis is also a stable equilibrium. In other words, *when trade costs are low and the share of manufacturing in final consumption is lower than $\frac{1}{2}$, the manufacturing sector is concentrated in a single region, while the agricultural sector is unevenly split between both regions.* Furthermore, this equilibrium is both stable and unique.[8]

Note that the share of the manufacturing sector can be determined analytically. Plugging $w_A^* = w_B^* = 1$ as well as $\lambda_B^* = n_B^* = 0$ into region A's equations (7.15)–(7.17) and solving the resulting expressions yields $\lambda_A^* = 2y$. This is an equilibrium so long as $y < \frac{1}{2}$ (which explains why we have made this assumption under $\lambda_A < 1$). It is also worth noting that, although the manufacturing share in total employment is the same under both high and low trade costs ($2y$), the two equilibria do not involve the same number of varieties, unlike the CP model, in which the number of varieties is the same regardless of the equilibrium reached.

7.2.1.3 Intermediate Trade Costs and Multiple Equilibria

Figure 7.3 illustrates the two iso-wage curves obtained for intermediate values of trade costs. By following the same reasoning as for the two previous cases, we find that both a locally stable symmetric equilibrium (S) and two locally stable asymmetric equilibrium (D and D′) now coexist, while two asymmetric interior equilibria (U and U′) are unstable.

---

[7] If one decreases manufacturing employment in both regions simultaneously, the economy moves back to point U. Therefore, point U corresponds to a saddle-path equilibrium, which is not a stable equilibrium.

[8] Up to a permutation of regions, as in the CP model.

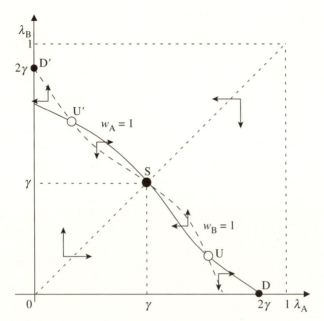

Figure 7.3. Employment distribution when trade costs are intermediate and final demand is low.

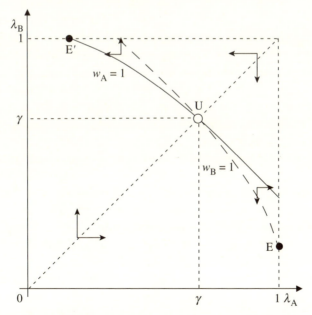

Figure 7.4. Employment distribution when trade costs are low and final demand is very high.

7.2.2   Complete Specialization of the Core ($y > \frac{1}{2}$)

The above analysis has a number of features in common with Krugman's
CP model: the manufacturing sector is fully agglomerated in one region
once trade costs are sufficiently low; dispersion prevails when these
costs are sufficiently high; and two different types of stable equilibria
coexist for intermediate values of trade costs. However, for this to be so,
the manufactured good's share in final consumption must be sufficiently
low ($y < \frac{1}{2}$). Indeed, under this assumption, the agglomeration force at
work has made manufacturing completely disappear from one region,
while the agricultural sector continues to exist in the other region. As
a result, wages remain the same and equal to 1 in both regions. This is
because the size, $2y$, of the manufacturing sector does not absorb the
entire regional labor force (which has been normalized to 1) since $y < \frac{1}{2}$.

These conclusions are no longer valid when $y > \frac{1}{2}$. Two cases may
arise. In the first case, when the manufactured good's share in final consumption is very high ($y \gg \frac{1}{2}$), simulations reveal the existence of a
new equilibrium characterized by *the complete specialization of the core
region with a wage rate exceeding* 1, along with the partial specialization
of the other region in agriculture. In other words, even though region A
is completely specialized in manufacturing, the final demand for the corresponding good is so large that manufacturing firms continue to exist
in region B in order to satisfy it. Figure 7.4 illustrates this scenario.

In this case, the asymmetric equilibrium is given by point E, situated
at the intersection of the curve $w_B = 1$ and the vertical line $\lambda_A = 1$. To
the left of E, the wage in region A is higher than 1, which attracts workers to this region's manufacturing sector. The same would be true in
region B if the size of the agricultural sector were to grow. If this sector
decreased in size, the wage would drop below 1, thus raising the number
of agricultural workers. These dynamics confirm that point E is indeed
a stable asymmetric equilibrium. Note that such an equilibrium, characterized by the complete specialization of one region in manufacturing
and the presence of both agriculture and manufacturing in the other, can
coexist with a symmetric equilibrium when trade costs are higher than
in the previous case: the iso-wage curves take on the same shapes as in
figure 7.3, but they lie more northeasterly and intersect lines $\lambda_A = 1$ and
$\lambda_B = 1$ before crossing the x- and y-axes.

The second case, illustrated in figure 7.5, shows what happens when
the share of final consumption is lower, but still greater than $\frac{1}{2}$. Here,
the equilibrium is characterized by a *reciprocal complete specialization*,
the final demand being insufficient to keep firms within the peripheral
region. In this case, while curve $w_A = 1$ intersects line $\lambda_A = 1$ before

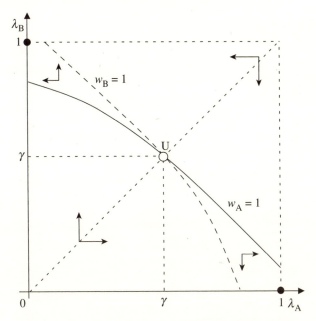

Figure 7.5. Employment distribution when trade
costs are low and final demand is high.

crossing the x-axis, the inverse occurs for curve $w_B = 1$. Consequently,
the point defined by $\lambda_A = 1$ and $\lambda_B = 0$ is a stable equilibrium.

Thus, as in the CP model, there are sets of parameter values that yield
multiple equilibria and, above all, that can bring about the coexistence
of equilibria *with and without* regional asymmetry. The novelty of the
present framework lies in the fact that *partial agglomeration may arise*.
In the CP model, the manufacturing sector disappears completely from
one region as soon as it becomes concentrated in the other, while here
industries can be split unevenly between two regions. That said, simulations reveal that only one sector can be unevenly split between the two
regions: there exists no equilibrium involving the two sectors unevenly
divided between the two regions. In other words, *an asymmetric equilibrium always implies the complete specialization of at least one of the
two regions*. We will see below that these asymmetric equilibria are at
the root of a new dynamics of regional disparities, which the CP model
does not account for.

7.2.3 The Impact of Trade Costs on Spatial Concentration

To sum up, figure 7.6 depicts the manufacturing sector's share in the
two regions as trade costs vary when the final demand share is high

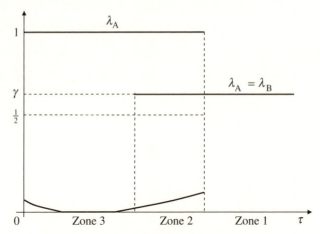

Figure 7.6. Manufacturing share and trade
costs when final consumption is high.

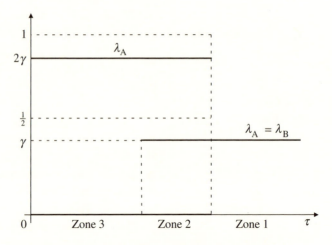

Figure 7.7. Manufacturing share and trade
costs when final consumption is low.

($\gamma > \frac{1}{2}$), while figure 7.7 does the same when the final demand share is
low ($\gamma < \frac{1}{2}$).

In the former case, when trade costs are high, only the symmetric
equilibrium is stable (zone 1). A decrease in trade costs leads to the
emergence of a stable asymmetric equilibrium, which coexists with the
symmetric equilibrium (zone 2). Under even lower trade costs, the latter equilibrium ceases to be stable (zone 3). However, in contrast with
the Krugman model, *partial* agglomeration in the core is possible. For
instance, the core is completely specialized in manufacturing as soon as

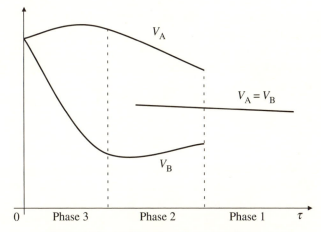

Figure 7.8. Welfare levels and trade costs.

a stable asymmetric equilibrium exists, but industry may still exist in the periphery. Over a domain of zone 3, however, industry completely vanishes from the periphery, even though it represents a large share of the final demand ($y \gg \frac{1}{2}$).

The latter case (figure 7.7) paints a fairly similar picture, the main difference being that, under any asymmetric equilibrium, *manufacturing completely disappears from the periphery* and so, because manufacturing represents a small share of the final demand ($y < \frac{1}{2}$), while some agricultural activities are maintained in the core. Here, trade costs play nearly the same role as in the Krugman model.

7.3 The Evolution of Regional Disparities

One of the main goals of economic geography is to study the impact of economic integration on spatial inequality. Trade costs serve as a proxy for economic integration, a reduction in these costs being tantamount to a greater degree of integration. Once again, we appeal to simulations to grasp their impact.

7.3.1 The Bell-Shaped Relationship between Economic Integration and Spatial Inequality

Figure 7.8 illustrates the welfare of a representative individual (i.e., his real wage) in each of the two regions as a function of the level of trade costs.

When trade costs are high, the spatial economy involves a symmetric pattern: manufacturing shares are the same in both regions as are nominal wages, both being equal to 1. Given that the fraction of imported varieties is also identical for both regions, the price indices must also be the same. Hence, there is no spatial inequality. So long as the symmetric equilibrium prevails, economic integration induces welfare gains that are distributed evenly between the two regions. Two positive effects are at work here: one is direct, the other indirect. First, the price index decreases because it increases with the level of trade costs (as in the CP model). Second, the drop in the price index leads to a decrease in both the marginal cost and fixed production costs via (7.8) and (7.9). Under lower production costs, some workers can be reallocated to the production of new varieties, thereby creating a further drop in the price index. This second effect is absent from the CP model, where the total number of varieties is constant.

Let us now consider the set of parameter values that yields both symmetric and asymmetric equilibria. At the asymmetric equilibrium, the existence of a larger manufacturing sector in one region generates higher profits for the firms located there. Indeed, firms benefit from both the supply-side and the demand-side: local intermediate demand is higher, thus making for a larger market than in the other region; production costs are smaller because of the lower price index. These two forces feed on each other, just as the growth of final demand is self-reinforcing in the CP model. Specifically, *the greater the size of the manufacturing sector in one region, the stronger the demand for intermediate varieties and the lower production costs in that region,* the combination of which contributes to a further increase in the size of the manufacturing sector.

A now familiar dispersion force comes to curb this agglomeration process. Indeed, very much as in the CP model, the demand for the manufactured good remains substantial in the periphery since the labor force is immobile, while a market-crowding effect occurs in the core. With this in mind, two cases may arise. First, assume the manufactured good's share in final consumption is low. Thus, the overall size of the manufacturing sector is not large enough for this sector to be present in the periphery. This is the asymmetric equilibrium illustrated by point D in figure 7.2, where both sectors are present in the core, while only the agricultural sector is active in the periphery, and wages are the same and equal to 1 for both regions. In the second situation, final demand for the manufactured good is high, making the cumulative mechanisms of agglomeration strong enough to lead to the core's complete specialization, while allowing for the manufacturing sector to be in the periphery. However, the core's nominal wage becomes strictly greater than 1, which gives rise to two opposing forces affecting the spatial equilibrium. The first is a further agglomeration force generated by the higher demand stemming from the core's workers higher income, since they enjoy a wage exceeding 1, the wage received in the periphery. The second, which is very intuitive but tends to be overlooked in CP models, is a new dispersion force. Given that regions have a fixed labor supply, the cost of labor is higher in the region characterized by a high concentration of economic activity. Beyond some point, this new dispersion force, combined with those of the CP model, stops, or even reverses, the process of agglomeration. In particular, *the rise in the cost of labor is a major force in triggering a reindustrialization of the periphery.*

We have seen that, when the core specializes in manufacturing, this sector may or may not cease to exist in the periphery. If this sector is present in both regions, the resulting equilibrium makes the producers of the manufactured good indifferent to location; the arbitrage is fairly involved, however. Let us consider the case in which the core is completely specialized. In choosing the periphery, a producer faces less competition on its local market as well as lower labor costs; however, it suffers from a lower intermediate demand, a weaker final demand because local wages are lower, and more costly intermediate inputs because trade costs apply to a larger fraction of the varieties used as inputs. When locating in the core, a producer's incentives are the inverse: there is more competition on the product market, a higher cost of labor as well as a lower cost for intermediate inputs, but intermediate and final demands are higher. When the core is not fully specialized, the above wage effects vanish.

Finally, as trade costs continue to decrease, the symmetric equilibrium ceases to be stable. Only the asymmetric equilibrium, in which the core hosts a larger share of the manufacturing sector, remains stable until full integration is achieved.

As in chapter 6, the agglomeration and dispersion forces have relative intensities that vary with the level of trade costs; thus, the resulting net outcome translates into different degrees of spatial inequality. In particular, the simulations above suggest that economic integration can be broken down into three main phases.

Phase 1. As discussed, at first economic integration occurs free of regional disparities, with both regions experiencing a simultaneous and equal increase in welfare.

Phase 2. As soon as an asymmetric equilibrium emerges, inequality follows. Indeed, while the nominal wage remains constant in the periphery, the fraction of imported varieties shoots up, which in turn pushes up the price index and reduces welfare in this region. Conversely, workers in the core not only benefit from a higher fraction of locally produced varieties but may also enjoy a higher nominal wage (in the case of complete specialization). In addition, *the interregional divergence may even continue to grow as economic integration deepens*. As illustrated in figure 7.8, the real wage gap becomes increasingly greater, because of

   (i) the increasing asymmetry in the share of locally produced varieties (see figure 7.6),

  (ii) the demand and cost feedback effects, and

 (iii) higher labor costs once specialization is complete (this is never the case in figure 7.8 but may occur in figure 7.11).

The decrease in trade costs and the resulting increase in the total number of varieties (which are welfare-enhancing for both core and periphery) do not necessarily outweigh the welfare-reducing effects experienced by the periphery, since it must import a larger number of varieties. Thus, the periphery workers may suffer a decrease in welfare.

Phase 3. With greater economic integration, the effects described in phase 2 are eventually reversed: not only does the periphery's welfare cease to decrease (if that was the case), but we are witness to *a phase of convergence between the regions*, the welfare gap between the two gradually diminishing. As the demand for labor keeps rising in the core, its cost increases once specialization becomes complete, an effect that amplifies competition in the core, giving (new) firms the incentive to relocate in the periphery once trade costs are low enough. Given the now decreasing fraction of imported varieties (see figure 7.6), workers in the periphery will enjoy a lower price index, while the opposite holds for their counterparts in the core. Furthermore, the latter see their nominal wages decline because of lower labor market tension in the core. The inhabitants of both regions continue to benefit from the reduction in trade costs and the greater number of varieties produced.

Ultimately, if full integration were possible ($\tau = 1$), the cost of labor and the price index would be equalized across both regions. In this case, regional disparities disappear altogether: regional welfare levels are equal and greater than they were at the initial symmetric equilibrium. However, inhabitants of the core may prefer intermediate integration over full integration, as the disappearance of spatial inequality may arise at the cost of a drop in their welfare.

In short, as mentioned in our foreword, *the relationship between the degree of economic integration and regional disparities traces out a bell-shaped curve*, which is depicted in figure 7.9. So long as the economy

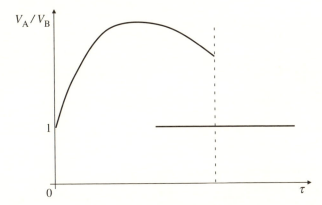

Figure 7.9. Welfare and trade costs: the bell-shaped curve.

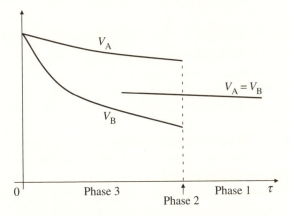

Figure 7.10. Welfare levels and trade costs
when the final consumption is high.

remains at the symmetric equilibrium, there is no spatial inequality and economic integration induces only efficiency gains. Switching to the asymmetric equilibrium sparks a positive hike in spatial inequality. Then, spatial inequality keeps increasing during the integration process. Once a certain threshold of integration has been reached, inequality progressively decreases.

7.3.2 The Structure of the Demand for the Manufactured Good

Two sources drive the demand for the manufactured good: workers and firms. As such, it is worth examining their respective impacts. Let us first assume that the manufactured good's share in final consumption y is greater than under the simulations considered in the previous section. Figure 7.10 illustrates the welfare levels reached in each region.

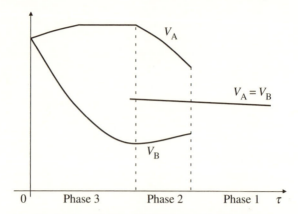

Figure 7.11. Welfare levels and trade costs when
the intermediate consumption is high.

Again, a bell-shaped curve emerges between trade costs and spatial inequality. Yet the divergence between regions is less pronounced when final demand for the manufactured good is lower (see figure 7.8). A higher manufacturing share is located in the periphery, which increases the relative number of varieties produced there and decreases the price index. This amounts to saying that *an increase in the manufactured good's share in final consumption accelerates the relocation of activities to the periphery.* This is corroborated by observing that, once the asymmetric equilibrium has been reached, the utility of periphery workers ceases to decrease and the utility of core consumers rises up to the level achieved under perfect integration, while never achieving a maximum as observed in figure 7.8.

As illustrated in figure 7.11, these results are reversed when the manufactured good's share in a firm's production μ takes a large value. In this case, regional inequalities are more pronounced than the scenario illustrated in figure 7.8. A greater jump occurs when moving from the symmetric equilibrium to the asymmetric equilibrium, with the periphery experiencing a sharp welfare decline during the divergence phase. The core's utility reaches a maximum and remains at this level for a whole range of trade costs. This corresponds to the case where all varieties are produced there, the periphery being fully specialized in agriculture, a situation that does not arise under the parameter values corresponding to figures 7.8 and 7.10. Finally, when the economy switches from the symmetric to the asymmetric equilibrium, spatial inequality rises sharply but keeps decreasing afterwards (in this case, phase 2 disappears).

A cursory reading of this discussion might suggest that these results are at odds with the CP model. Indeed, a central result in the Krugman model is that spatial inequality is stronger when the manufactured good's share in final consumption is large: a conclusion that runs opposite to ours. Actually, as the share of final consumption grows, the spatial immobility of labor implies here an increase in the periphery's demand. In turn, this demand becomes a stronger dispersion force. Thus, it makes sense for this hike in demand to lead to a decline in regional disparities. Conversely, when the share of the manufactured good in production increases, firms' mobile demand increases (the very demand that drives the self-reinforcing process of agglomeration). It is logical to witness the strengthening of inequalities in this case.

Therefore, the key issue is not so much whether the demand for the manufactured good increases because of final or intermediate consumption, but acknowledging instead the importance of the demand emanating from mobile versus immobile agents. In particular, an increase in the demand expressed by *mobile* agents (skilled workers in Krugman, firms here) reinforces the asymmetry between regions. On the contrary, an increase in the demand stemming from *immobile* agents (unskilled workers in Krugman, the whole labor force here) fosters a more balanced regional development. This explains our notational change of the share of varieties in final consumption in the two models. In particular, even though μ has a different economic meaning in the two models, this parameter's impact on interregional inequality is the same, as it captures the size of the inequality-fostering *mobile demand*, while parameters $1 - \mu$ and γ both capture the size of the *immobile demand*, which is conducive to a more balanced development.

As a final remark, it should be emphasized that Krugman and Venables' model enriches the study of the dynamics of regional disparities and brings to light a bell-shaped relationship between economic integration and spatial inequality. The underlying mechanisms are markedly different from those at work in the CP model. Empirically they are more in keeping with the limited degree of interregional migrations occurring within the European Union, and the importance of intermediate good in production processes. Including these two new variables sheds light on additional demand-side effects as well as an endogenous, competitive-advantage effect based on the cost of intermediate goods.

7.4 Concluding Remarks

Interpretation of the results drawn from the CP model warrants a degree of caution. Indeed, the analysis provided in this chapter suggests that the evolution of the spatial distribution of economic activity depends on the interaction between several forces, only a few of which are taken into account in the CP model. Accounting for such additional, empirically relevant effects (e.g., the demand for intermediate goods and the low spatial mobility of labor) brings to light a bell-shaped relationship between spatial inequality and economic integration. This relationship is at odds with the CP model's main conclusion, which suggests that a decreasing and monotonous relationship is at work instead. Including these additional variables leads us to believe that the twin goals of economic efficiency and spatial equality may be pursued simultaneously, at least once a certain level of integration has been reached. This concurs with Fujita et al. (1999, p. 260) for whom "declining trade costs first produce, then dissolve, the global inequality of nations." In the next chapter, we will see that similar bell-shaped relationships between economic integration and spatial inequality emerge in a number of other contexts, thus endowing this relationship with strong theoretical foundations.

To conclude, it should be emphasized that some of the forces leading to the relocation of firms are based on the existence of wage differentials across regions, wages being higher in the core. We may thus safely conclude that any policy or labor market institution preventing regional wage adjustments thwarts the spatial redistribution of firms, thereby consolidating the core–periphery structure (Faini 1999).

7.5   Related Literature

The models put forward by Krugman and Venables (1995) and Venables (1996) are difficult to handle. Aside from Puga (1999), there have been very few models that have built on these original works. By drawing on section 6.2, one could replace (7.5) by

$$l_A^{1-\mu} K_A^{\mu} = \frac{f}{C_\mu}.$$

This allows one to integrate the consumption of intermediate goods more easily, since only fixed costs depend on the varieties' price index, marginal costs now being constant. This simplification of the Krugman–Venables model has been studied by Ottaviano and Robert-Nicoud (2006) in the special case where $y = \mu < \frac{1}{2}$. They show that the set of equilibria is identical to those found by Krugman. This simplification, therefore, hides the bell-shaped curve, which is why we did not delve into it above. Fujita and Thisse (2002, chapter 9) consider another simplification in which the final sector produces a homogeneous good. They go on to demonstrate that two sectors agglomerate within the same region provided trade costs for intermediate goods exceeds a certain threshold.

Finally, Toulemonde (2006) has identified another mechanism of agglomeration, which bears some strong resemblance to what we have seen in this chapter. When workers are a priori unskilled and immobile, some of them may choose to become skilled in order to be able to work in the manufacturing sector. As a result, they earn a higher income and, therefore, have a higher demand for manufacturing goods, making their region a larger and more attractive market to firms. At the same time, the installation of new firms within this region gives a stronger incentive to workers to improve their skill. As above, we obtain a mechanism of cumulative causation in which spatial mobility is replaced by sector-based mobility. Combining this mechanism with skilled workers' greater spatial mobility may help to account for the strong spatial concentration of human capital observed in many developed countries (Moretti 2004), an issue that is further discussed in chapter 11.

8

The Bell-Shaped Curve of
Spatial Development

The two basic models of economic geography studied in chapters 6 and 7 are built on the Dixit–Stiglitz model of monopolistic competition. We have already seen that this model does not allow us to account for the procompetitive effects generated by falling trade costs and the formation of an agglomeration. This modeling strategy thus has the undesirable consequence of reducing the intensity of both agglomeration and dispersion forces. Indeed, the dispersion force is weaker because firms' markups are the same on the periphery and in the core, while we would expect them to be lower in the core due to tougher competition. Likewise, the agglomeration force is also weakened, as workers' real income is not positively affected by the price drop that should occur in the core. It is quite possible, therefore, that the predictions of the previous two chapters depend on this absence of procompetitive effects. This is why it is worth checking whether the main conclusions obtained so far hold true in a context that integrates these effects.

To do this, we use the linear model of monopolistic competition presented in chapter 3, as it allows us to integrate the aforementioned procompetitive effects but without accounting for strategic interactions, as will be done in chapter 9. It should be kept in mind, however, that this model neglects income effects. Furthermore, as observed in chapter 5, an iceberg-like trade cost looks like an *ad valorem* (multiplicative) tax (a customs duty, for example), while a transport cost often puts a strain on the real cost of every unit shipped, meaning that transport costs have the nature of a specific (additive) tax. In fact, these two modeling strategies correspond to different economic realities, which justifies our separate approaches to them. As seen in chapter 1, the two models are relevant because the two types of costs—tariffs and transport costs— have not changed in the same way or over the same periods. Moreover, when trade costs mainly comprise customs duties, they correspond to a transfer from a foreign producer to the importing country that is in turn redistributed to that country's residents. In contrast, the transport cost requires the consumption of scarce resources. In addition, resorting to an iceberg-type trade cost implies that both the mill price and trade costs move together. This is far from a natural assumption, so it is worth considering the case in which these two magnitudes are independent. Finally, as seen in chapter 4, the DSK model does not allow us to study firms segmenting their markets, even though this is common practice, especially on the international marketplace. All of this can easily be achieved by using the linear model.

In the next section, we show that the main results of the CP model remain true in the linear setting. Consequently, they do not seem to be specific to the assumptions of the DSK model or affected by the way in which trade costs are specified. One of the merits of the linear model is that it leads to a complete analytical solution. Furthermore, it will allow us to delve further into the study of new problems in economic geography, thus throwing light on aspects that are often difficult to examine within the Krugman model. In particular, the existence of a *bell-shaped relationship* between economic integration and regional disparities, highlighted in chapter 7, will be reexamined and developed here. More precisely, section 8.2 revisits this property in contexts that are strikingly different from the one explored in the previous chapter. Hence, the bell-shaped relationship can be grounded in very different principles, making it fairly robust. To do this, we account for positive trade costs for the agricultural good (Picard and Zeng 2005), the existence of increasing urban costs generated by the population growth in the core area (Ottaviano et al. 2002), and the heterogeneity of individual attitudes toward migration (Tabuchi and Thisse 2002).

The latter two extensions are fundamental in many respects. The first one captures in a simple but relevant way the idea of *congestion* that any agglomeration of activities brings about in the region concerned. To do this, we will use an urban metaphor, whereby an agglomeration is structured as a monocentric city. In this case, competition for land gives rise to land rent and commuting costs that both increase as the city expands. The second extension offers a much more satisfying approach to the migration processes than that of Krugman. Adam Smith observed long ago that human beings were the most difficult merchandise to move. Leaving aside migratory movements triggered by wars, *individual migration rests on a large number of considerations*, and the economic variables covered by the indirect utility represents only a small fraction of them. A more wide-ranging model of migration behavior is therefore needed.

Before proceeding, it is worth mentioning that many empirical studies suggest that the way a population is spatially distributed is linked to the stage of development of the economy (Williamson 1965). More precisely, an increase in spatial concentration would go hand in hand with the first stages of this process. Later on, there would be a spatial redeployment of activities. The empirical existence of a bell-shaped curve still sparks hot debates, which are beyond the scope of this chapter but will be addressed in chapters 12 and 13. Note, however, that our results throw new light on this subject, to the extent that it links the existence of such a curve to the degree of economic integration between regions: a variable that is likely to be correlated with the level of economic development.

8.1 A Linear Core–Periphery Model

Consider a linear core–periphery model with two regions, A and B. Unskilled labor is used in the agricultural and manufacturing sectors; as usual, it is equally split between the two regions ($\frac{1}{2}L_a$). Skilled labor is used only in the manufacturing sector; a share λ is located in region A, while a share $1 - \lambda$ is located in region B. Individual preferences are represented by a quasi-linear utility nesting a quadratic subutility, as in section 3.2. Consequently, a region A worker has the following indirect utility function:

$$
V_A = \sum_{r=A,B} \left\{ \frac{a^2 n_r}{2b} - a \int_{i \in \mathcal{N}_r} p_{rA}(i)\, di \right.
$$

$$
+ \frac{b + c n_r}{2} \int_{i \in \mathcal{N}_r} [p_{rA}(i)]^2\, di
$$

$$
\left. - \frac{c}{2} \left[\int_{i \in \mathcal{N}_r} p_{rA}(i)\, di \right]^2 \right\} + y + \bar{A}, \quad (8.1)
$$

where $\mathcal{N}_r$ is the set and n_r the mass of varieties produced in region $r = A, B$, $p_{rA}(i)$ is the delivered price in region A of the variety i produced in r, y is the worker's income and $\bar{A}$ is her initial endowment in the numéraire. Setting $N = n_A + n_B$, the demand in region A for the variety i produced in r is given by[1]

$$
q_{rA}(i) = (\tfrac{1}{2}L_a + \lambda L)[a - (b + cN)p_{rA}(i) + cP_A], \quad (8.2)
$$

where P_A is the price index in region A, given by

$$
P_A = \int_{i \in \mathcal{N}_A} p_{AA}(i)\, di + \int_{i \in \mathcal{N}_B} p_{BA}(i)\, di.
$$

---

[1] In what follows, the expressions for region B are obtained by permutating the indices A and B, and by replacing λ with $1 - \lambda$.

The technology is identical to that assumed by Forslid and Ottaviano (see section 6.3). The fixed requirement per firm in skilled labor is $f > 0$, while the marginal requirement m in unskilled labor is assumed to be equal to zero. Since this is formally equivalent to subtracting m from the intercept of the inverse demand function, this does not involve any loss of generality since marginal costs do not vary across locations.[2] Clearing of the regional labor markets implies that the number of firms located in a region is proportional to the number of skilled workers established there, so the following relationships must be satisfied:

$$n_A = \frac{\lambda L}{f} \quad \text{and} \quad n_B = \frac{(1 - \lambda)L}{f}.$$

Consequently, as in Krugman, the region receiving the larger number of skilled workers is also the one that attracts the larger number of firms.

The manufactured good is shipped between regions at the cost of t units of the numéraire per unit traded. As seen in chapter 4, Krugman's model cannot distinguish between *integrated* and *segmented* markets, while the linear model enables us to consider both mill and discriminatory pricing. In this chapter, we will focus on the latter case, in order to compare the possible impact of different spatial pricing policies. This means that each firm is able to choose a specific delivered price in the market in which it sells its variety, while bearing trade costs. In other words, there is spatial price discrimination, whereby the mill price varies according to the region in which the variety is sold. This assumption is fairly realistic in many sectors where firms are able to separate markets based on customers' locations. For example, Greenhut (1981) observes that the majority of American, German, and Japanese firms practice some form of spatial price discrimination. Likewise, Haskel and Wolf (2001) note that the price differences between national markets on identical products sold by IKEA stores can vary from 20 to 50% and show that these gaps cannot be explained by differences between tax rates and customs duties. Such price differences confirm what we have seen in chapter 5, i.e., the existence of significant and important border effects; other studies, reviewed in chapter 9, illustrate the various pricing strategies that firms might elect once they deliver their products and observe their customers' locations.

---

[2] Such a normalization would make no sense in the case of a DSK-based model. As CES preferences imply a constant relative markup, the equilibrium price would in effect be equal to zero. As the markup here, in contrast, is additive, our normalization is equivalent to a simple downward translation of the demand functions.

8.1.1   Equilibrium Prices and Variable Markups

We have seen in chapter 3 how prices are determined in the linear model within a closed economy. Under trade with segmented markets, each firm chooses a specific delivered price for each region. In other words, the firm i located in region A chooses its prices $p_{AA}(i)$ and $p_{AB}(i)$ in order to maximize its profits, taking the price index in each region as given. As the marginal requirement of labor has been normalized to zero, its profit function may be written

$$\pi_A(i) = p_{AA}(i)q_{AA}(i) + [p_{AB}(i) - t]q_{AB}(i) - fw_A,$$

where w_A is the region A wage of the skilled workers.

Using the demand functions (8.2) and differentiating $\pi_A(i)$ with respect to $p_{AA}(i)$ and $p_{AB}(i)$, we obtain two linear equations with two unknowns whose solution is given by

$$p_{AA}^*(P_A) = \frac{a + cP_A}{2(b + cn)},$$

$$p_{AB}^*(P_B) = \frac{a + cP_B}{2(b + cn)} + \frac{t}{2}.$$

Hence, firms established in the same region have the same domestic and delivered prices. Using the price index definition leads to

$$P_A = n_A p_{AA}^*(P_A) + n_B p_{BA}^*(P_A).$$

Plugging $p_{AA}^*(P_A)$ and $p_{BA}^*(P_A)$ into this expression allows us to obtain the equilibrium value of P_A and, then, the equilibrium prices:

$$P_A^* = \frac{aN + tn_B(b + cn)}{2b + cN},$$

$$p_{AA}^* = \frac{1}{2}\frac{2a + ctn_B}{2b + cN}, \tag{8.3}$$

$$p_{AB}^* = p_{BB}^* + \frac{t}{2}. \tag{8.4}$$

Note also that

$$p_{AA}^*(P_A) = \frac{P_A}{N} - \frac{tn_B}{2N},$$

$$p_{AB}^*(P_B) = \frac{P_B}{N} + \frac{tn_B}{2N}.$$

Because of trade costs ($t > 0$), firms sell in their local market at a price lower than the average price prevailing there (P_A/N), but sell at a price exceeding the average price in their foreign market (P_B/N). In particular, the price of imported varieties always exceeds the price of domestic varieties. Moreover, unlike what we have seen in Krugman's model, *equilibrium prices depend on firms' interregional distribution, as well as on the level of trade costs.* Specifically, it follows from (8.3) that the local equilibrium price p_{AA}^* decreases with the number of firms located in A since $n_B = N - n_A$ (local competition is tougher) and increases with the freight charges (the penetration of foreign varieties is more difficult). As a result, the relocation of firms from region B to region A pushes up domestic prices in the region of origin, but pushes them down in the host region. These procompetitive effects, which are absent from the DSK model, are the result of the interactions across firms brought to light by the linear model.

We also have

$$p_{AB}^* - p_{AA}^* = \frac{ct(n_A - n_B)}{2(2b + cN)} + \frac{t}{2}.$$

In other words, at the equilibrium prices, *arbitrage between regions is never profitable,* since we always have $p_{AB}^* - p_{AA}^* < t$, the largest value of

$$\frac{ct(n_A - n_B)}{2(2b + cN)}$$

being strictly smaller than $\frac{1}{2}t$ (it never pays for a consumer to buy in one place and to resell in another). This *partial freight absorption* arises because the foreign demand has a higher elasticity than the local demand once firms bear trade costs. This induces an exporting firm to lower its price in order to facilitate its penetration of the foreign market.[3] Such a practice, which characterizes spatial price discrimination, favors exported goods at the expense of local ones, as it biases the relative prices in favor of the former against the latter. Furthermore, $p_{AB}^* - p_{AA}^* > \frac{1}{2}t$ if and only if $n_A > n_B$. This means that a firm located in the big (respectively, small) region absorbs a lower (respectively, higher) share of the trade costs it bears to sell its variety in the foreign region.

By subtracting t from (8.3) and (8.4), it is readily verified that the mill prices are positive, whatever the distribution λ, if and only if

$$t < t_{\text{trade}} \equiv \frac{2a}{2b + cN} = \frac{2af}{2bf + cL}. \tag{8.5}$$

Moreover, this condition must also be verified in order for the consumers located in region B to buy from the firms set up in A, i.e., for the individual demands evaluated at equilibrium prices to be positive in each region. We assume throughout the rest of this chapter that (8.5) is always satisfied.

---

[3] The same logic explains the "reciprocal dumping" highlighted in models of international trade with oligopolistic competition (Brander and Krugman 1983).

A final comment is in order. Once trade costs are positive, there is no interregional trade when returns to scale are not increasing ($f = 0$) or varieties are homogeneous ($c = \infty$) because (8.5) does not hold. In each case, both regions offer all the varieties (there is an infinite number of them in the former case and they are all identical in the latter), which implies that each region is in autarky. More generally, it is readily verified that

$$\frac{dt_{trade}}{df} > 0 \quad \text{and} \quad \frac{dt_{trade}}{dy} < 0,$$

meaning that stronger scale economies and more differentiated varieties foster trade.

Note, finally, that the equilibrium consumption of the numéraire changes with the distribution of firms. Since individual preferences are quasi-linear, this consumption is given by the residual income after the spending on the manufactured good has been deducted.

8.1.2 Profits and Wages

Linear demand properties may be used to show that the equilibrium operating profits made in each market by a firm established in region A have the following form:

$$\pi^*_{AA} = (p^*_{AA})^2 (b + cN) \left(\frac{L_a}{2} + fn_A \right)$$

$$= (p^*_{AA})^2 \left(b + \frac{cL}{f} \right) \left(\frac{L_a}{2} + \lambda L \right),$$

$$\pi^*_{AB} = (p^*_{AB} - t)^2 (b + cN) \left(\frac{L_a}{2} + fn_B \right)$$

$$= (p^*_{AB} - t)^2 \left(b + \frac{cL}{f} \right) \left[\frac{L_a}{2} + (1 - \lambda)L \right].$$

It is clear from the first expression that an increase in the number of local skilled workers (and of firms) has two opposite effects on π^*_{AA}. On the one hand, it sparks a reduction in the equilibrium price (the competition effect) and in the quantity sold to a region A consumer (the consumer demand is more fragmented because of the larger number of locally produced varieties). On the other hand, the total population of consumers residing in this region increases, so the profits made by a region A firm from its local sales are higher. Despite the downward pressure on profits triggered by the relocation of some skilled workers, this positive market size effect, which originates from this very relocation, may compensate firms for the negative competition effect, which also stems from the increase in the number of firms located in the same region. This trade-off is similar to that found in Krugman. However, the concentration of firms within the same market makes competition fiercer here.

In partial-equilibrium settings, the consumer surplus is defined by the area between the demand curve and the market price. The surplus, $C_A^*(\lambda)$, of a region A consumer, evaluated at the equilibrium prices (8.3) and (8.4), is therefore given by

$$
\begin{aligned}
C_A^*(\lambda) = {} & \frac{a^2 L}{2bf} - \frac{aL}{f}[\lambda p_{AA}^* + (1 - \lambda)p_{BA}^*] \\
& + \frac{(bf + cL)L}{2f^2}[\lambda(p_{AA}^*)^2 + (1 - \lambda)(p_{BA}^*)^2] \\
& - \frac{cL^2}{2f^2}[\lambda p_{AA}^* + (1 - \lambda)p_{BA}^*].
\end{aligned}
$$

As shown by taking the first derivative of this expression with respect to λ, (8.5) implies that $C_A^*(\lambda)$ is always increasing over $[0, 1]$. This is because more varieties are produced in A and need not be imported. However, the second derivative shows that $C_A^*(\lambda)$ is strictly concave, meaning that the marginal gain brought about by a new local variety decreases. In other words, the consumer surplus increases with the size of the local market, but this effect gets weaker as the range of domestic varieties widens.

The free-entry assumption leads to zero equilibrium profit. By evaluating the zero-profit condition at the equilibrium prices, we obtain the skilled workers' equilibrium wage in each region. More precisely, the equilibrium wage prevailing in A is

$$
\begin{aligned}
w_A^*(\lambda) = {} & \frac{\pi_{AA}^* + \pi_{AB}^*}{f} \\
= {} & \frac{bf + cL}{4(2bf + cL)^2 f^2} \\
& \times \{[2af + tcL(1 - \lambda)]^2(\tfrac{1}{2}L_a + \lambda L) \\
& + [2af - 2tbf - tcL(1 - \lambda)]^2[\tfrac{1}{2}L_a + (1 - \lambda)L]\}. \quad (8.6)
\end{aligned}
$$

After simplification, this expression becomes a quadratic function of λ. It can then be shown that $w_A^*(\lambda)$ is increasing and concave in λ when f is high and/or t takes low values. However, it becomes a decreasing and convex function when f is low and/or t takes high values.

To sum up, both $C_A^*(\lambda)$ and $w_A^*(\lambda)$ increase with λ when trade costs are low, while they move in opposite directions when trade costs are high. These results provide important insights for the analysis of the agglomeration process, by suggesting that skilled workers and firms want to establish themselves in the bigger region once trade costs are low.

The linear model also allows us to study the wage differential between the two regions, as well as its evolution as a function of the trade cost level. Using (8.6), we obtain

$$w_A^*(\lambda) - w_B^*(\lambda) = \frac{(bf + cL)[2bf + c(L_a + L)]L}{2f^2(2bf + cL)}t(t_w - t)(\lambda - \tfrac{1}{2}), \quad (8.7)$$

where

$$t_w \equiv \frac{4af}{2bf + c(L_a + L)}.$$

Consequently, the nominal wage in the big (respectively, small) region exceeds the wage in the other region if and only if $t < t_w$ (respectively, $t > t_w$). In other words, *if trade costs are sufficiently low, the big region offers more attractive wages.* This is because firms in this region are able to exploit scale economies more effectively, having better access to consumers than firms located in the small region. Conversely, when trade costs are high, the small region proves to be more attractive in terms of wages because, as its market is less competitive, the gross profits are higher, allowing firms to pay higher wages. Moreover, it is readily verified that $t(t_w - t)$ increases once $t < \tfrac{1}{2}t_w$, but decreases when $t > \tfrac{1}{2}t_w$. As a result, provided that $t_w < t_{\text{trade}}$, when trade costs fall below t_{trade}, the nominal wage differential first increases and then decreases.

8.1.3 Agglomeration or Dispersion

Even though the linear demands for the manufactured good are independent of income, skilled workers' decisions to migrate are subject to an income effect through the indirect utility. Indeed, the indirect utility a worker achieves in a region is obtained by plugging the equilibrium prices (8.3), (8.4) and the equilibrium wage (8.6) into (8.1). The utility differential governing migration is thus given by the difference in consumer surpluses augmented by the difference in nominal wages. This takes a particularly simple form here:[4]

$$\Delta V(\lambda) \equiv V_A(\lambda) - V_B(\lambda) = C_A^*(\lambda) - C_B^*(\lambda) + w_A^*(\lambda) - w_B^*(\lambda)$$
$$= Kt(t^* - t)(\lambda - \tfrac{1}{2}), \quad (8.8)$$

where

$$K \equiv [2bf(3bf + 3cL + cL_a) + c^2L(L_a + L)]\frac{L(bf + cL)}{2f^2(2bf + cL)^2} > 0$$

is a positive constant and

$$t^* \equiv \frac{4af(3bf + 2cL)}{2bf(3bf + 3cL + cL_a) + c^2L(L_a + L)} > 0. \quad (8.9)$$

---

[4] The calculations are a little long but not particularly difficult. They are therefore left to the reader.

It immediately follows from (8.8) that $\lambda^* = \frac{1}{2}$ is always a spatial equilibrium (as in Krugman's model). Since the equilibrium prices have been determined under the assumption that firms always export to the other region, we now have to figure out whether or not t^* is lower than t_{trade}. The condition $t^* < t_{\text{trade}}$ holds if and only if

$$\frac{L_a}{L} > \frac{6b^2 f^2 + 8bcfL + 3c^2L^2}{cL(2bf + cL)} > 3, \qquad (8.10)$$

where the second inequality is verified because $b/c > 0$. This inequality means that the number of unskilled workers must be more than three times higher than that of the skilled workers. When (8.10) is not verified, we always have $t^* - t > 0$, so the coefficient of $\lambda - \frac{1}{2}$ in (8.8) is positive. In this case, the symmetric equilibrium is always unstable, which in turn implies that the manufacturing sector is always agglomerated (as in chapter 6 when the "black hole" condition is satisfied).

Let us now assume that (8.10) is satisfied. As $\Delta V(\lambda)$ is linear in λ and as $K > 0$, the utility differential has the same sign as $\lambda - \frac{1}{2}$ if $t < t^*$, but it takes the opposite sign if $t > t^*$. As expected, the value of the freight rate t with respect to the threshold t^* is crucial in determining the stability of the symmetric equilibrium. When $t > t^*$, the symmetric configuration is the only stable equilibrium since $d\Delta V(\lambda)/d\lambda < 0$. In contrast, when $t < t^*$, the symmetric equilibrium becomes unstable, so that skilled workers (and firms) are agglomerated in region A or B, according to whether the initial share of the workers residing in the corresponding region exceeds $\frac{1}{2}$. In other words, agglomeration arises when trade costs are sufficiently low, as in chapter 6 and for similar reasons.

To sum up, we have the following result.

Proposition 8.1. *Consider a two-region economy with segmented markets.*

(i) *Assume that (8.10) is not verified. Then, the core-periphery structure is the only stable spatial equilibrium with interregional trade.*

(ii) *Assume that (8.10) is satisfied. Then, if $t > t^*$, the symmetric configuration is the only stable equilibrium with interregional trade; if $t < t^*$, the core-periphery structure is the only stable equilibrium; finally, if $t = t^*$, any configuration is a spatial equilibrium.*

When t decreases from a certain threshold slightly lower than t_{trade}, we move from a pattern involving dispersion with two symmetric regions to a core-periphery structure. Since (8.8) is linear in λ, the break point and the sustain point are identical. We end up, therefore, with results similar to those obtained in chapter 6, although they are not identical. This leads us to believe that the nature of the results obtained by Krugman are robust against alternative specifications of preferences and trade costs.

Finally, when there are no increasing returns ($f = 0$), the coefficient of $\lambda - \frac{1}{2}$ is always negative since $t^* = 0$, which implies that dispersion is the only stable equilibrium. The same result holds as the degree of product differentiation vanishes ($c \to \infty$). This shows once more the role played by the combination "imperfect competition and increasing returns" for understanding the space-economy.

8.1.4 Some Redistributive Aspects of the Core–Periphery Structure

We saw in chapter 6 that the Krugman model is not easily amenable to a detailed welfare analysis. In contrast, the social surplus can be evaluated by adding up individual utilities since these are quasi-linear:

$$W = \tfrac{1}{2}L_a(C_A + 1) + \lambda L(C_A + w_A) + \tfrac{1}{2}L_a(C_B + 1) + (1 - \lambda)L(C_B + w_B).$$

Contrary to general belief, migration is not necessarily a force pushing for the equalization of standards of living. It may just as well reduce gaps in welfare levels or increase spatial inequality. From this perspective, the emergence of a core–periphery structure has several important implications regarding redistributive issues, which all echo the hot debates that arise each time new regional policies are to be designed. In order to dispel common misunderstandings, the following comment is in order: *both the planner seeking to maximize global efficiency and the market work with the same agglomeration and dispersion forces.* However, the CP structure involves two sources of inefficiency.[5] First, firms do not price at marginal cost; second, when skilled workers move from one region to the other, they do not take into account the impact that their relocation decision has on all the other workers. Nevertheless, the agglomeration and dispersion forces taken into account in a planner's calculations exist prior to the market, and they are also the forces shaping the market outcome. Since both solutions depend only upon the fundamental characteristics of the economy, these forces are common to the two institutional settings. What makes the difference is the institutional mechanism selected to solve the trade-off between these forces. The nature of the difference between the two approaches is often poorly understood, leading the public and some policy makers to believe that the socially optimal pattern of activities has nothing to do with what the free play of market forces yields.

---

[5] Note that the welfare analysis conducted here does not account for the optimal choice of the number of firms because this number is constant and given by L/f.

So long as the spatial structure of the global economy remains unchanged, falling trade costs are always favorable to all workers, as they imply a lower price index in each region. In this context the gradual opening-up of economies still has no impact on the location decisions made by economic agents. Such stability of the space-economy concurs with a common observation, i.e., *the first stages of an integration process take place at given locations.* Things get more complicated, however, once falling trade costs trigger the relocation of certain activities. In order to better understand what is going on here, let us compare the core-periphery and symmetric patterns from the viewpoints of the different groups of workers. As stated above, the surplus of the global economy can be measured using the sum of the individual utilities, which we may then use to assess the overall (in)efficiency of the two configurations.

First, unskilled workers living in the core always prefer the former configuration to the latter one, as they benefit from the lower prices of varieties caused by the agglomeration of the manufacturing sector. In contrast, for exactly the opposite reason, the same workers prefer the symmetric configuration when they live on the periphery, at least for the same level of trade cost.[6] The core-periphery structure, therefore, implies an asymmetric treatment of unskilled workers on account of their respective locations.

Second, somewhat paradoxically, it is worth stressing that skilled workers do not necessarily benefit from their concentration into a single region. Indeed, these workers do not account for the impact of their migration on their collective welfare, which here may differ from their individual welfare. This difference arises, on the one hand, because of the intensified competition that affects prices and wages and, on the other hand, because of the larger size of both the regional product and labor markets. The net effect is thus a priori undetermined. It can be shown, however, that this net effect is negative when trade costs, although lower than t^*, remain high, which means that the concentration of the manufacturing sector is not always desirable from the viewpoint of these workers. This is so because it may lead to very low prices, whence very low wages. The market failure here stems from the lack of coordination between skilled workers.

Lastly, when the skilled benefit from being agglomerated, the inhabitants of the core are potentially able to compensate the unskilled in the periphery. For this to become possible, the value of t must be lower than

---

[6] If the drop in trade costs is sufficiently large, the workers living on the periphery can achieve a higher level of welfare than they would have attained in a dispersed economy with high trade costs. To be meaningful, the comparisons made here are undertaken for the same cost level.

the threshold at which the economy's overall surplus is maximized when the manufacturing sector is concentrated. As agglomeration is often considered to give rise to wastefulness, it is not clear whether such a value of t exists. Yet Ottaviano and Thisse (2002) have proved that there is a critical threshold t^o under which the core–periphery structure becomes socially efficient. More precisely, as soon as trade costs are lower than

$$t^o \equiv \frac{4af}{2bf + c(L_a + L)} > 0,$$

the core–periphery structure generates the highest social surplus. Hence, once there are increasing returns ($f > 0$), *agglomeration is not necessarily inefficient from the social viewpoint*, as often claimed. The reason is simple to grasp: if trade costs are sufficiently low, firms take advantage of the larger market created by their concentration to exploit scale economies, while guaranteeing the inhabitants of the periphery good accessibility to their products. Clearly, $t^o = 0$ when there are no increasing returns ($f = 0$).

When $t < t^o < t^*$, the market yields agglomeration while the corresponding total surplus is high enough for those in the core to compensate those in the periphery. In this case, the brain drain is good for both the source and host regions. Of course, this requires transfers from the core to the periphery, a policy that has long been implemented in several countries with strong regional disparities (France, Italy, or Japan). For several years, however, we have witnessed the emergence, within regions considered to be rich, of political groups asking for more fiscal autonomy and, in many cases, for a reduction in the scope of interregional transfers. The existence of such movements leads us to doubt the political durability of mechanisms promoting interregional solidarity. It is reasonable to believe that the crumbling of patriotism in many European countries today, itself reinforced by both the process of European unification and the globalization of trade, largely explains the resurgence of regional sentiments. Such feelings are even stronger when they coincide with a transfer of resources to other regions. The difficulties that our societies are experiencing in thinking in collective terms will soon oblige us to reconsider the current format of solidarity across regions. At the same time, however, the analysis developed below suggests that the striking drop in the trade costs of all kinds favors the relocation of some activities toward the periphery, which should reduce, in the long run, the demand for transfers from the historical core.

As mentioned above, the situation in which $t^o < t < t^*$ is more problematic. In this case, the core region is incapable of compensating the peripheral region. This may give rise to the formation of pressure groups campaigning for or against an increased mobility of production factors. National governments rarely have the information needed to know when and how to thwart the emergence of large regions. Ever since the upsurge of political economy, it has been acknowledged that these groups can unwittingly help the central authorities to reduce their informational deficit. According to the (admittedly somewhat heroic) assumption that all possible interest groups can form and compete to implement the regional development policies that they want, results are less negative than one might think at first glance. By using the above model, it can be shown that the game involving these interest groups yields the second-best optimum, at which the planner chooses the spatial distribution of firms (Ottaviano and Thisse 2002). It is true that the assumptions underlying this result are bold ones, but the outcome nevertheless reveals a fairly unexpected trend.

8.2 When Does the Bell-Shaped Curve Arise?

We saw in chapter 7 that the conclusions of the CP model needed to be amended, in so far as the most likely outcome of economic integration would be not an increase in regional disparities, but rather the existence of a bell-shaped curve. We develop this idea further in the rest of this chapter by incorporating into the linear setting new and important elements liable to influence the choice of location, namely

  (i) the existence of positive trade costs in the agricultural sector,

 (ii) the existence of congestion costs caused by the spatial concentration of activities, and

(iii) the heterogeneity in individual migration behaviors.

What all these elements have in common is that they transform the monotone relationship between economic integration and spatial concentration into a bell-shaped curve, thus making this curve very plausible.

8.2.1 Agricultural Trade Costs

Agriculture is the "silent" sector in the CP model, although it seems awkward to introduce trade costs for the manufactured good and to neglect them for the agricultural one. When trade costs are positive, the prices of the agricultural good need not be the same in both regions. This would endow the symmetric configuration with more stability. Indeed, if a worker moves from A to B, the price of the agricultural good will become higher in B than in A, thus reducing the worker's incentive to move (Davis 1998).

The linear model permits a simple and elegant treatment of positive trade costs for both types of goods. In the manufacturing sector, technology and competition are the same as in the previous section. Regarding the agricultural sector, there are, as before, perfect competition and constant returns. However, in order to allow for two-way trade in the agricultural good, we assume that it is provided as two differentiated varieties, each region being specialized in producing one variety. In this case, the following subutility must be added to the individual preferences defined in section 3.2:

$$\alpha_a(q_A^a + q_B^a) - \tfrac{1}{2}(\beta_a - \gamma_a)[(q_A^a)^2 + (q_B^a)^2] - \tfrac{1}{2}\gamma_a(q_A^a + q_B^a)^2,$$

where q_r^a is the quantity of the variety of the agricultural good produced in region r, while all coefficients are positive with $\beta_a > \gamma_a$.

Denoting the indirect utility by V^a and following the same approach as that above, it can be shown that the interregional utility differential (8.8) becomes

$$\Delta V^a(\lambda) = [K t(t^* - t) - G t_a^2](\lambda - \tfrac{1}{2}),$$

where

$$G = \frac{L}{L_a + L}\frac{2}{\beta_a - \gamma_a} > 0$$

is a bundle of parameters independent of t and t_a, while t^* is still given by (8.9). Note that G tends to infinity when the agricultural good is homogeneous ($\beta_a = \gamma_a$). In this case, the manufacturing sector is always dispersed as the coefficient of $\lambda - \tfrac{1}{2}$ is negative. This explains our assumption that the agricultural good is differentiated: a fairly realistic assumption, after all.[7]

Clearly, there exists a value of t_a, denoted $\hat{t}_a$ such that the equation $K t(t^* - t) - G t_a^2 = 0$ has a single solution in t. When $t_a > \hat{t}_a$, the expression $K t(t^* - t) - G t_a^2$ is therefore negative, so that the industry is always dispersed. In contrast, when $t_a < \hat{t}_a$, the equation $K t(t^* - t) - G t_a^2 = 0$ has two positive roots t_1^a and t_2^a. Then, $K t(t^* - t) - G t_a^2 > 0$ so long as $t_1^a < t < t_2^a$, thus implying that the manufacturing sector is agglomerated. In short, we have the following proposition.

Proposition 8.2. *Consider a two-region economy with segmented markets. If $t_a > \hat{t}_a$, the symmetric configuration is the only stable equilibrium with interregional trade. If $t_a < \hat{t}_a$, then there exist two values*

---

[7] Thus, introducing positive trade costs for the agricultural good in the model of section 8.1 suffices to prevent the emergence of agglomeration.

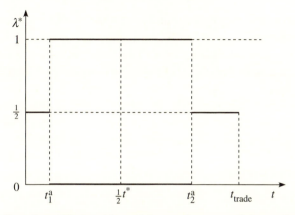

Figure 8.1. Set of equilibria with positive trade costs of the agricultural good.

$t_1^a \in (0, \frac{1}{2}t^*)$ and $t_2^a \in (\frac{1}{2}t^*, t^*)$ *such that the core–periphery structure is the only stable equilibrium if and only if* $t \in (t_1^a, t_2^a)$, *whereas* $t \notin (t_1^a, t_2^a)$ *implies that the symmetric configuration is the only stable equilibrium. Finally, for* $t_a = \hat{t}_a$, *every configuration is a spatial equilibrium.*

Here, economic integration has two facets, i.e., t and t_a. When shipping the agricultural good is not too expensive, the spatial distribution of industry follows a bell-shaped curve, described by the thicker lines in figure 8.1.

As shown by figure 8.1, agglomeration occurs during the second phase of the integration process. The dispersion in the first and third integration phases emerges for different reasons. In the former phase, the manufacturing sector is dispersed because shipping its output is expensive while, in the latter phase, dispersion occurs because the periphery develops a comparative advantage in terms of labor cost. Indeed, the agglomeration within a region (A, for example) lies at the origin of heavy imports of the agricultural good produced in region B. When trade costs of the manufactured good are sufficiently low, the price indices for this good are more or less the same in the two regions. On the other hand, the relative price of the agricultural good in region A increases provided that its trade costs remain more or less the same. This leads to a reduction in the nominal wages in region B such that skilled workers keep the same utility level as in region A. If the trade costs of the manufactured good keep decreasing, the wage differential becomes high enough to induce firms to move from A to B, a process that comes to a halt when symmetry is achieved. Note that, as in all the models studied so far, the transitions between the different equilibria are discontinuous and abrupt.

Observe, finally, that the domain (t_1^a, t_2^a) for which there is an agglomeration becomes smaller as t_a increases. In the limit, there is no further agglomeration, and spatial inequality disappears when shipping the agricultural good becomes sufficiently expensive. We may then safely conclude that the level of trade costs of the agricultural good matters for the location of industry. In particular, low trade costs for the agricultural good favor the agglomeration of the manufacturing sector.[8] Furthermore, even if the trade costs for all goods have fallen since the Industrial Revolution, *it is the relative trend of these various costs that ultimately determines the location of economic activity.*

8.2.2 Urban Costs

So far we have assumed that the agglomeration of firms and workers can be achieved without costs for migrants. Armchair evidence shows, however, that a human settlement of a sizable scale almost inevitably takes on the form of a city. In general, a city possesses its own employment center that gathers together firms, while workers are distributed all around it. Because everybody cannot live close to the city center, workers must commute between the workplace and their living place. Clearly, *commuting costs* go up as the number of inhabitants increases. Competition for land between workers gives rise to a *land rent* that varies with the distance to the city center. The land rent goes down as this distance increases, thereby compensating workers living far from their workplace.

Land rent augmented by commuting costs defines what we call *urban costs.* In most developed countries, they stand for a large, and growing, share of households' budgets. In the United States, housing accounts on average for 20% of household budgets while 18% of total expenditures is spent on car purchases, gasoline, and other related expenses. The latter does not account for the cost of time spent in traveling, which keeps rising. We thus find it reasonable to claim that almost 40% of the income of U.S. households is spent on urban costs. In France, between 1960 and 2000, housing and transportation expenses increased from 23% to 40% of household expenditures, which represents a growth of almost 75% despite an almost quadrupling of the real per capita income.[9] Moreover, as predicted by urban economics, urban costs increase with city size. In the United States, urban costs are less than $15,000 per year in cities like Pittsburgh, Baltimore, and Kansas City, but rise to nearly $20,000

---

[8] This result has been brought to light by means of simulations, in models based on the DSK approach, by Fujita et al. (1999, chapter 7).

[9] These numbers have been computed on the basis of the data presented by Rignols (2002). The index for the consumption expenditure of households was equal to 87.6 in 1960 and 78.7 in 2000. Housing expenses corresponded to 10.7% in 1960 and 19.1% in 2000, and transport expenses to 9.3% in 1960 and 12.2% in 2000. Consequently, we have $(10.7 + 9.3)/0.876 = 22.8$ in 1960 and $(19.1 + 12.2)/0.787 = 39.8$ in 2000.

per year in, e.g., San Francisco, Los Angeles, and New York. Looking at French data reveals that, in 2000, urban costs represented approximately 45% of individual incomes in Paris, but only 34% of individual incomes in small and medium-sized cities.[10]

Urban costs are likely to constitute a dispersion force more important than the demand stemming from immobile farmers/consumers. It is thus fairly surprising that the CP model did not integrate any of these elements, even though they are well-developed concepts in urban economics (Fujita 1989). It was not until Krugman and Livas Elizondo (1996) that such costs began to be taken into account in economic geography models.

The canonical model of urban economics is rooted in the pioneering work of von Thünen (1826), who sought to explain the location of crops around cities in preindustrial Germany. Provided that land is perfectly divisible and trade unfurls in a center whose location is fixed exogenously, von Thünen's model, later revisited by Alonso (1964) in an urban context, is consistent with the neoclassical paradigm involving constant returns and perfect competition. By combining the basic ingredients of urban economics with those of economic geography, we are able to study the interplay between trade costs and commuting costs.

To this end, we consider a one-dimensional space. Each region is now described by a *monocentric city* having a Central Business District (CBD) in which all manufacturing jobs are located. For simplicity, each center is treated as being dimensionless. Space is homogeneous, apart from the distance to the city center. The two cities are assumed to be sufficiently far apart for all the skilled workers to be able to live in either region. Finally, interregional trade takes place between the two city centers, and the transport costs of the manufactured good within each city are assumed to be zero.

We now add land to the two goods in the CP model. In other words, while firms do not consume land, skilled workers do consume land and travel to their employment center. To keep matters simple, we assume that each worker uses a unit lot size, while her unit commuting cost is given by $\theta > 0$ units of the numéraire. As the consumption of land is fixed, there is no need to make it appear in individual preferences, which thus remain unchanged. In contrast, a worker's budget constraint now depends on the distance x between her place of residence and her workplace (the CBD is situated at 0), via the land rent and the commuting

---

[10] In 2000, the total cost of people's journeys inside the Paris metropolitan area amounted to a staggering 34.3 billion euros, which is just over 8% of the local GDP. As for housing, the price per square meter is, on average, 80% higher in Paris than in the rest of France.

costs,

$$\sum_{r=A,B} \int_{i \in \mathcal{N}_r} [p_{rA}(i)q_{rA}(i)\,di] + A + R(x) + \theta x = y + \bar{A},$$

where the notation is the same as in the previous section, A is the quantity of the numéraire consumed, $R(x)$ is the land rent prevailing at x, and θx is the commuting cost between the city center and this location.

Assume that λL skilled workers live in region A. Competition for land can be described by means of a bidding mechanism, whereby each lot is attributed to the highest bidder. At spatial equilibrium, the skilled workers must achieve the same utility level. Since they consume the same lot and the prices of the varieties are the same all over the city, all region A workers must bear the same urban costs. These workers are equally split on each side of the center and the per capita urban cost is the same at any distance x to the CBD, which is equal to the cost paid by the resident who is furthest away. This resident is situated a distance $\frac{1}{2}\lambda L$ from the CBD. At this distance, the commuting cost is equal to $\frac{1}{2}\theta\lambda L$, while the land rent is equal to zero, the opportunity cost of land being assumed to be zero without loss of generality. Thus, we have

$$R^*(x) + \theta x = \tfrac{1}{2}\theta\lambda L.$$

Hence, the equilibrium land rent prevailing at distance x from the center is given by

$$R^*(x) = \theta(\tfrac{1}{2}\lambda L - x),$$

which is decreasing in x, thus compensating workers for their longer commute.

It remains to specify how a region's aggregate land rent is distributed among workers. The most common assumption is that it is redistributed among the skilled workers living in the city under consideration. As the aggregate land rent in region A is equal to

$$2 \int_0^{\lambda L/2} R^*(x)\,dx = \tfrac{1}{4}\theta\lambda^2 L^2,$$

each worker living in this region receives $\frac{1}{4}\lambda\theta L$, so the *net* urban cost she bears is $\frac{1}{4}\lambda\theta L$.

As the level of urban costs varies with the interregional distribution of skilled workers, the interregional utility differential must take into account the difference between urban costs, i.e.,

$$\tfrac{1}{4}\lambda\theta L - \tfrac{1}{4}(1-\lambda)\theta L = \tfrac{1}{2}(\lambda - \tfrac{1}{2})\theta L.$$

Consequently, the utility differential (8.8) becomes

$$\Delta V^u(\lambda) = [Kt(t^* - t) - \tfrac{1}{2}\theta L](\lambda - \tfrac{1}{2}).$$

As before, $\lambda^* = \frac{1}{2}$ is always a spatial equilibrium; it is unstable when the slope of $\Delta V^{\mathrm{u}}(\lambda)$ is positive. This is so if and only if t belongs to the interval defined by the two roots of the equation $Kt(t^* - t) - \frac{1}{2}\theta L = 0$:

$$t_1^{\mathrm{u}} \equiv \frac{t^* - \sqrt{(t^*)^2 - 2\theta L/K}}{2} \quad \text{and} \quad t_2^{\mathrm{u}} \equiv \frac{t^* + \sqrt{(t^*)^2 - 2\theta L/K}}{2},$$

where $t^* > 0$ is given by (8.9). Thus, we have the following proposition.

Proposition 8.3. *Consider a two-region economy with segmented markets. If $2\theta L > K(t^*)^2$, the symmetric configuration is the only stable equilibrium with interregional trade. If $2\theta L < K(t^*)^2$, then there exist two values $t_1^{\mathrm{u}} \in (0, \frac{1}{2}t^*)$ and $t_2^{\mathrm{u}} \in (\frac{1}{2}t^*, t^*)$ such that the core–periphery structure is the only stable equilibrium if and only if $t \in (t_1^{\mathrm{u}}, t_2^{\mathrm{u}})$, whereas $t \notin (t_1^{\mathrm{u}}, t_2^{\mathrm{u}})$ implies that the symmetric configuration is the only stable equilibrium. For $t = t_1^{\mathrm{u}}$ or $t = \tau_2^{\mathrm{u}}$, every configuration is a spatial equilibrium.*

Hence, as trade costs steadily decrease, the economy moves through three phases, namely dispersion, agglomeration, and redispersion of industry. We therefore obtain a diagram identical to that of figure 8.1. An increase in commuting costs favors the dispersion of industry by making broader the domain of the t values for which dispersion is the only stable equilibrium. In the limit, high commuting costs are sufficient to prevent the formation of a large metropolis and guarantee the continuation of industrial activities within several small cities, a situation fairly characteristic of preindustrial economies. In other words, *high urban costs prompt firms and workers to redisperse in order to lower these costs.*[11]

The spectacular drop in commuting costs sparked by the near-universal use of cars has led to a widening of the interval of trade-cost values, for which agglomeration is the equilibrium outcome. More precisely, this drop has the effect of delaying the interregional re-deployment of activities. So it is again the relative evolution of interregional trade costs and intraurban commuting costs that determines the structure of the space-economy. This has the following interesting implication: what matters for the global economy is not just the evolution of trade costs, as suggested by the CP model; what goes on inside the different regions is also crucial.

The reasons for the dispersion of industry are not the same for high and low trade costs. In the former case, meeting the demand for unskilled workers living on the periphery entails high supply costs; this explains

---

[11] Allowing for a variable lot size makes the analysis much more involved without affecting the nature of our results. See Tabuchi (1998) for a numerical study of the monocentric-city case.

why there is dispersion, as in the CP model. In the latter case, firms are dispersed because urban costs, and therefore wages, are too high for the agglomeration in a monocentric city to be an equilibrium (see, for example, Chaterjee and Carlino 2001). On the other hand, once it is recognized that the metropolis may become polycentric through the development of secondary employment centers, the redispersion process will be slowed down, so that the small region does not recoup all the activities that it boasted at the start of the integration process. In this case, we observe a decentralization process within the metropolis together with a partial redispersion of activities (Cavailhès et al. 2007).[12] Such results shed light on the interplay between different types of spatial friction affecting the location of economic activities between and within urban agglomerations. They also draw attention to two facts that policy makers often neglect: on the one hand, local factors may change the global organization of the economy and, on the other, global forces may affect the local/urban organization of production and employment. This calls for better coordination of transport policies at the urban and global levels.

It is worth noting that the existence of urban costs suffices as the sole dispersion force, as the model no longer requires the presence of immobile workers. Indeed, L_a can be set equal to zero without canceling out the dispersion force. In this case, the inequality $t_{\text{trade}} < \frac{1}{2}t^* < t_2^u$ is always satisfied. This implies the disappearance of the first phase of the bell-shaped curve. To put it another way, *the global economy is agglomerated when trade costs are high and dispersed when they are low.* This pattern of spatial development is exactly the opposite of that obtained by Krugman in the CP model. Such a difference in results can be explained as follows. When all workers live in the core region (remember that $L_a = 0$), firms are willing to pay them high wages so long as the geographical separation between regions involves high trade costs. Once these costs have decreased sufficiently, firms and workers prefer to be dispersed, as this new configuration permits a substantial reduction in urban costs. We fall back on the main result obtained by Helpman (1998) in a DSK-type model, in which all workers are mobile and the dispersion force lies in

---

[12] A recent study conducted in France sheds light on these various trends. Over the period 1989–92, Delisle and Laine (1998) found that three-quarters of firms' relocations between French municipalities did not move beyond a distance of 23 km, while one-half of them did not exceed a radius of 9.5 km. Only 15% of the relocated firms established themselves more than 50 km away, thereby probably moving out of the attraction field of their area of origin. As expected, big land-users were particularly involved in such moves, while the incentives to move away from the city increase with its size. Suburbs and peri-urban rings seem to be the main beneficiaries of this flight from the center.

the existence of a given housing stock.[13] This is also the result obtained by Krugman and Livas Elizondo (1996), who modify the CP model in two respects: on the one hand, all workers are mobile and, on the other, the dispersion force is a congestion cost in the core, which is similar to the approach used here.

A final remark is in order. The various results obtained above highlight the role of the *spatial scale*, a variable that economists often overlook. Although Krugman's model seems to provide a reasonable approximation of the space-economy at a macrospatial scale, this is not the case on a smaller scale, as it ignores variables that play a major role such as land and commuting. In other words, economic spaces do not fit into each other like Russian dolls. Each level requires a specific analysis and economic geography models must account for that fact.

8.2.3 Heterogeneous Migrants

The vast majority of economic geography models rest on a very simple, not to say naive, assumption regarding migration behavior: *individuals care only about prices and wages.* Yet migrants are not a representative sample of their region of origin's population but tend to self-select according to specific characteristics. For example, individual characteristics, such as age and family situation, weigh heavily in the balance. Moreover, regions are never totally identical and individuals often diverge in their perception of the noneconomic regional features; e.g., a warm weather can be evaluated positively by some, but negatively by others. In the same vein, European workers' low spatial mobility reflects, to a large extent, their attachment to their region of origin, where their families and friends live. In the European Union, cultural and linguistic differences are still very large, thereby acting as barriers to the mobility of labor. However, individual attitudes to these barriers diverge. What is considered as an almost insurmountable obstacle by some is seen as having little significance by others. In short, workers are *heterogeneous* in their perception of the noneconomic attributes of the different regions, and this heterogeneity is likely to affect the nature and intensity of migration flows. In other words, labor mobility is not driven only by economic variables, implying that workers may not react to economic inequalities once the noneconomic considerations they value become predominant.

Clearly, taking into account all the factors that matter in individual migration decisions is impossible. However, it is not so much the individual decision made by Mr. Smith or Ms. Jones, but their *aggregate*

---

[13] See Murata and Thisse (2005) for a detailed analytical treatment of the approach proposed by Helpman in a DSK-type setting.

migration behavior that is crucial for the spatial organization of the economy. At this level of analysis, discrete choice models, which we encountered in chapter 3, are very useful to the extent that their aim is precisely to describe the aggregated consequences of individual choices made by heterogeneous individuals. In what follows, we assume that the individual choice to live in a particular region is described by the *logit* model. This model represents a very good approximation of more general binary choice models, as is the case here (Anderson et al. 1992, chapter 2); it is, moreover, easy to handle.

So, we now assume that the direct utility of an individual located in region A is given by

$$V_A^h(\lambda) = V_A(\lambda) + \varepsilon_A,$$

where ε_A denotes the idiosyncratic part of her utility derived from living in region A, i.e., a random variable whose realization measures the quality of the match between the individual and region A. We also assume that the idiosyncratic terms ε_A and ε_B are independent and identically distributed. This does not imply that individual choices are identical. On the contrary, the realizations of ε_A and ε_B are different, as individual matches with the two regions typically differ. Under the logit, the probability of an individual choosing to live in region A is given by

$$P_A(\lambda) = \frac{\exp[V_A(\lambda)/v]}{\exp[V_A(\lambda)/v] + \exp[V_B(\lambda)/v]} \in (0,1), \qquad (8.11)$$

where v is the standard deviation (up to the factor $\pi/\sqrt{6}$) of the random variable ε_A. When $v = 0$, we fall back on the model studied above, as $P_A(\lambda) = 1$ if $V_A(\lambda) > V_B(\lambda)$ and $P_A(\lambda) = 0$ if $V_A(\lambda) < V_B(\lambda)$. Things are different when $v > 0$ because the probability of selecting region A is always smaller than 1, while the probability of choosing region B is always positive when $V_A(\lambda) > V_B(\lambda)$. In addition, as v rises, the former probability decreases and the latter probability decreases. In such a context, the parameter v can be interpreted as a measure of the heterogeneity of workers' preferences.

Workers' heterogeneity implies a dynamics that differs from that used so far. However, the stability of its steady state remains fairly standard and bears a strong resemblance to that used in the foregoing. First of all, the equation of motion of the CP model, which describes workers' migration, is replaced here by

$$\dot{\lambda} = (1 - \lambda)P_A(\lambda) - \lambda P_B(\lambda),$$

where the first term on the right-hand side of the equation represents the number of region B workers who choose to move to A, while the second represents the number of region A workers who choose to move to B. This modeling strategy is, therefore, compatible with the existence of cross-migration flows. Likewise, it allows one to account for the idiosyncratic repulsion and attraction factors emphasized in demographic studies.

A spatial equilibrium is achieved when the flow of immigrants is equal to the flow of emigrants, i.e., when $\dot{\lambda} = 0$. As the denominator of (8.11) is strictly positive, it follows that $\dot{\lambda} = 0$ if and only if the numerator is zero:

$$(1 - \lambda) \exp\left[\frac{V_A(\lambda)}{\nu}\right] - \lambda \exp\left[\frac{V_B(\lambda)}{\nu}\right] = 0 \iff \frac{\exp[V_A(\lambda)]}{\exp[V_B(\lambda)]} = \left(\frac{\lambda}{1 - \lambda}\right)^{\nu}.$$
(8.12)

Clearly, $\lambda = \frac{1}{2}$ is still a spatial equilibrium, and so because the deterministic parts of the utilities are equal, $V_A(\frac{1}{2}) = V_B(\frac{1}{2})$. In contrast, $\lambda = 0$ and $\lambda = 1$ are no longer spatial equilibria. In other words, *the fact that workers are heterogeneous in their migration behavior is sufficient to exclude the full agglomeration of firms and workers in a single region*, an extreme prediction of the CP model. This result marks the first major difference from this model.

It remains to check whether there exist other equilibria. By taking the logarithm of (8.12), we obtain a simpler expression to study:

$$J(\lambda; t) \equiv \Delta V(\lambda) - \nu \log \frac{\lambda}{1 - \lambda} = Kt(t^* - t)(\lambda - \tfrac{1}{2}) - \nu \log \frac{\lambda}{1 - \lambda},$$

where we have used the expression for $\Delta V(\lambda)$ given by (8.8). The value λ^* is a spatial equilibrium if and only if $J(\lambda^*; t) = 0$. Since $\dot{\lambda}$ and $J(\lambda; t)$ have the same sign, this equilibrium is stable if

$$\frac{\partial J(\lambda^*; t)}{\partial \lambda} < 0$$

in the neighborhood of λ^*. It can readily be verified that $J(\frac{1}{2}; t) = 0 > \lim_{\lambda \to 1} J(\lambda; t)$ and that

$$\frac{\partial^2 J(\lambda; t)}{\partial \lambda^2} = \frac{\nu}{\lambda^2} - \frac{\nu}{(1 - \lambda)^2}$$

so that $J(\lambda; t)$ is a strictly concave function of λ in the interval $(\frac{1}{2}, 1)$. This in turn implies that this interval contains at most one spatial equilibrium. Indeed, the existence of two equilibria would mean that $J(\lambda; t) = 0$ has at least two solutions belonging to the interval, which would contradict the strict concavity of $J(\lambda; t)$ and the values it takes on at the endpoints, $\frac{1}{2}$ and 1, of this interval. The same holds in the interval $(0, \frac{1}{2})$, apart from the fact that $J(\lambda; t)$ is now a strictly convex function of λ.

By differentiating $J(\lambda; t)$ with respect to λ, we obtain

$$\operatorname{sgn}\left(\frac{\partial J(\frac{1}{2}; t)}{\partial \lambda}\right) = \operatorname{sgn}(Kt(t^* - t) - 4v). \qquad (8.13)$$

The stability analysis of the spatial equilibria is thus based on the sign of the quadratic expression $Kt(t^* - t) - 4v$, very much as in section 8.2.2. Observe first that the symmetric equilibrium is stable if and only if $Kt(t^* - t) - 4v < 0$ holds for all admissible values of t. Note that the inequality $Kt(t^* - t) - 4v < 0$ holds for all the admissible values of t once v exceeds the threshold

$$v^{\mathrm{h}} \equiv \tfrac{1}{16}K(t^*)^2,$$

the value of which is obtained when $Kt(t^* - t)$ reaches its maximum, i.e., when $t = \frac{1}{2}t^*$. Hence, when v is sufficiently large, the equilibrium configuration always involves dispersion. This is because workers value the noneconomic regional characteristics more than the economic ones. In other words, economic gaps are too small to counterbalance differences between noneconomic characteristics. It is these characteristics that prevail in workers' decisions and, as they are equally distributed between the two regions in the eyes of the workers, the distribution of the manufacturing sector is therefore symmetric. In the special case $v = v^{\mathrm{h}}$, the inequality $Kt(t^* - t) - 4v < 0$ is also satisfied so long as $t \neq \frac{1}{2}t^*$.

Things are quite different when $v < v^{\mathrm{h}}$. In this case, the discriminant of the equation $Kt(t^* - t) - 4v = 0$ is always positive, so this equation has two real and distinct roots, given by

$$t_1^{\mathrm{h}}, t_2^{\mathrm{h}} = \tfrac{1}{2}t^* \pm \sqrt{\frac{(t^*)^2}{4} - \frac{4v}{K}},$$

where $0 < t_1^{\mathrm{h}} \leqslant \frac{1}{2}(t_1^{\mathrm{h}} + t_2^{\mathrm{h}}) = \frac{1}{2}t^* \leqslant t_2^{\mathrm{h}} < t^* < t_{\mathrm{trade}}$. As the coefficient of t^2 is negative, the expression $Kt(t^* - t) - 4v$ is negative when t takes values outside the interval $[t_1^{\mathrm{h}}, t_2^{\mathrm{h}}]$, but is positive when t belongs to this interval. Consequently, (8.13) implies that $\partial J(\frac{1}{2}; t)/\partial \lambda < 0$ as soon as trade costs are higher than t_2^{h} or lower than t_1^{h}, so that, in these two cases, the symmetric configuration is stable. Although the intervals $(0, \frac{1}{2})$ and $(\frac{1}{2}, 1)$ each contain a spatial equilibrium, they are unstable. Finally, we have seen that $\lambda = 0, 1$ are never equilibria. For $t < t_1^{\mathrm{h}}$ or $t > t_2^{\mathrm{h}}$, we may thus conclude that $\lambda^* = \frac{1}{2}$ is the only stable equilibrium.

We now come to the case where $t \in (t_1^{\mathrm{h}}, t_2^{\mathrm{h}})$. We have just seen that the interval $(\frac{1}{2}, 1)$ contains a single spatial equilibrium. As the symmetric equilibrium is unstable, the interior equilibrium must therefore be stable. Accordingly, there are two stable interior equilibria, belonging respectively to the intervals $(0, \frac{1}{2})$ and $(\frac{1}{2}, 1)$, which are the mirror images

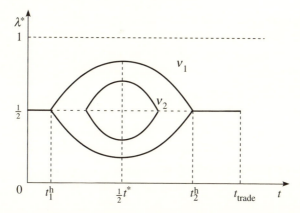

Figure 8.2. Bifurcation diagram when migrants are heterogeneous.

of each other. In other words, *when trade costs take on intermediate values, the manufacturing sector is partially agglomerated* $(0 < \lambda^* < \frac{1}{2}$ or $\frac{1}{2} < \lambda^* < 1)$. In this case, there is asymmetric intraindustry trade as more varieties are produced in one region than in the other.

Furthermore, when t decreases from t_2^h, the size of the agglomeration increases so long as t is higher than $\frac{1}{2}t^*$. In contrast, it decreases as soon as t is lower than $\frac{1}{2}t^*$ but greater than t_1^h. Indeed, for $\lambda^* > \frac{1}{2}$, we have

$$\mathrm{sgn}\left(\frac{\partial \lambda^*}{\partial t}\right) = \mathrm{sgn}\left(-\frac{\partial J(\lambda^*;t)/\partial t}{\partial J(\lambda^*;t)/\partial \lambda}\right)$$

$$= \mathrm{sgn}\left(\frac{\partial \Delta V(\lambda^*)}{\partial t}\right)$$

$$= \mathrm{sgn}(t^* - 2t)(\lambda^* - \tfrac{1}{2})$$

as $\partial J(\lambda^*;t)/\partial \lambda$ is negative, in so far as λ^* is a stable equilibrium. In other words, *the size of the agglomeration first increases and then decreases continuously with the trade cost level.* This is a second major difference from the CP model: workers no longer veer suddenly from one region to the other; they react differently, but smoothly, to the same differences in market conditions, giving rise to partial migrations. The agglomeration achieves its maximal size when $t = \frac{1}{2}t^*$.

The overall picture, which again implies a bell-shaped relationship between the degree of spatial concentration and the level of economic integration, is illustrated in figure 8.2, where $v_1 < v_2$ are two values of the parameter v smaller than v^h. Formally, it can be summarized as follows.

Proposition 8.4. *Consider a two-region economy with segmented markets.*

(i) *If $0 < v < v^h$, industry is dispersed for $t \geqslant t_2^h$. When $t_2^h > t > t_1^h$, industry is partially agglomerated. For $t_2^h > t > \frac{1}{2}t^h$, the interregional gap in the distribution of industry increases, but it decreases for $\frac{1}{2}t^* > t > t_1^h$. Finally, when $t \leqslant t_1^h$, industry is dispersed once again.*

(ii) *If $v \geqslant v^h$, industry is always dispersed.*

This proposition shows that *the heterogeneity in workers' individual preferences is a strong dispersion force*. Indeed, in so far as $v \geqslant v^h$, dispersion always prevails. Moreover, as soon as $v > 0$, in the interval $[0, t_1^h]$, firms and workers are dispersed, while they would be agglomerated if the population were homogeneous ($v = 0$). Similarly, in the interval (t_1^h, t_2^h), the agglomeration is partial instead of being complete since $t_2^h = t^*$ when $v = 0$. Finally, given that $\partial t_1^h / \partial v > 0$ and $\partial t_2^h / \partial v < 0$, the domain of the values of t for which the dispersion arises extends as workers become more heterogeneous.[14]

The above results can be reinterpreted within a broader context. It is, indeed, reasonable to believe that individuals bestow increasing relative weight on noneconomic factors affecting the quality of their life once they have achieved a sufficiently high material welfare.[15] In this case, we may expect an individual to choose her living and working place as described here. If this premise is correct, we may then safely conclude that both economic growth and the development of the welfare state combine to slow down individuals' mobility, by allowing them to satisfy their needs for socializing and/or their attachment to a certain environment. This would provide an explanation for the low mobility of European workers and, especially, its decline in regions that were formerly major sources of emigrants, such as southern Italy and southern Spain (Faini et al. 1996; Bentolila 1996). In the same vein, the approach developed here suggests that workers with a satisfying level of welfare will choose to stay put, thus challenging the dominant view that migration is induced only by income differentials.[16]

Before concluding, we would like to stress another fact that is often overlooked in the literature: the partial agglomeration or, better still, the dispersion of the manufacturing sector caused by the heterogeneity of

---

[14] One important implication of these results is the complete disappearance of regional disparities for positive levels of trade costs, not just when $t = 0$. Puga (1999) obtains a similar result in the Krugman–Venables model when the marginal productivity of labor in the agricultural sector is decreasing. The intersectoral mobility of labor is thus imperfect, very much as the spatial mobility of labor is here.

[15] Formally, this is equivalent to assuming that the parameter v is large enough.

[16] If economic integration involves reduced barriers to labor migration, this could increase the mobility of skilled workers.

preferences is likely to generate efficiency losses at the macroeconomic level. These are derived from the increase in trade flows that occur to the detriment of a relocation of activities, at least when trade costs are sufficiently low for the agglomeration to be socially efficient. If so, the low mobility of European workers thus presents two opposite facets: on the one hand, it corresponds to workers' greater attachment to their region, and thus responds to a real social need; on the other hand, it gives rise to losses with respect to productive efficiency, and these are liable to hold back the development of the economy as a whole.[17]

8.3 Concluding Remarks

We have seen that the conclusions of the CP model do not depend on the specific assumptions associated with the DSK model: its main message remains valid when we integrate the procompetitive effects that the spatial concentration of firms within the same region normally triggers. Furthermore, once we account for the fact that both the land rent and commuting costs increase with the spatial concentration of agents within the same area, Krugman's scenario is reversed, thereby supporting Helpman (1998). We thus find it reasonable to consider *the bell-shaped curve as a reconciliation of these two somewhat extreme approaches*, as this curve encapsulates these two complementary factors. While Krugman concentrates on the right-hand side of this bell, Helpman focuses on its left-hand side.

Above all, the strength of the bell-shaped curve lies in the fact that it holds under very different scenarios, but also under different assumptions with respect to workers' spatial mobility, whether they are immobile (chapter 7), imperfectly mobile (section 8.2.3), or perfectly mobile (section 8.2.2). Hence, it is to be expected that combining them in a more general setting leads to very similar conclusions. Moreover, the various additions considered in this chapter are united by the fact that they act along the same lines as the forces that underpin factor price equalization in neoclassical theory. As the interregional utility differentials associated with scale economies decrease once economic integration has reached a sufficiently high level, it is hardly surprising that, above a certain threshold, these forces become predominant and act in favor of a redeployment of activities to the benefit of the periphery.

Before this threshold is reached, however, the tendency toward agglomeration highlighted by the CP model remains relevant. In this case,

---

[17] Those losses may even be greater if agglomeration generates spillovers that are not taken into account here (see, for example, Belleflamme et al. 2000).

economic integration is likely to generate more regional disparities. As emphasized above, there could be a conflict in this phase between economic efficiency and spatial equity. Nevertheless, it would be misguided to call a halt to integration, as a significant part of these costs will already have been paid and integration will only produce all its positive effects once it has been taken to a sufficient point. If this scenario is correct, it is not hard to imagine the political difficulties it is bound to stir up in the populations affected by such a process of integration.

8.4   Related Literature

The versatility of the linear model has led to it being used in an increasing number of studies. Ludema and Wooton (2000) propose an alternative version in which the manufactured good is homogeneous, with firms competing in quantity. Belleflamme et al. (2000) show how external increasing returns and decreasing trade costs trigger a partial and progressive agglomeration of firms when workers are spatially immobile. Behrens (2004, 2005) studies the process of agglomeration when trade costs are too high to permit two-way trade. In particular, he establishes that prohibitive trade costs do not rule out the formation of regional disparities, thus showing that trade is not intrinsically responsible for the existence of spatial inequalities. Tabuchi et al. (2005) prove that the bell-shaped curve of spatial development is maintained in the case of an arbitrary number of equidistant regions. Ottaviano and van Ypersele (2005) and Behrens et al. (2007) use the linear model to study the impact of fiscal competition and commodity tax on trade and the location of industry, respectively. Tabuchi and Thisse (2006) study the interactions between industries supplying a nontradable and a costlessly tradable good; they show that both are partially agglomerated within the same region, but the industry producing the nontradable good is more agglomerated than the other. Finally, Melitz and Ottaviano (2008) deal with firms having different productivities, and hence different abilities to produce and to export.

9

Spatial Competition

Using concepts borrowed from location theory, this chapter seeks to test the robustness of the main results obtained in the previous chapters once it is recognized that firms have strategic behaviors. Location theory has a long history, which has been dominated by two models: the firm location model and the spatial competition model. The former is one of the oldest mathematical optimization problems and was posed by Fermat: find the point that minimizes the sum of the distances to the vertices of a triangle. It was taken up again by Weber (1909) to analyze a firm's optimal location. Weber assumes that the firm aims at minimizing total transport costs, which are defined by the sum of weighted distances to several markets, each weight expressing the importance of the corresponding market to the firm. This amounts to assuming that a firm seeks a location that gives it the best access to several markets, which have different sizes and relative positions. This is strongly reminiscent of the HME model developed in chapter 4. The main difference lies in the fact that competition is ignored in Weber's analysis whereas it is central to the HME model. Another important difference is that the Weberian firm trades with more than two spatially separated markets.

The aim of the spatial competition model is more ambitious, as it focuses on the location of several firms competing to attract consumers who are dispersed across space. Consumers' mobility is here confined to their shopping behavior, which takes place between their residence and the firm they patronize. The seminal contributions are Hotelling (1929) and Kaldor (1935). We must make it clear from the outset that what became known as *spatial competition* takes on a specific form: each firm has some market power over the consumers located in its vicinity. Indeed, as consumers and firms are spatially separated, buying from more distant firms may be more expensive. Hence, even if the total number of firms in the industry is large, each firm competes directly with a small number of rivals located nearby. The global market is, therefore, segmented into several submarkets formed by consumers who are more or less captive. Within each submarket, each firm is able to identify the rivals with which it must compete for the corresponding customers.

As observed by Kaldor (1935) in his review of Chamberlin's book, in such a context *spatial competition between firms is inherently strategic*, which of course invalidates the monopolistic competition approach. In other words, competition ceases to be global and monopolistic and instead becomes local and oligopolistic. One might think of the difference between the two settings as being the reflection of a difference in the spatial scale of reference: the former offers a good approximation of competition on the macrospatial level, while the latter better fits the microspatial level.

Spatial competition models have attracted a great deal of interest since the late 1970s, as game theory has enabled us to grasp the true nature of the various problems tackled by Hotelling. The reason for the success of these models is easy to understand: each consumer is characterized by her *address* within the geographical space. The same formal approach may then be used to study other settings involving heterogeneous agents distributed across more abstract spaces. Besides their price, firms also choose their location or, more generally, the type of good they supply. Section 9.1 provides the main results established in Hotelling's model. In this setting, consumers move to firms and bear the corresponding transport cost. As their locations are not observable, each firm charges the same *mill price* to all its customers. In section 9.2, we revisit the Hotelling model to deal with the case in which the good is delivered to consumers. Local markets are now segmented because customers' locations are observable. This in turn allows firms to choose a price specific to each local market. Roughly speaking, the model studied in the first section of this chapter may be viewed as describing the case of goods that are nontradable, in that they must be consumed where they are made available (*shopping*); those in the second section correspond to tradable goods, which are delivered and consumed at the customers' location (*shipping*).

Our purpose is to understand commonalities, distinctions, and potential combinations of economic geography and spatial competition. To this end, we consider a very simple economic and spatial environment in which consumers are distributed uniformly across space, production costs are the same across locations, while the market is supplied by two firms that each seek a location. This is because we want to focus on strategic interactions and their impact on firms' location choices.

9.1 Spatial Duopoly à la Hotelling

Compared with the previous models, the main distinctive feature of the spatial competition model is its focus on *a large number of locations* (or regions) and *a small number of firms*. In other words, we turn the model on its head by assuming that there is a continuum of locations (instead of two) and that two firms (instead of a continuum) set up within this space. At first glance, the two approaches thus seem to be unrelated. Things are not that simple, however. To show this, we use the prototype of spatial competition: the Hotelling model.

9.1.1 Competing for Market Shares

Consider a one-dimensional space represented by a linear segment; without any loss of generality, its length is normalized to 1. Each point x of the segment stands for the location of a consumer who wants to buy one unit of the good supplied by the firms. The segment $[0, 1]$ is thus the spatial representation of the market, the demand being distributed uniformly over that segment. The simplest version of the Hotelling model involves two firms, 1 and 2, selling a homogeneous product at the same fixed mill price. Firm $i = 1, 2$ chooses a location x_i along this segment, with $x_1 \leqslant x_2$ without loss of generality. The cost of moving to a firm is a linear function of distance. Specifically, a consumer living at $x \in [0, 1]$ bears a cost equal to $t|x - x_1|$ if she buys from firm 1, while this cost is equal to $t|x - x_2|$ if she buys from firm 2, where $t > 0$ is the unit transport cost. Though the unit transport cost is supposed to be the same for all consumers, the cost of moving varies with the distance between the consumer's location and the firm she patronizes.

Since the mill price is the same and the product homogeneous, a consumer always patronizes the nearer firm. Let $x_m = \frac{1}{2}(x_1 + x_2)$ be the midpoint between the two firms when $x_1 < x_2$. In this case, firm 1's market is $[0, x_m]$ and firm 2's market is $[x_m, 1]$. When both firms are located back-to-back ($x_1 = x_2$), they equally split the market. As the price is given to the firms, profit maximization amounts to maximizing market shares x_m and $1 - x_m$, respectively. If $x_2 < \frac{1}{2}$, then firm 1's best reply is to set up just to the right of firm 2. If $x_2 > \frac{1}{2}$, firm 1's best reply is to set up just to the left of firm 2. The same holds, mutatis mutandis, for firm 2. Hence, if they are not located at the market center, at least one firm has an incentive to change its location. This implies that $x_1^* = x_2^* = \frac{1}{2}$ is the unique Nash equilibrium in pure strategies. In other words, when prices are exogenous and identical, competition for market shares leads firms to agglomerate at the market center: there is minimum spatial differentiation.

However, once mill prices are chosen by firms, such a configuration is not part of the equilibrium. Indeed, each firm has an incentive to undercut its rival's price, so that both get trapped in a Bertrand situation in which they earn zero profits. Thus, price competition turns out to be a dispersion force leading firms to differentiate across space. An exhaustive approach, therefore, implies that we must deal with the choice of both location and price by each firm. Specifically, Hotelling has proposed a two-stage procedure to study this problem: in the first stage, firms choose their location noncooperatively; in the second stage, these locations being known to all parties, firms select their mill price noncooperatively. Using such a sequential procedure implies that firms anticipate the consequences of their location choices on their subsequent price choices. This endows the model with a dynamic structure that reflects the difference between selecting locations and prices, the latter being generally easier to revise than the former. Hotelling starts by solving the price subgame induced by the location choices made by firms in the first stage. The equilibrium prices thus obtained are then plugged into the profit functions, which now depend only upon firms' locations. These new profit functions are those used by firms in the first-stage game to determine their profit-maximizing location. This approach concurs with what has been known since Selten as a subgame perfect Nash equilibrium. The solution is obtained by backward induction: firms find the Nash price equilibrium of the subgame induced by any location pair; using these prices, firms determine the Nash equilibrium of the location game. Each stage is described in the next two subsections.

9.1.2   Competing in Prices

9.1.2.1   *The Case of Extreme Locations*

Assume that the two firms are established at the left-hand and right-hand endpoints of the segment, that is, firm 1 is located at $x_1 = 0$ and firm 2 at $x_2 = 1$. Each firm $i = 1, 2$ sets a mill price p_i that is the same for all its customers; in other words, firms do not discriminate in prices across space. In order to consume the good in question, each consumer must go to one of the two firms. As the good that they supply is homogeneous, each consumer chooses to buy from the firm with the lower *full price*, defined as the sum of the mill price and of the cost of moving to the firm. The idea that consumers compare full prices is an old one, which goes back at least to Cantillon (1755, p. 20) for whom a tailor who raises his price will see that "the villagers will find it more worthwhile to have their clothes made in another village, town or city, and waste time in going there and coming back again." This has one important consequence: consumers' individual choices are mutually exclusive, and thereby discontinuous.

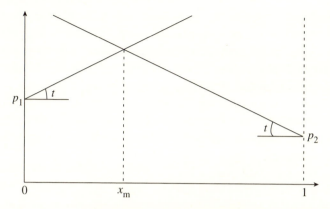

Figure 9.1. Market splitting.

For a consumer located in x, the full price associated with firm 1 is given by $p_1 + tx$, while the full price corresponding to firm 2 is equal to $p_2 + t(1-x)$. Because firms sell the same good, that consumer patronizes firm 1 if the following condition holds:

$$p_1 + tx < p_2 + t(1 - x).$$

This is equivalent to saying that

$$x < \frac{1}{2} + \frac{p_2 - p_1}{2t} \equiv x_m, \tag{9.1}$$

where x_m describes the location of the *marginal consumer*, who is indifferent between buying from firm 1 or firm 2. Consumers who buy from firm 1 are situated to the left of the marginal consumer, as firm 1's full price is lower for them than that of firm 2, while the other consumers go to firm 2. If $p_1 < p_2$, firm 1 has a bigger market than firm 2 because $x_m > \frac{1}{2}$, but the latter continues to sell to consumers close to it so long as $p_2 < p_1 + t$. The corresponding market splitting is illustrated in figure 9.1.

For x_m to belong to $[0, 1]$, the absolute value of the price gap $p_2 - p_1$ must not be too large. Formally, this condition is equivalent to $|p_2 - p_1| < t$, otherwise one of the two firms would serve the entire market, its competitor charging a mill price higher than its own augmented by the cost of moving borne by the most distant consumer. As consumers are uniformly distributed over the segment, firm 1's demand is defined by the length of its market segment, i.e., $D_1(p_1, p_2) = x_m$, while firm 2's demand is given by $D_2(p, p_2) = 1 - x_m$. Even though individual choices are discontinuous, *firms' aggregated demands are continuous.* This apparent contradiction is resolved because each consumer is assumed to be negligible, thus showing how it is possible, at the aggregated level, to get rid of individual discontinuities. In a context other than monopolistic competition, this shows once more how powerful is the assumption of a continuum of agents.

It is worth noting that, throughout this section, the market is covered, i.e., full prices are lower than consumers' reservation price. The model can be extended to deal with consumers who can refrain from buying. This makes the analytical treatment more complicated, without adding anything essential to the results.

Finally, the marginal production cost is supposed to be constant and the same for both firms. The underlying assumption is that firms are large with respect to their sector, but the sector is small with respect to the economy as a whole while production factors move freely across sectors. Hence, factor markets are unaffected by the two firms' behavior. Without loss of generality, we can normalize this cost to zero and reinterpret prices as markups. Hence, firm 1's profit function can be written as follows:

$$\Pi_1(p_1, p_2) = p_1 D_1(p_1, p_2) = p_1 \frac{p_2 - p_1 + t}{2t}. \tag{9.2}$$

The spatial duopoly problem may be interpreted as a noncooperative game in which the players are the firms and the strategies the mill prices, while the payoff functions are defined by the profits. We seek a Nash equilibrium, i.e., a pair of prices p_1^* and p_2^* such that firm 1 maximizes its profit at p_1^* when its competitor sets the price p_2^*, and conversely for firm 2. A firms's profit function is continuous with respect to both prices and concave with respect to its own price. As a result, the price game has a Nash equilibrium in pure strategies. It is well-known that such an equilibrium can be geometrically represented by the intersection of the two best-reply curves. We determine firm 1's best-reply function $p_1^*(p_2)$ by equalizing to zero the first derivative of Π_1 with respect to p_1:

$$p_2 - 2p_1 + t = 0 \tag{9.3}$$

so that $p_1^*(p_2)$ is given by

$$p_1^*(p_2) = \tfrac{1}{2}(p_2 + t).$$

Because each firm's best reply is an increasing function of the others' prices, firms' strategies are strategic complements.

As the model is perfectly symmetric, one expects the two equilibrium prices to be equal. Indeed, setting $p_1 = p_2$ in (9.3), we obtain the following solution:

$$p_1^* = p_2^* = t. \tag{9.4}$$

Moreover, as the best-reply functions are linear, the Nash equilibrium is unique and given by (9.4). Consequently, *firms' pricing involves an additive markup* (a common practice in the business world) *which depends positively on the unit transport cost*. The equilibrium prices being equal, the market is evenly split between the two firms, which make a profit equal to $\frac{1}{2}t$. Hence, firms' profits increase with the unit transport cost. This confirms a long-standing idea that goes back at least to Launhardt (1885), for whom

> the improvement of means of transport is dangerous for costly goods: these lose the most effective protection of all tariff protections, namely that provided by bad roads.
>
> Launhardt (1993, p. 150 of the English translation)

In other words, falling transport costs induce firms to be more aggressive. Everything works as if *distance protects the firms*. This protection becomes less effective, however, as transport and/or trade costs go down.

9.1.2.2 *Interior Locations*

In order to study the way firms choose their location, we need to determine their equilibrium prices for every location pair x_1 and x_2 belonging to $[0, 1]$ with $x_1 \leqslant x_2$. We define the distance separating the two firms as $\Delta = x_2 - x_1 > 0$.

If the marginal consumer is situated between firms 1 and 2, her location x_m is such that

$$p_1 + t(x_m - x_1) = p_2 + t(x_2 - x_m),$$

which leads to

$$x_m = \frac{p_2 - p_1}{2t} + \frac{x_1 + x_2}{2}.$$

It is between the two firms if and only if $|p_2 - p_1| \leqslant t\Delta$. The profit function is still defined by $\Pi_1(p_1, p_2) = p_1 D_1(p_1, p_2)$. In this case, the solutions of the two first-order conditions are as follows:

$$p_1^* = \tfrac{1}{3}t(2 + x_1 + x_2), \qquad p_2^* = \tfrac{1}{3}t(4 - x_1 - x_2). \qquad (9.5)$$

Firms' markups now depend on the unit transport cost as well as on firms' relative position within the market. We fall back on (9.4) in the special case in which $x_1 = 0$ and $x_2 = 1$.

By replacing prices with (9.5) in the profit functions, we obtain

$$\Pi_1^* = \tfrac{1}{18}t(2 + x_1 + x_2)^2, \qquad \Pi_2^* = \tfrac{1}{18}t(4 - x_1 - x_2)^2.$$

It can readily be verified that Π_1^* increases with x_1 while Π_2^* decreases with x_2. This observation has led Hotelling to conclude that firms would move closer to each other in order to establish themselves at the market center. This tendency toward agglomeration has come to be known under the name of the "principle of minimum differentiation." Hotelling's argument is incomplete, however. More precisely, are the prices in (9.5) the Nash equilibrium of the subgame induced by locations x_1 and x_2? It turns out that the answer can be negative.

As soon as $x_2 < 1$, firm 2 has a *hinterland* formed by the consumers situated between it and the right-hand end of the market ($x = 1$). If firm 1 gradually reduces its price to $\hat{p}_1 \equiv p_2^* - t\Delta$, its demand increases continuously to achieve the value x_2. If firm 1 reduces its price by a trifle below $\hat{p}_1$, its demand increases abruptly from x_2 to 1, as all the consumers belonging to firm 2's hinterland choose to buy from firm 1, the full price of firm 1 being lower than that of firm 2 for all these consumers (this situation was excluded in the argument above by assuming that the marginal consumer was situated between the two firms). Formally, the demand to firm 1 is, therefore, discontinuous at $\hat{p}_1$. Given this discontinuity, firm 1 may want to deviate from p_1^* in order to serve all the consumers at the price $\hat{p}_1$. Such a deviation is unprofitable if and only if the profit that firm 1 makes in p_1^* is greater than or equal to the profit that it makes at $\hat{p}_1$:

$$\Pi_1(p_1^*, p_2^*) = \tfrac{1}{18}t(2 + x_1 + x_2)^2 \geqslant \Pi_1(\hat{p}_1, p_2^*) = t[\tfrac{1}{3}(4 - x_1 - x_2) - \Delta],$$

which amounts to

$$(2 + x_1 + x_2)^2 \geqslant 12(2 + x_1 - 2x_2). \tag{9.6}$$

It is shown below that this condition is violated if the two firms are simultaneously close to each other and to the middle of the market. Consequently, if (9.6) does not hold, p_1^* is not the best reply of firm 1 against p_2^*. However, the pair $(\hat{p}_1, p_2^*)$ is not a Nash equilibrium either, as firm 2's profits are zero, whereas it can make positive profits by charging a price slightly below p_2^*. This implies that p_2^* is not firm 2's best reply against $\hat{p}_1$. As a result, *the price subgame has no Nash equilibrium in pure strategies* because the equilibrium prices, if any, must satisfy the first-order conditions.

The reason for this negative result lies in the fact that the profit function $\Pi_1(p_1, p_2^*)$ is not quasi-concave with respect to p_1 (see figure 9.2). Indeed, as the consumers located in firm 2's hinterland all shift to firm 1 as soon as $p_1 < \hat{p}_1$, this function has a second local maximum at price $\hat{p}_1$. So long as this maximum is higher than the one obtained at p_1^*, which

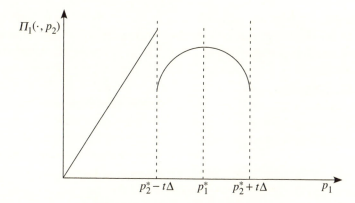

Figure 9.2. Firm 1's profit function.

is equivalent to $\Pi_1(\hat{p}_1, p_2^*) > \Pi_1(p_1^*, p_2^*)$, firm 1's best-reply curve displays an upward discontinuity at $\hat{p}_1$ and no longer intercepts that of firm 2.

When $x_1 > 0$, we obtain a similar condition for firm 2:

$$(4 - x_1 - x_2)^2 \geqslant 12(1 + 2x_1 - x_2), \tag{9.7}$$

so similar conclusions may be drawn when (9.7) is not satisfied.

Finally, in the special case where $\Delta = 0$, spatial differentiation disappears, thus implying that the two firms are trapped in a Bertrand-like duopoly in which they sell at the marginal production cost.

In short, we have the following proposition.

Proposition 9.1. *If $x_1 = x_2$, the price equilibrium is unique and given by $p_1^* = p_2^* = 0$. If $x_1 < x_2$, there is a price equilibrium if and only if*

$$(2 + x_1 + x_2)^2 \geqslant 12(2 + x_1 - 2x_2) \quad and \quad (4 - x_1 - x_2)^2 \geqslant 12(1 + 2x_1 - x_2).$$

Furthermore, this equilibrium is unique and given by

$$p_1^* = \tfrac{1}{3}t(2 + x_1 + x_2) \quad and \quad p_2^* = \tfrac{1}{3}t(4 - x_1 - x_2).$$

In the special case of symmetric locations ($x_1 + x_2 = 1$), the above existence conditions can be simplified to $x_1 \leqslant \tfrac{1}{4}$, i.e., $p_1^* = p_2^* = t$ is a Nash equilibrium if and only if the two firms are not located inside the second and third quartiles of the market. Proposition 9.1 is therefore easy to interpret. If the two firms are far from each other, the price drop that allows a firm to capture the entire market is quite substantial and thus unprofitable. By contrast, if the two firms are close to each other, this price drop becomes profitable because it is small. It is this idea that conditions (9.6) and (9.7) both describe in the case of nonsymmetric locations. It is worth noting here that *taking into account strategic* *interactions leads to new difficulties* (e.g., the nonexistence of an equilibrium) *that are not found with models of monopolistic competition.* This explains, at least partially, the modeling strategy selected in the previous chapters.

Another important implication of proposition 9.1 is the fact that we cannot seek a subgame perfect Nash equilibrium of the whole game as we have no solutions for a large number of subgames. One solution would be to appeal to mixed strategies because the existence of a price equilibrium is guaranteed. Another solution is to change some of the model's assumptions in order to restore the existence of a price equilibrium for any subgame. We will look at this option in the next subsection.

9.1.3 The Principle of Spatial Differentiation

In this section, we change Hotelling's model slightly by assuming that consumers' costs of moving to the firms are given by a quadratic function of the distance covered rather than being linear as above (d'Aspremont et al. 1979). One should keep in mind that we deal here with the movement of people (and not of commodities as in previous chapters). It is thus reasonable to expect that the marginal disutility attached to an incremental move rises with its length. This is precisely what the assumption of quadratic costs captures.

When $x_1 < x_2$, the marginal consumer is located at point x_m satisfying the condition

$$p_1 + t(x_m - x_1)^2 = p_2 + t(x_m - x_2)^2. \tag{9.8}$$

This equality is valid whatever the position of x_m with respect to the two firms. Whether x_m lies to the left or right of firm 1, in other words, whether x_m is greater than or less than x_1, nothing changes in the expression of x_m, which can belong to the hinterland of one of the two firms.

Equation (9.8) has a unique solution that is given by

$$x_m = \frac{p_2 - p_1}{2t(x_2 - x_1)} + \frac{x_1 + x_2}{2},$$

which is a linear function of the prices chosen by the two firms. Firm 1's demand is now continuous and is given by

$D_1(p_1, p_2)$

$$= \begin{cases} 0 & \text{if } p_1 > p_2 + t(x_2^2 - x_1^2), \\ x_m & \text{if } p_2 + t[(1 - x_1)^2 - (1 - x_2)^2] \leqslant p_1 \leqslant p_2 + t(x_2^2 - x_1^2), \\ 1 & \text{if } p_1 < p_2 + t[(1 - x_1)^2 - (1 - x_2)^2]. \end{cases}$$

If there is an equilibrium, it must be that the two firms are active ($0 < x_m < 1$). Indeed, when $x_m = 0$, firm 1 chooses to sell at a price that puts itself outside the market; and conversely for firm 2 when $x_m = 1$. Thus, any price belonging to one of these two domains necessarily leads to a suboptimal profit level for at least one firm.

By computing the first-order conditions and solving the system formed by the two linear equations thus obtained, we find that

$$p_1^*(x_1, x_2) = \tfrac{1}{3}t(x_2 - x_1)(2 + x_1 + x_2),$$
$$p_2^*(x_1, x_2) = \tfrac{1}{3}t(x_2 - x_1)(4 - x_1 - x_2).$$
(9.9)

As firms' profit functions are strictly concave over the relevant price intervals, this point is a Nash equilibrium of the price subgame. Moreover, this equilibrium is unique, as it is the solution of two linear equations.

Making the interfirm distance shorter by increasing x_1 and decreasing x_2 by the same amount, it is readily verified that both prices, and thus markups, go down. In other words, the two firms are better substitutes. In the special case of two symmetrically located firms ($x_1 + x_2 = 1$), we obtain $p_1^*(x_1) = p_2^*(x_1) = t(1 - 2x_1)$, which tends to zero as x_1 increases up to $\tfrac{1}{2}$. Moreover, the equilibrium prices also go up with the unit transport cost t. Last, the equilibrium prices are equal to the marginal production cost if and only if

(i) the two firms are located back-to-back ($x_1 = x_2$), or

(ii) the unit transport cost is zero ($t = 0$).

Plugging (9.9) into the profit functions yields two expressions Π_1^* and Π_2^*, which depend solely on x_1 and x_2. Applying the first-order conditions to these expressions yields the solution $x_1^* = -\tfrac{1}{4}$ and $x_2^* = \tfrac{5}{4}$. Hence, firms would locate outside the market. If we constrain locations to be within the market, then $x_1^* = 0$ and $x_2^* = 1$. In both cases, the location game has a unique Nash equilibrium (up to a permutation of indices). This result tells us something important, namely that price competition is a strong dispersion force as firms always want to move away from each other. This is because *spatial separation relaxes price competition.*

9.1.4 The Trade-off between Market Share and Price Competition

In short, the location of two competitors is the outcome of two opposite effects: the "market share" effect (the agglomeration force), which, when firms sell at given prices, encourages each to move closer to its competitor in order to increase its demand, and the competition effect (the dispersion force), which pushes firms to separate to restore their markups. We can, therefore, conclude that firms which are otherwise identical always choose to locate away from each other, but the amount of differentiation depends on the specifics of the model.

To illustrate the trade-off, consider the total derivative of firm 1's equilibrium profits of the first-stage game (taking into account the impact on the price subgame equilibrium):

$$\frac{d\Pi_1^*}{dx_1} = \frac{\partial \Pi_1^*}{\partial p_1} \frac{\partial p_1^*}{\partial x_1} + \frac{\partial \Pi_1^*}{\partial p_2} \frac{\partial p_2^*}{\partial x_1} + \frac{\partial \Pi_1^*}{\partial x_1}.$$

The first term is zero ($\partial \Pi_1^*/\partial p_1 = 0$) by definition of the equilibrium price p_1^* of the price subgame. The last term ($\partial \Pi_1^*/\partial x_1 > 0$) denotes the market share effect: at given prices, firm 1 wants to move closer to its rival to increase its market share and, hence, its profits; this derivative is therefore positive. The second term, however, is negative ($\partial \Pi_1^*/\partial p_2 \times \partial p_2^*/\partial x_1 < 0$). Indeed, when firm 1 moves closer to its competitor, the latter reacts by setting a lower price ($\partial p_2^*/\partial x_1 < 0$) (see (9.9) in the quadratic case). Furthermore, when firm 2 decreases its price, firm 1's profits go down ($\partial \Pi_1^*/\partial p_2 > 0$). It should then be clear that the equilibrium locations of the two firms depend on the intensities of these two effects.

Note, in passing, that this allows us to better understand the role played by the assumption of product differentiation in economic geography models, such as those studied in chapters 6–8. When firms sell a homogeneous good, they want to avoid spatial clustering because price competition has devastating effects upon them. By turning the picture around, this result suggests that firms selling differentiated goods may want to gather at some central market location, because price competition is now weakened.

Last, the spatial duopoly model can be extended to a multi-dimensional space. The introduction of a second dimension may seem natural, as economic agents do operate in a two-dimensional geographical space. It is more interesting, however, to consider a setting having one dimension which is geographical and one, or several, describing the characteristics of the products, as in the Lancasterian approach to product specification. In this way, taking into account several dimensions allows us to play with different types of horizontal differentiation (think of the different flavors of ice cream or colors of shirts). It can then be shown, via a long and fairly complex proof, that firms differentiate themselves along the dimension that is most important to them, whereas they minimize their differentiation with respect to other dimensions (Irmen and Thisse 1998). In order to gain more insight into this result, consider the simple case of a unit square. If firms want to maximize the distance between them, they locate at $(0,0)$ and $(1,1)$. In this case, prices are equal, while the boundary between the two market areas is given by the diagonal. On the other hand, when firms are established at $(0, \frac{1}{2})$ and $(1, \frac{1}{2})$, the market areas touch each other along the vertical segment passing through $(\frac{1}{2}, \frac{1}{2})$. It can be shown that these two locations define a Nash equilibrium of the location game, and so do $(\frac{1}{2}, 0)$ and $(\frac{1}{2}, 1)$. Therefore, everything works as if firms were seeking to reduce their contact zone as much as possible, as a bigger zone foments unleashed competition.

Having said that, we can therefore think of the following scenario as describing the selection of products and locations by firms. When transport costs are high, the spatial dimension dominates the others and firms have no incentives to differentiate their product. Their spatial separation protects them and each one supplies only its local market. If, on the other hand, there is a big drop in transport costs, distance ceases to offer a sufficient protection against competition. Consequently, each firm is now encouraged to differentiate its product in order to soften price competition. Such a behavior may then be viewed as firms' response to the tendency for profits to be eroded as a result of falling transport costs (chapter 1). We may thus safely conclude that the historical downward trend in the costs of shipping goods has played the role of a centripetal force, and so because *firms have substituted product differentiation for spatial differentiation*. So, we return to the story, although in a very different context, uncovered in the core–periphery model of chapter 6.

9.1.5 Spatial Competition and Preference for Variety

What we have seen above spurs us on to extend the Hotelling model to the case of firms offering differentiated products to consumers having a preference for variety. Their behavior is now described by a *purchasing probability* (or frequency) that depends on the prices and locations selected by firms. This approach, which enables us to make a direct comparison with the basic model of economic geography, was proposed by de Palma et al. (1985). It also allows us to integrate spatial competition and preference for variety within the same framework, as individual choices cease to be mutually exclusive.

Let us start by describing consumers' behavior when the two firms charge the same mill price. If, as in chapter 3, the first stage of the consumer choice process is described by the logit model, she buys one unit of the good, as in Hotelling's model, but with a positive probability for each firm. In other words, a consumer located in $x \in [0,1]$ is characterized by a probability (or a frequency) $P_1(x)$ of patronizing firm 1, given

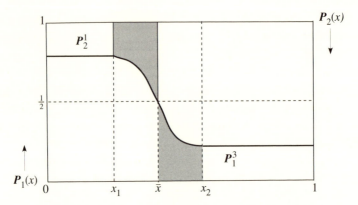

Figure 9.3. The purchasing probability function.

by

$$P_1(x) = \frac{\exp(-|x - x_1|)/v}{\exp(-|x - x_1|)/v + \exp(-|x - x_2|)/v}$$

$$= \frac{1}{1 + \exp(|x - x_1| - |x - x_2|)/v},$$

where v is a positive parameter measuring the quality of the match between a consumer and a firm, as in chapters 3 and 8, while $P_2(x) = 1 - P_1(x)$. Note that the random utility framework that stands behind this approach accounts for the various circumstances that govern consumers' daily shopping behavior, circumstances that lead to different matches between shops and consumers. When $v = 0$, we fall back on the situation in which each consumer goes to the closer firm since $P_1(x) = 1$ if, and only if, $x < \frac{1}{2}(x_1 + x_2)$.

When $v > 0$, all consumers have a strictly positive probability of buying from firm 1. Accordingly, market segments cease to be separated and do now overlap. The extent of the overlap depends on consumers' locations. By computing the derivative of $P_1(x)$ with respect to v, we can check that $P_1(x)$ decreases when v increases if the consumer is closer to firm 1 than firm 2 (i.e., $x < \frac{1}{2}(x_1 + x_2)$), while $P_1(x)$ increases in the opposite case. As seen in chapter 3, the intensity of the preference for variety increases with v, which implies that, from the consumer's viewpoint, the relative weight of distance in her decision is lower. Consumers close to firm 1 are, therefore, less inclined to go to this firm, while the opposite holds for those close to firm 2. However, $P_1(x) > P_2(x)$ if, and only if, $x < \frac{1}{2}(x_1 + x_2)$, which means that firm 1 remains more attractive than firm 2 if it is closer to the consumers. These different properties are illustrated in figure 9.3.

Everything works, therefore, as if the two firms sold differentiated goods, the differentiation of which is measured by v where, as in the CES, product differentiation is not modeled explicitly.

When prices come into the picture, distances are replaced by the full prices in the purchasing probability, which becomes (see chapter 3)

$$P_1(x) = \frac{\exp(-p_1 - t|x - x_1|)/v}{\exp(-p_1 - t|x - x_1|)/v + \exp(-p_2 - t|x - x_2|)/v}. \quad (9.10)$$

As $v > 0$, a firm can no longer supply the whole market by selling at a sufficiently low price because $0 < P_1(x) < 1$ for all x.

Firm 1 seeks to maximize its profit, given by

$$\Pi_1 = \int_0^1 p_1 P_1(x)\, dx.$$

As the probabilities P_i are continuous with respect to prices (p_1, p_2) and locations (x_1, x_2), the functions Π_1 and Π_2 are also continuous.

As the analysis of the simultaneous game is simpler than the analysis of the sequential game, we study this case here. First, it should be pointed out that the two firms no longer find themselves in a Bertrand-like situation when they are located together. This is due to the fact that they now sell differentiated products. If $x_1 = x_2$, (9.10) becomes

$$P_1(x) = \frac{\exp(-p_1/v)}{\exp(-p_1/v) + \exp(-p_2/v)}.$$

By studying the partial derivative of Π_1 with respect to p_1, we can show that this firm's best reply in price against $p_2^* = 2v$ is to sell its product at the price $p_1^* = 2v$. It is then easy to show that $p_1^* = p_2^* = 2v > 0$ is the only price equilibrium. When firms sell a homogeneous good ($v = 0$), we find ourselves back at Bertrand's solution. Conversely, when firms sell differentiated goods ($v > 0$), they are able to maintain positive markups.

Let us now assume that firm 2 is established at the market center ($x_2 = \frac{1}{2}$) and sets a price equal to $2v$. If firm 1 is located to the left of $\frac{1}{2}$, computing the partial derivative of Π_1 with respect to x_1 shows us that this firm's profit increases as it gets closer to the market center so long as $v \geqslant \frac{1}{2}t$. Hence, firm 1 has an incentive to locate at the market center. At such a location, firm 1's best reply is $p_1^* = 2v$. Accordingly, if $v \geqslant \frac{1}{2}t$, then $(x_1, p_1) = (\frac{1}{2}, 2v)$ is firm 1's best reply against $(x_2, p_2) = (\frac{1}{2}, 2v)$. There is, therefore, a symmetric Nash equilibrium in which both firms are located back-to-back at the market center and set prices equal to $2v$. However, when $v < \frac{1}{2}t$, either there is no pure strategy equilibrium or firms are separated (as in section 9.1.2). We can thus conclude that *a drop in shopping cost relative to the degree of product differentiation* *induces firms to cluster at the location with the highest market potential,* here at the middle of the segment. Such a result, which still holds with an arbitrary number of firms, may be viewed as the strategic counterpart of the main property of the core–periphery model studied in chapter 6.

9.2 Spatial Oligopoly à la Cournot

Most of the literature devoted to spatial competition has focused on mill pricing. When goods are homogeneous, each consumer thus seeks the firm that offers her the lowest full price. This approach seems unwarranted on at least three grounds.

1. First, firms endowed with market power are able to adopt pricing policies that are much more involved than mill pricing. In this context, a distant consumer turns to firms close by. However, competing firms need not remain inactive and can design discriminatory price schemes that make them more competitive in remote markets. To achieve their goal, they take on the responsibility of shipping goods and thus find it profitable to absorb part of the transport cost to offer lower delivered prices to distant customers. The numerous complaints about dumping in the automobile sector presented to the World Trade Organization is evidence of such behaviors in the international market place.

2. The dispersion force is always dominant in standard models of spatial competition. As seen above, firms want to soften the intensity of competition by being separated from each other. Firms can be agglomerated, however, if there is a device that reduces the intensity of competition. This is the case, for example, when firms sell sufficiently differentiated products. *Another way of reducing the intensity of competition is to retain quantity as a strategic variable in the second stage of the game.* Indeed, it is well-known that quantity (Cournot) competition results in market outcomes that are generally less competitive than those associated with price (Bertrand) competition. A body of work (albeit a small one, as it has emerged only recently) has revisited the strategic choice of location under Cournot competition.

3. Another drawback of the Bertrand-like spatial competition models is that they generally involve market areas that do not overlap, as each firm sells exclusively to a subsegment of consumers. Quantity competition, by contrast, is characterized by overlapping markets, i.e., by what is known as *intraindustry trade* in an international setting. This prediction agrees with economic reality as firms are seldom in a monopoly position over some territory. As soon as trade costs are sufficiently low, a mutual

invasion of markets occurs. Each firm not only sells its product close to its own production site, but also close to the sites of its competitors. This involves two-way trade of similar or homogeneous goods between different locations. According to Ecochard et al. (2005), trade within the EU-25 in 2002 involved a share close to 64% for this type of trade.

For all these reasons, we find it relevant to study the spatial version of the Cournot oligopoly.

9.2.1 Spatial Discrimination and Intraindustry Trade

As in the above, we assume that space is represented by the unit linear segment. Each point of this segment now stands for a particular market of each firm's product. Moreover, we also suppose that these markets are *segmented*, which means that firms choose a specific strategy for each of them (chapter 8). Such a practice is fairly common in international trade and has therefore been widely used in oligopolistic competition approaches to trade theory. The segmentation of markets allows us, furthermore, to tackle profit maximization separately in each market, since there are no direct interactions between supply and/or demand conditions among these markets so long as marginal costs are constant. Prices are determined as if no arbitrage between markets (a consumer buying in one place to sell in another) is possible. In fact, as will be seen later, there is no profitable arbitrage between markets at the equilibrium prices.

For simplicity, we assume that the inverse demand function in x is linear and is given by

$$p(x; x_1, x_2) = 1 - Q(x; x_1, x_2),$$

where $Q(x; x_1, x_2) = q_1(x; x_1, x_2) + q_2(x; x_1, x_2)$ represents the total quantity sold and consumed in this market. Each local market x is formed by consumers buying the good at the $p(x; x_1, x_2)$. Each firm chooses a quantity to supply to each local market.

When firm 1 serves market x from location x_1, it must bear a trade cost given by $t|x - x_1|$, while its marginal production cost is normalized to zero.[1] The profits made by firm 1 in x may then be written as a function of both firms' locations:

$$\Pi_1(q_1, q_2; x, x_1, x_2) = [1 - Q(x; x_1, x_2) - t|x - x_1|]q_1(x; x_1, x_2).$$

Cournot competition with segmented markets means that each firm chooses the quantity of the good it sells on each market. Applying

---

[1] We will see that, in such a setting, the possible nonexistence of a Nash equilibrium identified in section 9.1.2 disappears under market segmentation.

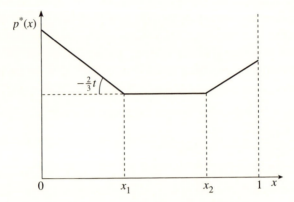

Figure 9.4. Equilibrium delivered prices.

the first-order conditions yields the equilibrium quantity and profits of firm 1 as follows:

$$q_1^*(x; x_1, x_2) = \tfrac{1}{3}(1 - 2t|x - x_1| + t|x - x_2|), \qquad (9.11)$$

and

$$\Pi_1^*(x; x_1, x_2) = [q_1^*(x; x_1, x_2)]^2 = [\tfrac{1}{3}(1 - 2t|x - x_1| + t|x - x_2|)]^2.$$

The equilibrium price in x is thus given by

$$p^*(x; x_1, x_2) = \tfrac{1}{3}(1 + t|x - x_1| + t|x - x_2|).$$

The delivered price prevailing in x is therefore an increasing function of the two firms' trade costs.

In all local markets situated between the two firms ($x \in [x_1, x_2]$), the delivered price is constant and equal to $\tfrac{1}{3}[1 + t(x_2 - x_1)]$. In all local markets belonging to one of the two hinterlands, for example, $x \in [x_2, 1]$, the delivered price is an increasing function of the distance between the market x and the two firms' locations:

$$p^*(x; x_1, x_2) = \tfrac{1}{3}[1 + |2tx - t(x_2 + x_1)|].$$

It is readily verified that no arbitrage is profitable, i.e., the price difference between two markets is lower than the cost of shipping the good between these markets. This is straightforward in $[x_1, x_2]$ because the equilibrium delivered price is constant. In $[x_2, 1]$, the equilibrium delivered price only increases at two-thirds the rate of the trade costs, so the price difference makes it impossible to cover the good's trade costs between the two markets. Likewise, no arbitrage is profitable in the other hinterland.

Figure 9.4 has two interesting implications. First, the difference between the equilibrium prices in a consumers' market and in a production site is generally an increasing function of the trade cost between these two markets, and therefore of the distance between them. In other words, spatial separation allows for price differences. Various empirical studies seem to confirm this prediction. For example, Engel and Rogers (1996) studied the evolution of price differences for very similar goods between American and Canadian cities. They found, in thirteen out of the fourteen products investigated, that distance plays a role in explaining observed price gaps, both within and between countries. More precisely, Engel and Rogers observed that distance explains around 20% of the volatility in prices between an American city and a Canadian city, while the national border explained a little over 30%. This impact of spatial separation on price differences has been confirmed by Parsley and Wei (2001) on American and Japanese cities, as well as by Engel and Rogers (2001) on fifty-five cities in eleven European countries. All these studies, which use comparable methods and data but come from different samples of cities, found that distance had a significant impact on price differences. Second, a reduction in the unit trade cost t leads to lower equilibrium prices in each market. In particular, the location of firms no longer matters in determining the equilibrium price once $t = 0$. Moreover, making competitors closer brings down the equilibrium prices in all local markets. All of this is reminiscent of what we have found in Hotelling's model.

In what follows, we assume that no location is sufficiently distant from the others for a firm located there not to find it profitable to serve the consumers living in *all* other places (this is the "complete market coverage" condition). Hence, we seek the condition that guarantees that the two firms are willing to serve *all* consumers whatever their location. This condition can be identified as follows: what is the least profitable situation for firm 1's profits? In a Cournot game, a firm's equilibrium profits are usually a decreasing function of its own cost and an increasing function of the cost of each of its competitors. The market share of firm 1 is therefore a decreasing function of its distance from the market and an increasing function of the distance separating firm 2 from that market. As firm 1 is located to the left of firm 2, the most extreme positions are such that $x_1 = 0$ and $x_2 = 1$. By replacing these locations in the equilibrium quantities (9.11), we obtain the complete coverage condition:

$$t < \tfrac{1}{2}. \tag{9.12}$$

This condition further guarantees that there is intraindustry trade in each market, regardless of firms' locations.[2] To simplify the analysis,

---

[2] This is similar to the condition identified by Brander and Krugman (1983) in the case of two countries and two-way trade of a homogeneous good under Cournot competition.

we assume that this condition holds. This assumption is not innocuous, however. The complete coverage of markets reduces firms' incentives to choose distant locations. Even though firms can increase their market power by locating close to the endpoints of the market segment, they are unable to enjoy a complete monopoly position over some local markets, which accordingly discourages dispersion.

We now seek to determine firms' equilibrium locations. Consider firm 1. Its total profits are equal to the sum of the profits made in each market x:

$$\Pi_1^*(x_1, x_2) = \int_0^1 \Pi_1^*(x; x_1, x_2)\, dx. \tag{9.13}$$

The first-order condition for its location to maximize $\Pi_1^*(x_1, x_2)$ is as follows:

$$\frac{\partial \Pi_1^*}{\partial x_1} = \frac{4t}{9} \left\{ -\int_0^{x_1} [1 - 2t(x_1 - x) + t(x_2 - x)]\, dx \right.$$

$$+ \int_{x_1}^{x_2} [1 - 2t(x - x_1) + t(x_2 - x)]\, dx$$

$$\left. + \int_{x_2}^1 [1 - 2t(x - x_1) + t(x - x_2)]\, dx \right\} = 0.$$

After integration and a few simple manipulations, this expression becomes

$$\frac{9}{4t} \frac{\partial \Pi_1^*}{\partial x_1} = (1 - 2x_1) + t[(x_1 - x_2)^2 + (2x_1 - x_2 - \tfrac{1}{2})] = 0.$$

To find the equilibrium locations, it remains to examine the incentives for firm 1 to change its location while its rival's location remains unchanged. Assume that firm 2 is located in the market center ($x_2 = \tfrac{1}{2}$). In this case, firm 1's first-order condition becomes

$$\frac{9}{4t} \frac{\partial \Pi_1^*}{\partial x_1} \bigg|_{x_2 = 1/2} = A(1 - 2x_1) = 0,$$

where

$$A = 1 - \tfrac{1}{4} t(3 + 2x_1) > 0.$$

Consequently, we have the following proposition.

Proposition 9.2. *If $t < \tfrac{1}{2}$, the agglomeration of the two firms at the market center is the unique Nash equilibrium.*

This proposition shows that Cournot competition leads to minimal spatial differentiation. This conclusion, which seemingly confirms Hotelling's intuition, contradicts the result obtained above under price competition. The reason for this difference lies in the fact that the agglomeration force here is magnified by the existence of a place where the cost of supplying the entire market is minimized (as in Weber), i.e., the market center. The dispersion force still stems from the strengthening of competition when firms get closer, but it is weaker than in the Hotelling model because competition takes place in quantities rather than in prices. In other words, the former effect dominates the latter one here.

We must now asses the robustness of proposition 9.2. First, this result depends on the geography under consideration. For example, Pal (1998) has shown that two firms competing over markets distributed along a circle end up located opposite to each other, thereby contradicting the property of agglomeration established above. This result underlines the importance of having a *central place* in the geographical setting. When markets are spread along a circle, there is no market center; thus, the agglomeration force is destroyed, while the dispersion force is left as it is. This finding remains valid if we consider two symmetric countries. In this case, there is again no central location, so that the dispersion force always prevails.

The agglomeration property also vanishes if, for the various reasons highlighted in previous chapters, we retain a distribution of production costs such that these costs are highest in the market center. In this case, firms tend to disperse to take advantage of the lower production costs in the periphery (Mayer 2000). Gupta et al. (1997) introduce an additional type of heterogeneity into consumers' geographical distribution and show that the market center accommodates all firms in special cases. By making the model more realistic, we therefore challenge the agglomeration property. These studies confirm one of the main points of this book, i.e., that, to understand firms' locational choices, it is crucial to have a precise description of the spatial distribution of production costs and demand: two effects not usually taken into account in spatial competition models.

Last, if trade cost increase beyond a certain threshold, thus implying that the complete coverage condition no longer holds, the market center ceases to be an equilibrium, as firms want to separate from each other to retain a sufficient number of consumers located close to the borders of the segment. A new force of dispersion thus appears, which bears some resemblance to the demand stemming from the immobile consumers in Krugman's core–periphery model (chapter 6). When trade costs are low, this force is not sufficient to prevent agglomeration. In contrast, when trade costs are sufficiently high, the equilibrium involves a gradual dispersion of producers. As above, agglomerated and dispersed equilibria may coexist for certain values of t (Gupta et al. 1997). All these results show the existence of a strong link between spatial competition models and those developed in economic geography.

9.2.2 Home-Market Effect and Spatial Competition

Given the role of the HME in economic geography, the following question suggests itself: is the HME still valid in a strategic context? We have just seen that the existence of strategic interactions between firms is a powerful dispersion force. It is, therefore, not clear that the big market still attracts a more than proportional share of firms once these interactions are taken into consideration.

Consider two regions, A and B. Region A has a fraction $\theta \geqslant \frac{1}{2}$ of consumers, whose total number is L. The total number of firms is fixed and given by the integer n, a fraction of which, λ, are located in region A. As before, the marginal production cost is normalized to zero. The price paid by a region A consumer is as follows:

$$p_A = 1 - [\lambda n q_{AA} + (1 - \lambda) n q_{BA}],$$

where q_{AA} and q_{BA} denote the quantity sold to a region A consumer by a firm located in region A and in region B, respectively. The profits of a region A firm are thus equal to

$$\Pi_A = p_A q_{AA} \theta L + (p_B - t) q_{AB} (1 - \theta) L.$$

Under Cournot competition, the equilibrium quantities can be obtained by applying the first-order conditions to Π_A and Π_B:

$$q_{AA}^*(\lambda) = \frac{1 + (1 - \lambda) nt}{n + 1}, \qquad q_{AB}^*(\lambda) = \frac{1 - t - (1 - \lambda) nt}{n + 1}.$$

Observe that firms choose not to export when n and/or t become sufficiently large. In this context, the complete coverage condition becomes

$$t < \frac{1}{n + 1}. \tag{9.14}$$

The equilibrium profits are then obtained by replacing the equilibrium quantities in the expression $\Pi_A^* = (q_{AA}^*)^2 + (q_{AB}^*)^2$, from which we are able to determine the incentive for a firm to set up in region A:

$$\Pi_A^*(\lambda) - \Pi_B^*(\lambda) = \frac{2Lt}{n + 1} \left[2 \left(1 - \frac{t}{2} \right) \theta - \left(1 - \frac{n + 1}{2} t \right) - nt\lambda \right].$$

As in chapter 4, each firm is pulled by the big market (the sum of the first two terms is positive by (9.14)) but the dispersion force (the third term is negative) gets stronger when the number of firms located in region A increases. The equilibrium distribution of firms is such that $\Pi_A^*(\lambda) - \Pi_B^*(\lambda) = 0$:[3]

$$\lambda^*(\theta) = -\frac{1 - (n+1)t/2}{nt} + \frac{2(1 - t/2)}{nt}\theta,$$

which exceeds θ so long as $\theta > \frac{1}{2}$ since $\lambda^*(\frac{1}{2}) = \frac{1}{2}$ and $\partial\lambda^*/\partial\theta > 1$, keeping (9.14) in mind. Moreover, $\partial^2\lambda^*/\partial t\partial\theta < 0$, so that falling trade costs increase the share of the firms established in the big market. We fall back, therefore, on the main properties of the HME uncovered in chapter 4.

9.2.3 Agglomeration under Spatial Competition

Spatial competition models make it possible to integrate a crucial element into firms' locational choices, namely, strategic interactions. The conclusions to which these models lead resemble those obtained in economic geography. Hence, with spatial Cournot competition we are at the point reached by Krugman (1980) in using the Dixit–Stiglitz model of monopolistic competition. All the ingredients, therefore, seem to be at hand for the study of the role of strategic interactions in economic geography settings in which location choices are endogenous and regional incomes depend on the share of activities established in each region. Unfortunately, this type of approach has barely been studied, for two reasons. The first one is easy to figure out: if each of the ingredients of the two approaches leads to comparable results, it is hard to see why we would not find similar results when the basic ingredients are combined. This remains to be proved, however. The second reason is that it very quickly becomes difficult to obtain analytical results in multimarket models with strategic interactions; thus, we are required to resort to numerical analyses.

9.2.3.1 *Regional Disparities and Unemployment*

Combes (1997) considers a model with two regions and two sectors. As usual, the agricultural sector produces a homogeneous good under constant returns and perfect competition. Trading the agricultural good is costless and this good is taken as the numéraire. The industry produces a homogeneous good under increasing returns. The cost function of a firm takes the form of a fixed cost expressed in the numéraire and a marginal cost evaluated in terms of labor. The trade cost of the industrial good, denoted t, is positive and additive as in chapter 8. Consumers

---

[3] This equality is generally not verified when n is an integer. It should, therefore, be replaced by two inequalities with opposite signs. This does not affect the conclusions, however.

have identical Cobb–Douglas preferences, which leads to the following aggregated demand for the manufactured good in region A:

$$Q_A = \frac{\mu Y_A}{p_A}, \tag{9.15}$$

where Y_A is the regional income, p_A is the price of the manufactured good in this region, and μ is the share of this good in the consumption structure. Finally, as above, markets are segmented and firms compete in quantity on each market. In other words, a firm located in region A chooses the quantities q_{AA} and q_{AB} that it sells in the two markets.

The major difference from the DSK-type model is that here *the differences in regional incomes stem from regional differences in unemployment*. To simplify matters, we make several assumptions regarding the working of regional labor markets. The total and agricultural populations, L and L_a, are exogenous and identical in each region. Moreover, there is no sectorial and spatial migration. Thus, the labor supply in the manufacturing sector is perfectly inelastic; it is also identical in each region, being equal to $L - L_a$. Wages in this sector are exogenous and the same in both regions: $w_A = w_B \equiv w$. In such a context there is no reason for the labor demand in the manufacturing sector (L_A for region A, which is endogenous and depends on firms' choice of location) to be equal to the labor supply. Consequently, region A experiences full employment when

$$L_A > L - L_a,$$

or faces unemployment when

$$L_A < L - L_a.$$

In the short run, the numbers of firms established in each region, n_A and n_B, are exogenous. The market equilibrium for the manufactured good in region A is

$$Q_A = n_A q_{AA} + n_B q_{BA}. \tag{9.16}$$

Thus, if f denotes the fixed production cost, (9.15) implies that the profits of a firm located in A are given by

$$\pi_A = \left(\frac{\mu Y_A}{Q_A} - w\right) q_{AA} + \left(\frac{\mu Y_B}{Q_B} - w - t\right) q_{AB} - f.$$

The first-order conditions for an equilibrium in which all the firms sell in both regions give the firm's share in each market:[4]

$$\frac{q_{AA}^*}{Q_A} = \frac{p_A - w}{p_A} \quad \text{and} \quad \frac{q_{AB}^*}{Q_B} = \frac{p_B - w - t}{p_B}. \tag{9.17}$$

---

[4] It is readily verified that the second-order conditions hold.

Finally, it remains to close the model by recalling that regional incomes are equal to the sum of the incomes of individuals who have a job:

$$Y_A = L_a + wL_A. \tag{9.18}$$

Using (9.15)–(9.18), the short-run equilibrium is characterized by the following expressions and their counterparts for region B[5]:

$$p_A^* = \frac{(n_A + n_B)w + n_B t}{n_A + n_B - 1},$$

$$[w - (n_A - 1)t]q_{AA}^* - (w + n_B t)q_{BA}^* = 0,$$

$$n_A(1 - \mu)q_{AA}^* - n_A \frac{\mu}{p_A}(p_B^* - t)q_{AB}^* + n_B q_{BA}^* = \frac{\mu}{p_A}(L_a - n_A f).$$

In the long run, the number of firms is endogenous and such that profits Π_A^* and Π_B^* (where prices and quantities are replaced by their equilibrium value) are zero:

$$\Pi_A^* = \Pi_B^* = 0.$$

At this stage, it is useful to distinguish the agglomeration and dispersion forces. As before, strategic interactions encourage firms to move away from their competitors and, therefore, to locate themselves in the region with the smallest number of firms, in order to face less competition. It is in the region with many firms, however, that employment is highest, and this results in a higher regional income. This generates an agglomeration force linked to the final demand: *the lower the regional unemployment and, therefore, the higher the regional income, the greater the incentives for firms to locate in the region.* We will see that the agglomeration force generated by a low level of regional unemployment is often sufficient to dominate the dispersion force stemming from competition, thus leading to regional disparities.

9.2.3.2 Numerical Analysis of Long-Run Equilibria

Even though the equilibrium profits are simpler than those obtained in the DSK model, they are still cumbersome to handle because the total number of firms is endogenous. So, as in chapter 7, we must appeal to numerical analysis to gain insights. For high trade costs and/or low fixed costs, Figure 9.5 depicts the regional dynamics that the economy may follow when new firms enter. Some points of the positive orthant must

---

[5] Note that some firms may find it unprofitable to export. The corresponding short-term equilibria must, therefore, be considered. It is then possible to compute the short-run profits made by a firm for all possible configurations of firms.

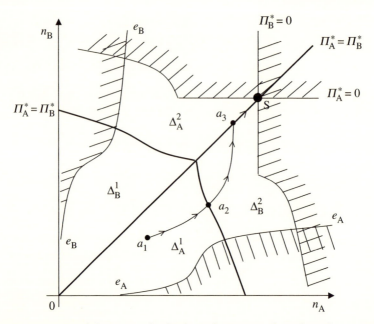

Figure 9.5. Regional dynamics for high trade costs and weak scale economies.

be eliminated because either profits are negative or one of the employment constraints is violated. The loci $\Pi_A^* = 0$ and $\Pi_B^* = 0$ as well as the full-employment loci $L_A = L - L_a$ (the curve $e_A e_A$) and $L_B = L - L_a$ (the curve $e_B e_B$) delineate the feasible (unshaded) area in which the economy may evolve. The loci along which profits are equal, $\Pi_A^* = \Pi_B^*$, are given by the bisector, since regions are strictly identical on this line, and by a downward sloping curve that stems from the balance between the agglomeration and dispersion forces. Both parts are represented by bold lines, which allow us to determine the four domains Δ_A^1, Δ_A^2, Δ_B^1, and Δ_B^2 that can contain short-run equilibria. In Δ_A^1, although the number of region A firms exceeds the number of region B firms, profits are higher in A; the opposite holds in Δ_B^1. In contrast, in Δ_A^2 the number of firms is still larger in region A but profits are now lower than in the other region. The same holds for region B in the domain Δ_B^2. In other words, in a short-run equilibrium such as a_1, the agglomeration force triggered by the higher volume of employment dominates the competition force, a configuration that cannot arise when incomes are exogenous.

Using figure 9.5, we are able to figure out what the entry process looks like. For example, starting at a_1, we first observe a *divergence phase* between regions with the economy moving from a_1 to a_2. As profits are higher in A than in B, more firms set up in region A. The gap between regions in terms of firms' share, and therefore of employment and

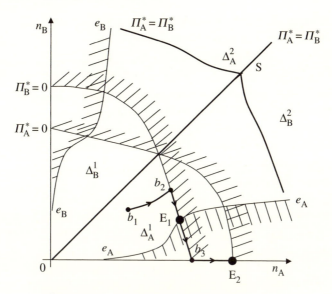

Figure 9.6. Regional dynamics for low trade
costs and strong scale economies.

wealth, grows. By contrast, from a_2, the degree of asymmetry between
the two regions becomes so high that the dispersion force becomes dominant, thus implying that profits become higher in the region in which
competition is weaker. In other words, we now face a *convergence phase*,
during which a growing number of firms set up in the region that has
only a few firms, thereby reducing regional asymmetries. From a_3, a symmetric equilibrium is achieved, although the profits are not yet equal to
zero. Firms therefore continue to enter one region or the other alternately until the long-run equilibrium S is achieved. For the chosen values
of the parameters (high trade costs and/or low fixed costs), the long-run
equilibrium is symmetric and does not display regional disparities.

What happens when trade costs go down or when the degree of increasing returns in the manufacturing sector rises? This is shown in figure 9.6,
where the long-run equilibrium is asymmetric. The zero-profit loci are
shifted in the southwest direction and, therefore, are now set further to
the left of the equal-profit locus. In other words, when fixed costs are
high with respect to trade costs, fewer firms enter the market. In this
case, *the entry process comes to a halt during the phase of regional divergence.* More precisely, following the path b_1–b_3, we first find a divergence
phase, as above, in which the number of firms increases in both regions,
but there is a relatively larger increase in the large region. However, once
b_2 is reached, profits in the small region vanish. Hence, the divergence

process is strengthened, since firms now have to leave region B, while others continue to set up in region A.

Two cases may then arise.

(i) When the regional population is low, the long-run equilibrium is given by E_1: there is partial agglomeration of the manufacturing sector. Profits are zero in region B but remain positive in region A, thus implying that more firms would like to enter and set up there. But no more workers are available in this region, so the entry process ends with a large number of firms in region A and a small number that stay put in region B.

(ii) When the regional population is high, the full-employment curve e_A-e_A moves downward.[6] In this case, region B ends up losing all its firms (in b_3), so full agglomeration prevails in A. The entry process comes to a halt in E_2 because profits are zero in region A while potential profits are negative in region B. In contrast, when the economy ends up in E_1, the dispersion force generated by full employment in region A softens the asymmetry in the distribution of firms.

In both cases, regional disparities emerge, since a larger number of firms are located in one region.[7]

To summarize, long-run asymmetric equilibria may emerge in a setting with strategic interactions. On this occasion we encounter the fundamental trade-off between increasing returns and trade costs (chapter 2), Krugman's core–periphery structure (chapter 6), and the right-hand side of the bell-shaped curve linking economic integration and spatial inequalities (chapter 8). Even though this model oversimplifies several aspects of local labor markets, it can hardly be denied that this type of research is too rarely undertaken.

9.3 Concluding Remarks

When firms sell a homogeneous good, price competition is a very strong dispersion force that pushes firms away from each other. This implies that, in one way or another, all devices that make it possible to lessen the impact of competition act in favor of agglomeration. In a linear market involving a very large number of locations, firms agglomerate at the market center once products are sufficiently differentiated and trade costs

---

[6] The other curves in figure 9.6 also move but keep the same shapes and relative positions.

[7] Clearly, the symmetric point of E_1 in case (i) is another possible long-run equilibrium, as region B is now more developed. The same holds for E_2 in case (ii).

sufficiently low. In this case, distance matters much less in consumers' behavior, which encourages firms to set up where the market potential is the highest. This agrees with one of the key messages of economic geography: low transport costs push firms selling differentiated goods to agglomerate. This is also true in the case of firms selling a homogeneous good once they compete in quantity. Finally, we have seen that oligopolistic competition can be integrated within the economic geography approach. Consequently, it seems fair to say that *strategic behaviors do not seem to vastly affect the conclusions obtained in settings based on monopolistic competition*, even though the underlying mechanisms differ.

9.4 Related Literature

Over the seventy-five years since it was written, Hotelling's article has remained a masterpiece that still deserves to be read. It has given rise to three different subfields: location theory, of course, but also product differentiation in industrial organization and the economic theory of competition between political parties. Somewhat surprisingly, this article contained a mistake that went uncorrected for fifty years (d'Aspremont et al. 1979). The correction was by no means minor, however, as it led to the replacement of the principle of minimum differentiation by the principle of differentiation. Hotelling's model has sparked a considerable number of publications, so that making a selection is not an easy task. A presentation of the basic ideas can be found in Eaton and Lipsey (1977) as well as in Gabszewicz and Thisse (1986). Chapter 8 of Anderson et al. (1992) offers an overview of the main results. We have assumed here that consumers always choose to buy; a more general analysis is provided by Hinloopen and van Marrewijk (1999). Finally, studies of spatial discrimination in the Cournot setting have been undertaken by Greenhut and Greenhut (1977), Brander (1981), Hamilton et al. (1989), and Anderson and Neven (1991).

Part III

Breadth and Determinants of Spatial Concentration

10

Measuring Spatial Concentration

The measurement of inequalities has long been of interest to economists, especially to those trying to evaluate inequalities across individual incomes (Sen 1973) or the degree of concentration in a given sector (Scherer 1980). In chapter 1, we presented some stylized facts regarding the spatial concentration of economic activities. However, our assessment of income distributions has been restricted to simple tools, such as numbers, tables, and maps depicting the GDP per capita. Although such tools succeed in conveying a general impression of the scope of spatial inequalities, their limitations are readily apparent. First, while the monotone increase in inequalities that characterizes the nineteenth century is easily captured by simple statistics, as soon as such inequalities become more complex and nonmonotone, we must turn to more sophisticated tools. Second, when the number of regions is large, it is no longer appropriate to simply rank all regions according to a given index of development. Third, extending our analysis to the sectoral level requires specific tools, as both predictions and policy prescriptions are likely to vary markedly across sectors. Last, with the ambition of *making better use of all available information* (modern databases often distinguish between more than 500 sectors) comes the need to move beyond simple maps and tables that cannot capture this breadth of information appropriately.

   Geographers and economists alike have sought to develop indices that capture inequality across industries, time, and space. It will become readily apparent that the issue is more complex than it seems at first glance. Although some indices have become standard, the *ideal index* remains to be discovered. Section 10.1 provides a set of properties that should be met by an ideal index, which gives us a benchmark by which to judge existing indices. The subsequent sections introduce the main approaches that are applied in the literature. The first approach is based on indices used for measuring inequality across individuals, such as the Gini index, an approach that can also be used to evaluate the industrial concentration of firms belonging to the same sector. This will allow us to find out how spatial inequalities imply new and specific constraints. Recently, attempts have been made to account for these constraints. An example of primary importance is the seminal work of Ellison and Glaeser (1997), which has generated a new family of indices allowing for more relevant comparisons of spatial concentration across industries. In the last section, we discuss the approach proposed by Duranton and Overman (2005), which constitutes an important step forward in conceptualizing and measuring spatial concentration. Based on the average distance between plants, this approach frees the analysis from the need to use spatial classifications, thereby reducing the corresponding biases.

10.1   The Properties of an Ideal Index of Spatial Concentration

Any empirical tool, ranging from the most basic to the most sophisticated, rests on a specific set of assumptions. This is true of linear regressions that presuppose that the error term has a very specific structure, but it is also true of more descriptive apparatus, such as inequality indices. It is, therefore, important to understand the implications of the assumptions made, and to compare them with the desirable properties that an ideal index should have. Some assumptions are less suggestive than others; as we will see, even the most obvious assumptions are not always satisfied.

To start with, given that most studies are carried out at the sector level, the first property that must be satisfied is as follows.

Property 10.1. Measures of spatial concentration should be comparable across industries.

In more concrete terms, this amounts to saying that we must be capable of comparing the degree of concentration in the automobile industry with, say, that in the chemicals industry. More generally, it means verifying whether a comparison of spatial concentration using a classification that describes a few sectors with spatial concentration using another classification that distinguishes more sectors is possible.

For example, is comparing the spatial concentration of poultry farmers with that of agriculture possible and meaningful? Although this property may seem obvious, it is nevertheless not satisfied by the simplest indices. The difficulty lies in the existence of differences regarding the size distribution of firms belonging to the same sector, a characteristic that is often called its "industrial concentration" (Scherer 1980). By affecting the average size, and hence the total number, of plants (or branches or stores), the degree of concentration of a sector impacts on its spatial concentration. It is, therefore, *highly desirable to distinguish industrial concentration from spatial concentration,* the latter having to be independent of the distribution of the activity among plants. As will be seen later on, this is only possible when data at the plant level are available or, at the very least, when the total number of plants in the sector under scrutiny is known.

The spatial counterpart of property 10.1 is as follows.

Property 10.2. Measures of spatial concentration should be comparable across spatial scales.

When this property holds, it allows for the meaningful comparison of spatial concentration across countries, or across different levels of spatial scales as, say, whether an activity is more concentrated at the national than the regional level. Somewhat surprisingly, property 10.2 has been more readily grasped than property 10.1, even though they are symmetric. For example, geographers have long pointed out that the number of regions considered in different countries is likely to have an influence on the comparison of their degree of regional concentration. Even though this problem has often been raised, only the most recent indices address this issue head-on.

Two other properties that deal with the definition of spatial units and sectors should also be satisfied. The first is as stated below.

Property 10.3. Measures of spatial concentration should be unbiased with respect to arbitrary changes to spatial classification.

For instance, let us suppose that the ninety-four départements of mainland France are replaced by ninety-four spatial units defined in a different way. In measuring the spatial concentration of a given sector, the index should have the same value under both definitions. This problem was brought to light long ago, and may be attributed to the delineation of borders separating spatial units. For any given geographical area, the underlying economic problem stems from the fact that homogeneous *economic* zones seldom coincide with *administrative* zones: tightly linked economic agents (such as employees and their workplaces, or firms and their subcontractors) are thus often split across different administrative spatial units. Hence, changing the definition of spatial units may result in a significant, but artificial, redistribution of economic activity. In other words, such changes can translate into different measures of concentration even though the degree of "real" agglomeration remains unchanged. More generally, the problems lying behind the difficulties encountered with properties 10.2 and 10.3 are related to *the discretization of a continuous space*, which is known as the modifiable areal unit problem (MAUP).[1]

For any given discretization, a related problem is that the standard indices generally do not take into account the *relative position* of spatial units (see Thomas (2002) and our discussion regarding two-region models in chapter 4). And yet proposition 10.3 requires that the index changes value when units are switched around (suppose for instance that you could invert the locations of London and Liverpool; the measured spatial agglomeration of activities in the United Kingdom would change). As a counterexample, the first two families of indices discussed below do not satisfy this property: they take the same values regardless of whether economic activities are located in adjacent or distant regions.

We find a criterion similar to property 10.3 with respect to the industrial dimension.

Property 10.4. Measures of spatial concentration should be unbiased with respect to arbitrary changes to industrial classification.

As seen above, the carving up of spatial units is arbitrary so that borders may separate regions with strong economic ties. Likewise, in defining a limited number of sectors, the industrial classification may also arbitrarily separate closely related economic activities. In particular, some related activities will inevitably be separated, while conversely others are likely to be grouped together despite marked differences. Furthermore, the precision of any given industrial classification often depends on the sector at hand. For instance, existing classifications typically distinguish between more items in the manufacturing sector than in services. This is another artificial source of difference between measures of concentration. Drawing from the idea of proximity in physical space, it may prove promising to consider the technological proximity that exists between industries by creating a measure of "technological distance." A generalized distance that would account for both spatial and technological distances could then be used when evaluating the spatial concentration of a sector.

The last two desirable properties are related to the possible existence of statistical criteria that enable us to test for the presence of spatial concentration.

Property 10.5. Measures of spatial concentration should be carried out with respect to a well-established benchmark.

---

[1] See Francis et al. (forthcoming) for a detailed analysis of the MAUP and Briant et al. (2007) for a detailed empirical assessment.

One benchmark that naturally comes to mind, and underlies a number of existing indices, is the uniform distribution. However, when studying the spatial distribution of a given sector, it seems more relevant and fruitful to use the overall distribution of activities. Although this is rarely done in practice, using a benchmark grounded in a specific economic model is also likely to lead to more consistent indices. In particular, such an approach would allow one to investigate whether the observed distribution differs from that derived from a specific theoretical framework.

Finally, regardless of the way the benchmark is defined, being able to determine whether the observed distribution is *significantly* different from its benchmark appears to be crucial. Furthermore, when do two estimators of spatial concentration differ significantly across areas, periods, or industries? This leads us to the last property an ideal index should satisfy.

Property 10.6. The measure should allow one to determine whether significant differences exist between an observed distribution and its benchmark, or between two situations (areas, periods, or industries).

Without these types of statistical tests, concentration indices have little value. This is because we are unable to determine whether we are dealing with high or low concentration, or whether there is even any spatial concentration at all.

10.2 Spatial Concentration Indices

10.2.1 The Gini Index

The most popular index for measuring inequality is undoubtedly the Gini index. It was originally used to evaluate inequalities across personal incomes (Sen 1973). In our context, it will be used to evaluate the spatial concentration of a given sector in terms of some given magnitude such as employment, production, or value-added. Let x_r^s be the level of the magnitude under consideration (e.g., employment) in sector $s = 1, \ldots, S$ and in region $r = 1, \ldots, R$. As with all the indices presented in this section, the Gini index is based on how regional shares of sector s, denoted λ_r^s, are distributed across regions:

$$\lambda_r^s = \frac{x_r^s}{x^s},$$

where $x^s \equiv \sum_{r=1}^{R} x_r^s$ is the total employment level in sector s.

Let us start with a graphical interpretation of this index, which will convey its intuitive meaning most readily. The main idea is to sort regions in ascending order by their degree of specialization in sector s (as measured by λ_r^s) and to draw what is known as the *Lorenz curve*. The x-coordinate corresponding to a point on this curve represents the fraction n/R of the n regions with the lowest employment shares in sector s. The y-coordinate corresponds to the cumulative share of these n regions in total employment, i.e.,

$$\lambda_{r(n)}^s = \sum_{r=1}^{n} \lambda_r^s.$$

If employment levels in sector s were uniformly distributed across all regions, each region would have $1/R$ of total employment, in which case the Lorenz curve would be given by the $45°$ line. As soon as the spatial distribution is not uniform, the Lorenz curve lies below the $45°$ line. In other words, the region with the lowest share of employment in sector s has a share of employment smaller than $1/R$; the first two such regions have a combined share that is smaller than $2/R$, and so on. In this case, a more unequal distribution translates to having greater levels of employment concentrated in a small number of large regions (and therefore lower levels in smaller regions): the greater the inequality, the more the Lorenz curve departs from the $45°$ line. The Gini index is given by the area that lies between the Lorenz curve and the $45°$ line (which needs to be multiplied by two for the upper bound of the index to be equal to one). The index ranges from zero, when the distribution of employment in the sector is uniform, to one, when all employment is concentrated in a single region.

Under the normalization $\lambda_{r(0)}^s = 0$, the *Gini index* is formally defined by

$$G^s = 1 - \sum_{n=1}^{R} \frac{1}{R}[\lambda_{r(n-1)}^s + \lambda_{r(n)}^s],$$

with each term in the sum corresponding to twice the area of the trapezoid situated below the Lorenz curve and delimited by the $(n-1)$th and the nth regions. This Gini index is called *absolute* because it uses the uniform distribution as a benchmark: each region is assigned the same weight $1/R$.

Another possibility involves comparing the distribution of sectoral employment with that of total employment, in order to determine the extent to which a given sector is more, or less, concentrated than the economy as a whole. This can be easily accomplished by replacing the x-coordinate values of the Lorenz curve: instead of using intervals of identical size $(1/R)$ for each region, as done with the uniform distribution, the intervals now have a varying length that corresponds to the total employment share of each region, which is given, for region r, by

$$\lambda_r = \frac{x_r}{x},$$

where $x_r = \sum_{s=1}^{S} x_r^s$ denotes the total employment in region r and $x = \sum_{s=1}^{S} x^s = \sum_{r=1}^{R} x_r$ the total employment in the area under study. What is called the *relative* Gini index uses an alternate Lorenz curve. Specifically, regions are now sorted in ascending order of their specialization with respect to their total size (as measured by λ_r^s/λ_r). Then we denote by $\lambda_{r(n)} = \sum_{r=1}^{n} \lambda_r$ the sum of the shares of total employment of the n least specialized regions in the sector under consideration. The shares $\lambda_{r(n)}$ are now used as the x-axis. Unlike the absolute index, where intervals are given by $1/R$, the relative index uses intervals of variable size given by $\lambda_{r(n)} - \lambda_{r(n-1)}$, which is merely the share in the total employment of the nth region. Formally, the relative Gini index equals twice the area that lies between the 45° line and this new Lorenz curve:

$$G^s = 1 - \sum_{n=1}^{R} \lambda_r [\lambda_{r(n)}^s + \lambda_{r(n-1)}^s]. \tag{10.1}$$

Unfortunately, both the relative and absolute Gini indices only satisfy a very limited number of the ideal index's properties. For example, they do not allow us to adequately compare industries having different market structures (property 10.1): a limitation that served as the catalyst for the development of a new wave of indices presented in the next section. Examining variations over time can also be biased by the fact that the total number of firms in a country varies over time, even if this variation is uniform across spatial units. It should also be clear that comparing different zones is problematic because they typically differ in their number of regions (property 10.2). For example, splitting a region into two smaller ones changes the ordering of regions, and thus modifies the Gini index.

When the first two properties are not satisfied, it follows that the third and fourth are also violated. On the other hand, the benchmark underlying both the absolute and the relative Gini indices is well-defined (property 10.5): the benchmark is the uniform distribution in the absolute index and the actual distribution of total activity in the relative index. However, to date, no statistical tests have been proposed for determining whether observed values depart significantly from their benchmark values (property 10.6).

It should be emphasized that indices measuring concentration across regions have a natural counterpart, i.e., absolute and relative *specialization indices* that measure the industrial structure of regions. While spatial concentration determines whether a given sector is more or less concentrated across regions, specialization determines whether a particular region accommodates a more or less equal distribution of all sectors. For example, we can construct a Gini specialization index to measure sector s employment shares within a given region r:

$$\mu_r^s = \frac{x_r^s}{x_r}.$$

Again, we sort the sectors in ascending order of their weight in region r, and construct a Lorenz curve by generating intervals on the x-axis that correspond either to $1/S$ (as with the absolute index) or to each sector's share of total employment (as with the relative index). The *Gini specialization index* for region r is given by twice the area between this new Lorenz curve and the 45° line, so that an expression similar to (10.1) holds. Given that indices of both concentration and specialization are founded on the same axioms, it must be that they share the same advantages and limitations.

10.2.2   The Isard, Herfindhal, and Theil Indices

Other indices that share more or less the same characteristics as the Gini index have been proposed in the literature. They are subject to the same drawbacks as the Gini index. They can also be defined by reference to the uniform distribution or the distribution of total activity. In what follows, our benchmark is the total employment distribution, thus making these indices comparable to the relative Gini index. Replacing λ_r with $1/R$ in the expressions given below allows one to obtain the corresponding absolute indices.[2]

1. The *Isard index*, which regained popularity through Krugman (1991c), consists of a measure of concentration based on the absolute distance

---

[2] In Bailey and Gatrell (1995), the reader can find a discussion of *spatial autocorrelation indices*, which are based on the pioneering work of Moran (1950). They have the important advantage of taking into account the relative position of the areas, i.e., these indices are no longer invariant to permutations of locations. However, an important caveat is that autocorrelation indices do not measure spatial concentration in the same way it has been understood so far. Such indices are more akin to an agglomeration index, as they evaluate the correlation between the value of an economic variable for a given area, and the distance-decay sum of the values of this variable for all the other areas. Unfortunately, this type of index shares the same limitations as all of the other indices presented in this section.

between the actual and benchmark employment distributions:

$$I^s = \frac{1}{2} \sum_{r=1}^{R} |\lambda_r^s - \lambda_r|.$$

2. The *Herfindhal index* is the weighted sum of the square of each region's sectoral employment share:

$$H^s = \frac{1}{R} \sum_{r=1}^{R} \lambda_r \left(\frac{\lambda_r^s}{\lambda_r} \right)^2,$$

which reduces to the standard expression $H^s = \sum_{r=1}^{R} (\lambda_r^s)^2$ for the absolute index, where $\lambda_r = 1/R$.

Note that both the Isard and the Herfindhal indices have an upper bound of 1 (when all firms belonging to sector s are located within the same region), while the lower bound is the inverse of the smallest region's share for the former, and the inverse of the number of regions for the latter. As the range of values of these indices depends on the spatial scale and the way regions are defined, they clearly violate the first four properties stated in section 10.1.

3. The idea of *entropy* is borrowed from physics, where it is used as a measure of disorder. It was subsequently used in economics as a measure of concentration/dispersion, and is closely related to the logit and CES models (Anderson et al. 1992, chapter 3).

The entropy indices are defined by

$$E^s(\alpha) = \frac{1}{\alpha^2 - \alpha} \left[\sum_{r=1}^{R} \lambda_r \left(\frac{\lambda_r^s}{\lambda_r} \right)^\alpha - 1 \right], \tag{10.2}$$

where α is a parameter which, when less than (respectively, greater than) 1, assigns more weight to observations corresponding to the lower (respectively, higher) tail of the distribution.

The most common version corresponds to the value $\alpha = 1$. By using l'Hôpital's rule, we obtain the following expressions:

$$\lim_{\alpha \to 1} E^s(\alpha) = \sum_{r=1}^{R} \lambda_r \lim_{\alpha \to 1} \frac{(\lambda_r^s/\lambda_r)^\alpha - 1}{\alpha^2 - \alpha} = \sum_{r=1}^{R} \lambda_r \lim_{\alpha \to 1} \frac{(\lambda_r^s/\lambda_r)^\alpha \ln(\lambda_r^s/\lambda_r)}{2\alpha - 1},$$

which yield the *Theil index*,

$$E^s(1) \equiv T^s = \sum_{r=1}^{R} \lambda_r^s \ln \frac{\lambda_r^s}{\lambda_r}. \tag{10.3}$$

When $\alpha = 2$, we get

$$E^s(2) \equiv C^s = \frac{1}{2} \left[\sum_{r=1}^{R} \lambda_r \left(\frac{\lambda_r^s}{\lambda_r} \right)^2 - 1 \right],$$

which is equivalent to

$$C^s = \frac{R}{2}\left(H^s - \frac{1}{R}\right).$$

Hence, C^s is equal to the difference between the Herfindhal index and its lowest value. Note that C^s also corresponds to the square of a coefficient of variation and varies from 0 to $\frac{1}{2}(R-1)$.

The most appealing property of entropy measures lies in their separability. For example, we can decompose the degree of concentration of European regions into a degree of concentration *between* countries and a degree of concentration across regions *within* each country. This property is especially intuitive when $\alpha = 2$ because the total variance of a variable with two indices (countries c and regions r) can be decomposed into a "between" and a "within" variance. More generally, for all values of α, we can obtain the following expression:

$$E^s(\alpha) = E_b^s(\alpha) + E_w^s(\alpha),$$

where $E_b^s(\alpha)$ is the level of entropy between countries (disregarding the regional dimension) and $E_w^s(\alpha)$ is a weighted average of the regional entropies within each country. Hence, the ratio $E_b^s(\alpha)/E^s(\alpha)$ may be interpreted as the share of total inequality due to international inequalities, while $E_w^s(\alpha)/E^s(\alpha)$ denotes the share due to interregional inequalities within countries.

Unfortunately, Bourguignon (1979) has shown that, except for $\alpha = 1$, the weights used in the within-entropy depend on the between-entropy, thus weakening the appeal of the separability property. As a result, this decomposition is almost exclusively used for the Theil index ($\alpha = 1$). In this case, the *between component*

$$T_b^s = \sum_{c=1}^{C} \Lambda_c^s \ln \frac{\Lambda_c^s}{\Lambda_c}$$

corresponds to the Theil index (10.3) computed over all countries, the Λs being defined by country exactly as the λs were defined by region. More precisely, the Λs represent country c's share of sectoral and total employment respectively:

$$\Lambda_c^s = \frac{X_c^s}{x^s} \quad \text{with} \quad X_c^s = \sum_{r \in c} x_r^s \quad \text{and} \quad \Lambda_c = \frac{\sum_{s=1}^{S} X_c^s}{x}.$$

As for the *within component*, it is given by the mean of the national Theil indices, weighted by the share of each country in the total employment in sector s:

$$T_w^s = \sum_{c=1}^{C} \frac{X_c^s}{x^s} T_c^s,$$

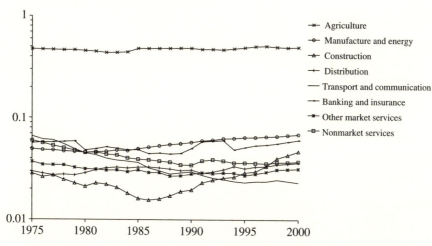

Figure 10.1. Theil indices for eight industries, EU-17, 1975–2000.
(Source: Brülhart and Traeger (2005).)

where T_c^s is the Theil index of country c, which is computed only over the regions belonging to this country (see (10.3)) and is given by

$$T_c^s = \sum_{r \in c} \frac{\lambda_r^s}{\Lambda_c^s} \ln \frac{(\lambda_r^s / \Lambda_c^s)}{(\lambda_r / \Lambda_c)}.$$

The Theil index suffers from the same weaknesses as those mentioned above. Still, it is evaluated with respect to a clear benchmark, and, equally importantly, significance tests based on bootstrap methods, have been proposed by Brülhart and Traeger (2005). These authors compute the Theil indices and apply their statistical significance test to eight industries in 236 European regions (NUTS2 or NUTS3) in seventeen Western European countries (EU-15 plus Norway and Switzerland). Figure 10.1 illustrates their results and reveals that agriculture is by far the most spatially concentrated sector with respect to total employment. Moreover, their analysis suggests that the concentration of industry (including energy) has increased regularly since the mid-1980s, whereas the transportation and communications industries have been characterized by dispersion during the last twenty-five years.

It is worth noting the unique nature of the construction industry, whose initial dispersion was later reversed to concentration. As discussed in the following section, however, intersectoral or intertemporal comparisons based on this index may be biased on account of differences across sectors in their degree of industrial concentration.

In order to illustrate the merits of the separability property in the case of the Theil index, figure 10.2 presents variations from 1982 to 1996 of

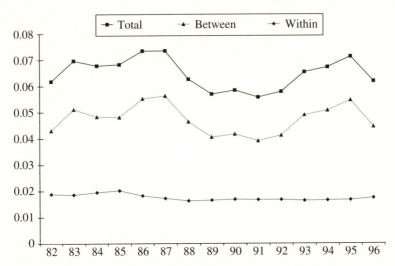

Figure 10.2. Decomposition of the Theil index for total employment, EU-12, 1982–96. (Source: Combes and Overman (2004).)

the overall concentration of total employment across European regions between and within countries.

This shows that short-run variations in the regional distribution of activity in Europe is due primarily to between-country variations, the within-country concentration remaining very stable over time. In the long run, overall spatial concentration varies little. At this stage, it is hard to say whether the above-mentioned differences really spring from changes in plant locations or from changes in the market structure (given by the number and size of firms) of the industries under consideration. We now go on to ponder such questions.

10.3 Indices Accounting for Industrial Concentration

Ellison and Glaeser (1997) radically depart from standard measures of spatial concentration by explicitly controlling for industrial concentration. To illustrate their point, they provide the following example: in the United States, 75% of employment in the vacuum-cleaner industry is covered by a mere four plants. Thus, necessarily, at most four regions account for three-quarters of the employment in this industry, which suggests a strong spatial concentration, as defined in the previous section. However, this strong spatial concentration is obviously tied to the fact that employment itself is concentrated in a very small number of plants. Conversely, a sector in which employment is spread across a large number of plants is more likely to be present in a large number of regions. The novel feature of Ellison and Glaeser's approach arises from recognizing that the existence of a limited number of plants confines employment to a small number of regions, which in turn influences the sector's spatial concentration. This is to be contrasted with the indices discussed above, which treat each employee as if she were to choose her location independently of the choices made by others. Specifically, Ellison and Glaeser compare the degree of the spatial concentration of *employment* in a given sector with the one that would arise if all *plants* in this sector were located randomly across locations. Note that, like the absolute and relative indices of concentration described above, there are two ways to define the weights associated with locations in those random choices. Locations may be given the same weight (in which case the probability that a given plant is located in each of them is the same, which corresponds to the uniform distribution) or different weights (matching, for instance, the total employment or the population share of the location).

Instead of following Ellison and Glaeser, we consider a slightly modified and more intuitive approach due to Maurel and Sédillot (1999). They use the correlation between the location choices of two plants i and j belonging to the same sector as an index of spatial concentration:

$$\gamma^s = \text{corr}(u_{ir}^s, u_{jr}^s),$$

where $u_{ir}^s = 1$ if plant i in sector s is located in region r, and $u_{ir}^s = 0$ otherwise. If $\gamma^s = 0$, location choices are independent, which corresponds to a random distribution of plants across space. If $\gamma^s = 1$, all plants in this sector are located together. If the distribution of economic activity is considered as the benchmark, the probability that a given plant in sector s chooses to be located in region r is given by the relative size of this region with respect to the overall level of economic activity. This amounts to assuming that the u_{ir}^s are nonindependent Bernoulli variables such that $P(u_{ir}^s = 1) = \lambda_r$.

It is fairly straightforward to derive an estimator of the concentration index γ^s from the observed distribution of plants. To this end, we begin by noting that the probability that two plants are located in the same region r is given by

$$P_r^s = E(u_{ir}^s u_{jr}^s) = \text{cov}(u_{ir}^s u_{jr}^s) + E(u_{ir}^s)E(u_{jr}^s) = \gamma^s \lambda_r (1 - \lambda_r) + \lambda_r^2,$$

while the probability that two plants are located within the same region is

$$P^s = \sum_{r=1}^{R} P_r^s = \gamma^s \left(1 - \sum_{r=1}^{R} \lambda_r^2\right) + \sum_{r=1}^{R} \lambda_r^2.$$

If an estimator P^s of this probability is available, we may derive an estimator for y^s as follows:

$$\hat{y}^s = \frac{\hat{P}^s - \sum_{r=1}^R \lambda_r^2}{1 - \sum_{r=1}^R \lambda_r^2}. \tag{10.4}$$

There are many possible estimators of P_r^s and, therefore, of P^s. For P_r^s, we could divide the number of plants located in region r by the total number of plants in sector s. Maurel and Sédillot choose to take into account the fact that plants have different sizes and assign a larger weight to the larger plants. Specifically, they use

$$\hat{P}_r^s = \frac{\sum_{i\in r, j\in r, i\neq j} z_i^s z_j^s}{\sum_{i,j,i\neq j} z_i^s z_j^s},$$

where z_i^s is the share of plant i in total employment in sector s.

Clearly, we have

$$(\lambda_r^s)^2 = \left(\sum_{i\in r} z_i^s \right)^2 = \sum_{i\in r, j\in r, i\neq j} z_i^s z_j^s + \sum_{i\in r} (z_i^s)^2.$$

Similarly, by summing across regions, we obtain

$$1 = \left(\sum_r \lambda_r^s \right)^2 = \left(\sum_r \sum_{i\in r} z_i^s \right)^2 = \left(\sum_i z_i^s \right)^2$$

$$= \sum_{i,j,i\neq j} z_i^s z_j^s + \sum_i (z_i^s)^2 = \sum_{i,j,i\neq j} z_i^s z_j^s + H^s,$$

where $H^s = \sum_i (z_i^s)^2$ is the Herfindhal index of sector s, which measures the degree of industrial concentration in this sector, disregarding any spatial considerations. Combing these expressions yields

$$\hat{P}^s = \sum_{r=1}^R \hat{P}_r^s = \frac{\sum_{r=1}^R (\sum_{i\in r, j\in r, i\neq j} z_i^s z_j^s)}{\sum_{i,j,i\neq j} z_i^s z_j^s} = \frac{\sum_{r=1}^R (\lambda_r^s)^2 - H^s}{1 - H^s}.$$

By plugging this value into (10.4), we obtain the spatial concentration index of Maurel and Sédillot (1999), denoted by $\hat{y}_{\mathrm{MS}}^s$:

$$\hat{y}_{\mathrm{MS}} = \frac{G_{\mathrm{MS}}^s - H^s}{1 - H^s},$$

where

$$G_{\mathrm{MS}}^s = \frac{\sum_{r=1}^R [(\lambda_r^s)^2 - \lambda_r^2]}{1 - \sum_{r=1}^R \lambda_r^2}$$

is a gross concentration index akin to those discussed in section 10.2. The main difference in using this spatial concentration index over those considered in section 10.2 is that it depends on the industrial concentration index H^s, not just on λ_r^s and λ_r. Instead of ignoring the fact that the distribution of employment in a given sector is conditioned by the way workers are grouped within firms, this fact is now explicitly taken into account. This new index better satisfies property 10.1, which requires comparability across industries, in that what is maybe the most crucial difference across industries, namely their industrial concentration, is explicitly taken into account. Unfortunately, most of the other properties are still violated, apart from property 10.5.

Although the literature reflects the lack of inclination to develop significance tests, any such efforts, based on bootstrap methods for instance, should lead to satisfying property 10.6. It is worth noting that these indices require very detailed (or fine) data, such as plants' sizes. If such data are not available, using the number of plants per industry on a national level, n_s, allows one to make a preliminary correction by assuming that all firms have the same size, which yields $H_s = 1/n_s$.

To conclude, it is worth comparing the index proposed by Ellison and Glaeser (1997) with that from Maurel and Sédillot (1999). The former is based on an Isard-type measure of gross spatial concentration (G_{EG}):

$$G_{EG}^s = \frac{\sum_{r=1}^{R}(\lambda_r^s - \lambda_r)^2}{1 - \sum_{r=1}^{R}\lambda_r^2}$$

from which we similarly obtain

$$\hat{y}_{EG} = \frac{G_{EG}^s - H^s}{1 - H^s}.$$

It can be shown that $\hat{y}_{EG}$ is also an unbiased estimator of y^s. Note the difference with the index of gross concentration used by Maurel and Sédillot (1999), which has the benefit of being derived directly from a probabilistic model of plants' location choices.

Table 10.1 provides a ranking of all the sectors in the two-digit classification for the United States and France, using Ellison and Glaeser's index. The similarities between the two rankings are striking. The two most spatially concentrated sectors are the same in both countries, while three of the four least concentrated sectors in the United States belong to the set formed by the four least concentrated sectors in France. Moreover, the sectoral rank correlation between the two countries is high (0.6).

10.4 The Duranton–Overman Continuous Approach

The additional contribution of the indices presented in the previous section, when compared with those drawn from other fields, is that

Table 10.1. Spatial concentration industries in the United States and France. (Source: Maurel and Sédillot (1999).)

Two-digit industries (U.S. definition)	U.S.A.		France	
	γ	Rank	γ	Rank
Textile mill products	0.127	1	0.036	2
Leather and leather products	0.029	2	0.039	1
Furniture and fixtures	0.019	3	0.008	10
Lumber and wood products	0.018	4	0.012	8
Primary metal industries	0.018	5	0.010	9
Instruments and related products	0.018	6	0.018	5
Transportation equipment	0.016	7	0.000	17
Apparel and other textile products	0.016	8	0.020	4
Miscellaneous manufacturing industries	0.012	9	0.014	6
Chemicals and allied products	0.009	10	0.012	7
Paper and allied products	0.006	11	0.007	11
Electronic and other electrical equipment	0.005	12	0.004	13
Printing and publishing	0.005	13	0.032	3
Fabricated metal products	0.005	14	0.003	14
Rubber and miscellaneous plastics	0.004	15	0.006	12
Stone, clay, and glass products	0.004	16	0.003	15
Industrial machinery and equipment	0.003	17	0.002	16

they explicitly take into account industry-level differences in market structure. These indices are not robust, however, in the way in which geographical areas are defined, and they do not take into account the relative positions of the areas, nor the distances separating them. The latter drawback is a crucial limitation: jobs can be permuted across areas and yet the indices still yield the same values. Moreover, developing methods that account for the distance between areas seems warranted if properties 10.2 and 10.3 are to be satisfied.

Building on earlier works developed by geographers (Bailey and Gatrell 1995), Duranton and Overman (2005) go much further by discarding any geographical classification and by basing their approach on the actual distances separating plants. As a result, properties 10.2 and 10.3 are both satisfied. They can even refine their conclusions by specifying the spatial scale on which the concentration is strongest. This calls for very precise data that give an accurate measure of the distance between plants. Duranton and Overman have access to plants' locations in the United Kingdom on the basis of their postal codes, which gives a precision level on the order of 100 m. With their data set, they are also able to work on a very detailed level, i.e., 234 sectors. This enables Duranton

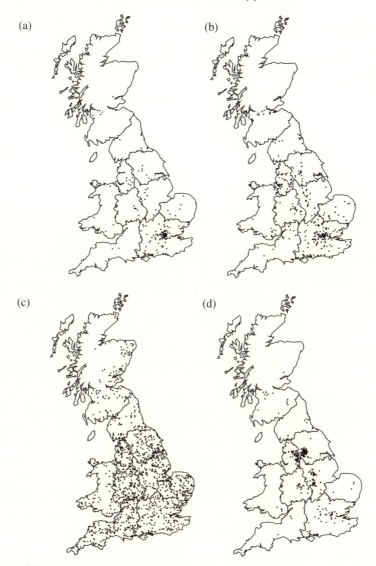

Figure 10.3. Maps of the distribution of plants in four industries in the United Kingdom: (a) basic pharmaceuticals; (b) pharmaceutical preparations; (c) other agricultural and forestry; (d) machinery for textile, apparel, and leather production. (Source: Duranton and Overman (2005).)

and Overman to draw maps such as those in figure 10.3, in which four industries are considered and where each point stands for a plant having more than ten employees.

The starting point for Duranton and Overman's approach is to count the number of plants that are separated by a given distance. By plotting

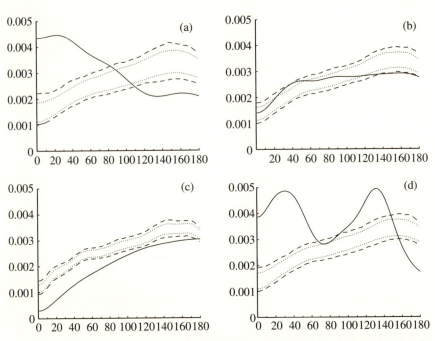

Figure 10.4. Densities and confidence intervals for four industries in the United Kingdom: (a) basic pharmaceuticals; (b) pharmaceutical preparations; (c) other agricultural and forestry; (d) machinery for textile, apparel, and leather production. (Source: Duranton and Overman (2005).)

this number against distance, one obtains a simple frequency graph of the distance between plants. The highest peaks correspond to the distance that most often separates any two plants. Let us assume that two peaks are present for a given sector, one at 30 km and the other at 110 km. This means that the spatial distribution of plants is characterized by a cluster of plants separated on average by 30 km, and that the mean distance between clusters is on average 110 km.

However, defining the spatial concentration as the number of plants separated by a *given* distance is unsatisfactory for the following two reasons. First, such an approach arbitrarily carves up distance into discrete intervals depending on which unit of length is used. Second, the measure of distance per se is debatable. For example, is measuring distance as the crow flies the most appropriate method? These two limitations imply that the distance between two plants is subject to measurement errors. With this in mind, it is preferable to smooth out the distribution of distances between plants. Intuitively, we can estimate the number of plants separated by a given distance d, say, 30 km, by taking the number of plants separated by a distance varying from 28 to 32 km and dividing this by four (corresponding to the distance between these two bounds if the unit of length is in kilometers), instead of the single number recorded in the database for 30 km. However, this type of smoothing remains incomplete as it still ignores the presence of plants separated by 27 or 33 km, and so on. Furthermore, it assigns the same weight to all points, regardless of the distance separating them from the reference distance (30 km in our example). Yet it seems reasonable to give extreme observations less weight and give more weight to, say, those at 29 or 31 km. Satisfying these two properties would require use of a kernel method, which is precisely what Duranton and Overman use. This method applies a weighting scheme that follows the normal distribution to all points lying a given distance from the reference point. Once this density is estimated, curves similar to those presented in figure 10.4 are obtained. In the case of textiles and apparel, the figure illustrates the two peaks discussed above.

The following question has yet to be answered: for every given distance, to what extent does the number of plants observed after smoothing *significantly* differ from the number obtained if their location were chosen randomly, or according to any benchmark distribution (property 10.6)? In contrast to previous indices, Duranton and Overman's approach allows them to address this question. Given the existing number of plants, they randomly assign each of them to one of any possible locations, and then calculate the number of plants separated by any distance. This operation is repeated, say, 1,000 times, which leads to a set of 1,000 values for each distance. They finally construct two-sided confidence intervals containing 90% of these values, i.e., with the upper and lower bounds given by the 95% and 5% percentiles of the generated values, respectively. This procedure generates two smooth curves, as illustrated by dotted lines in figure 10.4. If the number of plants observed after the smoothing procedure exceeds the upper bound of the confidence interval, the sector is said to be *locally concentrated* at the distance under consideration with a confidence level of 95% (as we ignore the 5% of observations situated above the upper limit of this interval). If the number of plants is smaller than the lower limit, the sector is said to be *locally dispersed* at the distance under consideration.

In addition to dealing with local concentration and dispersion, Duranton and Overman also work in a global way by defining the upper limit of the confidence interval in such a way that 95% of the whole set of draws (at any distance) lie below this upper bound. In this case, a sector is said to be *globally concentrated* if its density exceeds this limit at least once after smoothing out. They proceed analogously for the lower bound.

The corresponding curves are illustrated by broken lines in figure 10.4. Note that the basic pharmaceutical industry is locally concentrated for every distance below 80 km and globally concentrated, even if it is locally dispersed for distances exceeding 110 km.

Finally, it is worth noting that the continuous approach, by working with the actual number of plants when estimating confidence intervals, automatically takes into account differences in industrial concentration (property 10.1). By starting at a microscopic level, spatial classification is circumvented, which allows properties 10.2 and 10.3 to be satisfied. Moreover, this approach distinguishes itself from existing indices in that it also captures the firms' relative positions in space. By contrast, using a predefined industrial classification implies that property 10.4 is violated. Consequently, the Duranton–Overman approach may be sensitive to how sectors are defined, and should be extended to account for the technological distance between industries.

10.5 Concluding Remarks

The ideal index of spatial concentration still seems far from reach. Nevertheless, the growing availability of data on a very fine spatial scale has led to finer and more accurate methods than the standard indices of spatial concentration. These new indices account for a number of specificities that characterize spatial data. This type of approach allows us to satisfy several of the properties of an ideal index and, therefore, to better assess its variations over time or across industries. Collecting the required data can often prove very costly, however.

10.6 Related Literature

Marcon and Puech (2003) use an approach that is similar to that of Duranton and Overman (2005). The former were inspired by methods developed in forestry to study the spatial distribution of tree species. The latest version of their index (Marcon and Puech 2005) makes it possible to account for differences in industrial concentration between industries, and it can be modified to obtain a measure of co-location. In the spirit of Ellison and Glaeser's proposal, they can measure the likelihood that a given industry will locate in the same place as another industry. Barrios et al. (forthcoming) used Ellison and Glaeser's index to compare the spatial structure of industry in three small countries: Belgium, the Republic of Ireland, and Portugal. Feser et al. (2005) follow a different approach that rests on local spatial autocorrelation. Finally, we should mention Mori et al. (2005), who propose an alternative method based on aggregated data but which allows for a number of different tests to be run, such as the test of significant differences between an observed distribution and its reference, or between different industries, as required by property 10.6.

11

Determinants of Spatial Concentration and Local Productivity

The previous chapter discussed various approaches that measure the spatial concentration of economic activity. This line of research is part of a more comprehensive research program that has the ambition of answering the following fundamental questions. The first one, studied in chapter 10, can be formulated as follows: which industries are characterized by high spatial concentration, and how has this spatial concentration changed over time? The second question follows on naturally: what are the determinants underlying the spatial concentration, and are the corresponding explanatory variables consistent with those put forward by theoretical models?

We address these various issues in this chapter. In the first section, we present an approach that consists of regressing industry-specific indices of spatial concentration on a number of explanatory variables suggested by theoretical models, such as the intensity of increasing returns, the level of trade costs, or the importance of intermediate goods. Unfortunately, the selected explanatory variables are often not fully consistent with theory, while the results obtained may be given several conflicting interpretations.

With these shortcomings in mind, the second section introduces a markedly different approach, which focuses on the determinants of sectoral productivity, or growth in each geographical area under consideration, rather than studying solely the overall spatial concentration. This alternative approach makes better use of all available information and allows for a more rigorous interpretation of the results, which may be considered as the estimated specifications of simple theoretical models.

Introducing these two approaches serves to underscore some of the main difficulties encountered in empirical economic geography studies, namely missing variables and endogeneity. They will also allow us to bridge these approaches to the next two chapters, in which the empirical models used are more closely related to those presented in part II.

Before proceeding, the following comment is in order. The contributions discussed in this chapter often use the word "industry," while we have retained the word "sector" in previous chapters. For this reason, we will use industry and sector interchangeably.

11.1 The Determinants of Spatial Concentration

As seen in chapter 10, computing spatial concentration indices for a number of different industries is relatively easy when one has access to regional data, such as industry-specific regional employment. Several authors have taken up the ambitious task of understanding the *determinants* that underlie the values these spatial concentration indices can take.

11.1.1 The Framework

Kim (1995) may be viewed as a precursor in this field, and his work has inspired many researchers. His starting point was to regress a spatial concentration index on variables suggested by theory and, hence, expected to have a significant degree of explanatory power. Let $I_{s,t}$ be the index of spatial concentration for sector s at date t (across regions in a given country, for instance), and let $X_{s,t}$ be the vector of explanatory variables. The approach consists of estimating a vector of parameters β and two other sets of parameters γ_s and δ_t (one for each sector and one for each date, as discussed below in section 11.1.3) such that

$$I_{s,t} = X_{s,t}\beta + \gamma_s + \delta_t + \varepsilon_{s,t}, \tag{11.1}$$

where $\varepsilon_{s,t}$ is an error term. Kim (1995) considers two explanatory variables in the $X_{s,t}$ vector:

(i) the average size of firms in a specific sector at a given date and

(ii) the share of raw materials used in this sector.

These two variables are not as far-fetched as they may appear at first sight. In fact, they characterize the two main lines of research followed in explaining the spatial distribution of production, namely economic geography and standard trade theory.

As seen from chapter 2 onward, increasing returns appear to be necessary to account for the spatial concentration of economic activities, at least when space is homogeneous. An intuitive test is thus to verify whether the industries in which returns to scale are stronger do indeed correspond to those in which spatial concentration is greater. Unfortunately, data measuring the level of scale economies in a given industry are not available. Kim uses the average size of firms in each industry as a proxy: under zero profits, the stronger increasing returns are, the larger the size of plants. Specifically, finding a positive and statistically significant coefficient for a plant's average size would confirm the idea that increasing returns help to account for spatial concentration. When regressing the Gini indices computed on U.S. data in 1880, 1914, 1947, 1967, and 1987 for twenty industries, Kim finds that scale economies have a positive impact on the spatial concentration index. Several authors have tried to reproduce these results in the case of Europe. For example, Amiti (1999) adopts the same approach and also observes a positive correlation between scale economies and the spatial concentration of different industries. However, for reasons that will become clear below, the robustness of those results is questionable.

11.1.2 Omitted Variables

Economic theory typically focuses on one particular effect by controlling for (i.e., neutralizing) a large number of others that are at work in the real world. For instance, in order to isolate the trade-off between increasing returns and trade costs, we have assumed in part II that regions share the same technologies, endowments, and preferences. Such region-specific variables are sources of potential heterogeneity that could blur the trade-off we want to study. Yet these sources of heterogeneity are key variables in standard trade theories and, hence, could play an important role in shaping the spatial distribution of activity. Hence, while omitting these effects is legitimate from the theoretical standpoint, this approach makes little sense in empirical studies whose purpose is precisely to explain reality as well as possible, thus calling for the inclusion of as many relevant variables as necessary. Moreover, it is reasonable to believe that real-world patterns of activity are the outcome of the interplay between the main variables of economic geography and standard trade theory. The challenge is then to discriminate between these two approaches by determining which one accounts for the greater share of regional specialization or agglomeration. The set of economic geography variables must, therefore, be supplemented by control variables that account for the effects of regional heterogeneity. This is what Kim attempts, by using a country's share of raw materials as a control for natural endowments. The idea is that industries that are intensive in using raw material should be agglomerated because of their dependency on the supply of these inputs, and not because of increasing returns.

Unfortunately, this approach has severe limitations and there is little hope that it can provide convincing results. First, when attempting to account for the different degrees of spatial concentration observed across industries, the models presented in part II reveal that scale economies are not the only source of agglomeration. Several relevant explanatory variables are totally absent. Specifically, trade costs, which may vary substantially across goods, are missing (chapter 5). In the context of monopolistic competition, also absent is the elasticity of substitution that can vary substantially across industries and time (chapter 6). Another potential shortcoming is the fact that intermediate goods are not taken into account in the regression, a variable that has proved particularly important in some contexts (chapter 7). All the models presented in part II show that the list of omitted variables could be extended further. It is, therefore, somewhat naive to expect a single variable (here, the average size of firms in a given industry) to capture all these effects adequately. Obviously, if these effects happened to be distributed randomly across industries, their omission would have no impact as the error term's very function is to capture such effects in regression analyses. Unfortunately, such a strong assumption is rarely accurate in practice.

This problem goes under the general heading of *omitted variables*, and econometricians have long emphasized the biased estimates that can result. The omitted variable bias is not specific to a particular set of variables: it applies both to economic geography and other variables, which is the second main drawback of Kim's approach. In this respect, when he considers the share of raw materials in production and excludes any other explanatory variables, he makes other strong assumptions. For instance, absent from Kim's model are capital and labor intensities, two variables at the heart of Heckscher and Ohlin's theory. Along the same lines (and very relevant in modern economies), incorporating variables that distinguish between skilled and unskilled labor intensities might be an important addition. These variables are omitted in Kim (1995). Moreover, while controlling for factor intensities in production is undoubtedly important, it is misleading to study their role without taking into account how production factors are distributed across space. Indeed, factor intensities matter for spatial concentration in standard trade theory when the distribution of factors across regions is uneven.

11.1.3 Fixed Effects

A first solution to deal with omitted variables was implemented by Kim (1995) himself. It requires access to panel data across different industries and for different time periods, which allows one to use the method of *fixed effects*. In (11.1), y_s is an *industry* fixed effect, which is a dummy that equals 1 for all observations corresponding to sector s and 0 otherwise. When a complete set of fixed effects is included in an econometric specification, they are perfectly collinear with the intercept (the constant term), so one of them must be dropped in the estimation. Thus, the excluded industry becomes the reference for the others. For instance, the fixed effect corresponding to each of the remaining industries measures, everything else being equal, the difference in spatial concentration between the sector under consideration and the excluded sector. The concentration of the latter (net of the impact of explanatory variables) is measured by the intercept. Similarly, y_t is a *time* fixed effect; it takes a value of 1 for each observation corresponding to year t and a value of 0 otherwise. Again, one year dummy must be excluded to avoid collinearity.[1]

Fixed effects have the advantage of controlling for all variables that are constant over time but specific to each industry (the industry fixed effects) or constant across industries but proper to each time period (the time fixed effects), without the need for any data related to these variables. The major drawback of using fixed effects is that they allow for the estimation of the overall contribution of these variables but not for the estimation of the effect of each one separately.

In this context, β represents what is called the "between time and industry" effect. It captures the correlation between $I_{s,t}$ and $X_{s,t}$ across industry and time simultaneously, but not their cross-section correlation or their time correlation only. If $I_{s,t}$ varies only across industries and keeps the same value across time, β will be zero when the equation is estimated with industry fixed effects. Similarly, it would be also zero with time fixed effects if $I_{s,t}$ were to vary across time only. In other words, β is nonzero when $I_{s,t}$ and $X_{s,t}$ deviate in a correlated way once normalized by their industry averages (denoted $I_{s,\cdot}$ and $X_{s,\cdot}$) and by their time averages (denoted $I_{\cdot,t}$ and $X_{\cdot,t}$). In this case, estimating (11.1) or

$$I_{s,t} - I_{s,\cdot} - I_{\cdot,t} = (X_{s,t} - X_{s,\cdot} - X_{\cdot,t})\beta + \epsilon_{s,t}, \qquad (11.2)$$

obtained from (11.1) by simple manipulations, where $\epsilon_{s,t}$ is a new error term, leads to the same estimate of β (under certain conditions on the distribution of errors). This new formulation illustrates the fact that the correct interpretation is in terms of correlated departures of $I_{s,t}$ and

---

[1] Alternatively, one could choose to exclude both the constant and an industry (respectively, time) dummy in order to keep all time (respectively, industry) dummies. Such choices merely amount to different normalizations.

$X_{s,t}$ *from their industry and time averages.* By contrast, β will likely be different when estimated without fixed effects through

$$I_{s,t} = X_{s,t}\beta + v_{s,t}$$

despite the fact that this formulation also yields (11.2).

In short, the introduction of sectoral fixed effects is equivalent to assuming that the omitted variables remain constant over time: an assumption that is much less extreme than supposing they have no impact at all. For instance, over a fairly short period, it is reasonable to assume that differences in elasticities of substitution across industries barely vary, and are therefore controlled for by the fixed effects. However, such an assumption becomes more problematic when the time period is long. It becomes even more problematic when dealing with variables that often exhibit significant variations. In this case, turning to fixed effects does not help much. Similarly, time fixed effects control for macroeconomic-type shocks, provided these shocks affect all industries in the same way. For example, an increase in growth on a national scale could, in a given year, temporarily increase the average size of all plants across all industries, thus affecting equally their spatial concentration. Cyclical, macroeconomic effects of this nature do not provide any additional clues as to the determinants of spatial concentration: they are absorbed by time fixed effects that leave the impact of the other variables unchanged. This makes time fixed effects just as useful as their sectoral counterparts. Again, just as sectoral fixed effects are ineffective when the omitted variables are expected to vary over short time periods, the same caveat holds for time fixed effects when omitted variables vary across industries.

Furthermore, it is worth noting that fixed effects may be introduced to solve a problem that is specific to the determinants of spatial concentration. As noted above, a number of indices (e.g., the Gini index) are not comparable across industries (see property 10.1). Keeping this in mind, can we hope to infer anything about spatial concentration by comparing the different values these indices take across industries? For instance, estimating (11.1) only makes sense if we have been careful in choosing an index of spatial concentration that allows for comparisons between industries. However, under a less careful choice of indices, we can still rely on sectoral fixed effects to partly curb this problem. That said, correcting a gross concentration index to make it comparable across industries, as proposed by Ellison and Glaeser (1997), requires a more complex transformation than the log-linear rescaling corresponding to the fixed effects strategy.

11.1.4 Additional Variables

Using fixed effects requires panel data. Moreover, the existence of omitted variables that vary in both spatial and temporal dimensions remains problematic. Intuitively, an alternative remedy for correcting omitted variable bias is to add new explanatory variables to the vector $X_{s,t}$ in (11.1). A few additional variables that immediately come to mind are the degree of increasing returns and input–output linkages, trade costs, and the extent of technological spillovers, as well as the structure of local labor markets in terms of skilled and unskilled workers.

In this respect, Rosenthal and Strange (2001) adopt one of the most exhaustive specifications to date. Their estimations are conducted on three different spatial scales (U.S. municipalities, counties, and states) and each specification uses Ellison and Glaeser's index as a dependent variable, which accounts for differences in industrial concentration (chapter 10). Given the absence of any available time dimension, Rosenthal and Strange include industry fixed effects, but only at a more aggregated level than when computing the dependent and explanatory variables. Under each of the three spatial scales, their estimates reveal that labor market structure (in terms of skilled versus unskilled labor) has the most robust effect on spatial concentration. The variable accounting for technological spillovers also proves robust, but only at the municipal level, which seems reasonable given the local impact spillovers are expected to have. At the state level, intermediate inputs and natural endowments increase spatial concentration, while trade costs reduce it. Using European data, Amiti (1999) finds that vertical linkages have a statistically significant impact on spatial concentration within Europe.[2]

This approach is still wanting on a number of fronts. First, the compilation of comprehensive databases that cover the whole set of missing variables is often out of reach. Second, a more fundamental problem remains. To date, nobody has been able to show in a theoretical model how any of the spatial concentration indices presented in chapter 10 vary with the explanatory variables. This issue's persistence is hardly surprising, for its solution is extremely involved and requires computing these variables. To better grasp the difficulty of this exercise, it should be stressed that even more modest endeavors continue to look like stumbling blocks: in many models, the analytical expressions of the endogenous variables that underpin spatial concentration indices

---

[2] See Combes and Overman (2004) for a comprehensive review of this literature, which also discusses studies that examine simple correlations between spatial concentration and a given factor without adding control variables or fixed effects.

cannot be determined. To make matters even more involved, this procedure should be implemented in the context of a model involving several regions and industries, characterized by specific technologies and factor endowments. With these new difficulties, the task at hand seems almost impossible.

To conclude, the following comments are in order. Choosing a spatial concentration index as a dependent variable leads to a substantial loss of information. Indeed, such indices are aggregated variables, while the disaggregated information required to estimate their value is available for each region and sector. It is, therefore, questionable to only study the spatial concentration of a sector within a country, while it seems possible, using the same data, to identify, in any region, the determinants of employment, productivity, or growth of each sector. Furthermore, it seems more promising to use theoretical models to derive functional forms linking these disaggregated variables to explanatory variables. Providing estimations that respect theoretical models down to the last detail is a very difficult task, and we will cover such attempts in chapters 12 and 13.

In the next section, we will focus on a third approach, which, while still a far cry from economic geography models, has the advantage of being easier to interpret, as well as providing relevant results, using more robust methods than those initially put forward by Kim. In so doing, we will encounter endogeneity problems that are recurrent in empirical economic geography. We will see that the solution of endogeneity problems will allow us to solve some of the omitted variable problems discussed above.

11.2 The Determinants of Local Productivity

Our objective is now to discuss some studies that aim at evaluating the impact of the main variables considered in economic geography using what are known as nonstructural or *reduced form* specifications. Such specifications are not directly associated with a particular theoretical model, but can be useful in uncovering new ideas regarding the forces that underlie agglomeration economies.

11.2.1 The Theoretical Background

The main ideas of economic geography can be grasped with the help of a fairly simple model. Specifically, we consider a firm j located in region r and operating in sector s, which uses labor in quantity l_j and other inputs, viewed as a composite, in quantity k_j. We assume that its production is given by a Cobb–Douglas function:

$$y_j = A_j(s_j l_j)^\mu k_j^{1-\mu}, \tag{11.3}$$

where A_j is a Hicks-neutral factor-augmenting technology level, and s_j is the efficiency level of workers; both are specific to the firm. This firm's profits are given by

$$\pi_j = \sum_b p_{jb} y_{jb} - w_j l_j - r_j k_j,$$

where y_{jb} is the quantity exported to region b, p_{jb} is the mill price set in region b net of the marginal cost of intermediate goods, w_j is the wage rate, and r_j is the cost of inputs other than labor and intermediate goods. This function may then be rewritten as

$$\pi_j = p_j y_j - w_j l_j - r_j k_j,$$

where

$$p_j = \sum_b p_{jb} \frac{y_{jb}}{y_j}$$

is the average unit value, net of the cost of intermediate inputs, of the good produced by the firm. Hence, $p_j y_j$ denotes the firm's value-added and not the value of its production. This change is made in order to match data. Applying the first-order conditions to the firm's profit-maximizing problem and rearranging terms yields the following two equations:

$$w_j = \mu p_j A_j s_j^\mu \left(\frac{k_j}{l_j}\right)^{1-\mu} \quad \text{and} \quad r_j = (1-\mu)p_j A_j s_j^\mu \left(\frac{k_j}{l_j}\right)^{-\mu}. \tag{11.4}$$

By plugging the second expression into the first, we obtain

$$w_j = \mu(1-\mu)^{(1-\mu)/\mu} s_j \left(\frac{p_j A_j}{r_j^{1-\mu}}\right)^{1/\mu}. \tag{11.5}$$

Equation (11.5) requires individual-level wage data, which has only been made available very recently. Previous work relied on average wage in region r and sector s, which takes the following form:

$$w_{rs} = \frac{\mu(1-\mu)^{(1-\mu)/\mu}}{n_{rs}} \sum_{j \in (rs)} s_j \left(\frac{p_j A_j}{r_j^{1-\mu}}\right)^{1/\mu}, \tag{11.6}$$

where n_{rs} is the number of firms in region r and sector s.

In which region is the marginal productivity of labor, which is equal to the equilibrium wage, the highest? Equation (11.5) shows that wages are directly proportional to workers' efficiency, as reflected by s_j. While this finding is not specific to economic geography, we will see that it is crucial to keep it in mind when studying interregional wage differences. Moreover, (11.5) takes into account the variables p_j and r_j, which capture the main agglomeration and dispersion forces described in part II. A greater p_j (be it because demand is high, competition is weak, or because intermediate goods are cheap) translates to a higher wage, which in turn contributes to a higher degree of agglomeration of workers in that region. Conversely, low demand or fiercer competition brings down wages in a region, thus encouraging workers to leave it. The presence of r_j in the wage equation captures the effects transmitted through other factor prices. For instance, if a number of new suppliers were to move closer to their customers (i.e., an increase in the supply of a given production factor), the price of the corresponding factor would decrease. This, in turn, would translate to an increase in wages. Conversely, when production factors have a low elasticity of supply (land being the typical example), prices for these factors will be higher in areas characterized by more concentrated economic activity, which pushes down the wage rate. The models presented in part II serve the exact purpose of delving into these mechanisms, giving them micro-foundations, while they are conveniently expressed here by the "black boxes" p_j and r_j.

So far we have refrained from introducing technological externalities. This choice was made to avoid imposing any ad hoc components, with the objective of isolating phenomena that are micro-founded and endogenous. Yet Marshall has stressed the potential importance of technological externalities, such as knowledge and learning spillovers. They are taken into account here through the term A_j. Intuitively, regions characterized by an easy circulation of information and/or endowed with a high concentration of skilled workers are likely to benefit from more productive technologies, thus implying higher wages, as shown by (11.5). On the other hand, one would expect a heavily congested transportation network, or the emergence of high levels of pollution in densely populated areas, to worsen productivity and to act as dispersion forces through the corresponding decline in wages.

In short, the *wage equation* (11.5), or its aggregated version (11.6), captures the full breadth of agglomeration and dispersion forces, even though the microeconomic foundations of the underlying model are kept deliberately vague. For example, a number of details have been glossed over, including consumer preferences or the assumptions regarding the mobility of goods and factors. Recall that our goal here is not to construct a fully fledged economic geography model, as in previous chapters. Rather, constructing a simple framework in which prices and costs depend on both region and sector characteristics provides a clear vantage point from which to better understand the empirical results presented below.

Given that wage data are often available on a local scale for a number of different industries, most of the existing works use wages as the dependent variable. However, when data related to value-added and capital stocks are available, the possibility of conducting similar estimations by using the average productivity of labor, or total factor productivity, should not be overlooked. Specifically, it follows from (11.3) and (11.4) that the average labor productivity is given by

$$\frac{p_j y_j}{l_j} = (1 - \mu)^{(1-\mu)/\mu} s_j \left(\frac{p_j^{1-\mu} A_j}{r_j^{1-\mu}} \right)^{1/\mu} \tag{11.7}$$

and the total factor productivity is given by

$$\frac{p_j y_j}{l_j^{\mu} k_j^{1-\mu}} = p_j A_j (s_j)^{\mu}. \tag{11.8}$$

Observe that these two expressions are almost identical to (11.5) in that the left-hand side variables correspond to various productivity measures that are all linked to the same right-hand side variables: local input and output prices and the local levels of technology and labor efficiency.[3] Note also that the costs of inputs other than labor do not appear in (11.7) and (11.8).

11.2.2   The Econometric Analysis

One of the most important empirical questions in economic geography might read as follows: *is productivity higher in areas characterized by highly concentrated economic activity*, and if so, by how much? In other words, the first task is to uncover any existing correlation between the value of local productivity and the density of economic activities in the same region. A simple thought experiment is to consider the percentage change in productivity brought about by doubling employment or population density. Answering this type of question seems fairly straightforward. Specifically, we regress either the total factor productivity or, more often, the nominal wage on the employment (or population) density:[4]

$$\ln w_{rs} = \alpha + \beta \ln \text{den}_r + \varepsilon_{rs}, \tag{11.9}$$

---

[3] It should be kept in mind that talking about productivity is a slight abuse of language because $p_j y_j$ not the value of production but the value-added.

[4] In order to interpret the coefficient in terms of elasticity, we take the logarithm of all variables.

where ε_{rs} is an error term and $\mathrm{den}_r = \mathrm{emp}_r/\mathrm{area}_r$ is the total number of employees in region r (emp_r) divided by its surface area (area_r). The estimated coefficient that results from this regression indicates that a 1% higher density implies a β% higher productivity (if β is positive). For a density twice as high, wages increase by $(2^\beta - 1) \times 100\%$.[5]

As with nearly all of the studies presented in section 11.1, a number of econometric problems arise. To begin, it is worth noting that estimating (11.9) is equivalent to estimating (11.6) under the following assumption:

$$\ln \frac{1}{n_{rs}} \sum_{j \in (rs)} s_j \left(\frac{p_j A_j}{r_j^{1-\mu}} \right)^{1/\mu} = \beta \ln \mathrm{den}_r + \varepsilon_{rs}. \qquad (11.10)$$

Thus, the implicit assumption is that the density affects the wage level through the following variables:

   (i) the local level of technology, A_j,

   (ii) the output price, p_j,

   (iii) the input prices other than labor, r_j, or

   (iv) the local efficiency of labor, s_j.

However, we are not able to determine which variables are most affected. Furthermore, only the *net* effect of density is identified, leaving us in the dark as to whether the possible negative impact on some variables is compensated by the possible positive impact on others. That said, knowing the net effect is still of critical importance to public decision makers who might want to design policies that aim to concentrate or disperse activities. Once a given policy has been implemented, the present framework also allows for total net productivity gains or losses to be quantified.

When considering the sources of potential econometric bias, of chief concern are the potentially large number of omitted variables, an issue discussed above and which will be illustrated here using wage data. Before moving on, let us stress the main advantage of expressing all variables in logarithmic form. Aside from facilitating interpretation (the estimated coefficients become elasticities), taking logarithms brings residuals closer to the normal distribution (recall that, in regression analysis, a number of statistical tests assume that residuals are normally distributed).

A large fraction of regional differences in labor productivity stems not from the presence of local externalities but from the fact that some

---

[5] Consider two individuals located in regions 1 and 2, respectively, that differ only in terms of density. Then, (11.9) implies that their difference in productivity is such that $\log(w_2/w_1) = \beta \log(\mathrm{den}_2/\mathrm{den}_1)$. When $\mathrm{den}_2/\mathrm{den}_1 = k$, we have $w_2/w_1 = k^\beta$.

workers have a higher level of skill than others. Overlooking variables that account for differences in average regional skill levels is equivalent to assuming that labor skills are randomly distributed across regions and captured by the term ε_{rs}. Since this assumption is easily refuted empirically, it is standard practice to introduce control variables that capture workers' skills, qualifications, or academic achievement in the regression. It is straightforward to figure out what happens when these variables are omitted. If workers are more skilled in regions characterized by highly concentrated economic activity (which is generally the case), overlooking such variables overestimates the impact of density, because this variable also captures the influence of s_j.

Note that the variable w_{rs} we seek to explain depends on both the region r and the sector s, while the explanatory variable considered in (11.9) (density) varies across regions but not across sectors. Therefore, the literature usually also tries to control for the region's industrial mix, i.e., for the way in which local economic activity is distributed across a range of industries. Indeed, regions with the same density may have very different industries, or have the same industries but in very different proportions. For example, if the good is sold to a small number of industries, or if the factors used are industry specific, the industrial mix is crucial because it affects the level of productivity through the prices effects described above.[6] The industry's share in local economic activity is the first variable that is usually included in the specification:

$$\text{spe}_{rs} = \frac{\text{emp}_{rs}}{\text{emp}_r},$$

where emp_{rs} is employment in sector s and region r. By measuring the relative size of sector s in the local economy, the specialization index allows us to capture the effects of *intraindustry externalities* (resulting from the concentration of this sector only) and to distinguish them from *interindustry externalities* (resulting from the concentration of the overall activity), which are likely to be apprehended by the density variable. Knowing the relative importance of these two types of externalities is a major issue for the design of regional development policies. Indeed, this knowledge would allow public decision makers to design policies that would either favor the concentration of a handful of industries, as in the case of the Italian industrial districts, or welcome any industry because all of them would benefit from the externalities generated by the others.

---

[6] Note, however, that the industrial mix is much less important when the good under consideration is sold to most local industries and/or is designed for final consumers. The industrial mix is also rather unimportant when the inputs used to produce the good come from many local industries and/or mainly consist of labor.

Some authors further extend the set of explanatory variables and consider other kinds of intraindustry and interindustry externalities. Regarding the former, the number of local plants in the sector is a variable that allows us to determine whether intraindustry externalities depend on the average size of plants in the local industry rather than on the total number of employees (already captured by spe_{rs}). As for the interindustry externalities, an "industrial diversity" variable is often added. For given density and size of an industry, such a variable aims at evaluating how the distribution of employment spreads over the other local sectors and, therefore, at determining whether the industry benefits from the others. The inverse of the Herfindhal index in terms of industries' shares in regional employment is often used:

$$\text{div}_r = \left[\sum_s \left(\frac{\text{emp}_{rs}}{\text{emp}_r} \right)^2 \right]^{-1}.$$

Finally, it might be worth including each regions' surface area area_r in the explanatory variables. Indeed, for a given density, the absolute size of a region may play an important role, as it accounts for the total population on which externalities are built.

Note that several specifications expressed in logarithms are formally equivalent. For example, estimating the model

$$\ln w_{rs} = \beta \ln \text{den}_r + \eta \ln \text{area}_r + \varepsilon_{rs} \tag{11.11}$$

is equivalent to estimating

$$\ln w_{rs} = \beta \ln \text{emp}_{rs} + \varrho \ln \text{area}_r + \varepsilon_{rs}, \tag{11.12}$$

since $\varrho = \eta - \beta$. Interpreting econometric results, therefore, warrants a degree of caution. For example, the effect of an increase in density for a given surface area (β in (11.11)) is tantamount to an increase in the employment level for a given surface area (β in (11.12)). However, if the density is held constant, an increase in surface area (η in (11.11)) is not equivalent to the same increase when the employment level is kept fixed (ϱ in (11.12)), since the former requires a proportional increase in employment for the density to remain the same.

More variables that should be controlled for are known under the general heading of *natural amenities* and *local public goods*. Natural amenities are benefits ranging from a favorable climate, a coast-line location, and the presence of lakes and mountains to any natural endowments in raw materials. However, it should be stressed that the level of some amenities is the outcome of public policies; think of leisure facilities (theaters, swimming pools, etc.) or public services (schools, hospitals, etc.).

Public goods are said to be local when their benefits are only reaped by local consumers, while the access costs of using these goods by more distant consumers are very high. Local public goods can also be used by firms. Transport infrastructures, research laboratories, and job training centers are just a few examples. What happens when these amenities and local public goods are not included in the regressions? Local public goods inflate the productivity of production factors, such as labor and intermediate goods. If these local public goods were randomly distributed across space, their omission would be taken into account by the error term. Unfortunately, the supply of local public goods is the outcome of specific policies and often greater in areas characterized by concentrated economic activity. In this case, the effect of density is overestimated, as the density variable also captures the positive effect of these (omitted) local inputs. As shown by Roback (1982), dealing with natural amenities is slightly more involved. To see this, assume that a region is endowed with such amenities which attract migrants, all else being equal. The inflow of this new population exerts an upward pressure on the demand for housing, thereby pushing up rents. Higher land rents induce firms to substitute other production factors, such as labor, for land. As the marginal productivity of labor decreases, land–labor substitution leads to a drop in wages. When natural amenities are more abundant in heavily populated regions (as is the case for leisure facilities), the effect of density is thus underestimated. The key point is that omitted variables such as these can bias estimates in both directions, thus leaving us in the dark as to the magnitude and direction of the bias.

In the spatial context, there is still another group of omitted variables. All the explanatory variables considered so far have been restricted to the geographic area r under consideration; none have taken into account effects, such as interindustry or intraindustry externalities, that could emanate from *neighboring areas*. In other words, the implicit assumption so far has been a complete absence of nonmarket interactions between areas. Everything is estimated under the presumption that no spillover effects exist *between* regions or that those are randomly distributed across regions. If, as suggested in chapter 5, distance has a negative impact on interregional interactions (via trade flows or knowledge transfers), such an assumption seems untenable. It is undoubtedly the main weakness of the approach presented so far. Very few attempts have been made to correct the resulting biased estimates. First of all, a market-potential variable defined as the sum of each region's density weighted by the inverse of its distance to this area can be introduced.[7] Another

---

[7] See chapter 12 for a detailed discussion of the concept of market potential.

approach consists of using techniques borrowed from spatial econometrics, by adding spatially lagged variables and accounting for the potential
autocorrelation of the residuals.[8] In both cases, the objective of introducing such variables is to correct for an econometric bias, but they are
often introduced in an ad hoc manner (for instance, functional forms
for distance-decay effects are chosen arbitrarily) and might be difficult
to interpret. We will see in the next chapters how the introduction of
such variables may be better justified.

In a way, we find ourselves with the familiar quest of adding to our
regressions a seemingly endless string of control variables. As in section 11.1, using fixed effects is an option. Namely, when a panel of industries in different regions is available, we may introduce region and industry fixed effects to control for omitted variables. For instance, we can
evaluate the extent of interindustry externalities controlling for regional
fixed effects, provided that at least two years of data are available, and
making the reasonable assumption that amenity and public good endowments are constant during the short time period under consideration. In
the same vein, industry fixed effects can be introduced. Indeed, in addition to controlling for missing sector-specific variables, they are necessary to capture differences in labor shares across different industries:
replacing μ with μ_s in (11.6) implies in turn that the intercept α in (11.9)
should be industry specific. As more and more data become available,
we should even consider industry–time fixed effects in order to purge
the model of business cycle effects that are specific to some regions.

11.2.3 Endogeneity Bias

The above approaches shed light on a more general problem that often
plagues empirical studies in economic geography: the endogeneity of
some explanatory variables. Formally, OLS estimates are biased when
some explanatory variables are correlated with the residuals of the
regression. These variables are then said to be *endogenous*. The presence of such a correlation can be tested with the help of appropriate
statistical techniques, provided a sufficient number of exogenous variables are available. Using the density variable as an example, we first
want to obtain some clues as to the nature of the endogeneity problem.
To this end, assume that a given region experiences a shock observed
by economic agents but overlooked by the econometrician. For example,
a positive shock may stem from the decisions made by regional governments that lead to a higher local productivity; conversely, a hike in

---

[8] See Bailey and Gatrell (1995) for an introduction to these techniques, and Anselin
et al. (2003) for a more advanced presentation.

the oil price is a negative shock for regions having several oil-intensive industries. Some of these shocks may randomly affect the productivity of all inputs and may, therefore, be assumed to be independently and identically distributed across regions. In this case, they would be completely absorbed by the residual term, ε_{rs}. However, in economic geography, shocks are often localized and thus have an impact on the location of agents, who are attracted by regions benefiting from positive shocks (generating wage increases) and repelled by those suffering from negative shocks. These relocations obviously have an impact on regions' levels of economic activity and, consequently, on their density of regional employment. In other words, the employment density is necessarily correlated with the residuals (it is positive in our example):

$$\mathrm{corr}(\ln \mathrm{den}_r, \varepsilon_{rs}) \neq 0.$$

Density is thus endogenous, which contradicts one of the assumptions underpinning the validity of the OLS estimator, biasing it upwards here. Endogeneity is often framed as a problem of *reverse causality*: the unobserved shock initially affects wages, and thus density, through the mobility of workers, and not the other way around as equation (11.9) implies. If, however, the production factors were to be nearly immobile, one would expect the endogeneity bias to be weaker. That said, even in the context of immobile production factors, a given shock may affect the level of regional employment via the creation and destruction of jobs. As a result, the employment density variable would again be endogenous.

We want to stress the difference between the endogeneity problem in econometrics and the choice of endogenous variables in economic models, namely those that are determined in equilibrium. As mentioned above, in econometrics, endogeneity arises when some explanatory variables and the residuals are correlated. Thus, variables that are endogenous in the economic sense are likely to be endogenous from an econometric point of view. Even explanatory variables that are not directly correlated with the residuals may be tied to other endogenous variables (via the equation system describing the equilibrium outcome) which are themselves correlated with the residuals. This need not be the case, however. One may come across situations in which variables are endogenous in the economic sense but exogenous from the econometric standpoint, and vice versa. It all depends on the economic interpretation of the residuals, the determination of which is therefore a crucial step in the specification of an econometric model. Assessing the degree of econometric endogeneity of a given explanatory variable is only possible once the source of the economic model's residuals has been clearly identified.

The endogeneity problem is not specific to economic geography; the issues it generates are encountered in many other fields of economics. The issues' pervasiveness has one clear benefit: a wide variety of techniques have been proposed to address them. The most common approach involves using what are known as *instrumental variable techniques*. This consists of finding variables, called *instruments*, that are correlated with the endogenous explanatory variables but *not* with the residuals. The first step is to regress the variable whose exogeneity is suspect on the chosen instrument(s). In the present context, we may regress the density of regional employment at date t on the region's density several decades earlier. Such an instrumental regression may, for instance, be expressed as follows:

$$\ln \mathrm{den}_r = \rho \ln \mathrm{den}_{r,t-150} + v_r,$$

where $\mathrm{den}_{r,t-150}$ is the region's density 150 years before the year of interest and v_r is an error term. This provides us with a predicted value for the density given by $\widehat{\ln \mathrm{den}}_r = \hat{\rho} \ln \mathrm{den}_{r,t-150}$, where $\hat{\rho}$ is the OLS estimator for ρ. In the next step, the density in the initial regression (11.9) is replaced by its predicted value (the explanatory variable den_r is then said to be instrumented), which is uncorrelated with the residuals since the instrument is by definition exogenous:

$$\mathrm{corr}(\widehat{\ln \mathrm{den}}_r, \varepsilon_{rs}) = \mathrm{corr}(\hat{\rho} \ln \mathrm{den}_{r,t-150}, \varepsilon_{rs})$$
$$= \mathrm{corr}(\ln \mathrm{den}_{r,t-150}, \varepsilon_{rs})$$
$$= 0.$$

In this case, the OLS estimate of the equation

$$\ln w_{rs} = \alpha + \beta \widehat{\ln \mathrm{den}}_r + \varepsilon_{rs}$$

no longer suffers from endogeneity bias and provides an unbiased estimate of the effect of density (see Wooldridge (2002) for further details).

A few comments are in order. First, everything rests on the alleged exogeneity of the chosen instrument. Once again, both economic and econometric considerations must be taken into account. From the economic standpoint, in the density example, it is quite plausible that there is no correlation between past employment density and present-day productivity shocks. However, a time gap, be it 150 years or longer, is not necessarily a sufficient condition for exogeneity, because the source of a shock may be linked to unobserved factors that persist over time. Bearing this in mind, it is imperative to ponder all possible sources of endogeneity for both the explanatory variables and the possible instruments. Regardless of our confidence about the exogeneity of this or that variable, it is standard practice in econometrics to carry out *overidentification tests*, which can be interpreted as exogeneity tests for some of the proposed instruments. These tests are relatively straightforward, but they require the number of instruments to be greater than the number of instrumented variables. Regarding density, additional instruments might be given by past population levels at several different dates, or by former population growth rates. Other potential instruments may be based on regional skill endowments, as measured by the past regional levels of literacy or numbers of students.

Another advantage of using instrumental variable techniques is that it may address problems related to omitted variables. Indeed, as for reverse causality, they can also be framed in terms of a correlation between one or more explanatory variables and the residuals. To illustrate, let us assume we have omitted public infrastructure from our regression (whose effect is therefore captured by the residuals), and that such an infrastructure is more prevalent in dense areas. As a result, a positive correlation emerges between the residuals and one of the explanatory variables (the density again), generating the upward bias mentioned above. Given that the current level of public infrastructure can often be traced back only to recent governments' decisions, it should not be correlated with the population level several decades ago. In running the instrumental regression, any existing correlation between the current density and infrastructure is thus relegated to the residuals, which means that the new predicted value of density is free of omitted variable bias.[9]

Finally, it is worth noting that the endogeneity problem addressed in this subsection has been illustrated only for the density variable. Almost all other variables, discussed above and usually introduced in this type of regression, are, however, likely to be endogenous. For example, any variables related to the industrial structure are intimately linked to location decisions, which also leads to biased OLS estimators.

11.2.4   The Impact of Density on Wages

In practice, what is the extent of economies of density and of the biases arising from omitted variables and endogeneity? Results drawn from

---

[9] Note that the presence of omitted variables and the existence of reverse causality both bias OLS estimators by producing a correlation between one or more explanatory variables and the residuals. However, the source of this correlation is not the same. In the first case, the residuals are not random because they are correlated with omitted variables that are not random. In the second case, the residuals may be random *ex ante*, but their realizations, observed *ex post* by the agents, lead to decisions that affect the explanatory variables, thus making them correlated with the residuals.

Combes et al. (2008b) provide a useful starting point from which to address this question. This study estimates the magnitude of agglomeration economies on the basis of disaggregated French data, available at the individual level. Namely, the data set gives the location $r(i, t)$ and the sector $s(i, t)$ associated with each worker i at time t. Furthermore, it covers a time period spanning 1976 to 1998. The dependent variable is a worker's wage at a given date. The resulting specification bears some resemblance to the model presented above by assuming that the amount of efficient labor used in firm j at date t is expressed as follows (all variables now also depend on date t):

$$ s_{j,t} l_{j,t} = \sum_{i \in (j,t)} s_{i,t} \ell_{i,t}, $$

where $s_{i,t}$ is the efficiency of worker i at date t and $\ell_{i,t}$ is his supply of labor. In equilibrium, the first-order condition yields

$$ w_{i,t} = \mu(1-\mu)^{(1-\mu)/\mu} s_{i,t} \left(\frac{p_{j,t} A_{j,t}}{r_{j,t}^{1-\mu}} \right)^{1/\mu}, $$

so that the wage equation to be estimated is

$$ \ln w_{i,t} = \theta_i + \lambda \, \text{age}_{i,t} + \mu (\text{age}_{i,t})^2 + X_{r(i,t),t} \beta $$
$$ + Z_{r(i,t)s(i,t),t} \phi + y_{s(i,t)} + \delta_t + \epsilon_{i,t}, \qquad (11.13) $$

where $\epsilon_{i,t}$ represents an individual-specific productivity shock, while the remaining four groups of variables explain the wage rate. More precisely, $X_{r(i,t),t}$ is a vector of variables associated with the worker's location $r(i,t)$ at date t, the aim of which is to capture interindustry externalities (density, surface area, and diversity); $Z_{r(i,t)s(i,t),t}$ is a vector of variables that capture intraindustry externalities (specialization and number of firms); $y_{s(i,t)}$ and δ_t are industry and time fixed effects. Finally, the worker-specific variables, which depend directly on i and t, constitute the fourth group; they capture the impact of a given worker's skills $s_{i,t} \equiv \theta_i + \lambda \, \text{age}_{i,t} + \mu (\text{age}_{i,t})^2$, which is assumed to depend on a worker's fixed effect, θ_i, and her experience, which is reflected by her age and her age squared (note that μ is usually negative).

These last group of variables distinguishes estimations based on individual data from those using aggregate data. In particular, a specification that uses aggregate data explains the *average* wage $w_{rs,t}$ and includes as a covariate the *average* workers' average skills $Q_{rs,t}$ in sector s and region r at date t:

$$ \ln w_{rs,t} = Q_{rs,t} \theta + X_{r,t} \beta + Z_{rs,t} \phi + y_s + \delta_t + \varepsilon_{rs}. \qquad (11.14) $$

Typically, $Q_{rs,t}$ is assumed to depend on the average literacy, education, or skill levels of the employees in the local industry. This is to be compared with (11.13), in which θ_i is the efficiency pertaining to each worker, estimated as an individual-specific fixed effect. In other words, it need not depend only on the worker's education or skill level, as is the case when using aggregate data. It encompasses any effect specific to the worker that does not vary over time *whether it is observable* (i.e., available in the data set) *or not*. Access to data spanning several years allows for the introduction of such a fixed effect, the estimation of which is based on variations in a worker's wages over time and possibly across locations if she moves. This fixed effect does not, however, take into account time variations in an individual's skills. Thus, to complete the model, we add the worker's age and its square, the aim of which is to account for the large fraction of time fluctuations in an individual's skills (as shown by labor economists).

Ultimately, this type of estimation is much more general than models based on aggregate data on the following grounds:

(i) it exploits more information (e.g., using individual wages instead of average wages, and individual skills instead of average skills) and

(ii) the skill variables included in the model are no longer constrained to being proportional to other available explanatory variables.

Again, we use the density to illustrate the bias resulting from omitted variables and endogeneity. The most comprehensive estimation uses individual-specific data that include variables controlling for natural amenities, local public goods, and the market potential of neighboring areas; all variables that capture interindustry externalities are instrumented (as discussed above).[10] The elasticity of wage with respect to density is found to be 0.03, which means that *doubling the density of employment increases productivity by* $(2^{0.03} - 1) \times 100\% = 2.1\%$. When the endogenous explanatory variables are not instrumented, the same regression leads to a higher estimate of 0.037. Thus, failing to control for endogeneity would amount to overestimating agglomeration economies by more than 20%, which is still reasonable when compared with the larger bias caused by omitted variables. Let us now turn to this problem.

When working with aggregate data, the estimation of (11.14) shows that the impact of density on wages is 0.056 under the instrumented specification and 0.063 otherwise. Moreover, surface area is estimated

---

[10] The instruments used are lagged variables taken at dates distant enough to ensure their exogeneity. Combes et al. (2008c) confirm those results by considering either wages or total factor productivity as the dependent variable, and geological features as instruments.

to have an impact of 0.034, while in the context of individual data its impact is not statistically significant. This suggests that working with aggregated instead of individual data can be a very significant source of bias. This is because such data fails to capture differences in labor skills across regions accurately. Average skill levels taken into account as controls capture imperfectly, at best, real differences in skills across individuals. Adopting a fixed effect for each worker, together with age and its square, changes the estimated density by a factor of two, while the impact of the surface area disappears. The underlying reason is that workers are sorted across space according to their overall skills. Even when workers have identical observable skills (e.g., their levels of education or their qualifications), *the most efficient workers in terms of nonobservable characteristics* (e.g., their motivation or other psychological and cultural characteristics) *are located in the densest areas.* Therefore, overlooking or failing to adequately control for this selection of nonobservable skills across space (i.e., a problem of omitted variables) can lead to very inaccurate evaluations of agglomeration economies. This might bias estimations even more than edogeneity. For a public decision maker, the fact that doubling the density of economic activity increases factor productivity by either 2.1% or 4.5% makes a big difference.

Building on Combes et al., Mion and Naticchioni (forthcoming) study the spatial variation of wages in Italy. Also using individual data, their results corroborate what we have just seen, namely that the elasticity of wages with respect to density is largely explained by differences in worker skill levels (66% of the total variance), and that taking endogeneity into account reduces this elasticity by nearly 50%. Mion and Naticchioni also observe that the presence of skilled workers in the most populated areas can only be partly attributed to migration. More precisely, everything works as if the place of birth were a spatial sorting device. The authors' hypothesis is that the interregional distribution of skills is linked to the size of the cities as producers of knowledge, as suggested by Glaeser and Mare (2001) in the context of the United States. In this case, *the spatial selection of skills could be considered a dynamic process in which the largest cities play a crucial role*, in that the accumulation of skills occurs more rapidly in these areas than elsewhere. However, more research is called for before any definitive conclusion can be drawn on that important issue.

To put the above estimations into perspective, note that Ciccone and Hall (1996) and Ciccone (2002) have studied the impact of density, the former for the United States and the latter for the large EU countries. Both papers use instrumented wage equations and find that density has an estimated elasticity of approximately 0.04–0.05; they show that these estimates are barely affected by endogeneity bias. At first glance, this result is at odds with those obtained from French data. However, having noticed that differences in labor productivity were only controlled at the aggregate level in these two papers, it remains to be seen whether these estimates would be robust to omitted nonobservable characteristics.

11.2.5 Regional Dynamics

There are related, and sometimes older, branches of literature that have attempted to apply the same type of ideas to the analysis of regional economic dynamics. The underlying idea is readily grasped: rather than having an immediate impact on productivity, agglomeration economies could have a dynamic impact, thereby exerting an influence on regional growth. In other words, if $X_{rs,t}$ encompasses all local externalities (in logarithms), and if the logarithm of the marginal productivity of labor (11.6) is expressed as[11]

$$g_{rs,t} \equiv \ln\left[s_{rs,t}\left(\frac{p_{rs,t}A_{rs,t}}{r_{rs,t}^{1-\mu}} \right)^{1/\mu} \right],$$

it is also customary to estimate

$$g_{rs,t} - g_{rs,t-k} = X_{rs,t-k}\beta + \varepsilon_{rs,t},$$

where k is the lagged effect of externalities, measured in years, whereas the assumption made until now was

$$g_{rs,t} = X_{rs,t}\beta + \varepsilon_{rs,t}.$$

Glaeser et al. (1992) and Henderson et al. (1995) set the groundwork for an alternative specification that has been often used since then. The specification involves choosing a different dependent variable, i.e., replacing change in productivity by change in employment levels. While the choice of this alternative dependent variable is alluring because relevant data are often available on a very fine spatial scale, the drawback is that the resulting specification strays from its theoretical foundations, generating new issues in the interpretation of the estimations. For example, it is possible for the growth in productivity to lead to a drop in regional employment, which is at odds with the assumptions underlying this alternative specification (see Combes et al. (2004) for further details).

Another important issue in the literature is how fast externalities vanish across time. Finding a cogent answer to this question has clear and direct implications for the optimal timing of regional policies. Henderson

---

[11] As discussed above, one could use similarly the average labor productivity or the total factor productivity.

(2003) tackles this problem by considering lagged externalities, for each of a number K of years, as explanatory variables. The model estimated is given by

$$g_{rs,t} = \sum_{k=0}^{K} X_{rs,t-k}\beta_k + \varepsilon_{rs,t}.$$

Interpreting this specification warrants caution, however, as we run the risk of mixing the influence of lagged density values on local externalities with some simple possible inertia of productivity over time. The existence of such an inertia is plausible because it takes time to adjust production factors and/or to set up new plants. With this in mind, Henderson (1997) provides what seems to be the most appropriate model for testing the dynamics of local externalities:[12]

$$g_{rs,t} = \sum_{k=1}^{K} \alpha_k g_{rs,t-k} + \sum_{k=0}^{K} X_{rs,t-k}\beta_k + \varepsilon_{rs,t}.$$

This specification has the benefit of testing the persistence of externalities across time, while simultaneously controlling for the inertia effects of the dependent variable. Moreover, econometric techniques developed in the context of dynamic panels, such as generalized methods of moments, allow one to address endogeneity issues without finding specific instrumental variables. Indeed, it can be shown that sufficiently lagged values of the variables in level are valid instruments for the variables in first difference that are endogenous, and vice versa. In other words, the model is first rewritten as follows:

$$g_{rs,t} - g_{rs,t-1} = \sum_{k=1}^{K} \alpha_k (g_{rs,t-k} - g_{rs,t-k-1})$$
$$+ \sum_{k=0}^{K} (X_{rs,t-k} - X_{rs,t-k-1})\beta_k + \varepsilon_{rs,t} - \varepsilon_{rs,t-1}.$$

This specification also allows one to take into account the impact of region and industry fixed effects. Moreover, lagged values of $g_{rs,t-1}$ and of $X_{rs,t}$ are used as instruments whose validity can be checked by means of overidentification tests.[13]

Somewhat unexpectedly, Combes et al. (2004) find that the adjustment process shows greater inertia in the United States than in France, despite the lower mobility of French workers. Static externalities are found to be predominant in France (lagged values stop being significant after one

---

[12] This approach has been revisited by Combes et al. (2004) to allow for the simultaneous estimation of the dynamics of employment and of the number of firms.
[13] Arellano (2003) gives a detailed account of these techniques.

year), which is starkly at odds with the six- or seven-year lags found in Henderson (1997). Combes et al. also suggest that the elements conducive to the growth of existing firms (the intensive margin) are not necessarily the same as those that foment the creation of new firms (the extensive margin). More precisely, it appears that a large number of different-sized plants positively influences the growth of existing plants, whereas more new plants tend to be created where there are a small number of plants having a similar size. Finally, a large regional labor market with a small number of similar-sized industries would favor the growth of both new and existing firms. Hence, contrary to general beliefs, *a strategy that aims to diversify the local industrial structure is not necessarily a good strategy for boosting regional development.*

11.3   Concluding Remarks

While they can be alluring, simple regressions that rely on industry-specific characteristics to account for differences in spatial concentration give rise to a great many econometric and analytical problems that can be resolved imperfectly at best. Due caution needs to be exercised when running these regressions, paying particular attention to the potential for omitted variables and endogeneity biases. Despite their tenuous link with economic geography models, the other approaches discussed in this chapter lead to suggestively stylized facts about the magnitude of agglomeration economies and the regional structure of industries. Here also, we have encountered a number of econometric issues that are generic in empirical economic geography, namely omitted variables problems related to the imperfectly measured characteristics of the areas as well as endogeneity biases due to workers' and firms' endogenous location choices. Having said that, even when we account for a large number of explanatory variables and econometric issues, *agglomeration economies remain important*, thus inviting us to continue the exploration of the mystery of economic agglomeration.

The approaches we have covered are said to be *nonstructural* in the sense that they are not directly derived from a specific model, and do not have the aim of estimating the parameters of such a model (note that this did not preclude us from framing these nonstructural approaches within a general theoretical context). In the final two chapters of this book, the benefits of applying structural models will be presented in greater detail. As a preview, one such benefit is that structural models are more capable of capturing various types of interactions across regions, a task that is not often accomplished in the literature presented in this chapter. Common to all fields of economics, these two types of approaches (structural versus nonstructural) should be seen as complementary. The former is helpful in identifying robust correlations between variables that lie at the heart of economic geography, which involves a large number of variables. The latter intends to validate particular theoretical models with greater rigor, but this is often at the cost of a loss of generality.

11.4 Related Literature

The idea of agglomeration economies dates back at least to Weber (1909), while the potential role of industrial diversity in fostering local development was first discussed by Jacobs (1969). Intraindustry externalities are also called *localization economies* (Hoover 1936) or Marshall–Arrow–Romer (MAR) externalities. Interindustry externalities are called *urbanization economies* or Jacobs externalities. This cornucopia is a major source of confusion. It was not until the work by Glaeser et al. (1992) and Henderson et al. (1995), which both deal with employment growth in American cities, that a new strand of research has begun to estimate more precisely the magnitude of agglomeration economies. It took several more years for the many difficulties associated with such estimations to be fully understood. A fairly comprehensive review of the literature is provided by Rosenthal and Strange (2004). The reader will find in Cingano and Schivardi (2004) an analysis of regional productivity growth in Italy. Focusing on Chinese cities, Au and Henderson (2006) consider the impact of city size on wages. The existence of a bell-shaped relationship is confirmed, with the striking result that a large number of Chinese cities are undersized, as all agglomeration economies are not being fully exploited.

12

The Empirics of Economic Geography

As discussed in part II, one of the central problems studied by economic geography is the relative attractiveness of various locations for firms, as well as the underlying causes behind the observed differences in spatial patterns of firms. In particular, given that most firms are free to choose among a number of different regions, economic geography seeks to determine the characteristics of locations that are most consistently attractive to firms. Unearthing a set of convincing explanations for the observed spatial distribution of firms is thus another fundamental goal of economic geography. From this perspective, we will consider the insights that economic geography provides in corroborating or rejecting the assertion made in the *European Spatial Development Perspective*:

> Initial signs of liberalisation ... indicate that competition and commercial use are steering investment towards areas with high demand, since they appear to be the most promising. More remote regions with little market potential are threatened by further decline.
>
> European Commission (1999, p. 14)

   This chapter summarizes the methods and findings of a set of recent empirical research papers in economic geography. Although we have tried to provide a unifying framework that would account for most existing studies, this chapter fails to provide a fully integrated overview of this new literature because the dust has not yet settled. In the first section, the determinants making up a firm's locational decision are surveyed. Since firms locate in regions that provide them with the largest expected profits, a burgeoning line of research, presented in section 12.2, builds upon this assumption by using discrete choice models to assess the existence and impact of profit differentials across locations. Section 12.3 introduces a different approach: regions' shares of production and demand are used to estimate the home-market effect which, as seen in part II, lies at the heart of several economic geography models. Section 12.4 builds on the idea that profit differentials can also be expressed by differences in local factor prices, especially wages—an approach that is probably more in line with theoretical models. Section 12.5 introduces a relatively nascent literature that focuses on workers' migration within economic geography settings.

At this stage, we should make it clear that, despite significant and marked progress, empirical studies still fall short of the theoretical research that calls for general-equilibrium models. More precisely, the econometric models presented in this chapter exhibit many of the limitations inherent to partial-equilibrium analysis, such as endogeneity issues. Nevertheless, these studies may serve as a useful benchmark for assessing the empirical relevance and predictive power of economic geography models, as well as providing the seeds of new lines of research, some of which will be examined in chapter 13.

A last approach, presented in section 12.6, attempts to solve the problem of endogeneity by focusing directly on the main prediction of economic geography: the sensitivity of location choices with respect to the variables that are most relevant to firms. By drawing on methods borrowed from labor economics and other fields, this line of research aims to exploit large shocks (natural experiments) to uncover the key variables that determine firms' locations. Such shocks range from a sudden, unanticipated opening up of the economy to changes that affect firms' locational decisions more directly. Though fairly original, the fact that these works depart substantially from theory makes them somewhat difficult to interpret.

12.1   A General Framework

We begin by recalling the notation used in our benchmark setting: r and s are indices corresponding to any given region or country, p_r denotes the mill price of a variety sold by a firm located in r, m_r denotes its marginal production cost,[1] q_{rs} denotes the quantity that this firm sells on market s, and τ_{rs} denotes the iceberg-type trade cost from r to s. As seen in chapter 4, equilibrium operating profits (gross of fixed costs) made in market s are given by the following expression:

$$\pi_{rs}^* = (p_r^* - m_r)\tau_{rs}q_{rs}^* = m_r \frac{\tau_{rs}q_{rs}^*}{\sigma - 1},$$

since the equilibrium price is given by $p_{rs}^* = \tau_{rs}p_r^* = \tau_{rs}m_r\sigma/(\sigma - 1)$. In a short-run context in which the number of firms is exogenous and

---

[1] Note that m_r now designates the marginal *cost*, rather than the marginal *requirement* for labor as in the models presented in part II.

profits are positive, the quantity q_{rs}^* is determined on the basis of a CES-type demand function, which implies that

$$q_{rs}^* = (p_r^* \tau_{rs})^{-\sigma} \mu_s Y_s P_s^{\sigma-1},$$

where

$$P_s = \left[\sum_{r=1}^{R} n_r (p_r^* \tau_{rs})^{-(\sigma-1)} \right]^{-1/(\sigma-1)}$$

is the CES price index in s, Y_s is the income of this region, and μ_s is the share of the good considered in the consumption of region s. Thus, the total profits for a firm located in r are equal to

$$\Pi_r^* = \sum_s \pi_{rs}^* - F_r = c m_r^{-(\sigma-1)} \mathrm{RMP}_r - F_r, \tag{12.1}$$

where $c = \sigma^{-\sigma}/(\sigma-1)^{-(\sigma-1)}$, F_r denotes the firm's fixed cost and

$$\mathrm{RMP}_r \equiv \sum_s \phi_{rs} \mu_s Y_s P_s^{\sigma-1} \tag{12.2}$$

with $\phi_{rs} = \tau_{rs}^{-(\sigma-1)}$, where RMP stands for the *real market potential* with reference to the pioneering work of the geographer Chauncy Harris (1954). We will see that equation (12.1), called the *profit equation*, is at the root of various approaches used to estimate several predictions put forward by economic geography.

Harris's (1954) idea is simple: in many sectors, producers tend to locate in the regions that guarantee them a significant degree of accessibility to various markets. In particular, Harris's contribution consists of his definition of *market potential* as an indicator for the degree of accessibility to market r:

$$\mathrm{MP}_r \equiv \sum_s \frac{Y_s}{d_{rs}}, \tag{12.3}$$

where d_{rs} is the distance between r and s. This indicator is obviously inspired by the gravity equation, discussed in chapter 5, as Harris himself acknowledged:

> Market potential appears to gauge the possible spatial interaction between producers and markets, of the likely flow of goods from a point to accessible regions. A number of studies indicate that freight movement as well as many other types of relationships between any two points varies directly with their size and inversely with their distance apart.

> Harris (1954, p. 325)

To derive the expression proposed by Harris from the RMP defined above, we must make three additional assumptions. The first amounts to assuming that $\phi_{rs} = d_{rs}^{-\delta}$. Given that the estimation of the gravity equation yields values of δ close to 1 (see chapter 5), this expression reduces to $\phi_{rs} = 1/d_{rs}$. Moreover, it imposes a stronger assumption whereby each good's share in the total consumption is the same across regions. This simplifying assumption may be deemed acceptable when working with the consumption of final goods. However, regarding the consumption of intermediate goods, this assumption becomes more problematic, as it implies that either all sectors consume the same amount of each factor, or regional sectoral compositions are the same. Both are clearly inaccurate. It is worth noting one last and crucial difference between the RMP and Harris's market potential: while the price index is present in the former, it is absent from the latter. Yet we expect an increase in the number of competitors located in a given destination to generate a more fragmented demand, which in turn implies a decrease in the corresponding RMP. Thus, Harris's market potential is at best a rough approximation of the RMP, the latter taking into account more effects to explain a particular site's profitability.

The profit equation (12.1) shows that region r's profitability depends on two basic ingredients: the marginal production cost, m_r, which prevails there and its real market potential, RMP_r, taken as a general measure for the degree of accessibility to the overall set of markets available to firms located in region r. Equation (12.1) can thus be used in a number of empirical tests evaluating different determinants of firms' location choices. These tests can be described as follows.

1. *Location choice.* The simplest method consists of estimating the profit equation directly. This equation predicts how firms distribute themselves across space according to the relative accessibility of the regions under consideration, after controlling for the differences in regional costs. This type of research has primarily been applied to multinational firms, because the determinants underlying their locational decisions are more readily discernible than those for domestic (and therefore less "footloose") firms. In particular, multinational firms' location choices have occurred over the course of a relatively short time period, and they are free from the historical contingencies to which national firms are often subjected. This type of research will be examined in section 12.2.

2. *Home-market effect.* The existence of positive profit differentials between regions is incompatible with the existence of a long-term spatial equilibrium. The equalization of profits between regions can take two forms. First, it can occur via a relocation of firms, which should

ultimately result in the emergence of more intense economic activity in the regions with higher market potential. These studies correspond to the empirical counterpart of the literature devoted to the home-market effect presented in chapter 4; they will be discussed in section 12.3.

3. *Local factor prices.* Another way of adjusting profits is possible: the equalization of profits can be reached by allowing for higher production costs (e.g., higher wages) which would offset the greater market accessibility supplied by central regions. This type of mechanism has given rise to a large body of research that focuses on the *wage equation*, which is examined in section 12.4.[2]

4. *Migrations.* If wages tend to increase in the regions endowed with the greater market access, one should expect this situation to spark migratory movement, as in the core–periphery model presented in chapter 6; the extent of this movement depends on the degree of the workers' spatial mobility. Section 12.5 covers these types of validation.

5. *Stability of the spatial structures.* Economic geography models are characterized by the existence of multiple stable equilibria. This implies that far-reaching shocks could be capable of moving the economy as a whole from one pattern of agglomeration to another. The studies surveyed in section 12.6 have a historical emphasis; they suggest that large shocks have left spatial patterns unaffected.

Common to all these studies is the preeminence of market accessibility (measured by the RMP) as a major explanatory variable. However, the models studied in chapters 6 and 7 should be distinguished from international trade models with imperfect competition because of the following fundamental difference: in the former the location of demand is endogenous, whereas in the latter it is exogenous. Endogeneity can arise through a number of mechanisms, such as the migration of worker-consumers, as in Krugman (1991a), or because of the simultaneous location choices made by firms trading intermediate goods, as in Krugman and Venables (1995). In either case, a region's RMP is *endogenous* in that it depends on the location choices thus made. It is therefore crucial to take this feature into account in the empirical validations, a task that can prove very difficult.

---

[2] In the real world, both adjustment mechanisms are at work (see chapter 7). In particular, if the existence of a profit differential triggers a flow of firms to the region with high market potential, wages will be adjusted upwards: the higher the elasticity of the labor supply, the lower the wage increase. The measure of this elasticity is therefore crucial for determining which adjustment mechanism predominates in practice.

12.2 Location of Firms

This section describes the first strategy for estimating the profit equation, which entails the direct examination of firms' location choices. A firm wants to establish a subsidiary[3] in the region that offers it the highest profits. Consequently, it will locate in region r if $\Pi_r^* > \Pi_s^*$ for all $s \neq r$, where the profit function is given by (12.1). Drawing on a number of assumptions that we will explain below, the parameters of the profit function can be estimated by means of the *logit* model.[4] To the best of our knowledge, Carlton (1983) was the first to use this approach to study firms' location choices. Since then, many empirical studies have applied the same method to the subsidiaries of multinational firms.

12.2.1 An Econometric Model of Location

Any empirical work that studies location choices incorporates a set of variables with which we attempt to capture the two main determinants of profitability: the accessibility to existing demand and the level of production costs. Regarding demand, studies use very simple approximations that include the regional income or ad hoc specifications that include both the incomes of the regions under consideration as well as the income for more distant regions. Different formulations have been considered, ranging from the income of contiguous regions (Head et al. 1999) to Harris's market potential (Friedman et al. 1992). Nearly all of the studies conclude that these variables have a positive impact on firms' location choices, thus bolstering the idea that *firms seek the proximity of consumers*. Nevertheless, these results cannot be interpreted as an empirical validation of the predictions of economic geography models. Indeed, any theory focusing on firm location choices in the presence of positive trade costs will, in one way or another, predict that firms prefer to be close to their customers. Thus, more discriminating approaches and tests are required to empirically validate economic geography models, i.e., approaches that explicitly model the impact of the RMP on firms' locational decisions, as well as other variables specific to economic geography. It is worth stressing, however, that the above studies do not reject the main conclusions of economic geography.

---

[3] We assume that the firm wants to set up only one plant in the area under consideration. It would be interesting to consider firms with several plants that could split the fixed costs between them. Unfortunately, this is likely to make the models and their empirical testing extremely complex. We refer the reader to Navaretti and Venables (2004) for a survey of the literature devoted to foreign direct investments, which touches on this type of issue.

[4] See Train (2003) for a detailed presentation of the techniques for estimating this model.

Head and Mayer (2004a) propose the first location choice model fully consistent with theory. These authors examined a sample of 452 subsidiaries that Japanese firms have established in fifty-seven regions located within nine European countries (Belgium, France, Germany, the Republic of Ireland, Italy, the Netherlands, Portugal, Spain, and the United Kingdom) over the period 1984–95. Assuming that each firm's choice was made on the basis of (12.1), the profits made in each region can be calculated and sorted in decreasing order. Any transformation of the function Π_r^* that maintains the same ordering of profits would lead to the same location choices. With this in mind, Head and Mayer first make the (strong) assumption that fixed production costs are the same everywhere. Then, after this fixed cost is added to profits, the resulting expression is multiplied by σ, which is in turn raised to the power of $1/(\sigma - 1)$, and, finally, its logarithm is taken. The result, denoted by U_r, is as follows:[5]

$$U_r \equiv \frac{-\ln c + \ln(\Pi_r^* + F)}{\sigma - 1} = \frac{1}{\sigma - 1} \ln \mathrm{RMP}_r - \ln m_r. \qquad (12.4)$$

The structure of the term m_r must now be specified. One of the most common forms used to represent variable costs is through a Cobb–Douglas function whose exponents sum up to 1. Typically, this function includes labor, remunerated at the wage w_r, and other production factors (such as land and intermediate goods), the combination of which is understood as a composite input available to firms at the price v_r. The share of labor in the production process is α, while A_r represents the total factor productivity in region r. The logarithm of the marginal cost is thus given by

$$\ln m_r = \alpha \ln w_r + (1 - \alpha) \ln v_r - \ln A_r. \qquad (12.5)$$

Substituting (12.5) into (12.4), we obtain

$$U_r = \ln A_r + \frac{1}{\sigma - 1} \ln \mathrm{RMP}_r - \alpha \ln w_r - (1 - \alpha) \ln v_r. \qquad (12.6)$$

At this stage, the following question comes to mind: if all firms use the same expression (12.6), why do all firms not choose the same location? One possible answer rests on the following two ideas:

(i) locational decisions are sequential, and

(ii) there is some market congestion.

---

[5] To ease the burden of notation, we can omit the firms' index, so long as we bear in mind that we focus on the choice made by an individual firm. Indeed, some of the variables in the profit function will be specific to each firm.

The first firms to enter are attracted by the region offering the highest level of profit. The growing concentration of these firms strengthens competition within the region (lowering market potential), which in turn increases final demand (raising market potential). In other words, both downward and upward pressure is put on the real market potential RMP_r. So long as RMP_r remains high, firms will continue to flow into this region, but if RMP_r drops below some threshold, other regions will start attracting new entrants who will begin to locate there, and so forth. This adjustment process is based on the implicit assumption that firms have high relocation costs.

This explanation is one among many, and it is far from being the most convincing. In particular, firms that have similar observable characteristics (e.g., firms with the same investment date, sector, local labor market, markets for goods, etc.) may differ because of an underlying nonobservable or nonmeasurable heterogeneity. However, this heterogeneity can be partly accounted for by allowing A_r to be multiplied by a random variable ε_r. The random component specific to each firm–region pair reflects differences in total factor productivity across firms that are observed by the firms but not by the modeler.

Based on these assumptions, the expression encapsulating the variables that drive location choices becomes

$$\tilde{U}_r = \ln A_r + \frac{1}{\sigma - 1} \ln RMP_r - \alpha \ln w_r - (1 - \alpha) \ln v_r + \varepsilon_r. \qquad (12.7)$$

Under this formulation, location choice ceases to be deterministic and becomes probabilistic: the firm assigns a positive probability to each region so that each region is a potential candidate. In particular, location factors such as market access and production cost in region r become less important to firms when ε_r takes large absolute values.

The functional form for the probability of choosing a given region is determined by the underlying distribution function of the random variable ε_r. If we assume this variable follows the Gumbel law with the cumulative distribution function

$$F(\varepsilon_r) = \exp(-\exp(-\varepsilon_r)),$$

then the probability of choosing region r can be computed explicitly by the logit model (see chapters 3, 8 and 9):

$$\boldsymbol{P_r} = \frac{\exp U_r}{\sum_s \exp U_s}.$$

In turn, the logit model enables us to estimate the parameters of (12.6) using the maximum likelihood method.

The idea underlying this approach is thus straightforward. For any given firm, the potential profit corresponding to each region cannot be observed. However, the firm's actual location choice, as well as some characteristics of the regions where the firm could establish itself, is observable. These observations enable us both to sort regions according to their potential profits and to uncover the influence of the variables included in U_r.

12.2.2 The Determinants: Production Cost and Productivity

Data for regional wages w_r can often be obtained easily for quite a few sectors. This allows one to include directly one of the main components of labor costs into the estimation. We must bear in mind, however, that wages are only one of the components of labor costs. Efforts to account for labor market institutions that may vary across regions or countries should also be made. Moreover, it is worth recalling that labor is assumed to be homogeneous here while, as seen in chapter 11, the existence of regional differences in the workforce composition may generate substantial variations in productivity.[6] Data allowing for a precise measurement of regional labor heterogeneity are seldom available, and their impact is therefore rarely considered in the literature.

Furthermore, neither v_r nor A_r are observable directly, and overlooking these variables can lead to omitted variable bias, as discussed in the previous chapter. As a one seeks a certain number of observable variables to serve as suitable approximations for these two magnitudes. For instance, differences in the prices of industrial lots can be taken into account by including either the price of land or, in the absence of data, the regions' area as a proxy for v_r.[7] An obvious factor affecting A_r is the local level of education of the workforce. Note that high skills should naturally be translated into high wages, implying a rise in A_r. With perfectly competitive labor markets, including local wages in the regression should therefore be sufficient. Furthermore, another issue arises regarding wages. Indeed, we will see below that firms' location choices may also result in higher wages, thus raising important reverse causality issues. The same holds for the RMP whose role is discussed in the next subsection. This points to the need for an instrumentation strategy for wages. Local education is not a good candidate for an instrument because it likely affects the location of foreign direct investments (FDIs)

---

[6] As in chapter 11, we could add an extra term $\alpha \ln s_r$ to (12.5), where s_r reflects workers' skills in region r.

[7] If the local price of land is observable, the regional area naturally becomes redundant, at least as part of v_r.

directly through A_r. A possible solution to this problem has been put forward by Liu et al. (2006). They study the locations of FDIs in China, and use a particular aspect of the Chinese labor market, i.e., the duality between state-owned enterprises (SOEs) and private firms. Differences in the wages of SOEs across China seem to have desirable properties as an instrument for spatial disparities in private wages: an increase in the wages paid by SOEs in a particular city will affect the local labor market and therefore private wages. However, the formation process of those SOEs' wages probably has very little direct relation to the amount of FDI received by the city. Liu et al. (2006) implement this method in a conditional logit study of FDI location choices in China and find promising results. It seems hard, however, to generalize this type of instrumentation strategy because the divide in labor market used is quite specific to the case studied.

In addition to labor-costs issues, taxes and subsidies are also likely to have an impact on the cost of capital and, therefore, affect firms' locational decisions. Some studies thus include variables accounting for differences in the corporate tax rate, as well as other related measures for subsidies and regional policy. Indeed, it is an empirically robust fact that marginal differences in the tax rate imposed on profits have a substantial impact on firms' locational decisions. In a meta-analysis of the empirical studies devoted to this subject, Mooij and Ederveen (2003) report that an increase in the rate of taxation by one point reduces the amount of foreign investment received by around 5%. The impact of investment subsidies is much less clear, although certain types of subsidy do seem more effective than others. Targeted subsidies (for example, the $300 million received by Mercedes in 1993 from local authorities in Alabama to back a $250 million investment) do seem to have a significant impact on location decisions (Head et al. 1999). By contrast, these studies find the impact of subsidies arising from regional planning policies to be remarkably weak (Crozet et al. 2004). In the same vein, Devereux et al. (2007) confirm that grants have a small effect in attracting plants to specific geographic areas, but find that firms are less responsive to government subsidies in areas where there are fewer existing plants in their industry.

Empirical studies focusing on the location of multinational firms reveal a marked tendency for the agglomeration of firms with certain common traits, the most important being:

  (i) they belong to the same sector;

 (ii) the investors have the same country of origin;

(iii) plants are affiliated to the same firm or the same group.

One such type of group that has been studied in depth and exhibits these traits is the Japanese *keiretsu*, which is structured around input–output linkages in a number of sectors (automobiles, machine tools, and electronics). The spatial concentration of firms characterized by this type of relationship can lead to the formation of regional production systems in which firms trade intermediate goods between them, thus bringing down the level of v_r (see chapter 7). Moreover, via agglomeration economies similar to those described in chapter 11, firms can also share their respective knowledge and know-how, which is conducive to increasing their total productivity, A_r. Finally, the spatial concentration of firms also comes about on the basis of exogenous advantages such as natural resource endowments and access to coastal regions, among many other characteristics that account for lower factor prices and/or a higher productivity.

These different mechanisms can be accounted for through the use of regional fixed effects when data are available for several years and when the productivity and cost parameters vary little over time.[8] Alternately, additional control variables can be considered. As will be seen, implementing such controls is often a daunting task.

12.2.3   The Determinants: Market Potential

Aside from examining the key variables underpinning firms' production costs and productivity, economic geography also maintains that profits should be higher in areas where demand is high, which should spark the agglomeration of firms. Conversely, a region hosting many firms belonging to the same sector may lead to the fragmentation of demand, thus making this region less attractive to firms. It is precisely the interaction between these two effects that DSK-type models capture by means of the real market potential given by (12.2).

Unfortunately, estimating RMP_r is no simple matter. Indeed, it requires information regarding the values of ϕ_{rs} and P_s, neither of which are directly observable, as both depend on unknown parameters. The strategy then consists in estimating RMP_r by means of estimations of ϕ_{rs} and $\mu_s Y_s P_s^{\sigma-1}$ through the expression

$$\widehat{\text{RMP}}_r = \sum_s \hat{\phi}_{rs}\mu_s \widehat{Y_s P_s^{\sigma-1}}. \tag{12.8}$$

The method for estimating ϕ_{rs} via trade flows discussed in chapter 5 is not often feasible on a regional level, as data for trade flows on this spatial scale seldom exist. In addition, given that these trade flows depend

---

[8] See chapter 11 for a detailed discussion of this issue.

on firms' locational decisions (which is precisely what we would like to explain), adopting such a method would be rife with endogeneity problems. Similarly, estimating $\mu_s Y_s P_S^{\sigma-1}$ directly is impossible, mainly because of the lack of relevant data about regional prices and the need to estimate the elasticity of substitution, σ. Given that the only available data deals with bilateral trade between *countries*, the idea is to obtain an approximation of these magnitudes on the basis of their national counterparts. The procedure is outlined below.

If R and S denote two countries in the sample, the exports X_{RS} from R to S are expressed as

$$\ln X_{RS} = \text{FX}_R + \ln \phi_{RS} + \text{FM}_S + \varepsilon_{RS}, \tag{12.9}$$

where FX_R and FM_S are the variables used in the fixed-effects gravity model presented in chapter 5. In particular,

$$\text{FM}_S = \ln(\mu_S Y_S P_S^{\sigma-1}).$$

As also seen in chapter 5, free trade is hindered by the bilateral distance (d_{RS}), but also by the fact that the trading partners are different countries (with dummy variable B_{RS} set to 1 when R and S are different) or do not share the same language (in which case the dummy variable L_{RS} is equal to 0):

$$\ln \phi_{RS} = -\delta \ln d_{RS} - \beta_S B_{RS} + \lambda L_{RS} B_{RS}. \tag{12.10}$$

Estimating (12.9) after plugging (12.10) into it provides a first set of parameters, $\hat{\delta}$, $\hat{\beta}_S$, $\hat{\lambda}$, $\widehat{\text{FX}}_R$, and $\widehat{\text{FM}}_S$, the last two corresponding to fixed effects as in chapter 5. In turn, these parameters allow us to compute the regional indices $\hat{\phi}_{rs}$ by assuming that the same economic determinants of trade flows (see (12.9)) apply to both countries and regions:

$$\left.\begin{aligned} \hat{\phi}_{rs} &= \exp(-\hat{\beta}_S + \hat{\lambda} L_{RS}) d_{rs}^{-\hat{\delta}} \quad \text{for } r \neq s, \\ \hat{\phi}_{rr} &= d_{rr}^{-\hat{\delta}} = \left(\frac{2}{3}\sqrt{\frac{\text{area}_r}{\pi}}\right)^{-\hat{\delta}}, \end{aligned}\right\} \tag{12.11}$$

where r and s now denote regions.

In a second step, the real market potential can be determined for country S as follows:

$$\widehat{\mu_S Y_S P_S^{\sigma-1}} = \exp(\widehat{\text{FM}}_S).$$

To obtain the regional-level estimators, Head and Mayer (2004a) suggest allocating this value among regions in country S according to their relative weight in the national income, which amounts to ignoring price differences across regions of the same country. In this case, the second estimator that we need is given by

$$\widehat{\mu_s Y_s P_s^{\sigma-1}} = \left(\frac{Y_s}{Y_S}\right) \exp(\widehat{FM_S}). \tag{12.12}$$

Finally, by substituting (12.11) and (12.12) into (12.8), we obtain an expression of the RMP for each region, year, and sector. The corresponding values are used to estimate the profit equation (12.6) by means of a discrete choice model, as described above.[9]

In concluding their study on Japanese investments in Europe, Head and Mayer's assessment of the predictive power of economic geography is rather mixed. They find that the RMP does intervene in firms' locational decisions. Namely, for any given region, a 10% rise in the RMP corresponds to an increase in the probability of a firm choosing that region ranging from 3% to 11%, according to the specifications used. One failure of the RMP is that it leads to slightly less reliable predictions for firms' locational decisions than Harris's market potential. Furthermore, a number of variables absent from the DSK model (e.g., the size of the local economy, the number of domestic versus Japanese competitors, whether or not firms belong to the same kereitsu, etc.) have a considerable influence on firms' locational decisions. Such results suggest that the agglomeration forces stressed by the DSK model are far from being the only (or even most important) ones responsible for the observed spatial concentration of FDIs. In particular, agglomeration economies have a direct effect on firms' productivity (see chapter 11) and are, therefore, unquestionably at work.[10] The RMP, the level of activity, and the existence of local networks of firms being strongly correlated, distinguishing between these different mechanisms empirically is deceptively difficult and will undoubtedly require new methodological developments.

12.3   Home-Market Effect

We have just seen that firms make choices which, to a certain extent, agree with the main predictions of economic geography. In particular, firms establish themselves in regions with a high market potential and leave regions with poor access to markets. What kind of long-run equilibrium can arise from such individual choices? In theory, one should

---

[9] From an econometric standpoint, we note that certain explanatory variables used in the regression are estimated in a first step, and thus measured with error, which results in the familiar, biased standard deviations. However, correcting for this is difficult in the context of the logit model.

[10] This observation also invites us to pay more attention to the different spatial scales covered by theoretical and empirical models.

ultimately obtain a spatial pattern of firms such that no other locations would offer them opportunities for higher profits. In short, profits must be equalized between all occupied regions and lower in the remaining regions. One recent line of research starts from this assumption for assessing the predictive power of economic geography's main building block by using differences in the relative size of regions.

12.3.1 The Helpman–Krugman Model

Krugman (1980) was the first to examine what is known as the home-market effect (HME), which we have presented in chapter 4. Let us quickly review the theoretical model proposed by Helpman and Krugman (1985, chapter 10) as well as its corresponding empirical specification. Let λ denote the share of producers located in region r and let θ denote the demand share attributed to this region: $\lambda = n_r/N$ and $\theta = (\mu_r Y_r)/E$, where n_k is the number of firms in region k, $N = \sum_k n_k$ is the total number of firms, and $E = \sum_k \mu_k Y_k$ is total expenditure. When considering only two regions r and s, the spatial equilibrium is characterized by $\lambda^* \in (0, 1)$ such that $\Pi_r(\lambda^*) - \Pi_s(\lambda^*) = 0$. We can then use the profit equation (12.1) to obtain

$$\Pi_r(\lambda^*) - \Pi_s(\lambda^*) = c(m_r^{1-\sigma}\,\mathrm{RMP}_r - m_s^{1-\sigma}\,\mathrm{RMP}_s) - (F_r - F_s).$$

The empirical literature devoted to the HME makes several strong assumptions in order to obtain a solution amenable to estimation. The traditional sector is characterized by constant returns, perfect competition, and zero trade costs. Consumers care enough about the traditional good for both regions to produce it in equilibrium. Assuming that labor is the only production factor perfectly mobile across sectors, and that technology is identical across regions, the price of the traditional good is equalized between the two regions, which implies the interregional equality both of wages, $w_r = w_s$, and of fixed production costs, $F_r = F_s$.

Following the same approach as in chapter 4, the difference in profits between regions r and s can be written as

$$\Pi_r(\lambda) - \Pi_s(\lambda) = \frac{cE}{N}\left[\frac{\lambda(\phi - 1) - \phi + \theta(\phi + 1)}{\lambda(1 - \phi)(1 - \lambda) + \phi(1 - \phi)}\right]. \tag{12.13}$$

Solving $\Pi_r(\lambda) - \Pi_s(\lambda) = 0$, we obtain the following HME relationship:

$$\lambda^* = \tfrac{1}{2} + \mathcal{M}(\theta - \tfrac{1}{2}) \tag{12.14}$$

if

$$\frac{1}{2}\left(1 - \frac{1}{\mathcal{M}}\right) < \theta < \frac{1}{2}\left(1 + \frac{1}{\mathcal{M}}\right),$$

where $\mathcal{M} \equiv (1 + \phi)/(1 - \phi)$ and $\lambda = 0$ if $\theta < \frac{1}{2}(1 - 1/M)$. The equation (12.14) lends itself to several types of empirical verifications. The simplest amounts to carrying out a linear regression between λ^* and θ. The estimated coefficient has a theoretical value equal to $(1 + \phi)/(1 - \phi)$ and should therefore be greater than 1. Moreover, the above relationship acts as a guide in choosing the type of econometric model that should be used. Indeed, if region r were to exhibit very a very low demand for the manufactured good, it would be unlikely to attract any firm, in which case an increase in θ has no impact on λ^*. From the econometric point of view, the fact that the dependent variable can take a zero value implies that estimation by ordinary least squares leads to a downward bias in the coefficient; a Tobit-type estimation can remedy this problem. Last, the coefficient $\mathcal{M}$ is an increasing function of ϕ and is therefore a decreasing function of trade costs. This provides a second possible type of test: the relationship between λ^* and θ should have a steeper slope during, say, periods of trade liberalization.

12.3.2 Empirical Validations

Somewhat surprisingly, the first empirical studies of the HME did *not* consider equation (12.14) as the theoretical basis for their estimations. In particular, Davis and Weinstein (1996, 1999, 2003) used approaches matching theory much less closely in their work. The main difference lies in the fact that their specification uses variables in levels and not in shares, as required by (12.14). They estimate a relationship between the production y_r^k of a good k in country r and two variables labeled share_r^k and $\mathrm{idiodem}_r^k$:

$$y_r^k = \beta_1 \, \mathrm{share}_r^k + \beta_2 \, \mathrm{idiodem}_r^k + \varepsilon_r^k, \tag{12.15}$$

where

$$\mathrm{share}_r^k = \frac{y_R^k}{y_R} y_r,$$

given that $y_R^k = \sum_{s \neq r} y_s^k$ and $y_R = \sum_k X_R^k$ stand for the production of good k in the rest of the world (understood as the set of OECD countries in their applications) and its total production, respectively, while y_r is the total production in country r. It is worth noting that, in spite of its name, share_r^k is not expressed in terms of shares, but corresponds to the production of good k in country r when the share of sector k in this country is the same as in the rest of the world. The authors' central variable is $\mathrm{idiodem}_r^k$. It is defined as a deviation of country r's expenditure in good k relative to the rest of the world's expenditure pattern:

$$\text{idiodem}_r^k = \left(\frac{E_r^k}{E_r} - \frac{E_R^k}{E_R}\right) y_r,$$

where the expenditure variables E are analogous to the production variables y. In the absence of idiosyncratic differences in demand across countries (which amounts to assuming that $\text{idiodem}_r^k = 0$), Davis and Weinstein expect $y_r^k = \text{share}_r^k$ and, therefore, the coefficient β_1 to be close to 1. The coefficient β_2 captures the potential existence of the HME, i.e., the response of the equilibrium number of firms to spatial differences in demand. Imposing $\beta_1 = 1$ in equation (12.15) yields an expression more closely related to theory:

$$\frac{y_r^k}{y_r} - \frac{y_R^k}{y_R} = \beta_2\left(\frac{E_r^k}{E_r} - \frac{E_R^k}{E_R}\right) + \varepsilon_r^k.$$

In this way, we effectively work with an equation expressed in shares (or, more accurately, in differences in shares with respect to the rest of the world), which could be considered as the generalization of (12.14) to an R-country setting. For this reason, Davis and Weinstein (1996, 1999, 2003) see their specification as an approximation of (12.14), where β_2 would be an estimator of $\mathcal{M}$. We will discuss below the limitations of this interpretation.

Davis and Weinstein augment the specification (12.14) by a set of variables related to endowments in land, capital, and labor specific to each country and encapsulated in a vector labeled factors$_r$. This augmented specification is motivated by the need to distinguish between explanations relying on comparative advantage (via the variables factors$_r$) and explanations put forward by economic geography (via idiodem$_r^k$ controlled by share$_r^k$).[11] At the heart of Davis and Weinstein's analyses is the coefficient β_2, which serves to distinguish between these two sets of explanatory variables. Namely, $\beta_2 > 1$ lends credence to the economic geography model, whereas an estimate in which $\beta_2 < 1$ is only compatible with a model resting on compared advantage and constant returns.[12]

---

[11] The need to distinguish between the two families of models was also discussed in section 11.1 about the determinants of spatial sectoral concentration.

[12] Some studies have questioned this interpretation. Feenstra et al. (2001), Trionfetti (2001), and Head et al. (2002) have shown that it is possible to combine increasing returns, positive trade costs and $\beta_2 < 1$ in the absence of comparative advantage. Therefore, the only robust conclusion is that $\beta_2 > 1$ is incompatible with the presence of constant returns, thereby confirming the assumption of increasing returns, although the opposite case does not allow us to rule out increasing returns in favor of constant returns. Finally, it is difficult to find a theoretical model consistent with $\beta_2 < 0$. Thus, finding such an empirical result suggests the presence of a problem related to specification or to data.

Table 12.1. Davis and Weinstein (DW) estimators in pooled regressions.

		$\text{share}_r^k(\hat{\beta}_1)$		$\text{idiodem}_r^k(\hat{\beta}_2)$	
Article/sample	factors_r^k	Result	s.d.	Result	s.d.
DW96, OECD	No	1.103	(0.002)	1.229	(0.005)
	Yes	0.259	(0.198)	0.712	(0.033)
DW99, Japan	No	1.033	(0.007)	1.416	(0.025)
	Yes	−1.744	(0.211)	0.888	(0.070)
DW03, OECD	No	0.96	(0.01)	1.67	(0.05)
	Yes	—	—	1.57	(0.10)

The contributions of Davis and Weinstein (1999, 2003) are widely considered to provide an important empirical backing for the HME and for economic geography as a whole. For example, Fujita et al. (1999, p. 59) note that "[r]ecent work by Davis and Weinstein (1999) has attempted to measure the empirical importance of the home-market effect in patterns of international trade and has found surprisingly strong impacts," while Baldwin et al. (2003, p. 4) state with similar conviction that the two above-mentioned articles "find econometric evidence that one agglomeration force—the so-called home-market effect—is in operation." In fact, looking carefully at Davis and Weinstein's conclusions calls for a more cautious and nuanced interpretation.

Table 12.1 synthesizes the results obtained in the three articles by Davis and Weinstein (1996, 1999, 2003) when all sectors are pooled; the standard deviations are shown in parentheses; the second column shows whether or not the factors_r^k variable, which corresponds to a vector of controls for local endowments, is included. The 1996 and 1999 results indicate that, when adopting the authors' favorite specification, the Idiodem coefficient is less than one when the endowment variables are introduced into the equation. In other words, if we are to accept their econometric specification, the resulting estimations do *not* provide empirical backing for the HME. In their 2003 article, while their estimation reveals that $\beta_2 > 1$ even when endowments are controlled for, their specification in this case omits the share_r^k variable. This is problematic as it constitutes a substantial departure from the original theoretical framework.

If those first results tend to disqualify the HME, it is worth pondering the validity of the approach adopted by Davis and Weinstein. Indeed, a first criticism might draw attention to the heterogeneous nature of the sectors included in the pooled estimates. Trade costs, returns to scale, and intermediate inputs are a few characteristics among many that can

Table 12.2. Descriptive statistics for the sector-specific effect of idiodem$_r^k$, as estimated by Davis and Weinstein (1999, 2003).

Article	$\hat{\beta}_2$ Mean	$\hat{\beta}_2$ Median	N	$\hat{\beta}_2 > 1$ (%)	sgn > 1 (%)	$\hat{\beta}_2 < 0$ (%)	sgn < 0 (%)
DW99, Japan							
Table 6	1.63	0.45	20	45	40	40	5
DW03, OECD							
Table 2[a]	1.47	0.95	50	50	22	38	4
Table 3[b]	1.20	1.02	13	54	31	0	0
Table 4[c]	4.23	0.71	24	37.5	8.3	37.5	12.5

Notes: [a]four-digit classification, separate regressions; [b]four-digit classification, pooled regressions; [c]three-digit classification, separate regressions.

differ widely across sectors. Such differences in characteristics imply different theoretical relationships between production and demand shares. Thus, it seems fairly bold to assume that the estimated coefficients are the same across all sectors. For instance, in the two-region model, $\beta_2 > 1$ depends directly on the parameter ϕ, which varies across sectors since it captures trade costs. With this in mind, it may be more judicious to estimate the regressions sector by sector.

Table 12.2 presents the main descriptive statistics summarizing the results of Davis and Weinstein (1996, 1999), disaggregated by sector. At first sight, these are more encouraging for the HME. The mean of β_2, the coefficient for variable idiodem$_r^k$, is greater than 1 in this set of results. The mean values can, however, be influenced by extreme values. The median values are less sensitive to this problem and are less than 1. In particular, more than half of the coefficients are less than 1, and a significant fraction are even negative, which is not consistent with any model. With this in mind, it would seem the prevailing view of Davis and Weinstein's work, which lends credence to the HME, is unduly optimistic. Only eleven sectors out of fifty (for the four-digit classification in their 2003 article) verify in a strict sense the criteria defined by the authors themselves. A more circumspect interpretation would be that the results present too great a variance for any clear conclusions to be made regarding the existence or absence of the HME.

Let us go back to a stricter application of the theoretical predictions put forward by the HME. If we were to isolate two countries, A and B, and only consider their bilateral trade for different sectors k and dates t, equation (12.14) has a natural empirical counterpart. Production in country A can be defined as the sum of its production destined for its domestic market and its exports to B, and analogously, consumption as the sum of its production spent on its own market and its imports from B (vice versa for country B). This approach is essentially a linear regression for a panel of industries and years using the share of country A's production in the total production of the two countries (λ_t^k) as the left-hand-side variable, and country A's share of consumption in their joint consumption (θ_t^k) as the right-hand-side variable:

$$\lambda_t^k = \alpha_1 + \alpha_2 \theta_t^k + \varepsilon_t^k. \tag{12.16}$$

Despite α_2's similarity with Davis and Weinstein's coefficient β_2, there is a crucial difference that lies in the direct link between the estimated parameters and their structural counterpart derived from the theoretical model. Namely, under this interpretation, we obtain

$$\alpha_2 = \mathcal{M} = \frac{1 + \phi}{1 - \phi}.$$

Adopting the method presented in chapter 5, Head and Ries (2001) start off by calculating ϕ_t^k, using trade flows between Canada and the United States for different sectors. Then, they take ϕ_t^k for the median sector of their sample in order to gauge α_2's order of magnitude. This yields an estimated $\alpha_2 = 1.15$. They also propose a direct estimation of α_2 using their panel of sectors and years, studying each dimension independently. In other words, they first introduce time fixed effects and thus use only intersectoral variation; the second estimation uses sector fixed effects in order to estimate α_2 from intertemporal variations inside sectors. The results from the intersectoral ("between") dimension yield $\alpha_2 = 1.13$. This value, with its corresponding standard error of 0.07, corroborates, to some extent, the existence of the HME. However, the temporal ("within") dimension yields an estimated $\alpha_2 = 0.84$, which is significantly less than 1. As before, these results can be interpreted in various ways. An optimistic reading might only consider the sectoral results and eschew the temporal dimension for lack of robustness (it can be argued that six years of data is too meager). Yet the temporal dimension does annul the influence of comparative advantage, whose corresponding variables were omitted from the regression but potentially captured by the sector fixed effects, making for a potentially inflated estimate of α_2 in the intersectoral dimension.

There is a third strategy, which makes it possible to better evaluate and discriminate between these two interpretations. It consists of examining the impact of a change in trade liberalization over time. The theoretical model predicts that the lowering of tariffs between Canada and the United States should increase the value of α_2; this should translate to a lower fall in production for the sector with the greatest initial demand in the less populous country (here, Canada). This contradicts empirical observations by Head and Ries (2001), however, which raises further uncertainty about the validity of the HME.

At this stage, the following comments are in order. First, it is worth noting that, in Head and Ries's study discussed above, the authors isolate two countries in order to follow closely the theoretical model. This implicitly assumes that what happens within and between these two countries is not influenced by their relationship with the rest of the world, an assumption analogous to the "independence of irrelevant alternatives" often called upon in economic models, but which can raise criticism here. In fact, more often than not it is quite difficult to extend the HME to a higher dimensionality (with several regions/countries and sectors), even though a global economy composed of countries trading with a great many partners is precisely the proper context in which to examine the HME. In particular, as discussed in chapter 4, the notion of a dominant market becomes muddled as soon as more than two regions are involved. Moreover, the trading partners' relative locations is a crucial variable, and one that is ignored in all studies discussed above. For instance, Davis and Weinstein only estimate one β_2 for the entire set of countries, and this variable takes into account bilateral trade costs, which vary across pairs of countries. Attempts made to study the HME more generally have only very recently given rise to theoretical developments (Behrens et al. 2004), so it is probably premature to speculate on their empirical implications.

Finally, it should be pointed out that in both this section and the previous one, the econometric endogeneity of the explanatory variables is ignored altogether. This amounts to assuming that location choices are not endogenous, which is somewhat paradoxical in studies seeking to explain these very choices. This is tantamount to neglecting the main parameter of differentiation between the models of international trade with imperfect competition and those of economic geography. We will see that the studies presented in the following section are, in this respect, more rigorous.

12.4 Factor Prices and Economic Geography

The previous section makes the assumption that the profit surplus of the region with a strong market potential is entirely absorbed by the mechanism of firms' relocation, thereby equalizing profits across all regions in which firms from the same sector are established. The nominal wages are also assumed to be immediately equalized due to the unimpeded circulation of the traditional good. Another adjustment mechanism involves increasing the cost of the production factors in the regions exhibiting high market potential or, alternatively, lowering it in those regions where the profitability of production is lower.

By using the profit equation (12.1), the zero-profit condition can be written as

$$m_r = \left(\frac{c \, \mathrm{RMP}_r}{F_r}\right)^{1/(\sigma-1)}. \tag{12.17}$$

As before, the next part of the analysis depends upon which assumptions we adopt regarding the structure of production costs, i.e., the assumptions underlying the definition of m_r. Labor, taken here to be homogeneous and immobile across sectors, is the main factor of production, but firms also use other primary production factors and intermediate inputs. For these latter inputs, it is customary to assume (as in chapter 7) that each firm uses a combination of the manufactured good (with all varieties aggregated in a CES fashion) and of the primary inputs in its production function. The marginal production cost m_r is thus given by a Cobb–Douglas function analogous to the production function, which now depends on wages (w_r), the prices of the other primary factors (x_r), and the price index of the varieties (P_r):

$$m_r = w_r^\alpha x_r^\beta P_r^y, \tag{12.18}$$

where α, β, and y are three parameters summing to 1. Finally, if the fixed costs involve the same production factors and are used in the same proportion as the variable costs, we have $F_r = a w_r^\alpha x_r^\beta P_r^y$, where a is a constant measuring the degree of increasing returns to scale, which is assumed to be the same across regions. By equalizing (12.17) and (12.18) for the marginal production cost, we obtain a long-run equilibrium relationship linking the different factor prices in region r:

$$\ln w_r = \frac{1}{\alpha\sigma} \ln \mathrm{RMP}_r - \frac{y}{\alpha} \ln P_r - \frac{\beta}{\alpha} \ln x_r - \frac{1}{\sigma\alpha} \ln\left(\frac{a}{c}\right). \tag{12.19}$$

This equation, which is considered by Redding and Venables (2004), is analogous to a *wage equation*, as described in chapter 11. While regional wages show up on the left-hand side of (12.19),[13] regional wages also enter on the right-hand side (in the price index and market potential) and are thus only expressed implicitly. Furthermore, one important difference lies in the fact that the right-hand-side variables are in this case

---

[13] Note that w_r can be interpreted more broadly as the factor price for all the immobile factors, while x_r would be that of the mobile factors.

directly derived from the theoretical model (as opposed to being chosen in a more or less ad hoc fashion) and for this reason the estimation is characterized as *structural*. Following Hanson (1998), some authors have developed this equation in a simplified setting by assuming that labor is the only factor of production, i.e., $\beta = \gamma = 0$. It is worth noting that, even if the approaches are different, expression (12.19) is still directly linked to the notion of production site r's profitability, as considered in section 12.2. In particular, it specifies the level of factor prices needed for the profits of the firms established in r to be zero.[14] To date, two applications of this approach have been developed.

12.4.1 Regional Inequalities in Income per Capita

An obvious approximation of the logarithm of wages is given by the logarithm of the GDP per capita in region r ($\ln \mathrm{GDPC}_r$). If we make the somewhat strong assumption that the technological level and factor prices for other primary inputs are the same across regions (possibly because they are perfectly mobile), or that their differences are randomly distributed across space,[15] then we obtain the following equation:

$$\ln \mathrm{GDPC}_r = \frac{1}{\sigma \alpha} \ln \widehat{\mathrm{RMP}}_r + \frac{\gamma}{\alpha(\sigma - 1)} \ln \widehat{\mathrm{SP}}_r + \zeta + \varepsilon_r, \qquad (12.20)$$

where $\mathrm{SP}_r \equiv P_r^{1-\sigma}$ stands for what Redding and Venables (2004) call the "supplier potential," while ζ is a constant and ε_r is an error term capturing regional differences in the factor prices of other primary inputs or the productivity of those factors, which are both assumed to be randomly distributed. The central variable in the analysis is once again the real market potential, RMP_r. Note how high values of RMP_r clearly lead to high wages, which reflects the agglomeration mechanisms linked to the size of the final markets. As for the supplier potential variable, SP_r, this captures the role of the intermediate inputs described in chapter 7: the closer a firm is to its suppliers, the higher the wage it is willing to pay its employees, because of its greater profitability.

As in section 12.2, a preliminary regression using bilateral trade flows allows Redding and Venables to construct RMP and SP values for each country. Namely, along the same lines as in chapter 5, the bilateral flows between regions r and s are given by

$$\ln X_{rs} = \mathrm{FX}_r + \ln \phi_{rs} + \mathrm{FM}_s,$$

---

[14] Note also that the traditional sector has implicitly disappeared and that the nominal wages are therefore no longer equalized across sectors, and thus across regions.

[15] In particular, it must be assumed that factor prices in region r of the imperfectly mobile inputs are not linked to either the regions' market potential or the price index of the intermediate goods.

where

$$\text{FX}_r \equiv \ln(n_r p_r^{1-\sigma}) \quad \text{and} \quad \text{FM}_s \equiv \ln(\mu Y_s P_s^{\sigma-1})$$

and ϕ_{rs} can be approximated with the help of standard variables such as distance, contiguity, etc. In turn, the bilateral trade flows regression makes it possible to calculate the explanatory variables in (12.20):

$$\widehat{\text{RMP}}_r = \sum_s \exp(\widehat{\text{FM}}_s)\hat{\phi}_{rs} \quad \text{and} \quad \widehat{\text{SP}}_r = \sum_s \exp(\widehat{\text{FX}}_s)\hat{\phi}_{sr}.$$

As seen in chapter 11, wage equations require the inclusion of a certain number of control variables as a safeguard against potential omitted variable problems. It is particularly important to use such control variables to take into account international differences with respect to workers' skill levels, the level of technology, endowments, and the quality of institutions, all of which are absent in the theoretical model.[16]

With this in mind, Redding and Venables estimate (12.20) on the basis of a sample of 101 countries in 1994. The two variables RMP_r and SP_r are constructed from the same set of countries. In its simplest specification, the regression's explanatory power is impressive: RMP alone accounts for up to 73% of the variance in GDP per capita. Supplier potential, when considered as the sole explanatory variable, is the only one endowed with similar explanatory power.[17]

Unfortunately, this result is very sensitive to assumptions underlying the measure of parameters ϕ_{rs} and ϕ_{rr}. Redding and Venables assume that $\ln\phi_{rs} = -\delta\ln d_{rs} + \beta\text{bord}_{rs}$, with three alternate expressions for internal distance d_{rr} (and consequently for ϕ_{rr} as well). The specification chosen for internal distance is particularly important, as it partly determines the degree to which a region r's own GDP affects its RMP and therefore its GDP per capita. In the extreme case in which trade costs ϕ_{rr} and ϕ_{rs} are close to 1 and 0, respectively, region r's GDP is the only variable included in a regression that is supposed to explain r's GDP per capita. Even if ϕ_{rr} and ϕ_{rs} do not take such extreme values, other problems arise. When working within an economic geography framework with endogenous location choices, a regional wage or GDP

---

[16] Recent work by Head and Mayer (2006) and Herring and Poncet (forthcoming) has added measures for regional or individual skills to the Redding and Venables (2004) framework.

[17] The market and supplier potential variables retain a strong impact when control variables are included. They are never significant simultaneously, however, maybe because their correlation is high. Note that the econometric techniques used take into account both the presence of a great number of zero values in trade flows (this point is discussed in chapter 5) and the fact that some explanatory variables are estimated in a first stage (standard errors are bootstrapped), which is not the case in the studies presented in the previous sections.

shock that is observed by agents but not by the econometrician generates correlations between the error term and the explanatory variables. This is particularly true of the RMP, due to the presence of a region, since it involves this region's final demand. Such correlations give rise to problems of endogeneity comparable to those discussed in chapter 11 and earlier in this chapter.

One possible solution for reducing this potential bias involves estimating the model with only the nondomestic component of the RMP. Redding and Venables propose to distinguish between the *domestic* and *foreign* components of the market potential.[18] While this is likely to solve most of the endogeneity problems, this solution has the disadvantage of bringing about potential missing variables problems and specification errors. Adopting this approach, Redding and Venables find that the RMP variable alone accounts for 35% of the variance in GDP per capita in their sample. Even though this result is weaker than the previous one, it provides fairly strong empirical support to economic geography models (at the expense of HME approaches) by suggesting that *a country's level of development largely depends on the economic dynamism of the neighboring countries.* This result is similar to that of Gallup et al. (1999), who observe that physical geography has a significant impact on the level of development. More precisely, these authors show that having a tropical climate and being landlocked are characteristics that negatively affect a country's GDP per capita. However, even though Singapore is very close to the equator and Austria and Switzerland are landlocked, these three countries rank among the richest in the world. Simply put, *physical geography does not explain everything.* By contrast, taking into account economic geography cogently accounts for both the poverty of Rwanda and the wealth of the three countries mentioned above. The main problem with this type of approach is the fact that the theoretical model predicts factor prices that increase with the size of neighboring countries *and* with the size of the local market. If we were to apply only the first component of market potential, Canada would be expected to have significantly higher wages than the United States, which is not the case.

The best solution involves constructing the RMP variable by including both its domestic and foreign components, but using instrumental

---

[18] For instance, the market potential of the United States is "split" between a term accounting only for the American demand and another term accounting for the (trade cost-weighted) demand from all other countries in the world. Note that this divide is not fully consistent with the model's actual prediction. First, in terms of functional form, the model calls for taking the logarithm of the sum of demands and not the sum of the logarithm of demands. Second, there is no theoretical reason why separate terms should have a different impact.

variables for RMP to adequately remedy the endogeneity problem. Redding and Venables (2004) take a first step in this direction, by using the distances to New York, Brussels, and Tokyo as instruments.[19] This approach has the advantage of not being subject to the problem of endogeneity if these instruments are thoroughly exogenous. However, the choice of these reference cities is far from trivial: the underlying forces that have made these three cities so affluent are likely to be included in the model itsel, making these instruments endogenous (in the econometric sense). Further progress still needs to be made if we are to obtain truly satisfactory estimators for the effect of the RMP in this type of model.[20]

12.4.2 Regional Wage Inequalities

Redding and Venables (2004) sought to explain international wage inequalities through economic geography models using income-per-capita differences. However, the first study of this kind regarding spatial inequalities focused on wage differences at the regional level.

If in (12.19) labor is the only production factor ($\beta = \gamma = 0$ such that $\alpha = 1$), we obtain an equation, put forward and estimated by Hanson (1998, 2005), which defines the equilibrium wage of region r as follows:

$$\ln w_r = \frac{1}{\sigma} \ln \text{RMP}_r - \frac{1}{\sigma} \ln \left(\frac{a}{c} \right). \tag{12.21}$$

Wages are again a function of RMP_r, as in the previous setting. However, the effect of the supplier potential has now disappeared, since the production process no longer involves intermediate goods. Hanson further uses the structure of the theoretical model in order to estimate this new wage equation without using a preliminary gravity equation. In this context, he considers two additional equilibrium conditions:

(i) workers' migration equalizes the *real* wages across regions as in Krugman (1991a); and

(ii) the agricultural good in household consumption is replaced by housing, as in Helpman's model (1998) discussed in chapter 8.

---

[19] These cities were chosen as instruments because they lie in the center of the world's three major economic zones, which form what is known as the Triad.

[20] Rice et al. (2007) use NUTS3 data for Great Britain to analyze the determinants of spatial variations in income and productivity. They identify a robust relationship between spatial variations in productivity (but not income) and proximity to economic mass. Mayer (2008) extends the Redding and Venables (2004) regressions to a large set of countries for the period 1965–2003. This makes it possible to apply panel data techniques, and new instruments. Results prove to be robust to the use of country fixed effects and time-varying instruments. This recent finding confirms the empirical success of the wage equation.

Thus, if H_r is the stock of housing in r and P_r^H is its price, the equalization of real wages implies that

$$w_r P_r^{-\mu_r} (P_r^H)^{-(1-\mu_r)} = w_s P_s^{-\mu_s} (P_s^H)^{-(1-\mu_s)} \quad \text{for all } r \text{ and } s.$$

The second equilibrium condition reflects the fact that at the equilibrium price supply and demand with respect to housing must be equal:

$$H_r = (1 - \mu_r) \frac{Y_r}{P_r^H}.$$

Drawing from (12.21), we can replace the two price terms in RMP$_r$ in order to obtain[21]

$$\ln w_r = B + \frac{1}{\sigma} \ln \left[\sum_s Y_s^{(\sigma(\mu-1)+1)/\mu} w_s^{(\sigma-1)/\mu} H_s^{(\sigma-1)(1-\mu)/\mu} \phi_{sr} \right] + \varepsilon_r,$$

$$(12.22)$$

where B is a constant and ε_r is an error term analogous to the one described in the previous section.

Hanson estimates two versions of (12.22) using nonlinear least squares on a sample of 3,075 American counties:[22] a simplified version that replaces the RMP with Harris's market potential, and the structural version that is derived directly from the theoretical model. The estimations have the following characteristics: variables are time-differenced, which is equivalent to adopting county fixed effects in the case of two time periods; numerous control variables are introduced especially to account for skill heterogeneity across counties; and instrumental variables are used in order to tackle the endogeneity problem linked to the endogenous location choices.[23]

A purely structural estimation makes it possible to identify all parameters underlying the theoretical model and possibly to reject it if those parameters do not satisfy the structural constraint. Without imposing any constraints *ex ante* on housing costs, the structural estimation

---

[21] Hanson assumes that the share of housing costs in income is the same across regions and, above all, that the incomes in this sector are uniformly redistributed across space. This is tantamount to suppressing an agglomeration force, since land prices (and therefore landlords' incomes and consumption) would have been higher in the central regions if this assumption had not been formulated (see chapter 8).

[22] Equation (12.22) is not linear in the unknown parameters σ and μ, which does not allow Hanson to use ordinary least squares. An alternative solution, used by Mion (2004), consists in undertaking a Taylor expansion of this equation before estimating it by ordinary least squares. While this specification constitutes a small deviation from the theoretical model, the extent of this deviation is potentially testable and quantifiable. Moreover, ordinary least squares has the advantage of greater robustness (by not depending on the way in which the fixed-point algorithm research is initialized) and better-known asymptotic properties.

[23] We refer the reader to chapter 11 for details regarding the estimation of wage equations.

reveals that the share of housing costs in consumption is indeed between 0 and 1, the elasticity of substitution is greater than 1, and trade costs are positive. *The economic geography model considered by Hanson is therefore not rejected by the data.* The prevailing wage in one region increases with both the income level and the stock of housing in the neighboring regions. The no-black-hole condition (see chapter 6) is also satisfied. For the period 1980–90, the R^2 value is equal to 0.35, confirming the relative success of this type of empirical strategy. The estimated values for the elasticity of substitution σ are bounded by 4.9 and 7.6, which is consistent with the levels presented in the literature. Moreover, structural estimations are of interest as they allow us to determine possible values for other variables in the model. For instance, the producers' markup, $\sigma/(\sigma-1)$, is found to be bounded by 15% and 25%, which seems reasonable. On the other hand, the share of income spent on nontransportable goods (accommodation and nontransferable services) would lie between 3% and 7%, which is lower than observed empirically.

Finally, it is interesting to note that the econometric specification that most closely follows the theoretical model (Hanson 2005) provides better overall results than the specification involving Harris's market potential. This result makes a more convincing case for economic geography than those obtained by Head and Mayer (2004a), for whom the specification most consistent with economic geography explained location choices in a less convincing manner. Having said that, the scope of Hanson's empirical confirmation should be assessed with caution. While the parameter values invoked for the structural estimation are consistent with theory, they are not all consistent with armchair evidence.

Mion (2004) and Brakman et al. (2004a) build on Hanson's (1998, 2005) pioneering analysis for data on Italy and Germany, respectively. Without being identical, these authors' results are quite close to Hanson's. First, the model is not rejected for these two countries. The elasticity of substitution σ is equal to 6.2 for Germany and lies between 5.9 and 6.7 for Italy. After controlling for endogeneity, a value of 3.9 is found for Germany and of 1.9 for Italy. As in Hanson, the estimate for the non-transportable goods sector's share in the overall economy is too small to conform with reality but is higher for Italy when the Taylor expansion of (12.20) is estimated.

12.4.3 Wage Equation: The Case of Mexico

The two types of empirical analysis described above correspond to strict applications of theoretical economic geography models. However, other studies have investigated the relationship between factor prices and accessibility to markets. Although departing from theory, these models account for markets' relative positions as in the previous section (this was lacking in the estimations of agglomeration economies presented in chapter 11). To illustrate this, Hanson (1996) uses the example of Mexico's rapid international trade liberalization. In 1985, this country emerged somewhat abruptly from forty years of protectionism, and soon after was admitted into GATT (1986) and NAFTA (1994). These transformations in Mexican firms' economic environment, coupled with the predominant role played by Mexico City in national production, make this country an almost ideal experiment for economic geography's main predictions. Hanson uses the distance from the capital and the distance from the closest U.S. border crossing to explain Mexican wages. In particular, the dependent variable is the wage in each Mexican region relative to the prevailing wage for the same sector in Mexico City. He examines the values and explanatory power of the model before and after 1985. Hanson finds that a 10% rise in the distance from Mexico City corresponds to a reduction in wages by 1.9%, while the same increase in the distance from the American border generates a 1.3% drop. This suggests that *the accessibility to markets is significant in determining regional wages.* The other conjecture put forward, namely that after 1985 the distance to Mexico City has become less important in determining regional wages than the distance to the northern border, is, however, not confirmed.

In short, it seems that market potential has a significant impact on wages at both the international and interregional levels. These results are in line with economic geography, although many methodological questions remain to be investigated.

12.5 Migrations

The empirical studies discussed in the previous section suggest that regions having a strong market potential offer higher nominal factor prices than other regions. This is particularly true of wages. Consequently, if workers are mobile, they should be attracted by the regions with a strong market potential and there should be positive net migration flows toward these regions (provided that the cost of living is not too high there). In Krugman's model (1991a), workers choose their location on the basis of the regional gap in real wages. In a model with more than two regions, it is assumed that region r attracts or repels workers depending on whether the real wage offered there is higher or lower than the real wage across other regions. Crozet (2004) applies this idea to analyze the migratory flows between European regions,[24] but he also wants to incorporate the fact that these regions might experience fairly high levels of unemployment. In a simple approach à la Harris and Todaro (1970), Crozet assumes that the expected real wage in r is given by the real wage, w_r, multiplied by the probability, e_r, that a worker finds a job in this region. This value is assumed to be inversely proportional to the unemployment level. Moreover, changing places imposes migration costs, so that individuals make their residential choice by maximizing their expected real wage after deducting these costs. As workers are also assumed to be heterogeneous (for the reasons presented in chapter 8), they do not all move at the same time, and do not necessarily choose the same region.

As seen in chapter 8, discrete choice models allow for a simple but realistic treatment of migration decisions. More precisely, Crozet assumes that the satisfaction of individual i in region r is given by $\ln(w_r e_r) + \varepsilon_r(i)$, where $\varepsilon_r(i)$ accounts for the quality of the match between individual i and region r. Migrating from r to s involves a cost $1/\rho_{rs}$, which is generally taken to be positively correlated with the distance separating the two regions. By assuming that the migration cost merely reduces the utility of living in the destination region, the satisfaction derived from living in region s for an individual initially living in r can be expressed as

$$V_{rs} + \varepsilon_s(i) \equiv \ln(w_s e_s \rho_{rs}) + \varepsilon_s(i).$$

The individual i will choose s as her region of residence if this utility is greater than that provided by any other region. As in section 12.2, we can only describe the choice in a probabilistic way. This implies giving a functional form to the distribution of the random variables $\varepsilon_s(i)$. As in section 12.2, assuming that the random term follows a Gumbel law yields a logit-type probability for a worker residing in region r to move to region s:

$$\boldsymbol{P}_{rs} = \frac{V_{rs}}{\sum_t V_{rt}} = \frac{w_s e_s \rho_{rs}}{\sum_t w_t e_t \rho_{rt}}.$$

As in section 8.2.3, the aggregated flow of r to s (mig_{rs}) is then obtained by multiplying the individual migration probability by the population living in r, $\boldsymbol{P}_{rs} L_r$, while the total flow leaving region r (mig_r) is given by $L_r(1 - \boldsymbol{P}_{rr})$. Consequently, the share of migrants from region r that are

---

[24] The sample consisted of gross migratory flows between regions in Germany (1983–92), Italy (1983–93), the Netherlands (1988–94), Spain (1983–93), and the United Kingdom (1980–85).

heading for s is given by

$$\frac{\text{mig}_{rs}}{\text{mig}_r} = \frac{\omega_s e_s \rho_{rs}}{\sum_t (\omega_t e_t \rho_{rt} - \omega_r e_r \rho_{rr})}. \qquad (12.23)$$

The final step is to specify the real wage variables in (12.23), in order to obtain an equation that can be estimated. Similar to work in the preceding sections, Crozet (2004) draws equilibrium wages from the Krugman (1991a) framework.

As is the case for firms, *a good access to markets proves more attractive to individuals*, but through different mechanisms: high market potential attracts both firms and individuals, the former because it gives rise to higher profits (see (12.1)), and the latter via the nominal wage that factors in the migration equation (see (12.21)). For workers, greater proximity to producers also gives rise to a lower price index. The analogous benefit for firms is a better access to intermediate goods in central regions, as described by the supplier potential of Redding and Venables (2004) described in section 12.4.1.

Crozet uses a quasi-structural version of this model that has the dual benefit of exhibiting good predictive power and generating parameter estimates whose signs and values are consistent with theory. The parameters estimated are

  (i) the manufacturing sector's elasticity of substitution, σ, and

  (ii) the elasticity of trade costs with respect to distance, δ (the share of nontradable goods in consumption cannot be identified and needs to be chosen in an ad hoc way).

Note that μ cannot be identified separately from σ and has to be fixed to an ad hoc value. All estimates of σ are significantly greater than 1, ranging from 1.3 for the United Kingdom to 4.3 for the Netherlands, when the share of nontradable goods is fixed at 0.4. Moreover, the estimates for the elasticity of trade costs with respect to distance are all positive and have a very high mean value (approximately 1.8), although this elasticity varies significantly depending on the country and the value adopted for the share of nontradable consumption goods.

This analysis has been replicated by Pons et al. (2007), who use a completely different sample: the migration flows between Spanish provinces in the interwar period. Again, migrating workers were attracted by the regions characterized by a high degree of centrality. Note that workers of that period were already sensitive to migration costs, and the source of Madrid- and Barcelona-bound migration was primarily from regions close to these two cities. Indeed, Madrid and Barcelona received significantly fewer workers from more distant regions, even though these regions are among the poorest.

12.6   The Stability of Spatial Patterns

The existence of multiple stable equilibria is often presented as one of
the main features of economic geography. The empirical detection of
multiple equilibria does not in itself mean that the agglomeration mechanisms discussed in this book are confirmed, as other forces also trigger cumulative mechanisms and, therefore, multiple equilibria (see, for
example, Farrell and Klemperer 2007). On the other hand, an empirical
refutation of the existence of multiple equilibria would provide support
for comparative-advantage models of agglomeration, as such models
yield unique equilibria, which are determined by the regions' specific,
exogenous characteristics.

Davis and Weinstein (2002) study major changes in the distribution of
Japanese cities which could reveal the existence of multiple equilibria.
Their results are summarized succinctly below, and suggest that they
found little evidence for the existence of multiple equilibria:

> An important practical question, then, is whether such spatial catas-
> trophes are theoretical curiosa or a central tendency in the data. Our
> results provide an unambiguous answer. Even nuclear bombs have little
> effects on relative city sizes over the course of a couple of decades. The
> theoretical possibility of spatial catastrophes due to temporal shocks
> is *not* a central tendency borne out in the data.
>
> Davis and Weinstein (2002, p. 1284)

To start with, let us return to figure 6.8, and assume that the economy's parameters take values consistent with three stable equilibria (one
equilibrium is symmetric and the other two are agglomerated). While the
effects of a minor shock can be quickly undone, each equilibrium being
locally stable, a large shock is likely to thrust the agglomeration equilibrium toward dispersion, and vice versa. Even when the only stable equilibria are of the agglomerated type, a major shock is liable to change
the location of the agglomeration, which would move from one region
to another. Two empirical methods have been proposed to examine the
stability of spatial economic patterns: examination of the correlations
between the degree of agglomeration across sectors and across time,
and study of the spatial robustness of agglomerations to identifiable
shocks.

12.6.1   The Historical Stability of Agglomerations

The first method consists of computing the correlation between region
r's share $\lambda_{r,t}$ in the total population at time t, and this share b years
earlier, $\lambda_{r,t-b}$. Although a high correlation is to be expected for short

periods, it is reasonable to believe that the correlation is markedly lower over longer periods subject to substantial demographic and economic developments, or over periods subject to important shocks. A city is the natural geographical unit for the calculation of $\lambda_{r,t}$, provided it maintains the same administrative definition over the relevant time period. As this continuity rarely exists in the long run, Davis and Weinstein (2002) examine thirty-nine Japanese regions, dividing the population by the region's surface area in order to use density as a measure of agglomeration, which is likely to cancel out the effect of an administrative change in a city border. The most striking result is that the intertemporal correlation between population densities in 1998 and in 1600 ($b = 398$) is equal to 0.76. The rank correlation coefficient is even higher, i.e., 0.83. In other words, over the course of four centuries, during which time the Japanese population multiplied tenfold and the economy moved from being predominantly rural to industrial to even service-based, *the regions' hierarchy has nonetheless remained extremely stable.*

Brakman et al. (2004b) repeated this exercise with German cities. The advantage of the German example is that physical geography plays less of a role than in Japan, where the presence of mountains confines the country's populous inhabitants to a small fraction of the territory (30% of Japan is usable in practice). After examining sixty cities, these authors found a rank correlation equal to 0.84 between the populations of 1939 and 1999. Bearing in mind that Davis and Weinstein found a correlation of 0.93 for Japan (between 1920 and 1998), it would appear that the German urban structure displays less stability than the Japanese one; that said, the correlation for Germany is still very high. Thus, a central message in Davis and Weinstein (2002) is that *physical geography is an important determinant of economic geography* and that the existing body of literature has paid too little attention to this aspect.[25]

Conversely, Acemoglu et al. (2002) illustrate a case in which initial geographical advantages are turned into a disadvantage: the European colonization of the American, African, and Oceanic continents from 1500 onward. The tenets of economic geography would lead one to expect that Europeans chose to establish themselves in areas providing good access to factors and markets before their arrival. In this case, the colonizers would have chosen regions that already had dense, urbanized populations, in order to build on these initial advantages. Acemoglu et al. tried to investigate whether an area's prosperity in 1500 is a good indicator of

---

[25] Some recent studies, and particularly Gallup et al. (1999) already described in section 12.4.1, have, however, emphasized the predominant role of physical geography in the economic destiny of a nation.

its level of development in 1995. The response was unequivocally negative. The level of income per capita in 1995 is negatively linked to the level of urbanization and density in 1500. In fact, according to Acemoglu et al., the colonizers tended to consider existing population centers in terms of resource extraction, and thus only established institutions that made very little contribution to future development. These authors account for this phenomenon by noting that regions with high human density also had the greatest prevalence of diseases, which discouraged settlement by Europeans, and in turn hindered the establishment of institutions conducive to the growth of a market economy. In other words, at this time, *physical geography would have played against economic geography*. This type of fascinating historical analysis, although in need of methodological refinement, provides a number of opportunities for quantifying the respective roles played by physical geography, endogenous agglomeration phenomena, and shock in the distribution of activities.

Dumais et al. (2002), building on the work of Ellison and Glaeser (1997), study the evolution of the latter's concentration index over the course of 1972-92 in U.S. counties. Although significant historical accidents did occur, we should nevertheless observe great stability in the relative concentration of sectors, as well as a high degree of stability where the main centers corresponding to each sector are located. Remember that the concentration indices used here are invariant to any permutation of nearby geographical units, and only help in evaluating the first statement (see chapter 10). This leads Dumais et al. to tackle the second statement by estimating a model with mean reversion of each region's share in any given sector. Mean reversion allows for a certain degree of geographical mobility in each sector, while still keeping the same geographical concentration index. One important, preliminary result is that the degree of concentration is very stable over time: the correlation coefficient for geographical concentration indices in the manufacturing sectors between 1972 and 1992 is 0.92. Using a different index of concentration (but still examining the United States), Kim (1995) obtains a weaker correlation, of 0.64, for the period 1860-1987. This relatively high historical agglomeration stability is consistent with firms' highly variable spatial behaviors. One possible explanation is that, in any given sector, new firms replace old ones, but choose the same locations. Another possibility accounting for the extremely high resilience of agglomeration over time, even in light of major changes in the location of sectors, may be that each sector's basic structures are stable over time. In fact, Dumais et al. also find that firms' mobility is generally very high. Moreover, the most concentrated sectors do not seem to be characterized by a lower mobility than the dispersed ones. Economic geography models seem to suggest the opposite, namely that once sectors are spatially concentrated, they acquire a certain degree of spatial inertia.

Using the same method as Dumais et al., Barrios et al. (2005) also observe a certain stability in the degree of agglomeration for Irish and Portuguese industries between 1985 and 1998, a significant period for the industrialization of these two countries. However, this stability is not as high as the level observed by Dumais et al.: the correlation was 0.68 for Portugal, and 0.41 for the Republic of Ireland. This observed stability is again accompanied by fairly high geographical mobility of firms. These various results give rise to a natural question: what are the specific reasons underlying firms' relocation decisions if geographical concentration remains more or less constant?

12.6.2 Do Temporary Shocks Have a Long-Run Impact?

Studying historical correlations becomes particularly appealing when there is reason to believe that over long periods of time some cities have been subjected to shocks important enough to alter the existing spatial equilibrium. It may be fruitful to examine directly this type of shock and its impact on the location of economic activities. If we assume that shocks are multiplicative, we obtain the following expression:

$$(\ln \lambda_{r,t+a} - \ln \lambda_{r,t}) = \alpha + \beta(\ln \lambda_{r,t} - \ln \lambda_{r,t-b}) + \varepsilon_{r,t}, \qquad (12.24)$$

where a is the time that has elapsed since the end of a shock occurring at time $t - b$, and b is the duration of the shock. The estimated value for β tells us about the adjustment dynamics subsequent the shock. If $\hat{\beta} \approx 0$, this suggests that the size of cities evolves randomly: temporary shocks would then have a permanent effect. Conversely, if $\hat{\beta} \approx -1$, this means that the shocks are totally absorbed after a years. In Davis and Weinstein (2002), the shock extended from 1940 to 1947 ($b = 7$), i.e., during Japan's heavy bombing by the U.S. Air Force. The period following the end of the shock covers 1947 to 1960 ($a = 13$). Davis and Weinstein's results show that $\hat{\beta} \approx -1$. The cities that experienced the greatest drops in population after the bombings witnessed the most significant demographic growth in the immediate postwar period. In general, the shocks borne by each city had been completely absorbed by 1960. Even Nagasaki and Hiroshima (which suffered nuclear bombings that reduced their population by 8.5% and 20%, respectively) saw their population growth rates revert to those of the prewar years of 1925–40 by 1960 for Nagasaki and by 1975 for Hiroshima, while prewar population levels had been reached long before these dates in both cities.

Simply put, contrary to what some economic geography models would have us believe, these results do not lend credence to the existence of major shocks in the urban hierarchy. Nevertheless, the gap between theory and empirical evidence in this type of research makes interpretation difficult. For instance, what is the extent of the shock needed for the model to predict a change in the equilibrium selected? Did the bombings suffered by Japan correspond to a shock of sufficient magnitude to change the existing equilibrium? Relying on a simulated version of the model would be essential in answering this question properly. The problem becomes even more complex if we bear in mind that the "required" magnitude of a shock also depends on the area's level of economic integration at the time of the shock. The spectrum of trade-cost values allowing for the existence of multiple equilibria is in fact fairly small: a range of $1.63 < \tau < 1.81$ is found when evaluated for $\mu = 0.4$ and $\sigma = 5$, as used by Fujita et al. (1999, table 5.1). Outside of this range, two situations are possible: when τ is higher than 1.81, any existing symmetry is stable, whatever the extent of the shock; when τ is lower than 1.63, *very* substantial shocks are required to alter the existing spatial concentration.

Davis and Weinstein are very evasive about their assumption with respect to the relevant value of τ at the time of the bombings. It is therefore impossible to know whether their result really invalidates the existence of abrupt changes in spatial configurations, as it is not inconceivable that the economy of the time required an even greater shock than the American bombings to bring about a change in spatial equilibrium. Taking into account the conditional nature of the theoretical predictions (which vary according to the value of trade costs, the degree of product differentiation, the share of goods in consumption, the mobility of workers, etc.) might be a welcomed nuance in this type of analysis.

The article by Davis and Weinstein (2002) gives rise to another problem: their choice of a case in which physical geography is liable to play a predominant role. On account of its particularly mountainous nature, and the meager amount of land that lends itself to building a sizable city, Japan may constitute an exceptional case in which economic activity reverts to its original location by default, i.e., in the absence of viable alternatives. Although this criticism is valid with respect to the activities considered as a whole, it is much less convincing on a sectoral level. For instance, Davis and Weinstein (2008) demonstrate that after the bombing of various Japanese cities, each sector tended to return to its original location, despite the fact that the massive destruction had a great, but temporary, impact on the distribution of sectors across different cities.

Brakman et al. (2004b) follow a similar approach for Germany. They find a greater persistence of the shocks due to bombardment, with an estimate of $\hat{\beta} = -0.42$ for cities in West Germany, setting the window for recovery at four years ($a = 4$). This coefficient reaches -0.52 when the window is extended to seventeen years. This can be contrasted with East Germany, for which the authors did not observe any tendency for cities to revert to their initial size after the bombings, which could suggest that the nature of economic institutions is a crucial determinant.

To conclude, it is fair to say that the group of studies undertaken to date seem to converge in invalidating the existence of phenomena such as catastrophes and historical accidents. Namely, the distribution of city sizes remains stable even in the presence of substantial shocks (no catastrophes); and the same degree of mobility is observed between sectors, regardless of their degree of spatial concentration, thus suggesting the absence of locked-in effects generated by historical accidents. This leads us to think that the catastrophic changes predicted by standard models of economic geography (see chapter 6) should not be part of the core principles of economic geography. Rather, they are similar to the prediction of the Bertrand model in industrial organization: theoretical curiosities that serve as stepping stones.

Finally, it is impossible not to think that these approaches take the DSK model *too* seriously. In any case, these models are bound to raise a few eyebrows for historians (among others), who are well aware that the inertia of urban structures can be explained by a wealth of other determinants that never factor into these parsimonious economic specifications. For example, these upheavals rest on Krugman's assumption that workers are inherently indifferent between two regions that offer them the same real wage. Allowing for heterogeneous preferences, agglomeration in the region deemed less attractive by workers as a whole is an equilibrium for a much smaller range of trade costs than is the case in the other region (Tabuchi and Thisse 2002). In other words, the Japanese citizens' attachment to their respective cities could be sufficient to explain why the migrations predicted by Krugman (1991a) stand very little chance of being observed in reality. More generally, reintroducing heterogeneity in preferences, technology, or endowments in economic geography models is feasible and would make them fit reality much better while their fundamental intuitions remain.

12.6.3 The Division of Germany as a Natural Experiment

Finally, we consider the approach recently developed by Redding and Sturm (forthcoming), which is more robust in its attempt to discern the effects of major shocks on spatial equilibria. Unlike the research strategies discussed in the two previous subsections, these authors adopt an approach that faithfully respects theory and draws on the profit equation (12.1). In addition, they propose an original set of solutions for tackling the endogeneity issues regarding market potential. Finally, by applying a method known as difference-in-difference (i.e., differencing with respect to both spatial and temporal dimensions), they safeguard themselves from a large number of time–area fixed effects. These fixed effects are characteristic of noneconomic geography models, and were potentially uncontrolled for in the previous studies.

Regarding the endogeneity of market potential, let us recall that one of the main problems lies in the fact that the evolution of a region's income or factor prices plays an important role in the evolution of its market potential which, in turn, is supposed to explain those very same variables. Finding an instrument for market potential boils down to isolating a source of unexpected variation for any given region's market access. A major historical shock can be a good candidate for exogenous variability, provided it can be proven that the sudden variation in market potential, and therefore in the shock, is not directly linked to wages or other immobile factor prices in the region.[26]

With this in mind, Redding and Sturm used the separation of Germany at the end of World War II as a natural experiment capable of revealing the incidence of an exogenous variation in market potential on the economic activity of various German regions. Indeed, both parts of Germany were highly integrated when the escalation of the Cold War brought any form of exchanges between the two new states to a virtual standstill. Moreover, the new border was drawn arbitrarily, as it was the result of the allied forces' power-sharing negotiation. In this experimental context, the predictions put forward by economic geography are clear: *the regions close to the border dividing Germany should become less attractive.* In other words, mobile factors should seek to avoid these locations, while immobile factor prices should drop. All in all, we would thus expect markedly lower growth in economic activity in regions close to the border, in comparison to regions situated further to the west, where the levels of activity only marginally depended on trade links with the eastern part of Germany before the country's partition.

---

[26] For example, a natural disaster that destroys transport infrastructure such as a port in a nation open to international trade would provide us with a good approximation of an exogenous variation in market potential. By contrast, the construction of an airport would be a more questionable instrument, for this decision is certainly linked to the development of the region's trade and, therefore, to its own market potential.

Redding and Sturm test this prediction by comparing the population growth for twenty German cities situated within 75 km of the East–West border (99 cities in their overall sample), before and after the partition of the country.[27] This method examines the growth differential between the two parts of Germany subsequent a far-reaching shock. More precisely, the goal was to account for each city's population growth rates over the course of the seven periods, by means of a regression that (in its simplest form) includes a common trend for all cities as a whole as well as the impact of proximity with East Germany. Since the idea is that the distance from the new border only has an effect on growth after partition, an extra variable is introduced to multiply the border proximity expression by a dummy variable equal to 0 before the partition and 1 after it. Redding and Sturm find a marked difference between the evolution of the two parts of Germany only after the partition. By using their coefficients, the accumulated difference in growth during the thirty-eight-year period of separation is an estimated 33%.

Aside from the drop in market potential, are there any other convincing explanations accounting for this growth differential? It is certainly possible to think of alternative explanations of this phenomenon. For example, differences in endowments or institutions could account for a large portion of observed differences in levels of development. In this particular case, however, the institutions were the same in West Germany as a whole after the constitution of 1949, while the differences in natural endowments between the eastern and western parts of West Germany were certainly not affected by the separation from East Germany. Thus, this approach has the added benefit of allowing us to discriminate between different possible explanations for the evolution of economic activity. To ensure that the growth differential is indeed the result of a drop in market potential, the authors introduce Harris's version of market potential into the same regression (which takes into account the partition, since demand from cities in East Germany is assumed to be zero after the partition). This variable, which departs significantly from theory due to a dearth of data, is nonetheless capable of almost fully explaining the post-partition growth differential.

Another interesting issue is the size of cities. In the regions close to the new eastern border, there are several cities of different sizes. Now, according to economic geography, the large cities should suffer less from the partition, as they are more dependent on their initial local demand, which is more likely to be unaffected by the partition. By separating the

---

[27] Their benchmark regression excludes the observations relative to the growth rates of cities during World War II, and after reunification. The seven periods considered are 1919–25, 1925–33, 1933–39, 1950–60, 1960–70, 1970–80, and 1980–88.

sample into two parts, Redding and Sturm do indeed find that the small cities were substantially more affected than the large ones.

Finally, another conjecture is that the growth differential arises as a result of differences in the specialization of cities. If intuition leads us to believe that cities' specialization is spatially correlated, then we would expect border cities to be less conducive to specialization after World War II. To ensure that both the cities close to the border and the other cities (the control group) are comparable, Redding and Sturm match the cities among the two groups. This means (i) finding a city at least 75 km away from the border that matches the industrial structure of a given border city, and (ii) comparing the difference in the evolution of both cities, using a reduced control group comprised only of the matched cities. The results are very much in line with the previous ones; this again supports the importance of market potential as an explanatory variable.

12.7   Concluding Remarks

Although there has been a burgeoning of empirical studies in economic geography (which in itself calls for rejoicing), it is difficult not to walk away from this chapter without a trace of disappointment. Indeed, there still seems to be a substantial gap between theory and empirical evidence. Furthermore, it often proves difficult to discriminate between different contending explanations. However, these criticisms should not be pushed too far, as a number of fairly robust conclusions emerge from the existing literature. In particular, it appears that *the structural approaches, directly rooted in specific theoretical models, are often more convincing than the reduced forms that are traditionally used.* This should be interpreted as a call for new and more rigorous theoretical reflections. Conversely, the burgeoning of empirical studies observed in recent years has prompted researchers to tackle problems from different perspectives. More precisely, the empirical line of research has underscored the need for hypotheses that are sufficiently simple to be tested, sufficiently general to make sense on an empirical level, but precise enough to allow one to discriminate between economic geography models and alternative explanations. This type of work is not necessarily consistent with theorists' spontaneous inclination, but it serves an indispensable function if theoretical predictions are ever to be tested.

Although some conclusions are undoubtedly disappointing from a theoretical standpoint, a number of findings have stood the test of empirical analysis. First, as seen in chapter 5, economic geography provides a solid microeconomic foundation for the gravity and market potential models. Second, we do not observe the home-market effect with sufficient frequency to presume that it is relevant in the real world. This result, however, does not mean that economic geography fails to explain observed patterns of activities. One compelling frustration, which is undoubtedly responsible for the lackluster results, lies in the fact that the current empirical models used to test theory are unduly specific and restricted. To reiterate, economic geography models are all too often restricted to two regions and a single sector, whereas reality is clearly far more complex. Extending the simple case to several regions and several industries constitutes somewhat of a naive leap of faith. A recent study by Behrens et al. (2004) lends credence to this idea by showing that a region's industrial share depends not only on its size but also on its relative accessibility within a multi-regional system. There is no question that future empirical studies must move beyond testing hypotheses within a simple bilateral linear relationship, as is so often characteristic of existing studies. Finally, we have seen that the home-market effect and the wage equation are dual relationships in economic geography. In the absence of a significant degree of labor mobility, regions with a strong market potential will therefore tend to see an increase in their factor prices, which in turn reduces the intensity of the home-market effect.

This is indeed the third main lesson of the models discussed in this chapter: *empirical backing for the wage equation is fairly strong.* In other words, labor tends to be better remunerated in regions with a high market potential. On the other hand, this relationship seems to imply that the spatial mobility of labor would be insufficient to guarantee the equalization of wages. However, before we can draw any definitive conclusions on this matter, it would be appropriate to take into account the interregional differences in housing prices, which have only been considered by Hanson (2005) to date, and which represent a significant fraction of household budgets (see chapter 8). In this respect, a preliminary study by Rice and Venables (2003) indicates that this type of realignment mechanism is actually at work in Great Britain.

Be that as it may, empirical analyses of migratory flows lead us to believe that it is unlikely that the European Union will take on a core–periphery structure with one single core and a large periphery. A more realistic scenario is one that involves *several core–periphery structures emerging on an infracommunity scale.* In fact, this type of structure is already observed in several of the member states. In the next chapter, we will see that approaches based on the simulation of calibrated models lead to similar conclusions for a number of sectors.

12.8   Related Literature

Brakman et al. (2001) contains an introduction to the empirical testing of many of the issues tackled in this chapter. Head and Mayer (2004b) offer a more complete synthesis of the various empirical studies seeking to corroborate economic geography models, while Overman et al. (2003) provide a synthesis of the empirical studies devoted to trade and geography.

13
Theory with Numbers

In order to go beyond descriptive empirical studies of the mechanisms underlying spatial concentration described in chapter 11, chapter 12 presented the body of work that provides estimates and econometric tests for DSK-type models of economic geography. These models constitute an important branch of economic geography, and their empirical counterpart is characterized by the attempt made to depart as little as possible from the underlying theoretical framework. In some cases, predominantly in the context of studies relating to the wage equation and migrations, it was possible to estimate fundamental parameters (e.g., trade costs, the elasticity of substitution between differentiated goods, the share of the differentiated good in consumption, etc.) for completely specified models. These estimates can be used in two ways. First, they can serve as a battery of tests for economic geography models. In particular, while one can rarely accept a model with certainty, *rejecting* a model through the structural constraints it imposes is straightforward. For example, the DSK model only makes sense if the elasticity of substitution across varieties is larger than 1. If the estimations lead to values less than 1, the model must be rejected. As mentioned earlier, however, substantial progress needs to be made in this direction, particularly when it comes to validating one model over another one.

Moreover, structural estimates can serve as a basis for simulations that deepen our understanding of the working and implications of more comprehensive models of economic geography that include a large number of regions and sectors. Indeed, with many industries and locations, most economic geography models cannot be fully solved analytically. This makes it necessary to resort to simulations and, thus, to assign values to a large number of parameters. The interest of such exercises is questionable. Setting these values is often an arbitrary process, and the resulting explanations of spatial concentration can hardly be reconciled with simple frameworks involving only two regions. In other words, there is not a lot of value-added in extending models to more regions or sectors when parameter values have to be arbitrarily assigned. In contrast, simulations are much more useful when one has access to parameter values that have been estimated from real data. In this case, when a large-scale model has not been rejected in a first phase of econometric estimation, it is admissible and potentially illuminating to simulate it. For instance, such simulations may be used to provide accurate projections for the real effects of specific policies. Unfortunately, this type of exercise (estimations followed by simulations) is rarely undertaken.

However, this approach is still a far cry from a complete analysis of all the predictions set out by economic geography. For one, it is particularly surprising that so few authors have attempted to determine whether the bell-shaped curve between spatial concentration and economic integration is traced out by real data, as economic geography would expect. This chapter presents the few studies that specifically focus on such an issue and are also strictly in line with theoretical economic geography models. It is regrettable that, to date, testing this relationship has been conducted with a systematic disregard for the first "estimation" phase. In other words, authors have predominantly conducted simulations of large-scale economic geography models by using parameter values derived from real data, which have not been obtained from the estimation of the corresponding models. Deriving parameter values from strict econometric estimations would provide us with standard errors and the added benefit of being able to construct confidence intervals for the models' output. The existing simulations can nevertheless provide insights into one important issue: does more economic integration lead to more spatial concentration once realistic values for parameters are chosen?

In section 13.1, we present studies based on economic geography models derived from the DSK framework. Some of these studies rely on an initial estimation of the underlying parameters à la Hanson (2005). Unfortunately, they prove incomplete and do not examine the bell-shaped curve. Conversely, the studies that *do* deal with the bell-shaped curve omit the preliminary estimation phase. Rectifying this oversight should be possible in the near future by adopting, for instance, the approach proposed by Redding and Venables (2004) and presented in chapter 12, thus "closing-off" the process. In section 13.2, we will present a slightly less standard approach based on economic geography models that abandon the monopolistic competition assumption in order to examine competition with strategic interactions (like the models discussed in chapter 9). In this type of approach, all parameter values are calibrated, except for the sector-specific trade-cost parameter, which is estimated. This allows one to conduct large-scale simulations based on real cases, and to make a certain number of predictions stemming from this alternative family of models.

13.1   Predictions Based on the Dixit–Stiglitz–Krugman Model

Given that DSK-type models have been subject to both theoretical extensions and empirical validations, they naturally take precedence over all other studies trying to evaluate how economic geography fares in real settings. With this in mind, the first section is devoted to these models.

13.1.1   Simulations Derived from Estimations

Hanson (1998) was the first to proceed along these lines, applying U.S. data to an economic geography model and obtaining the relevant estimates presented in chapter 12. In the initial version of his article, he focuses on simulating the impact of a local shock on a set of U.S. counties. In the final version, Hanson (2005) examines the spatial diffusion of a positive shock of 10% on the market potential of a given county. Structural but noninstrumented estimations revealed the importance of distance, as the shock had an effect of about 1% on local wages, but this effect fully disappeared beyond a radius of 250 km. However, these estimations overlook the fact that when agents' location choices are endogenous most of the explanatory variables are also endogenous (as seen in chapter 12). Thus, technically, the most appropriate estimations should be both structural and instrumented. This provides a slightly weaker distance-decay effect. For estimates covering the period 1980–90, the impact of the shock on local wages is 4%; at 200 km, it is 0.5%; and it vanishes only after 450 km. For any given distance, the estimated impact is more substantial over the period 1970–80. This result, which suggests that the role of distance has grown stronger over time, has long been considered puzzling. Yet this finding is consistent with the increasingly important impact distance has had on trade flows (see chapter 5). Note that such an evolution could stem from the structural increase in the size of the nontradable sector, a possibility that Hanson cannot control for with the data at hand. Finally, Hanson carries out the same simulations based on nonstructural estimates of the model, replacing the main explanatory variable with Harris's market potential. For the period 1980–90, the shock increases local wages by an estimated 2.6%; at 200 km it increases them by 1%; at 400 km it increases them by 0.5%, and the effect disappears after 700 km. Once again, the impact of distance is stronger during the period 1980–90, with the local effect rising to 3.7% but disappearing after 300 km.

In any case, the role played by distance on how wages respond to an initial shock appears to be very marked. This may be due to the particularly high value of the estimated trade cost parameter. Specifically, Hanson uses a functional form $\tau_{rs} = \exp(td_{rs})$, where the bilateral distance d_{rs} is measured in thousands of kilometers; he obtains a value of t equal to 3.2. Such a value implies that traveling a distance of 2000 km is tantamount to multiplying the price of a good by $\exp(2 \times 3.22) = 626$, a value that is highly implausible for a market as integrated as the U.S. economy. This result could partly be explained by Hanson's choice to build from a specification that directly links wages and distance, without first estimating the link between trade flows and distance. Recall that gravity model estimates suggest that trade costs are described by a different functional form; $\tau_{rs} = d_{rs}^{\delta}$ since the logarithm of trade flows has systematically been shown to exhibit a more or less linear relationship with the logarithm of distance.

In the context of Italy, Mion (2004) reexamines Hanson's approach by applying the above-mentioned log-linear relationship for trade costs, and obtains more plausible results. A negative shock on incomes of 10% in the Latium provinces has a local impact of 1% but it affects every Italian province, and the effect gradually weakens to about 0.1%. Another interesting, stylized finding emerges from this study. Although Latium is situated in the center of Italy, a shock emanating from this location has a greater effect on the southern Italian provinces than the northern ones. This is because, relative to the north, the south's market potential depends more heavily on Latium's economic activities, thereby making the latter more vulnerable to a shock of this kind. When applying the specification of trade costs used by Hanson (2005), Mion finds that the estimated impact of distance is more substantial. The functional form used for the relationship between trade flows and distance is, therefore, important for the results obtained.

Crozet (2004) uses his own estimates to obtain predictions related to both the size of the fields of attraction for populations in large regions and the magnitude of interregional migrations.[1] Such results must be handled with care because Crozet assigns an ad hoc value to the share of the nontradable consumption good. Interestingly, it appears that such distances are fairly small, thus suggesting that, in Europe, *polarization should arise on a relatively small scale.* For example, whereas Lombardy has an internal distance of 58 km, the model suggests that this region should attract firms within a radius ranging from 95 to 150 km from its

---

[1] Such results must be handled with care because Crozet assigns an ad hoc value to the share of the nontradable consumption good.

center. Consequently, Lombardy is not expected to threaten any other major Italian region, since the largest city closest to Milan, i.e., Turin, is situated 141 km away, while Genoa and Rome are 164 and 576 km away, respectively.

In short, these different results suggest that *although individuals in the European Union are indeed attracted by regions with a high market potential, the corresponding forces are very localized and are thus incapable of giving rise to core-periphery structures on a large spatial scale.* Unfortunately, there are few studies proposing simulations of DSK economic geography models founded on real estimates of their parameters. We now turn our attention to studies in which these parameters are calibrated in a more ad hoc manner, but which have the advantage of providing a richer framework which goes beyond the simulations considered above.

13.1.2 Simulating the Bell-Shaped Curve

A DSK model of economic geography tracing out a bell-shaped curve relationship between integration and spatial concentration was proposed by Puga (1999). This is an extension of the model described by Krugman and Venables (1995) (discussed in chapter 7): the main novelty is the introduction of a supplementary input (e.g., land) into the production function of the agricultural good. This results in the manufacturing sector facing an imperfectly elastic labor supply, since a wage increase triggers a labor-land substitution in the agricultural sector. This approach differs from that of Krugman (1991a) (where labor is sector-specific, thus implying zero elasticity in the labor supply), but also from that of Krugman and Venables (1995) (where the labor supply is infinitely elastic, so that the agricultural sector disappears as soon as the manufacturing wage rises above the agricultural wage). As the labor supply is now imperfectly elastic, competition for this factor is much more intense than in the two previous models. In particular, the agglomeration of the industry in one region sparks a more substantial wage increase. Puga shows that this dispersion force leads to the progressive redispersion of activities once the level of trade falls below some threshold value, the symmetric pattern being reached for strictly positive trade costs (see also chapter 8). In other words, there would be two threshold values for trade costs, so that one region is more industrialized than the other between these two values. For values of trade costs outside this interval, the location of activities is symmetric. Puga (1999) shows that the upper and lower threshold values of trade costs, denoted respectively by $\bar{\phi}_s$ and $\underline{\phi}_s$, are the solutions to the following quadratic equation:

$$[\sigma(1 + \alpha) - 1][(1 + \alpha)(1 + \eta) + (1 - \alpha)\mu]\phi^2$$
$$- 2\{[\sigma(1 + \alpha^2) - 1](1 + \eta) - \sigma(1 - \alpha)[2(\sigma - 1) - \mu\alpha]\}\phi$$
$$+ (1 - \alpha)[\sigma(1 - \alpha) - 1](\eta + 1 - \mu) = 0. \quad (13.1)$$

These solutions depend on the model's parameters: σ, the elasticity of substitution between varieties, which is assumed to be identical for both final and intermediate consumptions; μ, the share of the manufacturing good in final consumption; and α the share of intermediate inputs in the final sector. Note that a sector consumes only its own intermediate varieties. This is an improvement over the Krugman (1991a) model, in which these goods are omitted altogether. However, this framework, though more general, fails to capture the fact that different sectors use intermediate inputs from other sectors. The new parameter, η, is the elasticity of the region's labor supply, which is potentially endogenous, but considered as constant here.

The thought experiment now reads as follows: if we assume that the model under consideration reflects reality, what are its predictions regarding the degree of spatial concentration for different sectors? In other words, rather than seeking to estimate and test the model, the aim is to focus on the specific implications of a model's conclusions, with the intent of assessing (a posteriori) whether these conclusions are realistic and acceptable. When subscribing to this framework, one obvious limitation is that it only applies to situations with two countries or regions.

Head and Mayer (2004b) present a first calibration of (13.1) for two pairs of countries (France-Germany and United States-Canada) artificially isolated from the rest of the world. For each sector s, they collected data relating to μ and α, which are in general easily accessible from national accounting statistics, with definitions closely corresponding to those found in the theoretical model. However, assigning values to σ is a tricky matter, as this parameter does not correspond to a national accounting concept. With this in mind, these authors refer to Hummels (1999), who estimated these values by means of gravity estimates that include tariffs. Indeed, in this model, the price elasticity of demand, captured by the tariff coefficient, is exactly equal to the elasticity of substitution σ (as seen in chapter 5). Regarding η, a proper estimate is still absent from the literature. To obtain a better estimate, Head and Mayer adopt a (very high) arbitrary value of 200 that is identical across all sectors.[2]

---

[2] This is one of the limitations of this exercise. Values of η need to be very high in order to obtain real solutions to the equation (13.1). More work is called for to make this setting compatible with more realistic values.

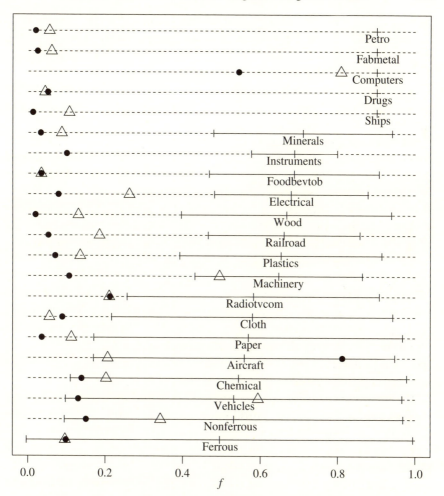

Figure 13.1. Degree of integration in various industrial sectors.
(Source: Head and Mayer (2004b).)

Using these values, the now numerical equation (13.1) can be solved for each sector, which allows Head and Mayer to obtain the $[\phi_s, \bar{\phi}_s]$ interval for which sector s should be concentrated Then, they estimate directly each sectors' degree of economic integration, $\hat{\phi}_s$, on the basis of bilateral trade flows (as described in chapter 5). The results obtained are presented in figure 13.1.

The solid horizontal lines represent the intervals in which the symmetric equilibrium is unstable for each sector. This interval is not defined for some sectors, namely when (13.1) does not have real roots (the top five cases). The left-hand side of the equation is thus positive for every $\phi \in [0, 1]$, which implies that the symmetric equilibrium is stable. The dots and the triangles correspond to the values of $\hat{\phi}$ for the France–Germany and United States–Canada pairs, respectively. Thanks to the position of these points, we can identify the sectors which, according to the model, should be dispersed (outside the $[\underline{\phi}_s, \bar{\phi}_s]$ range) or agglomerated (inside this range). For example, the vehicles sector is expected to be agglomerated, while sectors such as textiles or paper should exhibit dispersion.

Furthermore, sectors that fall to the right of the $[\underline{\phi}_s, \bar{\phi}_s]$ interval and those that lie on its left must be distinguished. The former have attained a level of integration such that any additional reduction in trade costs would generate less spatial concentration. In light of figure 13.1, it seems that none of the sectors has yet reached this level of integration. Conversely, in the latter case, the sectors are positioned before the peak of the bell, so that a deeper degree of economic integration would first increase spatial concentration, while more substantial integration could reduce it.

Figure 13.1 reveals that most of the sectors fall either outside the interval, to the left, or inside it but closer to its left-hand border. This suggests that, apart from the five sectors characterized by a symmetric and stable equilibrium whatever the level of integration, more integration implies more agglomeration (at least in the initial phase). Caution is warranted in interpreting these results, however, as the estimates are fairly sensitive to the values chosen for the parameters. It would be beneficial to have better estimates of the structural parameters, possibly via the methods presented in chapter 12, to strengthen this conclusion.[3]

The next phase would involve verifying whether the prediction made on the basis of figure 13.1 in terms of future variations in spatial concentration conforms with the real world. One initial approach would be to link an indicator of concentration with the position of the sector on the bell-shaped curve. In adopting this approach, however, we run the risk of taking this model's predictions a little too seriously. For instance, when adopting a strict reading of this model, in areas outside of the $[\underline{\phi}_s, \bar{\phi}_s]$ range, a sector should be characterized by a perfectly symmetric spatial configuration. Yet this model does not take into account exogenous differences across regions (e.g., technology, endowments, etc.), which means that observing either full dispersion or full agglomeration for any given sector is unlikely. Nevertheless, ranking sectors according to their degree of concentration and assessing how closely this ranking

---

[3] Brakman et al. (2006) have applied this approach to different pairs of EU countries. Their findings confirm the idea that the trade freeness estimates lie mostly to the left of the agglomeration interval, suggesting that more trade integration could lead to geographic agglomeration in the EU.

corresponds to the results presented in figure 13.1 would be useful in corroborating or rejecting the model.

Though interesting, this approach is still bound by the limitations underpinning the theoretical model. Even when disregarding the simplifying assumption that the elasticity of substitution is the same for both final and intermediate consumption, and even after turning a blind eye to the assumption that sectors only use their own varieties as the intermediate input, we cannot possibly brush aside two other severe limitations: only two regions are considered, and differences in endowments and technology are ignored altogether. Amending this initial approach requires developing a richer theoretical framework.

13.1.3 The Effects of European Integration

Forslid et al. (2002) calibrate and simulate a fully fledged general equilibrium model for the European Union of 1992. Their aim is to assess the properties of this model by extending it to a large-scale, realistic setting. They also eschew the simplifying assumption that comparative advantages are equal across regions, an assumption retained in most theoretical models but which fails to hold empirically.

It is worth noting that, as soon as we reincorporate comparative advantages into the analysis, both types of models (comparative advantage and economic geography) differ in one major respect: the comparative-advantage models predict that the integration of trade increases countries' specialization and, therefore, the spatial concentration of sectors. In contrast to economic geography models, however, this relationship is *monotonous*. Thus, in a Heckscher–Ohlin world, the greater the degree of market integration, the higher the spatial concentration, unlike the situation with bell-shaped curve models, in which very low trade costs lead to a more balanced spatial pattern. With this in mind, Forslid et al. sought to distinguish the sectors in which comparative-advantage models accurately capture reality, from those sectors that seem to obey the bell-shaped curve underlying most economic geography models.

Ten large regions were considered in their computable spatial equilibrium model: four large European areas (Central, North, South, and West) encompassing the eighteen countries of Western Europe; the United States and Canada; Southeast Asia (including Japan); China and South Asia; former Soviet countries; Eastern Europe; and the rest of the world.[4]

---

[4] Central includes Austria, Denmark, Germany, and Switzerland; North includes Finland, Iceland, Norway, and Sweden; South includes Greece, Italy, Portugal, and Spain; and West includes the Benelux countries, the Republic of Ireland, France, and the United Kingdom.

The study specifically focuses on the effects of a deeper integration between the latter four regions. Fourteen sectors are distinguished; these are linked by input–output matrices specific to each of the regions defined. In other words, Forslid et al. construct a rich framework that

(i) introduces a large number of regions and sectors,

(ii) takes into account differences in technology and endowments across regions, and

(iii) allows for a sector to use its own as well as other intermediate inputs.

Of the fourteen sectors under consideration, two (agriculture and energy) are assumed to produce homogeneous goods under perfect competition and decreasing returns with respect to labor, the only factor used. Trade costs are assumed to be nil in those industries. This is formally equivalent to the agricultural sector of Puga (1999) and implies an imperfectly elastic labor supply for the other sectors. Two sectors (public services and private services) represent the local nontradable service subject to monopolistic competition. Finally, the ten remaining sectors are assumed to be characterized by a DSK-type market structure, with iceberg trade costs varying by origin, destination, and sector. Capital, skilled, and unskilled labor are the three primary factors of production, along with intermediate goods drawn from other sectors. All primary factors are assumed to be immobile across regions but mobile across sectors.

Forslid et al. also try to achieve greater realism by extending and generalizing the assumptions made on consumer preferences and firm technology. The former are defined on two levels: a Cobb–Douglas function of the consumptions from all fourteen sectors, while the varieties produced in each sector are aggregated as composite CES goods (except for the homogeneous goods), with an industry-specific elasticity of substitution. Along the same lines, the production function of the manufacturing sectors consists of nested CES functions. Varieties of the tradable goods from the same sector are first aggregated using the CES function that applies to final consumption (which is a strong assumption). The composite goods obtained for each sector are in turn aggregated via a CES function with a different elasticity, and the set of goods under perfect competition are aggregated among themselves via the same CES function. Finally, the primary inputs are also aggregated using a CES function and the three types of inputs are ultimately aggregated via a last CES function (with different elasticities). Moreover, each CES function adopts different weights to properly capture the proportion of elements they aggregate, as was assumed in chapter 5. These weights are given by the budget coefficients of final consumption and by the elements making up input–output matrices, all available through national accounting consumption and production databases. Regarding trade costs and elasticities of substitution, Forslid et al. draw estimates from other studies. To sum up, this approach reflects an ambition to render the model as realistic as possible and to use real data to the extent possible. Unfortunately, some values (the elasticities of substitution and the trade costs) are still to be determined. Ideally, these values should have been drawn from estimations internal to the study; here they are simply borrowed from outside sources, i.e., chosen in a more or less ad hoc manner.

Calibrated in such a way, the model can then be simulated. In other words, every sector's share in each region, along with the corresponding wages and prices, can be calculated numerically at the general equilibrium of the model. Only ten regions and fourteen sectors were included to facilitate data collection and avoid unduly lengthy or involved calculations. In order to examine how economic integration influences the distribution of economic activities across each of the four Western European regions, Forslid et al. change the level of trade costs in one percentage-point increments (both upward and downward). The entire model is rerun for each value. The authors begin by studying the distribution of sectors across the different regions. This approach reveals that *for certain sectors, changes in the relative sizes of regions due to changes in the degree of integration are small; for other sectors, variations in relative size are more pronounced and result in greater specialization or deindustrialization.* These results are synthesized by differences in a spatial concentration index across sectors, which we now examine in more detail.

Figure 13.2, from Forslid et al. (2002), illustrates how a simple indicator of spatial concentration varies across sectors. This index captures how the standard deviation of the distribution of production shares of each sector across the four European areas varies according to trade costs (normalized to 1 as a benchmark). The most striking result is that four sectors (metals, chemical products, transport equipment, and machinery) display a bell-shaped relationship between trade costs and spatial concentration consistent with the relationship obtained in models with one sector and two regions. The other tradable goods sectors, especially textiles, leather, and food products, are characterized by a continuous rise in the degree of agglomeration, consistent with a comparative-advantage interpretation. As expected, the sectors exhibiting a bell-shaped curve are those with the highest returns to scale and

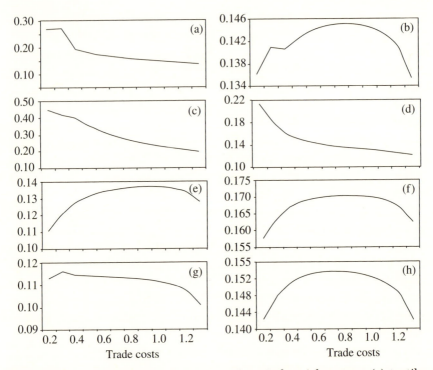

Figure 13.2. Spatial concentration in various industrial sectors: (a) textiles, (b) chemicals, (c) leather products, (d) food products, (e) metals, (f) transport equipment, (g) minerals, (h) machinery. (Source: Forslid et al. (2002).)

with the most substantial share of intermediate consumption drawn from their own sector.

Moreover, it is worth noting that figure 13.2 also suggests that the sectors exhibiting a bell-shaped curve are at the start of the agglomeration process, which parallels the predictions of Head and Mayer (2004b) discussed in the previous section. Note, however, that sectors supposedly characterized by the bell-shaped curve relationship exhibit less pronounced changes in their level of concentration than those sectors that are more consistent with comparative-advantage models. Even though theoretical work has predominantly focused on how industrial sectors have been subject to the forces of economic geography, it could very well be that fundamental changes in the future distribution of European activities may actually take place in more traditional activities that would concentrate themselves more readily. Note, however, that Forslid et al. also obtain a bell-shaped relationship with respect to the degree of concentration of manufacturing sectors *as a whole*. This overall curve reveals that a substantial part of changes in concentration have already taken place

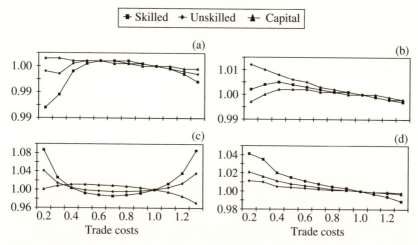

Figure 13.3. Real factor returns: (a) Central, (b) South, (c) North, (d) West. Production in $U.S. billion. (Source: Forslid et al. (2002).)

at the aggregate level. Concentration levels are likely to increase until current trade costs drop by another 30%, at which point concentration levels will start to fall slightly.

It is also possible to simulate the differences in the level of agents' indirect utility across regions. This is done by plotting real factor returns across a number of regions, as displayed in figure 13.3.

Different production factors do not all experience the same real gains following economic integration: some factors even experience losses. The West experiences a continuous increase in its real factor prices, but the gains enjoyed by skilled workers (and, to a lesser extent, capital) are more substantial than the gains obtained by unskilled workers. Factor price dynamics are more complex in North, where at first labor (skilled and unskilled) suffers a decline in wages, while capital makes gains. This trend is later reversed, however, as skilled labor gains more than other factors at the highest level of integration. Conversely, in South, it is unskilled labor that benefits most from more intensive economic integration, while skilled labor and capital start off with gains and then suffer losses. The same pattern is observed in Central with respect to capital and unskilled labor, whereas skilled labor always benefits slightly from greater integration.

Ultimately, these results are consistent with the Stolper-Samuelson theorem, although somewhat modified by effects specific to economic geography. Forslid et al. also provide the variations in each regions' total GDP. *Every region benefits from economic integration, but the gains are meager and interregional differences tend to widen.* In fact, GDP is nearly constant in Central, whereas it increases slightly in South. The increase is more marked in West, but overall North is expected to benefit most from integration. Moreover, reverting to less intensive integration should still benefit North (the effect is U-shaped), while losses are predicted for the other three regions in this context.

Using a model with vertical linkages, which is calibrated on 194 European regions, Bosker et al. (2007) go one step further. They first estimate the parameters of a trade cost function given by

$$\tau_{rs} = \alpha d_{rs}^{\beta}(1 + \text{bord}_{rs})^{y},$$

where α is a trade cost parameter, d_{rs} is the distance between regions r and s, β is a parameter measuring the distance-decay effect, bord_{rs} is a dummy equal to 1 if regions r and s are separated by a border and 0 otherwise, and y is a parameter measuring the strength of border impediments (chapter 5). Bosker et al. (2006) estimate β and y, and then simulate the changes in the spatial distribution of activities obtained when lowering the parameter α. Two scenarios are considered. In the first one, labor is mobile: decreasing trade costs strengthen the process of agglomeration, and extremely low costs may even yield a catastrophic agglomeration in the metropolitan area of Paris. In the second one, labor is immobile: decreasing trade costs now lead to the bell-shaped curve. Such results confirm the main theoretical predictions of economic geography (chapters 6–8).

All in all, as if to respond to the call by Fujita et al. (1999) for computable spatial equilibrium models, Forslid et al. (2002) developed the first such model, which provides a number of theoretical predictions. Their predictions, as well as those obtained by Bosker et al. (2007), are bolstered by facts and figures drawn from a realistic economic geography model, which takes into account the role of differences in technology and factor endowments. As Forslid et al. (2002) acknowledge, the method used in their study is more comparable to *theory with numbers* than to strictly empirical results. The next logical step will be the estimation and testing of models, before moving to these types of simulations.

13.2 Simulations in an Estimated Model of the French Space-Economy

Another attempt to simulate a computable spatial equilibrium model was proposed by Combes and Lafourcade (2001). They build on the setting discussed in section 9.2.3. Intermediate inputs are incorporated into the model via the input–output matrix. This increases the incentives firms have to agglomerate because cost-linkages are now at work. The tougher the competition in a region, the lower the goods' prices and, therefore, the lower the intermediate good component in the marginal cost (see chapter 7 for the presentation of such an effect in the DSK framework). The objective is to determine the predictions that emerge from such a model when it is applied to a large number of regions (the 341 French employment areas) and of sectors (ten or sixty-four sectors). Furthermore, the impact of trade costs is estimated in a preliminary phase that precedes the simulation, whereas the remaining parameters are drawn from data in the French national accounts.

13.2.1 Estimations

The first goal is to avoid adopting arbitrary values for a number of parameters. Combes and Lafourcade draw all technological, budgetary, and wage values from national accounting statistics. There is only one group of parameters left to determine: *trade costs specific to each sector and every origin–destination pair.* Once these are estimated, it is possible to compute the values of the endogenous variables using the equilibrium conditions. It is assumed that, within the same sector, the level of trade costs between two regions is proportional to an index of generalized road transport costs. Such an index is available for every pair of employment areas. The proportionality coefficient varies across sectors. This is the parameter (one for each sector) estimated in the econometric step. If the estimated coefficients are significantly negative, the model is rejected.

Another distinctive feature of the model is that it leads to linear equations for prices and quantities in the short-run equilibrium that are easy to solve. However, the size of firms in a given region and sector (the variable on which the estimation is based) is not a linear function of the parameters to be estimated. Instead of using nonlinear econometric techniques as in Hanson (2005), Combes and Lafourcade expand the equilibrium relationships in the neighborhood of the perfectly integrated equilibrium (zero trade costs). While this approach gives way to burdensome algebra, it has the advantage of resulting in a specification that can be estimated by ordinary least squares. Such an estimation is deemed more robust and, to date, its properties are better known than those of nonlinear estimation techniques.

The model is not rejected by French data. Among the sixty-four sectors considered, only the gas and petroleum sector displays a significantly negative coefficient. Two other sectors exhibit a negative, but statistically insignificant, coefficient, while all remaining sectors have a positive coefficient, being statistically significant in forty-seven cases. When the sectors are aggregated into ten items, all estimated coefficients are positive, nine of them being different from zero. Moreover, when dropping the intermediate input effects from the model, the resulting estimates are markedly lower and less significant for manufacturing sectors, which lends credence to the importance of input–output linkages in explaining the spatial distribution of economic activities. By contrast, removing intermediate inputs from the model leaves estimates for services nearly unchanged, which should not come as a surprise given the predominance of labor over other production factors in services. In addition, adding geographical variables (e.g., proximity to a coast or border) or regional fixed effects markedly improves the estimates. This suggests that *physical geography and the history of the regions are also likely to play an important role in the determination of local employment.*

13.2.2 Simulations

By using its equilibrium relationships, calibrating a model allows one to obtain values of variables for which no data are available. For example, the maps in figure 13.4 illustrate the exports from the employment areas located in Île de France (figure 13.4(a)) and in the Rhône-Alpes region (figure 13.4(b)) to all French employment areas. The equipment goods sector is used as an illustration.

Aside from providing data that could be useful for policy purposes, calibrating the model also allows further study of its theoretical properties in a large-scale framework. For example, the model appears to respect the main principles of gravity theory discussed in chapter 5. That is, figure 13.3 shows thatexports to nearby employment areas are higher and, conversely, exports are low for distant areas. However, exports to large employment areas are also sizable, even over long distances. Cities like Bordeaux, Toulouse, Marseille, Nice, and Strasbourg distinguish themselves as major destinations for both Île-de-France and Rhône-Alpes regions. Combes and Lafourcade also show that, at a spatial scale involving the twenty-one French administrative regions, the correlation between predicted regional flows and their true values (which are observable) is equal to 0.48, which is quite satisfactory given the many assumptions underpinning the model.

Let us now move on to the simulations that shed light on the model's agglomeration and dispersion forces. The simulation of the short-run equilibrium allows Combes and Lafourcade to compute firms' operating profits, i.e., gross of fixed costs. Those made in the equipment goods sector, shown in figure 13.5, reveal a strong core–periphery structure.

(a)   (b)

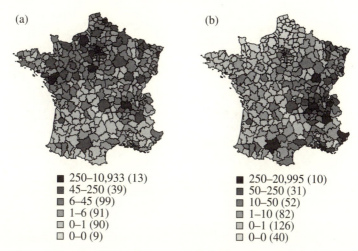

- ■ 250–10,933 (13)
- ■ 45–250 (39)
- ■ 6–45 (99)
- ◻ 1–6 (91)
- ◻ 0–1 (90)
- ◻ 0–0 (9)

- ■ 250–20,995 (10)
- ■ 50–250 (31)
- ■ 10–50 (52)
- ◻ 1–10 (82)
- ◻ 0–1 (126)
- ◻ 0–0 (40)

Figure 13.4. Exports of equipment goods (average = 100) from the employment areas of (a) Île-de-France and (b) Rhône-Alpes (number of employment areas in parentheses). (Source: Combes and Lafourcade (2008).)

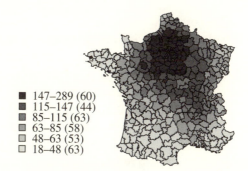

- ■ 147–289 (60)
- ■ 115–147 (44)
- ■ 85–115 (63)
- ◻ 63–85 (58)
- ◻ 48–63 (53)
- ◻ 18–48 (63)

Figure 13.5. Operating profits in equipment goods (average = 100; number of employment areas in parentheses). (Source: Combes and Lafourcade (2008).)

Operating profits are higher in areas close to Paris, and they decrease in an almost monotonic way as the distance from Paris increases. Thus, if fixed production costs are more or less the same across employment areas, we would expect new firms to set up in the French core (the metropolitan area of Paris) to the detriment of peripheral regions. It is worth trying to understand the underlying causes of such a process. Figure 13.6 illustrates two determinants of operating profit, i.e., the average markup given in part (a) and the volume of production given in part (b).

Although the simulated markups are higher around Paris than within the central part of the country (which we will refer to as the "middle band") of employment areas, they can be very high in the periphery. Combes and Lafourcade show that this pattern comes from a set of

(a)   (b)

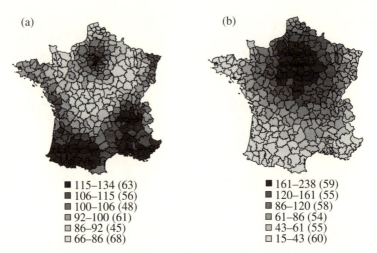

■ 115–134 (63)   ■ 161–238 (59)
■ 106–115 (56)   ■ 120–161 (55)
■ 100–106 (48)   ■ 86–120 (58)
▣ 92–100 (61)   ▣ 61–86 (54)
▢ 86–92 (45)   ▢ 43–61 (55)
▢ 66–86 (68)   ▢ 15–43 (60)

Figure 13.6. (a) Markups and (b) output per firm in equipment goods (average = 100; number of employment areas in parentheses). (Source: Combes and Lafourcade (2008).)

forces that are fairly complex. In the areas around Paris, competition is strong, which implies low prices and markups. However, because of better access to most markets, trade costs are low. The same holds for marginal production costs, as these depend directly on the prices of goods, which are lower in the more competitive, central region. Resulting from these two contending forces, it appears that in the core the lower marginal production and trade costs outweigh the profit-skimming effect of competition. The opposite is true in the peripheral regions: competition is weak, which has a positive impact on prices and markups, but trade costs are high, owing to large distances from the large markets. The same is true of the marginal production costs because of weaker competition, which pushes up factor prices. In this case, however, the positive effects of competition more than offset the cost effects, which accounts for the high markups in the peripheral regions. The intermediate areas do not benefit from either of the two effects (low costs or weak competition), which results in low markups.

It remains for us to grasp how the volume of production per firm across different areas, shown in figure 13.6(b), can make consistent both the distributions of profits (figure 13.5) and of markups (figure 13.6(a)). It is easily seen that production decreases sharply when moving away from Paris. As a result, the core region benefits from both high markups and fairly large volumes of production, which explains the high profits there. However, in other areas, production and markups have opposite effects on profits. The middle band of regions receives low markups but

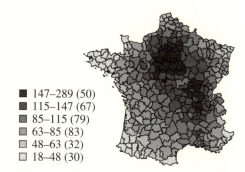

147–289 (50)
115–147 (67)
85–115 (79)
63–85 (83)
48–63 (32)
18–48 (30)

Figure 13.7. Operating profits after a 30% decrease in trade costs in equipment goods (average = 100; number of employment areas in parentheses). (Source: Combes and Lafourcade (2008).)

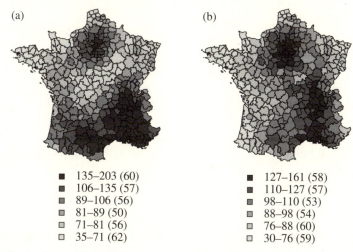

(a)

■ 135–203 (60)
■ 106–135 (57)
■ 89–106 (56)
□ 81–89 (50)
□ 71–81 (56)
□ 35–71 (62)

(b)

■ 127–161 (58)
■ 110–127 (57)
■ 98–110 (53)
□ 88–98 (54)
□ 76–88 (60)
□ 30–76 (59)

Figure 13.8. Operating profits after a 30% decrease in trade costs for (a) construction and (b) insurance (average = 100; number of employment areas in parentheses). (Source: Combes and Lafourcade (2008).)

sells more than the periphery (but less than the core), which yields intermediate profit levels. Finally, despite high markups in the periphery, the offsetting effect of low sales is too strong for profits to rise.

Finally, we should mention one last simulation that aims to evaluate the impact of a substantial drop in trade costs. To date, it has been impossible to simulate the processes underlying the entry of new firms, mainly because of limitations in computing capabilities. Consequently, Combes and Lafourcade can only assess the impact of a drop in trade costs assuming that firms do not change location. In this case, the drop in trade costs affects only firms' size, prices, employment, and sales across regions. Figures 13.7 and 13.8 give the levels of operating profits per firm, which represent the incentives for new firms to concentrate in a particular region after a drop in trade costs of 30% (which is comparable to the 38.5% drop in transport costs observed in France over the last twenty years; see chapter 5).

For the equipment goods sector, we observe that a second peak of high profits emerges around Lyon. In other words, if new firms were to enter, they would concentrate not only around Paris, but also near Lyon, a result that agrees with the left part of the bell-shaped curve. The profit gradient does, however, increase around these cities. In other words, *if there are now two core regions instead of one, the profit differential between them and their neighboring areas is strengthened*. In other words, while concentration incentives decrease at the national level, they may simultaneously increase at a local level. All manufactured sectors exhibit the same behavior.

Some noticeable differences emerge in the construction sector and in a services activity, the insurance sector. Simulating the model shows that the initial pattern is different, in that these sectors have three main centers (Paris, Lyon, and Marseille), instead of a single center (Paris) as in the other manufacturing industries. As shown in figure 13.8(a) for construction, following the drop in trade costs, Lyon and Marseille now merge to form a single southeast peak that spreads westward as far as Toulouse and becomes larger than that of Paris. Regarding the insurance sector (figure 13.8(b)), while the peak around Paris shrinks, profits get higher all along the Rhône Valley, from Lyon to Marseille, with a sharp decline when one moves either eastward or westward.

Computing the spatial concentration index à la Ellison and Glaeser (chapter 10) reveals that a 30% drop in trade costs leads to a decrease in employment concentration on the national level, but to varying degrees depending on the sector. When these indices are considered region by region, it is found that spatial concentration increases in a large number of regions. Thus, still taking firm location choices as constant, a 30% drop in trade costs yields a decrease in interregional disparities, but an increase in intraregional disparities. In other words, *there would be less polarization at the national level but more at the local level*.

The study by Combes and Lafourcade was reproduced by Teixeira (2006) using Portuguese data. This gives us a unique opportunity to compare the same model in two distinct real contexts that differ with respect to two variables that are crucial in economic geography: the initial degree of spatial concentration, and the transport infrastructure's configuration. Estimates reveal that trade costs have a positive impact in all twenty-five sectors under consideration, bearing in mind that the geographical classification used covers eighteen regions. Accounting for endogeneity improves the quality of the estimates. One striking finding is the degree to which Portugal is less integrated than France; the ratio of transport costs to marginal production costs is estimated to be five to ten times greater in Portugal. Moreover, two candidate sites for agglomeration appear around Lisbon and Porto, which are Portugal's most developed regions. This agglomeration occurs despite the fact that markups are also high in the smaller regions (as in France). Assuming again that existing firms' locations are fixed, a simulation modeling the impact of a new infrastructure planned for 2010 yields an increase in the peripheral regions' employment levels, and a corresponding decrease in the spatial concentration of activities, as suggested by the left part of the bell-shaped curve. As in the case of France, this impact must be qualified by recognizing that the entry of new firms in central regions, where profitability is higher than at the periphery, would simultaneously take place. Again, simulating the impact of a drop in trade costs and allowing for the entry of new firms remains prohibitively burdensome.

13.3 Concluding Remarks

Adopting a "theory with numbers" approach allows one to accurately illustrate how the main forces underlying economic geography models can generate spatial equilibria in the real world. Unearthing new spatial theories was not the aim here; our goal was instead to apply different theoretical models to real contexts with real data, and to move beyond unrealistic frameworks that work with a $2 \times 2 \times 2$ setting. The conclusions drawn from this richer setting should allow for a better understanding of the processes driving regional development, and may help policy makers discriminate between different economic projects.

It would be an oversight not to mention that these studies are only in their infancy. At the very least, current theoretical frameworks need to be further enriched by freeing themselves of the same, strong assumptions, and by testing new ones. Most models assume the same market structure across all sectors and do not account for the fact that some firms have plants located in different regions. This is a challenging but promising avenue for future research. Two trends are likely to be fruitful in future endeavors: available data sets are constantly improving in quality, which makes for more accurately calibrated parameters, and improvements in computing technologies will allow one to carry out more far-reaching simulations.

As a final note, there is no doubt that these advances will only be achieved by means of a two-step process in which a number of relevant parameters are first estimated, as described in chapter 12, and then the model is simulated using these estimates. Although some have started to venture in this direction, much remains to be done.

13.4   Related Literature

The exercises in computable spatial equilibrium under imperfect competition applied to European integration are rooted in studies by Smith and Venables (1988), Haaland and Norman (1992), and Gasiorek et al. (1992). Gasiorek and Venables (1997) produced the first study that is close to economic geography: it focuses on the impact that improvements in infrastructures have on the spatial concentration of activities.

14
Concluding Remarks

That we now live in a *flat world* is a widely held belief. Distances are no longer prohibitive; borders are sometimes thought of as arbitrary constructs inherited from the past. Accordingly, the spatial separation of nations and regions should be of little importance in economic life. At the same time, a number of debates regarding the emergence of economic spatial disparities have been thrust into the political arena, and have made a clear place for themselves in the consciousness of the public. At first glance, a paradox emerges: should the integration of markets not be leading us toward an increasingly global village? This question masks the simple fact that proximity and spatial homogeneity do not necessarily go hand in hand. To this end, economic geography offers a set of tools that aim at unearthing some of the complex interactions between globalization and spatial inequalities. Its main point is subtle and may be summarized as follows: even though trade costs must be positive for space to matter, one should not infer from this observation that location matters less when trade costs decrease. Quite the opposite in fact: by rendering firms more footloose, lower trade costs make them more sensitive to minor differences between regions. A tiny difference may then have a big impact on the spatial distribution of economic activity. Consequently, despite progress in integration, economic geography shows that "*physically, culturally, and economically, the world is not flat*" (Leamer 2007, p. 123).

14.1 The Paradox of the Global Village

Many commentators have touted the novelty of our recent wave of globalization. With the progressive disappearance of borders and trade costs, it is often held that the world has seen an unprecedented degree of integration in both markets and societies. Such statements merit qualification. As described in chapter 1, World War I interrupted an important wave of globalization: the first free trade agreements were struck during some of the decades leading up to the war, and transport costs dropped precipitously during this time as well. An anthology recently published by Ferri (2005) lends credence to the idea that *globalization is not a new phenomenon*. In particular, the fear and fascination it brings about are recurrent themes. From as far back as antiquity, it appears that Seneca had already witnessed some of these changes:

> All the barriers have been cast aside.
> Cities have been built on virgin land.
> The world is crisscrossed by roads.
> Everything is changing.
> Nothing is as it was.
>
> Cited in Ferri (2005, p. 20) [our translation]

While every wave of globalization is similar in fomenting both apprehension and fascination, the mechanisms underlying each wave are often quite unique: *technological and institutional conditions endow each one with distinct properties*. However, these specificities must not become an end in themselves and hinder our understanding of the forces that are common to all globalization phases. In particular, all waves of globalization are accompanied by some unease, probably because economic integration imposes lifestyle changes that force agents to think, act, and work on a new spatial scale.

An incomplete list of contemporary issues with a *strong territorial component* would include:

- nations' unequal economic and social developments;
- the persistence of strong regional imbalances in terms of employment and income within the European Union;
- the globalization of trade, and the new international division of labor that it is likely to trigger;
- the spatial fragmentation of production processes and the relocations of activities in the context of dwindling trade costs;
- urban violence and the emergence of poor areas with limited access to local labor markets;
- the role played by large urban metropolises in driving innovation and growth;
- the sprawl of housing around urban centers and the concomitant challenge of financing local public services;
- the various types of pollution (air, noise, etc.) caused by new transport infrastructures, or simply by the extension of older ones (freeways, high-speed trains, airports); and
- all problems arising from the congestion of transport networks.

14.2 The Objective of Economic Geography

The paradox of the global village mentioned above is illusory. In no way does tempering the tyranny of distance through various technological advances necessarily imply that spatial considerations should disappear from economic and social life. On the contrary, the study of spatial phenomena has actually become *more* complex on two accounts. First, individual or firm-specific location decisions are made on the basis of an increasingly richer set of factors. Given a wealth of explanatory variables, it is then easy for researchers to "see what they want to see" and find support for virtually any thesis. Second, the relative importance of location decisions depends on which spatial scale is taken as a reference. This complication can be likened to trying to build a railway network from rails of different gauges.

Economists have addressed the above issues with an embarrassed silence. The absence of cogent answers is in no small way related to the woeful neglect and disinterest economists have had for spatial questions. Needless to say, such an attitude has made them incapable of providing relevant answers, and has rendered other disciplines sceptical of the role economics can play in furthering our understanding of spatial phenomena. It is therefore high time to give spatial considerations a rightful place in economic analysis.

This book has addressed only a limited number of problems. The relative absence of regional and urban economics in teaching programs has led us to focus on a few major issues. Specifically, while research in urban economics has been growing steadily and has acquired greater relevance, study of regional economics has long been dormant. That said, the last decade has seen a noticeable upsurge in research investigating the causes and effects of inequality across regions and nations, on both theoretical and empirical grounds. With this in mind, we have restricted our analysis to the study of *interregional* inequalities, which has clear limitations. In particular, the macrospatial dimension is studied to the exclusion of microspatial aspects, even though these latter variables are bound to play an important role in spatial phenomena.

In the end, what have we learnt? No simple statements or ready-made recipes will do. Since this book aims to be of educational value, we could desist from offering any answer at all and leave readers to formulate their own responses. We will attempt, however, to sum up the main lessons, as these often run counter to conventional wisdom. Furthermore, in doing so, we hope to convince any student or teacher who may have skipped to this chapter that perusing the rest of the book may provide topics for reflection that are both new and relevant. The final section of this chapter will underscore the limits of current studies and propose avenues for future research.

14.3   What Have We Learned?

For clarity, our main findings are presented as a short list of fundamental points.

1. Trade is not synonymous with homogenization. It is often claimed that the development of trade tends to foster the homogenization of consumption, to the detriment of preexisting varieties. It is far from obvious that more trade necessarily gives rise to a reduction in the diversity of goods supplied and consumed. In fact, the opposite is probably more likely to hold. Those deploring the homogenization of lifestyles often overlook a key point: ultimately, from the individual's perspective, the total number of products available throughout the world is of little significance; what matters to people is the total number of products they have *access* to (see chapter 4). Overall, it seems untenable to argue that international trade foments less variety, aside from the cases in which new products sideline old ones because they are of better quality or less expensive or both.[1] Indeed, one of the tenets of industrial organization is that firms have an interest in differentiating and/or improving their products, at least when existing technology makes this possible. Such strategies take on an even greater importance in the context of international markets, where competition is harsher. To sum up, it should be clear that *trade increases the range of opportunities available to everyone*, even when the overall number of products is reduced, as national products are not the same as foreign ones. Italian wines are not French wines, and opening up the market allows consumers to discover a panoply of new products, even if such trade is made at the expense of certain domestic varieties that disappear after a while.

A further point to be noted is that benefits from increased trade are not distributed uniformly across partners. The gains are higher in the country producing the smallest number of varieties, as its inhabitants benefit from greater access to a more substantial share of varieties: those produced abroad (see chapter 4). From a theoretical standpoint, only trading partners of equal size can have equal gains.

---

[1] This could also occur when network externalities in consumption are strong. For example, François and van Ypersele (2002) show that openness to trade in cultural goods industries can lead to the extinction of local varieties, and therefore to a fall in cultural diversity. In the same vein, Grilo et al. (2001) show that a growing market size may trigger the exit of network goods.

2. Distance continues to play an essential role in economic and social life. Advances in information and communication technologies have cut trade costs considerably, and trade agreements have contributed to the progressive disappearance of customs barriers, a traditional obstacle to trade. It would be wrong, however, to infer that the transfer of goods, services, and information has become instantaneous and virtually free of charge. Upon inspection, most markets are still a long way from this frictionless world. The nineteenth century witnessed the first revolution in transport and communications to have a lasting effect on societies and economies, but this has not led to the disappearance of distance in economic relationships. Even today, it continues to influence the behavior of economic agents, albeit more subtly than before. Many journalists and commentators "observing" or "predicting" the death of distance are guilty of taking quite a few shortcuts. For example, when applying the gravity model to a large variety of flows, distance continues to have a strong influence, even though this conclusion probably merits qualification when dealing with immaterial goods.

It should be kept in mind, however, that distance is often a "black box" in most studies, masking a number of complex interactions and forces. But it is still empirically clear that, contrary to general beliefs, *globalization does not seem to lead to the relative disappearance of local trade.* Although it is unquestionable that global trade is increasing, local transactions are increasing even more rapidly, for reasons that have yet to be fully understood. The drop in transport and communication costs could hide another important fact: the trade of highly sophisticated and differentiated goods requires an increasing number of transactions, which in turn could outweigh the drop in trade costs.[2]

Moreover, in spite of a few noticeable counterexamples, trade costs (especially international costs) are still sizable. In many regions of the world, transport costs alone continue to be a significant barrier to trade: a barrier comparable to the woefully deficient or nonexistent infrastructure during the time leading up to the Industrial Revolution. In other words, distance-related costs are still relevant and should not be overlooked in theories of interregional and international trade. These costs become all the more important when considering the mobility of different production factors, since it allows for the choice of production sites that are fairly remote from one another.

---

[2] This reasoning is analogous to the explanation of vertical specialization put forward by Yi (2003): when transport costs decline, at some point firms find it profitable to spread their production across different sites. In this case, lower transport costs lead to a more than proportional increase in trade, and trade may become more local than before if production processes are split across neighboring regions for coordination purposes.

As Bertil Ohlin stated back in 1933, and reiterated at the *Nobel Symposium* organized in his honor in 1976, the above facts and observations point to the need for the synthesis of international trade and location theories. This is precisely the ambition of economic geography. Hence, it differs from urban economics, although they share some common features.

3. The emergence of spatial inequalities. By focusing on trade in commodities *and* on the mobility of production factors, economic geography provides a novel framework to work with. Recall that neoclassical theories of international trade tend to model nations as a pool of *internationally* immobile factors, which are nonetheless perfectly mobile on the *national* scale (e.g., factors can move from one industry to another, or from one region to another, without friction). In a perfectly competitive environment with constant returns to scale, the neoclassical model predicts that factor prices converge. It is thus hardly surprising that differences in size have no bearing on the dynamics of spatial inequality.

By adopting imperfect competition and increasing returns, economic geography departs from standard models and captures the influence of country and market size. This is a primary and often striking source of inequality (see chapters 4, 11, and 12). In turn, allowing for the spatial mobility of skilled labor and/or intermediate goods, we may predict *greater* inequalities, the manufacturing sector being almost totally agglomerated in a small number of regions (see chapters 6–8). While this result is probably too extreme, even a watered-down reading of these results suggests the existence of growing economic disparities across space. In other words, trade and factor mobility foster a growing *divergence* across regions.

Hence, economic geography provides insights that are diametrically opposed to the conventional wisdom. For instance, the neoclassical model maintains that convergence (and the resulting equalization of factor prices) is inversely related to the strength of existing barriers to trade; economic geography, on the other hand, suggests that convergence arises when these costs are high. In the latter setting, regional differences are more likely to appear once trade costs are low, although one would expect these lower trade costs to make economic agents entirely footloose. As we have seen, below some threshold the intensity of agglomeration forces is reduced under decreasing trade costs, but so is the intensity of dispersion forces. Economic geography tells us that the former tends to outweigh the latter under low trade costs, while the reverse holds under high trade costs. Namely, even if various forms of congestion can spark the redeployment of economic activity to the periphery, this only occurs under *very* low trade costs.

Similarly, while the divergence phase is characterized by a widening GDP gap across regions, this phase may give way to forces that curb (and even undo) the increasing difference between welfare levels. Indeed, price differences tend to fade away with the erosion of trade costs. Meanwhile, disparities in welfare levels can continue to grow and it is hard to know when (or whether) the critical threshold below which they decrease will be reached. Moreover, nominal wage gaps may persist because of existing heterogeneity *between* workers and *across* firms, two characteristics that have only very recently begun to be modeled in the context of economic geography. When combined, these various elements may give rise to stark regional disparities that manifest themselves through strong political tensions between spatial entities.

Finally, it is important to distinguish between individual and spatial inequalities. Indeed, it should be kept in mind that individuals having similar socioeconomic characteristics tend to congregate. This creates a self-reinforcing, dynamic process that sorts individuals according to these characteristics and accentuates initial income gaps, thus generating a vicious circle. In other words, *spatial inequalities cannot be considered as the mere accumulation of individual inequalities.*

4. Improvements in transport infrastructure may be harmful to some regions. The building or improvement of large transport infrastructures is expected to yield a substantial drop in transport costs. Such a policy may have remarkably different impacts, depending on whether agents' locations are taken to be *exogenous* or *endogenous* (see chapter 4). In the former case, we have just pointed out that both regions come out as winners. Under endogenous location decisions, while all workers have better access to the total set of goods, the new infrastructure may push a number of firms to relocate into the large region, and cause deindustrialization of the small region. Hence, inhabitants of the large region are likely to benefit most from the new infrastructure, except when wages or urban costs are much lower in the small region. Policy makers must, therefore, bear in mind that *public transport policies should not treat spatial patterns as exogenous*; modifying the existing transport infrastructure is likely to trigger the relocation of some agents, thus planting a seed of a self-reinforcing dynamic process that may lead to a drastically different space-economy. Such consequences may be easily overlooked by transport planners, who then run the risk of being dismayed at the unforeseen and undesirable rise in activity in the prosperous region at the expense of the poorer region (see chapters 6 and 7). In fact, this phenomenon was corroborated empirically after the construction of large highways in France and Italy during the 1960s (Plassard 1977).

5. What does the future hold for regional trade blocks, especially the European Union? Europe's low labor mobility is not conducive to the emergence of a large, EU-wide core–periphery structure. This prediction is confirmed by empirical studies and simulations carried out on calibrated models. However, both types of studies suggest *the existence of core–periphery structures on a smaller scale* (see chapters 12 and 13). In this case, the most likely pattern would involve a few large urban regions, each having a periphery formed by nearby regions. Hence, the advent of greater spatial equity on the *interregional* level may be accompanied by increasingly large disparities on the *intraregional* level. In other words, deeper economic integration would reorganize spatial differences and inequalities, but it would not suppress them.

In addition, using more realistic migratory models has proved useful in curbing some of the core–periphery model's extreme findings. Specifically, by better capturing the idiosyncrasies of potential migrants, we have been able to cast doubt on the rather unrealistic full concentration of skilled workers predicted by the Krugman model (see chapter 8). In particular, the strong attachment of European workers to their region of origin results in weaker migration flows. Moreover, beyond a certain threshold of integration, such a behavior may spark a new redispersion of economic activity. This scenario fosters spatial equity, not necessarily at the expense of economic efficiency once the heterogeneity of workers' preferences is taken into account. On the other hand, if we restrict our attention to directly observable economic magnitudes, this lower concentration of economic activity can lead to the emergence of small disparities across large economic spaces. Over time, this may give rise to significant differences in GDP per capita. If such a mechanism is indeed at work, the low mobility of European labor would sustain the emergence of substantial income disparities with respect to other large economic entities, such as the United States.

Finally, chapter 7 suggests that the supply of intermediate goods plays an important role in the agglomeration of economic activity, especially when the corresponding services are provided by workers with low spatial mobility. Bearing this in mind, one may expect the spatial fragmentation of production processes to result in highly specialized activities located in a few large urban regions. Simultaneously, the gradual drop in trade costs should favor the relocation of other, less specialized activities to regions with lower labor costs.[3] Indeed, owing to the pioneering work of Coase (1937), we know that transaction costs are one of the main reasons for the existence of firms. Given that the cost of trading commodities is just one special case of transaction cost, globalization should lead to a two-pronged movement involving the outsourcing of tasks and the vertical disintegration of firms. And, in fact, current trends indicate such a move toward the reorganization of firms around their core competencies, which typically rest on durable, specialized, and nontradable factors. If this trend is confirmed in the future, we can see how different types of cores and peripheries could coexist within the same economic space, thus generating a socioeconomic patchwork of wealthy and poorer districts, which we can observe in many cities.

6. Modeling strategies in economic geography. During the last decade, economics has underscored the heterogeneity of agents as a key element in the functioning of market economies. By focusing on the *spatial differentiation* of economic agents, economic geography is in keeping with this approach and conforms to the dominant pattern of contemporary research.

On several occasions, we have noted that increasing returns to scale (be they internal or external to the firm) are crucial in explaining the emergence of agglomeration and spatial inequalities (chapters 2, 6, 7, and 8). In their absence, dispersion forces are likely to prevail, thereby ensuring the equalization of factor prices obtained in the neoclassical model. It remains for us to explain how a large number of firms can operate under these conditions, since a downward sloping average cost curve allows a firm to influence the market. This is where the second key assumption, i.e., product differentiation, comes into play. Firms selling differentiated varieties do indeed benefit from a degree of market power that grants them some leeway in setting their price. Combining these two assumptions (increasing returns and product differentiation) is at the heart of Chamberlin-like models of monopolistic competition.

Moving on, we have also noted that both the DSK and linear models of monopolistic competition retain their flexibility once trade costs are added to the picture, thus making them especially well suited to addressing the main research questions in economic geography. Above all, these models allow for a consistent study of the macroeconomic consequences of market integration, by taking into account the general-equilibrium effects that link the different parts of the economy. This feature, which

---

[3] This result was established by Fujita and Thisse (2006) in a DSK-like model of economic geography.

makes monopolistic competition models so appealing, finds its origin in the absence of strategic interactions between firms; indeed, these interactions are reduced to their bare elements in order to isolate the forces most relevant to the question at hand. The fact that both models lead to the same conclusions should not be considered a weakness. Quite the contrary: it should lend credence to the existence of a wider set of models that all yield the same (qualitative if not quantitative) results.

Accounting explicitly for strategic interactions, as in spatial competition, yields results that do *not* contradict those put forward by using monopolistic competition (see chapter 9). It should be emphasized, however, that spatial competition models require either a number of nontrivial simplifications (such as resorting to partial-equilibrium analysis) or a move to an almost intractable framework. Using monopolistic competition thus seems warranted, given its greater flexibility. There is also a need to better understand how these two types of market structures are related to the reference spatial scale.[4]

Finally, one of the main stumbling blocks in the economic geography literature is undoubtedly the fact that the models used are very *specific*, which means they must only be considered as examples. This forces a researcher to continually question the robustness of her results, no matter how many individual examples corroborate each other. Building a full-fledged general-equilibrium model that combines imperfect competition with increasing returns to scale is a formidable task, which is still beyond our reach. Meanwhile, a research strategy that involves different examples may be considered reasonable. Examples of this kind may also serve as the impetus for more fundamental research into the building of general models.

14.4   Where Next?

As always, there is more to do than has already been done. Below are just a few key issues that call for further work.

1. One distinctive feature of the space-economy is that it seems to obey some *strong empirical regularities.* Think of the gravity model that accounts for the flows of goods, capital, and people, as well as the existence of wage gradients that vary according to distance from large cities. Another example is Zipf's law, which suggests that the hierarchy of cities follows a specific distribution. Economic geography provides a rationale

---

[4] Somewhat unexpectedly, Pinkse et al. (2002) show that the spatial competition model is relevant on the macrospatial level for some industries, i.e., at a scale at which competition would be expected to be global.

for some of these stylized facts, while at the same time proposing a more rigorous analysis, from both the theoretical and empirical standpoints. Nevertheless, much work still needs to be done before we have a good understanding of the "laws" governing the economic space.[5]

The evolution of those regularities also presents a number of challenges that need to be overcome. Regarding the gravity model, recent works suggest that trade flows have become more sensitive to distance. This is counterintuitive at best. Furthermore, why have goods been traded over shorter and shorter distances over the past fifty years? Has time become more important than distance in modern economies, as suggested by the development of just-in-time strategies? Might these shorter distances be explained by the upsurge of preferential agreements that bring together neighboring countries? Furthermore, might this distance paradox be linked to the emergence of increasingly complex products, which make local goods more appealing?[6] Yet the possibility remains that this paradox might just be a statistical artifact stemming from the evolution of trade statistics available for long-distance and short-distance trading partners, respectively.

2. The assumed symmetry between firms and the varieties they produce places us in what can be considered as a symmetric market environment. Yet we have seen that the heterogeneity of consumers vastly affects the CP model's main conclusions. Accordingly, it is legitimate to wonder if the heterogeneity of firms also affects the main results found in part II of the book. If, more likely than not, the answer is yes, then to what extent is this the case? Heterogeneity can take different forms, many of which are not directly relevant to spatial issues. Yet future insights and findings developed in other economic fields are likely to help us understand the role of heterogeneity. Specifically, they should act as a catalyst for more research in economic geography.[7]

Along the same lines, the homogeneity of the labor force is probably the least credible assumption of all. In the real world, national and regional labor markets are often fragmented, giving rise to local labor markets, which are often characterized by a low intersectoral mobility. In this case, spatial mobility may be viewed as a substitute for choosing a new career. Human capital endowments and worker reorientation programs are, therefore, two additional elements to take into account. More generally, it is well-known that regions and countries differ vastly in their labor market institutions. In short, one of the most unsatisfactory

---

[5] Duranton (2007) is a good case in point.

[6] See Duranton and Storper (2008) for more on this explanation.

[7] Nocke (2006) and Baldwin and Okubo (2006) are the first steps in this direction.

aspects of today economic geography lies in its oversimplified treatment of labor markets.

3. An increasing number of empirical studies reveal that the high degree of competition that characterizes large metropolitan areas sparks a *selection* of agents: only the (most) innovative firms and the (most) highly qualified workers are likely to be found in such places (see Syverson 2004; Combes et al. 2008a). While the emergence of such clusters is crucial in shaping the space-economy, it has been overlooked in economic geography models.[8] It also raises a number of challenging and thorny policy issues such as spatial sorting and segregation, the self-sustaining nature of spatial and individual inequalities, and the design and relevance of regional policies and urban planning. All in all, economic geography should pay greater attention to the microeconomic and microspatial mechanisms of *local development* and, consequently, to the role of the spatial scale in building models. For this, we must focus on spillovers and local interactions, which leave few paper trails but whose impacts are (partially) capitalized in land rents. At such a spatial scale, economic geography must be combined with urban economics in order to uncover the modus operandi of such externalities.

4. So far, economic geography models have assumed that products are horizontally differentiated. Although this assumption can be justified during the first stages of theory-building, one should keep in mind the increasingly important role that *quality competition* plays in international trade. This type of competition accounts for the exit of many firms unable to maintain their market share, a fact that lies at the root of many spatial inequalities. It should be clear that improving the current framework by taking into account quality differentiation would provide more accurate and relevant results; the main difficulty lies in the absence of an industrial organization model involving vertical differentiation which is as simple to handle as the Dixit–Stiglitz model. Thus, here too, the research agenda should focus on an issue that is not directly related to economic geography.

5. Choosing a location is typically a long-run decision in that it often involves sunk costs. Thus, when making this decision, an agent is expected to maximize her intertemporal profit or utility, based on the expectations she has regarding regional and market evolution. In turn, the accuracy of her expectations depends on the location choices made

---

[8] Melitz and Ottaviano (2008) is probably the first attempt made to account for selection phenomena in an economic geography setting.

by others, who also acted according to their own expectations (see Krugman 1991b). How workers form their expectations in such a context is an incredibly challenging question. The perfect foresight assumption used in the literature is hardly tenable and should be used as a benchmark at best.[9] The problem becomes even more complex when pondering the location decision of firms running several plants. While economic geography brings to light a number of relevant questions regarding globalization, the literature has yet to take a serious look at the spatial behavior of multinational firms. This may very well be the most challenging puzzle to unravel. Indeed, a multinational firm runs a network of plants that are coordinated by its headquarters, but it must also pay close attention to the behavior of its rivals.

6. While economic geography suggests the existence of multiple equilibria, history shows that large urban agglomerations are highly resilient to external shocks and exhibit great inertia in their evolution. It is reasonable to conjecture that this inertia is, to a large extent, due to the existence of different types of infrastructure, such as housing, public facilities, and transport networks, the use of which spans several generations (see, for example, Glaeser and Gyourko 2005). The durability of infrastructure has been completely overlooked until now, and is undoubtedly a domain in which intertemporal considerations play an important role. Here, empirical approaches might be most apt for revealing the reasons for the coexistence of a very persistent and stable urban structure and a fairly high degree of volatility with respect to regional specialization.

7. Economic geography maintains that regional disparities can be very strong. That said, most models overlook many elements that can contribute to the well-being of individuals, such as urban costs, natural amenities, schooling, and social networks. In order to better assess the real disparities across space, one should account for these various elements, which may contribute to a leveling-out of welfare levels (see chapter 8). In other words, merely comparing GDP per capita provides a pretty fuzzy picture of the welfare implications.

8. Empirical studies also suffer from several serious shortcomings. It should be emphasized, however, that they are more recent and often provide richer perspectives than their theoretical counterparts. We have seen that assessing a particular industry's degree of concentration and comparing the result across industries or time remains a difficult task.

---

[9] See Oyama (2006) for a rigorous analysis of the CP model with forward-looking agents.

We also need to better understand the links between industrial and spatial concentration, the relationships between firms' locations, and the role of spatial scale.

Moreover, variables accounting for location choices and local productivity have yet to be evaluated by means of more rigorous methods. Furthermore, these variables are often found to have a tenuous link with the underlying theoretical model, while a number of econometric problems arise. The rise in the availability of individual-level data should enable a greater degree of industry- and location-specific heterogeneity to be taken into account, and help researchers refine their understanding of spatial selection and sorting phenomena. Econometric panel techniques should make it easier to discriminate between issues specific to the mechanisms stressed by economic geography and the respective positions of regions in the global space. Furthermore, such techniques should also be useful in addressing endogeneity problems, which affect a great number of explanatory variables and are endemic to any model that aims to explain the choice of locations.

As we have seen, sticking closely to theoretical models by adopting a structural approach allows for a more precise interpretation of the results. There is no doubt that this nascent body of work needs to be expanded. Nevertheless, provided methodological precautions are taken, nonstructural approaches should also continue to provide increasingly robust stylized findings. Such models are required in order for new lines of theoretical research to emerge; they will also serve as the basis for more sophisticated empirical approaches.

While the lack of interest manifested by many economists about spatial issues is regrettable, the opposite attitude (disinterest in economic theory as a whole on the grounds that it is aspatial) is untenable. This attitude long characterized traditional regional economists, and it largely explains the stagnation of this field. In particular, as we have seen, space is the common denominator for a large number of real-world issues, while key advances in economic theory often overlook spatial considerations. In this respect, it is appropriate to recall two salient examples from the history of spatial economic theory. Harold Hotelling used Cournot and Bertrand as the catalyst for what would later become the spatial competition framework. Paul Krugman started to apply the Dixit–Stiglitz setting to trade theory. When he included factor mobility in his framework, economic geography had been launched. These two examples should leave us with plenty of food for thought.

References

Acemoglu, D., S. Johnson, and J. Robinson. 2002. Reversal of fortune: geography and institutions in the making of the modern world income distribution. *Quarterly Journal of Economics* 117:1231-94.

Ago, A., I. Isono, and T. Tabuchi. 2006. Locational disadvantage of the hub. *Annals of Regional Science* 40:819-48.

Ahearne, A., W. Griever, and F. Warnock. 2004. Information costs and home bias: an analysis of US holding of foreign equities. *Journal of International Economics* 62:313-36.

Alonso, W. 1964. *Location and Land Use*. Cambridge, MA: Harvard University Press.

Amiti, M. 1999. Specialisation patterns in Europe. *Weltwirschaftliches Archiv* 134:573-93.

Amiti, M., and C. A. Pissarides. 2005. Trade and industrial location with heterogeneous labor. *Journal of International Economics* 67:392-412.

Anas, A. 1983. Discrete choice theory, information theory, and the multinomial logit and gravity models. *Transportation Research* B 17:13-23.

——. 1987. *Modeling in Urban and Regional Economics*. Chur, Switzerland: Harwood Academic Publishers.

Anderson, J. 1979. A theoretical foundation for the gravity equation. *American Economic Review* 69:106-16.

Anderson, J., and E. van Wincoop. 2003. Gravity with gravitas: a solution to the border puzzle. *American Economic Review* 93:170-92.

——. 2004. Trade costs. *Journal of Economic Literature* 42:691-751.

Anderson, S. P., and D. Neven. 1991. Cournot competition yields spatial agglomeration. *International Economic Review* 32:793-808.

Anderson, S. P., A. de Palma, and J.-F. Thisse. 1992. *Discrete Choice Theory of Product Differentiation*. Cambridge, MA: MIT Press.

Anselin, L., R. Florax, and S. Rey. 2003. *Advances in Spatial Econometrics*. Springer.

Arellano, M. 2003. *Panel Data Econometrics*. Oxford University Press.

Armington, P. 1969. A theory of demand for products distinguished by place of production. *IMF Staff Papers* 16:159-78.

Arrow, K., and G. Debreu. 1954. Existence of an equilibrium for a competitive economy. *Econometrica* 22:265-90.

Arthur, W. B. 1994. *Increasing Returns and Path Dependence in the Economy*. Ann Arbor, MI: The University of Michigan Press.

Au, C.-C., and J. V. Henderson. 2006. Are Chinese cities too small? *Review of Economic Studies* 73:549-76.

Aumann, R. J. 1964. Markets with a continuum of traders. *Econometrica* 32:39-50.

——. 1966. Existence of competitive equilibria in markets with a continuum of traders. *Econometrica* 34:1-17.

Bade, K. J. 2002. *Migration in European History*. Oxford: Basil Blackwell.

Baier, S. L., and J. H. Bergstrand. 2001. The growth of world trade: tariffs, transport cost, and income similarity. *Journal of International Economics* 53: 1-27.

———. 2004. Do free trade agreements actually increase members' international trade? Mimeo, University of Notre-Dame.

Bailey, T. C., and A. C. Gatrell. 1995. *Interactive Spatial Data Analysis*. Essex: Longman Scientific & Technical.

Bairoch, P. 1988. *Cities and Economic Development: From the Dawn of History to the Present*. University of Chicago Press.

———. 1993. *Economics and World History: Myths and Paradoxes*. University of Chicago Press.

———. 1997. *Victoires et déboires. Histoire économique et sociale du monde du XVIᵉ siècle à nos jours*. Paris: Editions Gallimard.

Baldwin, R. E. 1999. Agglomeration and endogenous capital. *European Economic Review* 43:253-80.

———. 2006. *In or Out: Does It Make a Difference? An Evidence Based Analysis of the Trade Effects of the Euro*. London: CEPR.

Baldwin, R. E., and P. Krugman. 2004. Agglomeration, integration and tax harmonisation, *European Economic Review* 48:1-23.

Baldwin, R. E., and T. Okubo. 2006. Heterogeneous firms, agglomeration and economic geography: spatial selection and sorting. *Journal of Economic Geography* 6:323-46.

Baldwin, R. E., R. Forslid, P. Martin, G. I. P. Ottaviano, and F. Robert-Nicoud. 2003. *Economic Geography and Public Policy*. Princeton University Press.

Barbieri, K. 2003. *The Liberal Illusion. Does Trade Promote Peace?* Ann Arbor, MI: The University of Michigan Press.

Barrios, S., L. Bertinelli, E. Strobl, and A.-C. Teixeira. 2005. The dynamics of agglomeration: evidence from Ireland and Portugal. *Journal of Urban Economics* 57:170-88.

———. Forthcoming. Agglomeration economies and the location of industries: a comparison of three small European countries. *Regional Studies*, in press.

Beckmann, M. J., and J.-F. Thisse. 1986. The location of production activities. In *Handbook of Regional and Urban Economics* (ed. P. Nijkamp), volume 1, pp. 21-95. Amsterdam: North-Holland.

Behrens, K. 2004. Agglomeration without trade: how non-traded goods shape the space-economy. *Journal of Urban Economics* 55:68-92.

———. 2005. How endogenous asymmetries in interregional market access trigger regional divergence. *Regional Science and Urban Economics* 35:471-92.

Behrens, K., and Y. Murata. 2007. General equilibrium models of monopolistic competition: a new approach. *Journal of Economic Theory* 136:776-87.

Behrens, K., A. Lamorgese, G. I. P. Ottaviano, and T. Tabuchi. 2004. Testing the home market effect in a multi-country world: the theory. CEPR Discussion Paper no. 4468.

———. 2005. Testing the "home market effect" in a multi-country world. CORE Discussion Paper no. 2005/55.

Behrens, K., J. H. Hamilton, G. I. P. Ottaviano, and J.-F. Thisse. 2007. Commodity taxation harmonization and the location of industry. *Journal of International Economics* 72:271-91.

Belleflamme, P., P. Picard, and J.-F. Thisse. 2000. An economic theory of regional clusters. *Journal of Urban Economics* 48:158-84.

Bénabou, R. 1994. Working of a city: location, education and production. *Quarterly Journal of Economics* 106:619-52.

Bénassy, J.-P. 1991. Monopolistic competition. In *Handbook of Mathematical Economics* (ed. W. Hildenbrand and H. Sonnenschein), volume 4, pp. 1997-2045. Amsterdam: North-Holland.

———. 1996. Taste for variety and optimum production patterns in monopolistic competition. *Economics Letters* 52:41-47.

Bentolila, S. 1996. Sticky labor in Spanish regions. *European Economic Review* 41:591-98.

Bergstrand, J. H. 1985. The gravity equation in international trade: some microeconomic foundations and empirical evidence. *Review of Economics and Statistics* 67:474-81.

Bonanno, G. 1990. General equilibrium theory with imperfect competition. *Journal of Economic Surveys* 4:297-328.

Bosker, M., S. Brakman, H. Garretsen, and M. Schramm. 2007. Adding geography to the New Economic Geography. CESifo Working Paper 2038.

Bossuyt, A., L. Broze, and V. Ginsburgh. 2001. On invisible trade relations between Mesopotamian cities during the Third Millennium B.C. *The Professional Geographer* 53:374-83.

Bourguignon, F. 1979. Decomposable income inequality measures. *Econometrica* 47:901-20.

Brakman, S., and B. J. Heijdra. 2004. *The Monopolistic Competition Revolution in Retrospect.* Cambridge University Press.

Brakman, S., H. Garretsen, and Ch. van Marrewijk. 2001. *An Introduction to Geographical Economics.* Cambridge University Press. (Second edition published in 2008: *The New Introduction to Geographical Economics.*)

Brakman, S., H. Garretsen, and M. Schramm. 2004a. The spatial distribution of wages and employment: estimating the Helpman–Hanson model for Germany. *Journal of Regional Science* 44:437-66.

———. 2004b. The strategic bombing of German cities during WWII and its impact on city growth. *Journal of Economic Geography* 4:201-17.

———. 2006. Putting new economic geography to the test: free-ness of trade and agglomeration in the EU regions. *Regional Science and Urban Economics* 36: 613-35.

Brander, J. 1981. Intra-industry trade in identical commodities. *Journal of International Economics* 11:1-14.

Brander, J., and P. R. Krugman. 1983. A "reciprocal dumping" model of international trade. *Journal of International Economics* 15:313-21.

Braudel, F. 1979. *Civilisation matérielle, économie et capitalisme, XVe-XVIIIe siècle: le temps du monde.* Paris: Armand Colin. (English translation, 1985: *Civilization and Capitalism 15th-18th Century: The Perspective of the World.* New York: Harper Collins.)

Braunerhjelm, P., R. Faini, V. Norman, F. Ruane, and P. Seabright. 2000. *Integration and the Regions of Europe: How the Right Policy Can Prevent Polarization.* London: Centre for Economic Policy Research.

Briant, A., P.-P. Combes, and M. Lafourcade. 2007. Do the size and shape of spatial units jeopardize economic geography estimations. Mimeo, Paris School of Economics.

Broda, C., and D. E. Weinstein. 2006. Globalization and the gains from variety. *Quarterly Journal of Economics* 121:541–85.

Brülhart, M., and R. Traeger. 2005. An account of geographic concentration patterns in Europe. *Regional Science and Urban Economics* 35:597–624.

Campbell, J. R., and H. A. Hopenhayn. 2005. Market size matters. *Journal of Industrial Economics* 53:1–25.

Cantillon, R. 1755. *Essai sur le nature du commerce en général.* London: Fletcher Gyles. (English translation (H. Higgs), 1964: *Essay on the Nature of Trade in General.* New York: A. M. Kelley.)

Carey, H. C. 1858. *Principles of Social Science.* Philadelphia, PA: J. Lippincott.

Carlton, D. 1983. The location and employment choices of new firms: an econometric model with discrete and continuous endogenous variables. *Review of Economics and Statistics* 65:440–49.

Carrère, C. 2006. Revisiting the effects of regional trade agreements on trade flows with proper specification of the gravity model. *European Economic Review* 50:223–47.

Casetti, E. 1980. Equilibrium population partitions between urban and agricultural occupations. *Geographical Analysis* 12:47–54.

Cavailhès, J., C. Gaigné, T. Tabuchi, and J.-F. Thisse. 2007. Trade and the structure of cities. *Journal of Urban Economics* 62:383–404.

Ceglowski, J. 2006. Does gravity matter in a service economy? *Review of World Economics* 142:307–29.

Chamberlin, E. 1933. *The Theory of Monopolistic Competition.* Cambridge, MA: Harvard University Press.

———. 1951. Monopolistic competition revisited. *Economica* 18:342–62.

Chaney, T. 2007. Distorted gravity: heterogeneous firms, market structure and the geography of international trade. Mimeo, MIT. (Also forthcoming in *American Economic Review.*)

Charlot, S., C. Gaigné, F. Robert-Nicoud, and J.-F. Thisse. 2006. Agglomeration and welfare: the core–periphery model in the light of Bentham, Kaldor, and Rawls. *Journal of Public Economics* 90:325–47.

Chaterjee, S., and G. A. Carlino. 2001. Aggregate metropolitan employment growth and the deconcentration of metropolitan employment. *Journal of Monetary Economics* 48:549–83.

Ciccone, A. 2002. Agglomeration effects in Europe. *European Economic Review* 46:213–27.

Ciccone, A., and R. E. Hall. 1996. Productivity and the density of economic activity. *American Economic Review* 86:54–70.

Cingano, F., and F. Schivardi. 2004. Identifying the sources of local productivity growth. *Journal of the European Economic Association* 2:720–42.

Cipolla, C. M. 1962. *The Economic History of World Population,* 7th edn. Harmondsworth: Penguin.

Clark, W. A. V. 1986. *Human Migration.* Thousand Oaks, CA: SAGE.

Clark, X., D. Dollar, and A. Micco. 2004. Port efficiency, maritime transport costs, and bilateral trade. *Journal of Development Economics* 75:417–50.

Coase, R. 1937. The nature of the firm. *Economica* 4:386–405.

Cohen, D. 2007. *Globalization and Its Enemies.* Cambridge, MA: MIT Press.

Combes, P.-P. 1997. Industrial agglomeration and Cournot competition. *Annales d'Economie et de Statistique* 45:161–82.

Combes, P.-P., and M. Lafourcade. 2001. Transport costs decline and regional inequalities: evidence from France. CEPR Discussion Paper no. 2894.

——. 2005. Transport costs: measures, determinants, and regional policy. Implications for France. *Journal of Economic Geography* 5:319–49.

——. 2008. Competition, market access and economic geography: structural estimations and predictions for France. Mimeo, Paris School of Economics (available at www.enpc.fr/ceras/lafourcade/artinf270207.pdf).

Combes, P.-P., and H. G. Overman. 2004. The spatial distribution of economic activities in the European Union. In *Handbook of Regional and Urban Economics* (ed. J. V. Henderson and J.-F. Thisse), volume 4. Amsterdam: North-Holland.

Combes, P.-P., T. Magnac, and J.-M. Robin. 2004. The dynamics of local employment in France. *Journal of Urban Economics* 56:217–43.

Combes, P.-P., M. Lafourcade, and T. Mayer. 2005. The trade creating effects of business and social networks: evidence from France. *Journal of International Economics* 66:1–29.

Combes, P. P., M. Lafourcade, J.-F. Thisse, and J.-C. Toutain. 2008a. The rise and fall of spatial inequalities in France (1860–1930–2000). Mimeo, Paris School of Economics.

Combes, P.-P., G. Duranton, and L. Gobillon. 2008b. Spatial wage disparities: sorting matters! *Journal of Urban Economics* 63:723–42.

Combes, P.-P., G. Duranton, L. Gobillon, and S. Roux. 2008c. Estimating agglomeration economies with history, geology, and worker effects. CEPR Discussion Paper no. 6728.

Crafts, N., and A. Mulatu. 2005. What explains the location of industry in Britain, 1871–1931? *Journal of Economic Geography* 5:499–518.

Cronon, W. 1991. *Nature's Metropolis. Chicago and the Great West.* London: W. W. Norton.

Crozet, M. 2004. Do migrants follow market potentials? A calculation of a new economic geography model. *Journal of Economic Geography* 4:439–58.

Crozet, M., T. Mayer, and J.-L. Mucchielli. 2004. How do firms agglomerate? A study of FDI in France. *Regional Science and Urban Economics* 34:27–54.

d'Aspremont, C., J. J. Gabszewicz, and J.-F. Thisse. 1979. On Hotelling's "Stability in Competition". *Econometrica* 47:1045–50.

d'Aspremont, C., R. Dos Santos Ferreira, and L.-A. Gérard-Varet. 1996. On the Dixit–Stiglitz model of monopolistic competition. *American Economic Review* 86:623–29.

Davis, D. R. 1998. The home market, trade and industrial structure. *American Economic Review* 88:1264–76.

Davis, D. R., and D. Weinstein. 1996. Does economic geography matter for international specialization? NBER Working Paper 5706.

——. 1999. Economic geography and regional production structure: an empirical investigation. *European Economic Review* 43:379–407.

——. 2002. Bones, bombs, and break points: the geography of economic activity. *American Economic Review* 92:1269–89.

——. 2003. Market access, economic geography and comparative advantage: an empirical assessment. *Journal of International Economics* 59:1–23.

——. 2008. A search for multiple equilibria in urban industrial structure. *Journal of Regional Science* 48:29–65.

Debreu, G. 1959. *Theory of Value.* Wiley.

Delisle, J.-P., and F. Laine. 1998. Les transferts d'établissements contribuent au desserrement urbain. *Economie et Statistique* 311:91–106.

de Palma, A., V. Ginsburgh, Y. Y. Papageorgiou, and J.-F. Thisse. 1985. The principle of minimum differentiation holds under sufficient heterogeneity. *Econometrica* 53:767–81.

——. 2007. Firm location decisions, regional grants and agglomeration externalities. *Journal of Public Economics* 91:413–35.

Diamond, J. 1997. *Guns, Germs, and Steel. The Fate of Human Societies.* New York: W. W. Norton.

Dierker, E., H. Dierker, and B. Grodal. 2003. Cournot competition in a general equilibrium model with international trade. Mimeo, University of Vienna.

Di Mauro, F. 2000. The impact of economic integration on FDI and exports: a gravity approach. Centre for European Policy Studies (Brussels) Working Document 156.

Dinopoulos, E., K. Fujiwara, and K. Shimomura. 2007. International trade and volume patterns under quasi-linear preferences. Mimeo, University of Florida.

Disdier, A. C., and K. Head. 2008. The puzzling persistence of the distance effect on bilateral trade. *Review of Economics and Statistics* 90:37–48.

Dixit, A. K., and J. E. Stiglitz. 1977. Monopolistic competition and optimum product diversity. *American Economic Review* 67:297–308.

Dumais, G., G. Ellison, and E. L. Glaeser. 2002. Geographic concentration as a dynamic process. *Review of Economics and Statistics* 84:193–204.

Duranton, G. 2007. Urban evolutions: the fast, the slow, and the still. *American Economic Review* 97:197–221.

Duranton, G., and V. Monastiriotis. 2002. Mind the gaps: the evolution of regional earnings inequalities in the U.K. 1982–1997. *Journal of Regional Science* 42:219–56.

Duranton, G., and H. G. Overman. 2005. Testing for location using microgeographic data. *Review of Economic Studies* 72:1077–106.

Duranton, G., and M. Storper. 2008. Rising trade costs? Agglomeration and trade with endogenous transaction costs. *Canadian Journal of Economics* 41:292–319.

Eaton, B. C., and R. G. Lipsey. 1977. The introduction of space into the neoclassical model of value theory. In *Studies in Modern Economics* (ed. M. Artis and A. Nobay), pp. 59–96. Oxford: Basil Blackwell.

——. 1997. *On the Foundations of Monopolistic Competition and Economic Geography.* Cheltenham, U.K.: Edward Elgar Press.

Eaton, J., and S. Kortum. 2002. Technology, geography and trade. *Econometrica* 70:1741–80.

Ecochard, P., L. Fontagné, G. Gaulier, and S. Zignago. 2005. Intra-industry trade and economic integration. CEPII report for JETRO-IDE.

Economist Intelligence Unit. 2001. *International Price Comparisons. A Survey of Branded Consumer Goods in France, Germany, Sweden, the U.K. and the U.S.* London: *The Economist.*

Eichengreen, B. 1993. Labor market and European monetary unification. In *Policy Issues in the Operation of Currency Unions* (ed. P. Masson and M. Taylor), pp. 130–62. Cambridge University Press.

Ellison, G., and E. L. Glaeser. 1997. Geographic concentration in U.S. manufacturing industries: a dartboard approach. *Journal of Political Economy* 105: 889–927.

Engel, C., and J. Rogers. 1996. How wide is the border? *American Economic Review* 86:1112–25.

———. 2001. Deviations from purchasing power parity: causes and welfare costs. *Journal of International Economics* 55:29–57.

Estevadeordal, A., B. Frantz, and A. M. Taylor. 2003. The rise and fall of world trade, 1870–1939. *Quarterly Journal of Economics* 118:359–407.

Ethier, W. 1982. National and international returns to scale in the modern theory of international trade. *American Economic Review* 72:389–405.

European Commission. 1999. *ESDP The European Spatial Development Perspective. Towards Balanced and Durable Development of the Territory of the European Union.* Luxembourg: Office for Official Publications of the European Communities.

Evenett, S., and W. Keller. 2002. On theories explaining the success of the gravity equation. *Journal of Political Economy* 110:281–316.

Faini, R. 1984. Increasing returns, non-traded inputs and regional development. *Economic Journal* 94:308–23.

———. 1999. Trade unions and regional development. *European Economic Review* 43:457–74.

Faini, R., G. Galli, P. Gennari, and F. Rossi. 1996. An empirical puzzle: falling migration and growing unemployment differentials among Italian regions. *European Economic Review* 41:571–80.

Farrell, J., and P. Klemperer. 2007. Co-ordination and lock-in: competition with switching costs and network effects. In *Handbook of Industrial Organization* (ed. M. Armstrong and R. Porter), volume III, pp. 1967–2072. Amsterdam: North-Holland.

Feenstra, R. C. 2004. *Advanced International Trade: Theory and Evidence.* Princeton University Press.

Feenstra, R. C., J. Markusen, and A. Rose. 2001. Using the gravity equation to differentiate among alternative theories of trade. *Canadian Journal of Economics* 34:430–47.

Ferri, L. 2005. *Ils racontent la mondialisation. De sénèque à Lèvi-Strauss.* Paris: Saint-Simon.

Feser, E., S. Sweeney, and H. Renski. 2005. A descriptive analysis of discrete U.S. industrial complexes. *Journal of Regional Science* 45:395–419.

Findlay, R., and K. H. O'Rourke. 2003. Commodity market integration: 1500–2000. In *Globalization in Historical Perspectives* (ed. M. D. Bordo, A. M. Taylor, and J. G. Williamson), pp. 13–64. University of Chicago Press.

Fontagné, L., T. Mayer, and S. Zignano. 2005. Trade in the Triad: how easy is the access to large markets. *Canadian Journal of Economics* 38:1401–30.

Forslid, R., and G. I. P. Ottaviano. 2003. An analytically solvable core–periphery model. *Journal of Economic Geography* 3:229–40.

Forslid, R., J. Haaland, and K.-H. Midelfart-Knarvik. 2002. A U-shaped Europe? A simulation study of industrial location. *Journal of International Economics* 57:273–97.

Francis, R. L., T. J. Lowe, B. Rayco, and A. Tamir. Forthcoming. Aggregation error for location models: survey and analysis. *Annals of Operations Research*, in press.

François, P., and T. van Ypersele. 2002. On the protection of cultural goods. *Journal of International Economics* 56:359–69.

Frankel, J. 1997. *Regional Trading Blocs.* Washington, DC: Institute for International Economics.

Friedman, J., D. Gerlowski, and J. Silberman. 1992. What attracts foreign multinational corporations. *Journal of Regional Science* 32:403–18.

Fujita, M. 1989. *Urban Economic Theory: Land Use and City Size.* Cambridge University Press.

Fujita, M., and J.-F. Thisse. 2002. *Economics of Agglomeration: Cities, Industrial Location and Regional Growth.* Cambridge University Press.

———. 2003a. Agglomeration and market interaction. In *Advances in Economics and Econometrics: Theory and Applications* (ed. M. Dewatripont, L. P. Hansen, and S. T. Turnovsky), pp. 302–38. Cambridge University Press.

———. 2003b. Does geographical agglomeration foster economic growth? And who gains and loses from it? *Japanese Economic Review* 54:121–45.

———. 2006. Globalization and the evolution of the supply chain: who gains and who loses? *International Economic Review* 47:811–36.

Fujita, M., P. Krugman, and A. J. Venables. 1999. *The Spatial Economy: Cities, Regions and International Trade.* Cambridge, MA: MIT Press.

Gabszewicz, J. J., and J.-F. Thisse. 1986. Spatial competition and the location of firms. In *Location Theory* (ed. J. J. Gabszewicz, J.-F. Thisse, M. Fujita, and U. Schweizer), pp. 1–71. Chur, Switzerland: Harwood Academic Publishers.

Gallup, J. L., J. D. Sachs, and A. Mellinger. 1999. Geography and economic development. *International Regional Science Review* 22:179–232.

Gasiorek, M., and A. J. Venables. 1997. Evaluating regional infrastructure: a computable equilibrium approach. "Modelling Report" by The European Institute and the London School of Economics.

Gasiorek, M., A. Smith, and A. J. Venables. 1992. "1992": trade and welfare. A general equilibrium model. In *Trade Flows and Trade Policies* (ed. L. Winters), pp. 35–63. Cambridge University Press.

Giersch, H. 1949. Economic union between nations and the location of industries. *Review of Economic Studies* 17:87–97.

Ginsburgh, V., Y. Y. Papageorgiou, and J.-F. Thisse. 1985. On existence and stability of spatial equilibria and steady-states. *Regional Science and Urban Economics* 15:149–58.

Glaeser, E. L., and J. Gyourko. 2005. Urban decline and durable housing. *Journal of Political Economy* 113:345–75.

Glaeser, E. L., and J. E. Kohlhase. 2004. Cities, regions and the decline of transport costs. *Papers in Regional Science* 83:197–228.

Glaeser, E. L., and D. C. Mare. 2001. Cities and skills. *Journal of Labor Economics* 19:316–42.

Glaeser, E. L., H. Kallal, J. Sheinkman, and A. Schleifer. 1992. Growth in cities. *Journal of Political Economy* 100:1126–52.

Glaeser, E. L., J. Kolko, and A. Saiz. 2001. Consumer city. *Journal of Economic Geography* 1:27–50.

Greenhut, J. J., and M. L. Greenhut. 1977. Nonlinearity of delivered price schedules and predatory pricing. *Economica* 45:1871–75.

Greenhut, M. L. 1981. Spatial pricing in the United States, West Germany and Japan. *Economica* 48:79–86.

Greenhut, M. L., G. Norman, and C.-S. Hung. 1987. *The Economics of Imperfect Competition: A Spatial Approach.* Cambridge University Press.

Greenwood, M. L. 1997. Internal migration in developed countries. In *Handbook of Population and Family Economics* (ed. M. R. Rosenzweig and O. Stark), pp. 648–719. Amsterdam: North-Holland.

Grilo I., O. Shy, and J.-F. Thisse. 2001. Price competition when consumer behavior is characterized by conformity or vanity. *Journal of Public Economics* 30:385–408.

Guiso, L., P. Sapienza, and L. Zingales. 2004. Cultural biases in economic exchange. NBER Working Paper 11,005.

Gupta, B., D. Pal, and J. Sarkar. 1997. Spatial Cournot competition and agglomeration in a model of location choice. *Regional Science and Urban Economics* 27:261–82.

Haaland, J., and V. Norman. 1992. Global production effects of European integration. In *Trade Flows and Trade Policies* (ed. L. Winters), pp. 67–88. Cambridge University Press.

Hamilton, J., J.-F. Thisse, and A. Weskamp. 1989. Spatial discrimination: Bertrand vs. Cournot in a model of location choice. *Regional Science and Urban Economics* 19:87–102.

Hansen, N. 1990. Do producer services induce regional development? *Journal of Regional Science* 30:465–78.

Hanson, G. 1996. Localization economies, vertical organization, and trade. *American Economic Review* 86:1266–78.

———. 1997. Increasing returns, trade and the regional structure of wages. *Economic Journal* 107:113–33.

———. 1998. Market potential, increasing returns, and geographic concentration. NBER Working Paper 6429.

———. 2005. Market potential, increasing returns, and geographic concentration. *Journal of International Economics* 67:1–24.

Harrigan, J. 1996. Openness to trade in manufactures in the OECD. *Journal of International Economics* 40:23–39.

Harris, C. 1954. The market as a factor in the localization of industry in the United States. *Annals of the Association of American Geographers* 64:315–48.

Harris, J. R., and M. P. Todaro. 1970. Migration, unemployment and development: a two sector analysis. *American Economic Review* 60:126–42.

Haskel, J., and H. Wolf. 2001. The law of one price. A case study. *Scandinavian Journal of Economics* 103:545–58.

Head, K., and T. Mayer. 2000. Non-Europe: the magnitude and causes of market fragmentation in Europe. *Weltwirtschaftliches Archiv* 136:285–314.

———. 2002. Illusory border effects: distance mismeasurement inflates estimates of home bias in trade. CEPII Working Document 2002-1.

———. 2004a. Market potential and the location of Japanese investment in the European Union. *Review of Economics and Statistics* 86:959–72.

———. 2004b. The empirics of agglomeration and trade. In *Handbook of Regional and Urban Economics* (ed. J. V. Henderson and J.-F. Thisse), volume 4, pp. 2609–69. Amsterdam: North-Holland.

———. 2006. Regional wage and employment responses to market potential in the EU. *Regional Science and Urban Economics* 36:573—94.

Head, K., and J. Ries. 2001. Increasing returns versus national product differ-
    entiation as an explanation for the pattern of U.S.-Canada trade. *American
    Economic Review* 91:858-76.

Head, K., J. Ries, and D. Swenson. 1999. Attracting foreign manufacturing:
    investment promotion and agglomeration. *Regional Science and Urban Eco-
    nomics* 29:197-218.

Head, K., T. Mayer, and J. Ries. 2002. On the pervasiveness of the home market
    effect. *Economica* 69:371-90.

——. 2007. How remote is the offshoring threat? Mimeo, University of British
    Columbia.

Helpman, E. 1998. The size of regions. In *Topics in Public Economics: Theoret-
    ical and Applied Analysis* (ed. D. Pines, E. Sadka, and Y. Zilcha), pp. 33-54.
    Cambridge University Press.

Helpman, E., and P. R. Krugman. 1985. *Market Structure and Foreign Trade.*
    Cambridge, MA: MIT Press.

Henderson, J. V. 1974. The sizes and types of cities. *American Economic Review*
    64:640-56.

——. 1988. *Urban Development: Theory, Fact and Illusion.* Oxford University
    Press.

——. 1997. Externalities and industrial development. *Journal of Urban Eco-
    nomics* 42:449-70.

——. 2003. Marshall's scale economies. *Journal of Urban Economics* 53:1-28.

Henderson, J. V., A. Kuncoro, and M. Turner. 1995. Industrial development in
    cities. *Journal of Political Economy* 103:1067-90.

Herring, L., and S. Poncet. Forthcoming. Market access impact on individual
    wages: evidence from China. *Review of Economics and Statistics,* in press.

Hicks, J. H. 1969. *A Theory of Economic History.* Oxford: Clarendon.

Hinloopen, J., and Ch. van Marrewijk. 1999. On the limits and possibilities of
    the principle of minimum differentiation. *International Journal of Industrial
    Organization* 17:735-50.

Hohenberg, P. M. 2004. The historical geography of European cities. An inter-
    pretative essay. In *Handbook of Regional and Urban Economics: Cities and
    Geography* (ed. J. V. Henderson and J.-F. Thisse), pp. 3021-52. Amsterdam:
    North-Holland.

Hoover, E. M. 1936. *Location Theory and the Shoe and Leather Industries.*
    Cambridge, MA: Harvard University Press.

Hotelling, H. 1929. Stability in competition. *Economic Journal* 39:41-57.

Hummels, D. 1999. Toward a geography of trade costs. Mimeo, University of
    Chicago.

——. 2007. Transportation costs and international trade in the second era of
    globalization. *Journal of Economic Perspectives* 21(3):131-54.

Hummels, D., and V. Lugovskyy. 2006. Are matched partner trade statistics a
    usable measure of transportation costs? *Review of International Economics*
    14:69-86.

Husson, C. 2002. *L'Europe sans territoire.* La Tour D'Aigues: Editions de l'Aube.

Irmen, A., and J.-F. Thisse. 1998. Competition in multi-characteristics spaces:
    Hotelling was almost right. *Journal of Economic Theory* 78:76-102.

Isard, W. 1956. Regional science, the concept of region, and regional structure.
    Papers of the Regional Science Association 2:13-26.

Jacobs, J. 1969. *The Economy of Cities*. New York: Random House.

——. 1984. *Cities and the Wealth of Nations*. New York: Random House.

Jaffe, A., M. Trajtenberg, and R. Henderson. 1993. Geographic localization of knowledge spillovers as evidenced by patent citations. *Quarterly Journal of Economics* 108:577-98.

Kaldor, N. 1935. Market imperfection and excess capacity. *Economica* 2:35-50.

——. 1970. The case for regional policies. *Scottish Journal of Political Economy* 17:337-48.

Keller, W. 2002. Geographic localization of international technology diffusion. *American Economic Review* 92:120-42.

Keynes, J. M. 1919. *The Economic Consequences of the Peace*. London: Macmillan.

Kim, S. 1995. Expansion of markets and the geographic distribution of economic activities: the trends in U.S. regional manufacturing structure, 1860-1987. *Quarterly Journal of Economics* 110:881-908.

Kirman, A. 1992. Whom and what does the representative individual represent? *Journal of Economic Perspectives* 6:117-36.

Koopmans, T. C. 1957. *Three Essays on the State of Economic Science*. New York: McGraw-Hill.

Kremer, M. 1993. Population growth and technological change: 1,000,000 B.C. to 1990. *Quarterly Journal of Economics* 108:681-716.

Krugman, P. R. 1979. Increasing returns, monopolistic competition, and international trade. *Journal of International Economics* 9:469-79.

——. 1980. Scale economies, product differentiation, and the pattern of trade. *American Economic Review* 70:950-9.

——. 1991a. Increasing returns and economic geography. *Journal of Political Economy* 99:483-99.

——. 1991b. History versus expectations. *Quarterly Journal of Economics* 106: 651-67.

——. 1991c. *Geography and Trade*. Cambridge, MA: MIT Press.

——. 1995. *Development, Geography, and Economic Theory*. Cambridge, MA: MIT Press.

Krugman, P. R., and R. Livas Elizondo. 1996. Trade policy and the Third World metropolis. *Journal of Development Economics* 49:137-50.

Krugman, P. R., and A. J. Venables. 1995. Globalization and the inequality of nations. *Quarterly Journal of Economics* 110:857-80.

Lampard, E. E. 1955. The history of cities in the economically advanced areas. *Economic Development and Cultural Change* 3:321-42.

Landes, D. S. 1998. *The Wealth and Poverty of Nations*. London: Abacus.

Launhardt, W. 1885. *Mathematische Begründung der Volkswirtschaftslehre*. Theipzig: B. G. Teubner. (English translation, 1993: *Mathematical Principles of Economics*. Cheltenham, U.K.: Edward Elgar.)

Leamer, E. E. 2007. A flat world, a level playing field, a small world after all, or none of the above? A review of Thomas L. Friedman's *The World is Flat*. *Journal of Economic Literature* 45:83-126.

Leamer, E. E., and J. Levinsohn. 1994. International trade theory: the evidence. In *Handbook of International Economics* (ed. G. Grossman and K. Rogoff), pp. 1339-94. Amsterdam: North Holland.

Léon, P. 1976. La conquète de l'espace national. In *Histoire économique et sociale de la France* (ed. F. Braudel and E. Labrousse), volume III, pp. 241–73. Paris: Presses Universitaires de France.

Lepetit, B. 1988. *Les villes dans la France moderne (1740–1840)*. Paris: Albin Michel.

Limão, N., and A. J. Venables. 2001. Infrastructure, geographical disadvantage and transport costs. *The World Bank Economic Review* 15:451–79.

Liu, X., M. Lovely, and J. Ondrich. 2006. The location decisions of foreign investors in China: untangling the effect of wages using a control function approach. Mimeo, Syracuse University.

Lösch, A. 1940. *Die Räumliche Ordnung der Wirtschaft*. Jena: Gustav Fischer. (English translation, 1954: *The Economics of Location*. New Haven, CT: Yale University Press.)

Ludema, R. D., and I. Wooton. 2000. Economic geography and the fiscal effects of regional integration. *Journal of International Economics* 52:331–52.

Maddison, A. 2001. *The World Economy: A Millennial Perspective*. Paris: OECD.

Marcon, E., and F. Puech. 2003. Evaluating the geographic concentration of industries using distance-based methods. *Journal of Economic Geography* 3: 409–28.

———. 2005. Measures of the geographic concentration of industries. Mimeo, Université de Paris-I.

Marshall, A. 1890. *Principles of Economics*. London: Macmillan. (The eighth edition was published in 1920.)

Martin, P., and C. A. Rogers. 1995. Industrial location and public infrastructure. *Journal of International Economics* 39:335–51.

Matsuyama, K. 1992. The market size, entrepreneurship, and the Big Push. *Journal of the Japanese and International Economies* 6:347–64.

———. 1995. Complementarities and cumulative process in models of monopolistic competition. *Journal of Economic Literature* 33:701–29.

Maurel, F., and B. Sédillot. 1999. A measure of the geographic concentration in French manufacturing industries. *Regional Science and Urban Economics* 29: 575–604.

Mayer, Th. 2000. Spatial Cournot competition and heterogeneous production costs across locations. *Regional Science and Urban Economics* 30:325–52.

———. 2008. Market potential and development. CEPR Discussion Paper no. 6798.

McCallum, J. 1995. National borders matter: Canada–U.S. regional trade patterns. *American Economic Review* 85:615–23.

McFadden, D. 1974. Conditional logit analysis of qualitative choice behavior. In *Frontiers in Econometrics* (ed. P. Zarembka). New York: Academic Press.

Melitz, M. J. 2003. The impact of trade on intra-industry reallocations and aggregate industry productivity. *Econometrica* 71:1695–725.

Melitz, M. J., and G. I. P. Ottaviano. 2008. Market size, trade, and productivity. *Review of Economic Studies* 75:295–316.

Midelfart-Knarvik, K. H., and H. G. Overman. 2002. Delocation and European integration: is structural spending justified? *Economic Policy* 35:321–59.

Mills, E. S. 1972. *Studies in the Structure of the Urban Economy*. Baltimore, MD: The Johns Hopkins Press.

Mion, G. 2004. Spatial externalities and empirical analysis: the case of Italy. *Journal of Urban Economics* 56:97–118.

Mion, G., and P. Naticchioni. Forthcoming. The spatial sorting and matching of skills and firms. *Canadian Journal of Economics*, in press.

Mooij, R. A., and S. Ederveen. 2003. Taxation and foreign direct investment. A synthesis of empirical research. *International Tax and Public Finance* 10: 673-93.

Moran, P. A. P. 1950. Notes on continuous stochastic phenomena. *Biometrika* 37:17-23.

Moretti, E. 2004. Human capital and cities. In *Handbook of Regional and Urban Economics: Cities and Geography* (ed. J. V. Henderson and J.-F. Thisse), pp. 2243-91. Amsterdam: North-Holland.

Mori, T., and A. Turrini. 2005. Skills, agglomeration and segmentation. *European Economic Review* 49:201-25.

Mori, T., K. Nishikimi, and T. E. Smith. 2005. A divergence statistic for industrial localization. *Review of Economics and Statistics* 87:635-51.

Mossay, P. 2006. The core-periphery model: a note on the existence and uniqueness of short-run equilibrium. *Journal of Urban Economics* 59:389-93.

Mundell, R. 1957. International trade and factor mobility. *American Economic Review* 47:321-35.

Murata, Y., and J.-F. Thisse. 2005. A simple model of economic geography à la Helpman-Tabuchi. *Journal of Urban Economics* 58:137-55.

Murphy, K. M., A. Shleifer, and R. W. Vishny. 1989. Industrialization and the Big Push. *Journal of Political Economy* 79:1003-26.

Muth, R. F. 1971. Migration: chicken or egg? *Southern Economic Journal* 3:295-306.

Myrdal, G. 1957. *Economic Theory and Underdeveloped Regions*. London: Duckworth.

Navaretti, G. B., and A. J. Venables. 2004. *Multinational Firms in the World Economy*. Princeton University Press.

Neary, J. P. 2001. Of hype and hyperbolas: introducing the new economic geography. *Journal of Economic Literature* 39:536-61.

———. 2003. Globalization and market structure. *Journal of the European Economic Association* 1:245-71.

Neven, D., G. Norman, and J.-F. Thisse. 1991. Attitudes toward foreign products and international price competition. *Canadian Journal of Economics* 24:1-11.

Nitsch, V. 2005. Zipf zipped. *Journal of Urban Economics* 57:86-100.

Nocke, V. 2006. A gap for me: entrepreneurs and entry. *Journal of the European Economic Association* 4:929-55.

Ohlin, B. 1968. *Interregional and International Trade*. Cambridge, MA: Harvard University Press. (First edition published in 1933.)

O'Rourke, K. H., and J. G. Williamson. 1999. *Globalization and History: The Evolution of a Nineteenth Century Atlantic Economy*. Cambridge, MA: MIT Press.

Ottaviano, G. I. P., and F. Robert-Nicoud. 2006. The "genome" of NEG models with vertical linkages: a positive and normative synthesis. *Journal of Economic Geography* 6:113-39.

Ottaviano, G. I. P., and J.-F. Thisse. 2002. Integration, agglomeration and the political economics of factor mobility. *Journal of Public Economics* 83:429-56.

———. 2004. Agglomeration and economic geography. In *Handbook of Regional and Urban Economics: Cities and Geography* (ed. J. V. Henderson and J.-F. Thisse), pp. 2563-608. Amsterdam: North-Holland.

Ottaviano, G. I. P., and J.-F. Thisse. 2005. New economic geography: what about the N? *Environment and Planning* A 37:1707–25.

Ottaviano, G. I. P., and T. van Ypersele. 2005. Market size and tax competition. *Journal of International Economics* 67:25–46.

Ottaviano, G. I. P., T. Tabuchi, and J.-F. Thisse. 2002. Agglomeration and trade revisited. *International Economic Review* 43:409–36.

Overman, H. G., S. Redding, and A. J. Venables. 2003. The economic geography of trade, production, and income: a survey of empirics. In *Handbook of International Trade* (ed. J. Harrigan and K. Choi), pp. 353–87. Oxford: Basil Blackwell.

Oyama, D. 2006. Potential methods in a core–periphery model with forward-looking expectations. Mimeo, Hitotsubashi University.

Pal, D. 1998. Does Cournot competition yield spatial agglomeration? *Economics Letters* 60:49–53.

Papageorgiou, Y. Y., and T. R. Smith. 1983. Agglomeration as local instability of spatially uniform steady-states. *Econometrica* 51:1109–20.

Parsley, D. C., and S.-J. Wei. 2001. Explaining the border effect: the role of exchange rate variability, shipping costs and geography. *Journal of International Economics* 55:87–105.

Pascoa, M. 1993. Non-cooperative equilibrium and Chamberlinian monopolistic competition. *Journal of Economic Theory* 60:335–53.

Peri, G. 2005. Determinants of knowledge flows and their effects on innovation. *Review of Economics and Statistics* 87:308–22.

Pflüger, M. 2004. A simple, analytically solvable, Chamberlinian agglomeration model. *Regional Science and Urban Economics* 34:565–73.

Picard, P., and D.-Z. Zeng. 2005. Agricultural sector and industrial agglomeration. *Journal of Development Economics* 77:75–106.

Pinkse, J., M. Slade, and C. Brett. 2002. Spatial price competition: a semiparametric approach. *Econometrica* 70:1111–55.

Plassard, F. 1977. *Les autoroutes et le développement régional*. Paris: Economica.

Pollard, S. 1981. *Peaceful Conquest: The Industrialization of Europe 1760–1970*. Oxford University Press.

Pons, J., E. Paluzie, J. Silvestre, and D. A. Tirado. 2007. Testing the new economic geography: migrations and industrial agglomeration in Spain. *Journal of Regional Science* 47:289–313.

Portes, R., and H. Rey. 2005. The determinants of cross-border equity flows. *Journal of International Economics* 65:269–96.

Puga, D. 1999. The rise and fall of regional inequalities. *European Economic Review* 43:303–34.

———. 2002. European regional policies in light of recent location theories. *Journal of Economic Geography* 4:373–406.

Rauch, J. E., and V. Trindade. 2002. Ethnic Chinese networks in international trade. *Review of Economics and Statistics* 84:116–30.

Ravenstein, E. G. 1885. The laws of migration. *Journal of the Royal Statistical Society* 48:167–227.

Redding, S., and D. Sturm. Forthcoming. The cost of remoteness: evidence from German division and reunification. *American Economic Review*, in press.

Redding, S., and A. J. Venables. 2004. Economic geography and international inequality. *Journal of International Economics* 62:53–82.

Reilly, W. J. 1931. *The Law of Retail Gravitation.* New York: Pilsbury.

Ricardo, D. 1817. *On the Principles of Political Economy and Taxation.* London: John Murray.

Rice, P., and A. J. Venables. 2003. Equilibrium regional disparities: theory and British evidence. *Regional Studies* 37:675-86.

Rice, P., A. J. Venables, and E. Patacchini. 2007. Spatial determinants of productivity: analysis for the regions of Great Britain. *Regional Science and Urban Economics* 36:727-52.

Rietveld, P., and R. Vickerman. 2004. Transport in regional science: the "death of distance" is premature. *Papers in Regional Science* 83:229-48.

Rignols, E. 2002. La consommation des ménages depuis quarante ans. INSEE Première, no. 832.

Roback, J. 1982. Wages, rents and the quality of life. *Journal of Political Economy* 90:1257-78.

Robert-Nicoud, F. 2005. The structure of simple "New Economic Geography" models. *Journal of Economic Geography* 5:201-34.

Romer, P. 1992. Increasing returns and new developments in the theory of growth. In *Equilibrium Theory with Applications* (ed. W. A. Barnett, B. Cornet, C. d'Aspremont, J. J. Gabszewicz, and A. Mas-Colell), pp. 83-110. Cambridge University Press.

Rosen, S. 2002. Markets and diversity. *American Economic Review* 92:1-15.

Rosenthal, S., and W. Strange. 2001. The determinants of agglomeration. *Journal of Urban Economics* 50:191-229.

———. 2004. Evidence of the nature and sources of agglomeration economies. In *Handbook of Regional and Urban Economics* (ed. J. V. Henderson and J.-F. Thisse), volume 4, pp. 2119-71. Amsterdam: North-Holland.

Samuelson, P. A. 1952. Spatial price equilibrium and linear programming. *American Economic Review* 42:283-303.

———. 1954. The transfer problem and transport cost. II. Analysis of effects of trade impediments. *Economic Journal* 64:264-89.

———. 1983. Thünen at two hundred. *Journal of Economic Literature* 21:1468-88.

Santos Silva, J., and S. Tenreyro. 2006. The log of gravity. *Review of Economics and Statistics* 88:641-58.

Scherer, F. M. 1980. *Industrial Market Structure and Economic Performance.* Boston, MA: Houghton Mifflin.

Scitovsky, T. 1954. Two concepts of external economies. *Journal of Political Economy* 62:143-51.

Scotchmer, S., and J.-F. Thisse. 1992. Space and competition: a puzzle. *Annals of Regional Science* 26:269-86.

Scott, A. J. 2004. A perspective of economic geography. *Journal of Economic Geography* 4:479-99.

Scott, A. J., and M. Storper. 2003. Regions, globalisation, development. *Regional Studies* 37:579-93.

Sen, A. K. 1973. *On Economic Inequality.* Oxford: Clarendon Press.

Sen, A. K., and T. E. Smith. 1995. *Gravity Models of Spatial Interaction Behavior.* Springer.

Smith, A., and A. J. Venables. 1988. Completing the internal market in the European Community. Some industry simulations. *European Economic Review* 32: 1501-25.

Spence, M. 1976. Product selection, fixed costs, and monopolistic competition. *Review of Economic Studies* 43:217-35.

Spulber, D. F. 2007. *Global Competitive Strategy.* Cambridge University Press.

Starrett, D. 1978. Market allocations of location choice in a model with free mobility. *Journal of Economic Theory* 17:21-37.

Stein, E., and C. Daude. 2002. Longitude matters: time zones and the location of foreign direct investment. Mimeo, Inter-American Development Bank.

Syverson, C. 2004. Market structure and productivity: a concrete example. *Journal of Political Economy* 112:1181-222.

Tabuchi, T. 1998. Urban agglomeration and dispersion: a synthesis of Alonso and Krugman. *Journal of Urban Economics* 44:333-51.

Tabuchi, T., and J.-F. Thisse. 2002. Taste heterogeneity, labor mobility and economic geography. *Journal of Development Economics* 69:155-77.

——. 2006. Regional specialization, urban hierarchy, and commuting costs. *International Economic Review* 47:1295-317.

Tabuchi, T., J.-F. Thisse, and D.-Z. Zeng. 2005. On the number and size of cities. *Journal of Economic Geography* 5:423-48.

Teixeira, A. C. 2006. Transport policies in light of the new economic geography: the Portuguese experience. *Regional Science and Urban Economics* 36:450-66.

Tharakan, P. K. M., I. Van Beveren, and T. Van Ourti. 2005. Determinants of India's software exports and goods exports. *Review of Economics and Statistics* 87:776-80.

Thomas, I. 2002. *Transportation Networks and the Optimal Location of Human Activities: A Numerical Geography Approach.* Cheltenham, U.K.: Edward Elgar.

Tinbergen, J. 1962. *Shaping the World Economy: Suggestions for an International Economic Policy.* New York: Twentieth Century Fund.

Tirado, D. A., E. Paluzie, and J. Pons. 2002. Economic integration and industrial location: the case of Spain before World War I. *Journal of Economic Geography* 2:343-63.

Tirole, J. 1988. *The Theory of Industrial Organization.* Cambridge, MA: MIT Press.

Toulemonde, E. 2006. Acquisition of skill, labor subsidies, and agglomeration of firms. *Journal of Urban Economics* 59:420-39.

Train, K. 2003. *Discrete Choice Methods with Simulation.* Cambridge University Press.

Trionfetti, F. 2001. Using home-biased demand to test trade theories. *Weltwirtschaftliches Archiv* 137:404-26.

U.S. Department of Labor. 2002. *Labor Markets in the 21st Century: Skills and Mobility. Proceedings of a Joint United States and European Union Conference* (available at www.dol.gov/ilab).

Venables, A. J. 1996. Equilibrium locations of vertically linked industries. *International Economic Review* 37:341-59.

Verdon, J. 2003. *Voyager au moyen age.* Paris: Editions Perrin.

Vickerman, R., K. Spiekermann, and M. Wegener. 1999. Accessibility and economic development in Europe. *Regional Studies* 33:1-15.

von Thünen, J. H. 1826. *Der Isolierte Staat in Beziehung auf Landwirtschaft und Nationalökonomie.* Hamburg: Perthes. (English translation, 1966: *The Isolated State.* Oxford: Pergamon Press.)

Weber, A. 1909. *Über den Standort der Industrien.* Tübingen: JCB Mohr. (English translation, 1929: *The Theory of the Location of Industries.* University of Chicago Press.)

Williams, E. E. 1896. *Made in Germany.* London: William Heinemann.

Williamson, J. G. 1965. Regional inequality and the process of national development. *Economic Development and Cultural Change* 14:3–45.

———. 1990. *Coping with City Growth during the British Industrial Revolution.* Cambridge University Press.

Wilson, A. G. 1970. *Entropy in Regional and Urban Modelling.* London: Pion.

Witzgall, C. 1964. Optimal location of a central facility: mathematical models and concepts. National Bureau of Standards (Washington, DC) Report 8388.

Wolf, H. 2000. Intranational home bias in trade. *Review of Economics and Statistics* 82:555–63.

Wooldridge, J. 2002. *Econometric Analysis of Cross Section and Panel Data.* Cambridge, MA: MIT Press.

———. 2006. *Introductory Econometrics: A Modern Approach.* Belmont, CA: South-Western.

World Bank. 1991. *World Development Report: The Challenge of Development.* Oxford University Press.

———. 1995. *World Development Report: Workers in an Integrating World.* Oxford University Press.

World Trade Organization. 2000. *International Trade Statistics 2000.* Lausanne, Switzerland: World Trade Organization.

———. 2001. *Market Access: Unfinished Business. Post-Uruguay Round Inventory and Issues.* Special Studies 6. Lausanne, Switzerland: World Trade Organization.

———. 2005. *International Trade Statistics 2005.* Lausanne, Switzerland: World Trade Organization.

Wrigley, E. A. 1988. *Continuity, Change and Chance: The Character of the Industrial Revolution in England.* Cambridge University Press.

Yi, K.-M. 2003. Can vertical specialization explain the growth of world trade? *Journal of Political Economy* 111:52–102.

Young, A. A. 1928. Increasing returns and economic progress. *Economic Journal* 38:527–42.

Young, E. C. 1924. The movement of farm population. Cornell Agricultural Experimental Station (Ithaca, New York), Bulletin 426.

Yu, Z. 2005. Trade, market size, and industrial structure: revisiting the home-market effect. *Canadian Journal of Economics* 38:255–72.

Zweig, S. 1944. *Die Welt von Gestern—Erinnerungen eines Europäers.* Stockholm: Bermann-Fischer. (Translated, 1964: *The World of Yesterday: An Autobiography.* Lincoln, NE: University of Nebraska Press.)

Index